PROLOGUE

At the end of World War II ⊦
Prisoner of War detained in a c⻊ _
a switchboard operator, and against the back drop of post war predjudice a budding romance is played out in secret. Meanwhile his mother (Mutti), and younger brother, Horst, a hairdresser, were forced to flee their home in Pyritz, Western Pomerania, ahead of the advancing Russian army. They were refugees, destitute and alone and desperate for Hans to return home. Also left behind in Germany was his childhood sweetheart Vera.

At the age of 19, injured in battle, Hans had been taken prisoner in France in 1944. He spent 15 months detained as a POW in the US before being shipped to the UK after the end of the war.

This three way conversation builds a story of heartache, determination, loyalty and longing exposing the dire contrast of the lives of ordinary people on either side of defeat and victory. Their lives are played out in these letters meticulously kept by Hans for over half a century and not discovered until after his death. Hans had carefully marked each of the letters he received from family and friends with both the date of receipt and the date of his reply. The letters that follow are in the order Hans received them.

Acknowledgements

This book could not have been presented to you without the invaluable help of a number of people. Thankyou to Fiona Quinton who helped to transcribe Hans and Jean's letters. Brigitte Shade and Irmgard Gökova who saved the day by translating the letters written in the old German Sütterlin script, firstly into modern German and then into English; also to Judith Usiskin, Helene Alderman, Thamara Freeman and Tom E Morrison for painstakingly translating Mutti and Horst's German letters into English.

1

Family tree of some of the people you will be meeting.

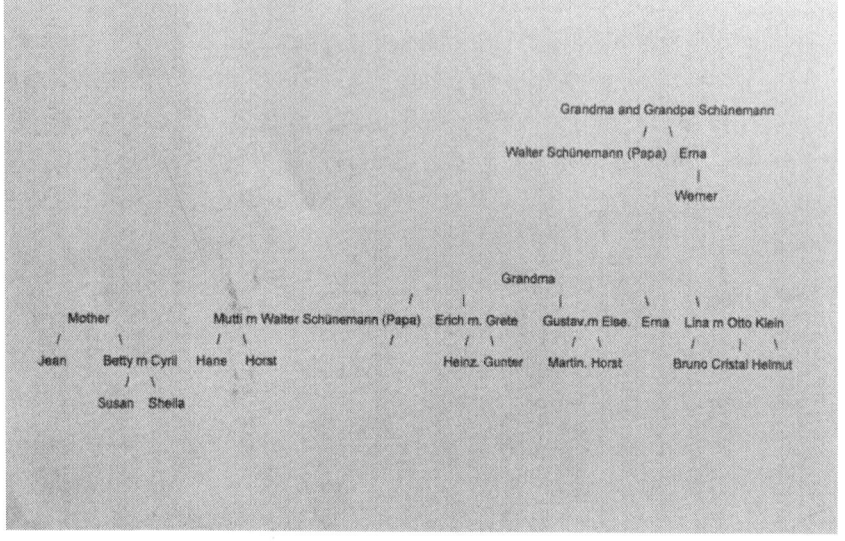

```
                                                    Grandma and Grandpa Schünemann
                                                         /  \
                                                 Walter Schünemann (Papa)  Erna
                                                                 |
                                                              Werner


                                                         Grandma
                                       /        |               |            \        \
          Mother            Mutti m Walter Schünemann (Papa)  Erich m. Grete  Gustav.m Else.  Erna  Lina m Otto Klein
         /       \           /   \            /        / \            / \           /    |    \
     Jean    Betty m Cyril  Hans  Horst              Heinz  Gunter  Martin. Horst  Bruno Cristal Helmut
             /    \
          Susan  Sheila
```

Hans

     29.4.46

Finally, I am getting around to sending you a few lines. Thank you very much for your two lovely cards dated 2.1, which I received two days before leaving America on 3.4.1946. I was so happy to hear from you. I am glad to read that you have already received one lot of mail from me. I can well imagine that you are awaiting my arrival anxiously. I also wished I could be on my way to you. When they discharged me I gave them your address, which means that I can come straight to you. But when will it be? I hope soon. The post is not taking quite so long anymore, because it's a shorter distance. I have got the 'big water' behind me already. In a way I am pleased about that because it means every kilometre towards the East means I am one step closer to you. I am very well and hope you are too. Mum and Horst are well too I am glad to say. Where are they now? I have not received any mail from them.

Did you think of us on 21.3.43? Never forget the main thing. I am sending you my love and loving kisses. Yours Hans. Please pass on my best wishes to all.

(a note he made to himself)

Today cards sent to grandmother and search card to mum

14.5.46	card to Vera.
14.5.46	card to family Kuger.
20.5.46	card to Vera.
26.5.46	letter to Vera.
31.5.46	card to Horst (old address).

To: Ms Vera Halling,
              Prenzlau/Mark Brandenburg,
              Neubrandenburher Strasse 7b,
              Germany -Russ. Zone.

From: Johannes Klawitter,

4

Prisoner's No.:   A672859,
               Gaulby-Road-Camp
         No. 94 Camp Wartnaby,
            Billesdon-Leicester, Great Britain.

      2.9.46

I received your letter dated 30.7.46 on 24.8.46, in which
you describe your very hard and difficult life. Initially, I
was overjoyed to hear from you but as I read on, the blow
it dealt me was almost unbearable. Vera! I cannot take anymore. Does this mean my only enjoyment in life have been
destroyed? I cannot possibly comprehend this. I have been
through the war and seen its consequences and would never
dream of judging you. We are only human and nobody is perfect. I have been thinking about it a lot and it caused me to
have sleepless nights. There are moments in our lives one
cannot control. I have read your letter dated 30.5.46 again
in which you are begging me to stay with you in Prenzlau.
You will have received my answer in the meantime. I cannot see from your letter whether you ever got married. In
spite of everything I still believe in you and will accept your
apologies, if you can promise me that these things never
happen again. I do not wish to be seen as a martyr but if it
is your own inner wish not to see me again, I would never
stand in your way. You once put your fate into my hands.
Please accept my heartfelt condolences on your dad's passing.

I am now sending you my greetings, which come from the
bottom of my heart, and I remain, still, your Hans.

Replied   15/9   Aschersleben 18.8.46

                                    12.9.46

My dear Hans,
Today we are sending you warm Sunday greetings again. I
have just finished my work. This morning Horstel and I collected corn. It is definitely reassuring to know that we have
harvested grain for the winter, so that we have somthing

'put by'. I have been collecting corn for four weeks already and it was crippling. But then, at least when you come, we will have something to eat. I really do hope that you have received our post at long last. So far 5 letters have been returned to us.

I am really sorry that you have had to be without news from us for so long. A year has passed since dear Grandma was laid to rest on 3.8.45 in Rosow, Kreis Greifenhagen near the river Oder. My dear, she asked me to send you her love- she thought about you so often. On 26.12.1945 we buried Grandpa Shünemann in Altenpleen, Stralsund. Little Irma "Irmchen" has been at rest since March 1945 in Anklam and Uncle Otto and Helmut are buried near Wolgast in Kröslin. If it were to be granted to us to return once more to our beloved homeland so many people would no longer be there. Now, nearly one and a half years have passed since we had to leave our beloved homeland. When will we ever see it again? We were only able to bring very little with us as we went to Friedrichsthal. One can barely even think back to our beautiful home, it is all rubble and ashes. Gotthilf Büchholz is at Greifswald with Heidemann, he has no idea where his parents might be. My dear boy, I would so dearly love to fulfil your wish and send you a photo, only we no longer possess anything anymore, neither Bank books, nor documents. When you eventually return home to us, we will tell you about everything that has happened. The only good thing is that Horst still has his profession, so he can at least provide for us. If only the day would come that you return to us and good news were to come from our dear Papa!

We are all in good health and we hope you are too. Please write with your news as soon as you can. Warm greetings from your mother who is always thinking of you and from Horst. Hoping that you return soon and in good health.

Dear Hans, return to us soon. Greetings from Horst

Aschersleben   11.8.1946

My dear son,

I finally received your lovely card of 16.7.46 yesterday and thank you warmly for it. We are so pleased to hear from you. All the letters that we wrote to you have been returned to us. So now I will use this new address.

Today I sent you a card via the Red Cross and hopefully this will actually reach you. It makes me very sad to have no news of you now that you are 22 . My very dear boy. The day before yesterday I received a letter from Vera's mother that shocked me unspeakably. I should have been with you, as in it she reveals everything. Before yesterday, I was completely unaware: but in the letter she says that in August of last year Vera had a little girl, who died on Christmas Eve, shortly before Christmas.

Healthwise, we are well, which is what we hope for you, dear Hans. Perhaps you can soon be with us? Who knows whether one day we shall be able to return to our beloved homeland. If only we could be together! Then the burden would be lighter! How happy I would be to eventually receive a sign of life from Papa. Perhaps that day will actually come ! Heinz Ludwig is already at Herta's in Tenzerow. From Vera's letters I understand that her father is very ill, hopefully he will get better. I have also written a letter to Vera.

Now, my dear boy, stay in good health. We are very much looking forward to receiving your first letter. Warm greetings from us - we are longing to see you again. Mutti and Horst

Hoping for your healthy return. At the same time, we wish you a healthy Whitsun. Hopefully you will be with us in time for your birthday.

7

Wishing for your healthy return as soon as possible. (This is
at top of letter, written upside-down)

Aschersleben, 25.8.46

23.9.46

My dear Hans

Thank you very much for your lovely card dated 2 August,
which we were very happy to receive. We hope you have, by
now, received our post because you sent previous cards to
the old relocation camp and it appeared to have been there
for several days before it finally reached us. We left the camp
3 months ago and we now live in a pretty little room. We
take it everything is fine with you and, most of all, hope you
are well – we can say the same from us.

We had great success with the wheat this year, having collected 5 hundredweights, and we are now looking forward
to the winter with confidence.

I can well believe you are enjoying working in the fresh air
and sunshine. Have you already received Vera's post? Don't
take it too much to heart. You are still so very young! I wonder when we shall see each other again? Horst went to Calbe
on the river Saale today to collect cucumbers. We shall have
a photo done as soon as possible and we will send it to you.
Can you also send us a photo of you? We have not seen you for
two and a half years now. We should be so happy to receive a
long letter from you

Now, my dear boy, please take care of yourself, stay fit and
well and write as often as you can. We are sending you our
love and a thousand kisses. Your mum, who is always thinking of you, and your brother Horst.

8

Replied   13/10.46   Aschersleben 8.9.46

5.10.46

My dear Hans

I am thanking you with all my heart for your card dated 11.8.46. We are always happy to receive your news. Would you not be able to write us a letter one day? You could then write a bit more.

Our lovely summer is coming to an end. Horst is studying for his exam. Uncle Gustav and family and Auntie Lina are sending their love, especially Judith. Have you still not received any post from us? I have written quite often! We suppose you still don't know when you are coming back to us. We would be happy to have you here. Herta and Heinz Ludwig have moved. Heinz Bieck went to France 8 months ago. He works in a mine. Have you heard from Vera in the meantime? Don't worry too much about this. Try to get over it. Perhaps it was meant to be. You, my dear boy can then come back to us and stay with us as long as you want, so that the two of us are not always so alone in this world. And I think that you too would love to come home and stay with us again. Who knows whether and if we shall ever be able to return to our home country.

Dear Hans, please write to us as often as you can. We are always very happy to receive your post. How are you coping with your farm work? Maybe one day you will be a real farmer. That would be very nice. My dear boy, we are sending you our love and wish you all the best.

Your ever loving mum and brother Horst.

Hoping for a healthy reunion isoon.

replied 13.10.46 Aschersleben, 15.9..46

5.10.46

My dear boy

I am confirming, with thanks and great happiness,the receipt of your lovely card dated 25.8.46. Well, you have now received Vera's letter! I understand you very well and I know exactly how you feel, especially when you were looking forward very much to a reunion. The letter I received from Vera's mother also upset me. I would never have thought Vera could do such a thing. However, it obviously was not proper love, otherwise she would never have done this to you. You, my lovely son, are now asking me for my opinion, now that the first pain has gone and you have calmed yourself a little, you might come to the conclusion yourself, that it is better for you if you forget her. You would never have had a happy marriage with her. I was very upset for several days, because I loved Vera like my own daughter. Vera stayed with us for 8 days at Christmas 1944 you were already in A,* she already carried somebody else's child under her heart. We went to see grandmother and were on our way to escape when we (Gertrud, Horst and Vera) stayed for 6 weeks with the Hallings. I had no idea about anything. I only got to know about it from her mother in August this year. Dear Hans, this

10

hurt me deep in my heart and I wondered if it was meant to be. When a mother, who loves her son, realises he is being cheated in such a way, it hurts deeply!! I have had such a lot of worry and upset in my life and wonder when there might be an end to it. I beg you, be strong and don't show how upset you are. There is time to find happiness again. Only this hope gives me peace. Had you cheated on her it would have hurt me even more. My most inner wish is now for us all to be together again. Life is so hard for a refugee, separated from loved ones. I also wanted to tell you, my dear Hans, when I was with Vera's parents last year, I was somewhat disappointed. Even Vera seemed embarrassed, because everything was so different to what it is here with us. You would have been disappointed too. Vera had to promise her father on his deathbed that she would marry the father of her child, and – believe you me my boy – it would be for the best! Otherwise, one day might come in the future, when you two would have quarrelled about this. Just think of Werner from Repenow and Edith from Selchow who have gone through the same and so have many others!! The only good thing is that it has happened before the marriage. When you come back to us, we shall make our lives as good as possible. It is very, very hard for me to be in a foreign country without being heaering from our lovely Papa. Perhaps the day will come which will bring us the happiness of his return. I am busy going to the fields every day to collect onions, beans and potatoes. It has been a worthwhile job and I am very happy so far. Horstel is working very hard towards his exam that is coming up soon. Hopefully we shall be going to Vorpommern in October to see all our relatives once more.

Dear Hans, please send us a letter. Take care of yourself, stay healthy, and never forget that your mum and your brother worry a lot about you. With lots of love and kisses from your mum, who is always thinking of you, and from your brother Horst.

Looking forward to seeing you again very soon.

* America

Replied 27.10.46   Aschersleben, 4.10.46

                                    19.10.46

My dear Hans

We were so happy to receive your lovely letter dated 15.9.46 and also your card from 2.9.46, and thank you from the bottom of our hearts. We are so happy to know that, finally, you are getting our mail. You have been waiting for such a long time. Sorry about my bad handwriting. I squashed the ring finger of my right hand in the garden gate, which makes writing very difficult, but I don't want to make you wait any longer.

I bet you were really pleased when you met Gerhard Fenner. I know his mother well. She used to be so desperate and I used to console and talk to her when her son went missing, then in November 1944, when they got the news, I also received your card telling me that you were taken prisoner. We were so happy to know that you were still alive. A long time has passed since then. And look what all of us have gone through in the meantime!! The main thing is you are alright, and I can say the same about us. We are waiting for you here and when you return, who knows whether we will ever be able to return to our home country!!! What kind of injury did you have? Has it not healed yet?

I have got a lot of potatoes in reserve now. I wish I did not have to go such a long way, but we shall just have to manage. I heard from Auntie Erna, she is sending her love to you. I am sure she would love to hear from you some time.

Miss Erna Bieck c/o Mueller
Gerdeswalde

Horst – 3
Grimmeswalde/Vorpommern

Also Mr. Eichhorn from Thuringia is sending his best wishes. He came to see us last week. Please write to us as often as you can, If only we could see you again. My dear boy, take care of yourself and stay well.

Lots of love and kisses from your mum, who is always worried about you, and your brother Horst.
Hoping to see you again very soon.

Prenzlau,
1 9.9.46

23.10.46

My dear Hans

Today I received your letter dated 2.9.46. I cannot describe the emotions it awoke in me. But I have to tell you straight away, that your letter came one day too late. I have now calmed down a little and am able to write to you. You speak with such love and magnanimity that someone like me can only wish for. I would love to come to you and thank you and just leave everything here behind. Only yesterday I decided, after a lot of thought, to get married. I arranged the wedding to take place in the Registrar's Office. Oh Hansi, I am at the end of my tether. What am I to do? I know that every one of my words will feel like a stab in your heart, and to know this causes me such pain. What's going to happen? I have never been so sad and felt so lonely in my whole life. As soon as I received your first letter I wanted to tell you everything. I wanted you to decide if our lives could ever be built together. I was simply too much of a coward to talk about what has happened, and now this has come to be my downfall. I did not intend to leave you to your fate in a foreign country. You must understand me. I always hoped you would stay with me forever, and at the same time I had this terrible thought in my mind that it would not happen. I have often asked myself why I had to betray your love. I cannot excuse what I have done and I will never be happy and satisfied in the knowledge that you are so unhappy. I thank you from the bottom of my heart for your kind and understanding words. You are such a good and lovely person. I wish I could make amends for everything I did to you. I would promise you the earth and would fulfil your every wish so that you would never ever be disappointed again for the rest of your life. I wanted to regain your love and trust but these two words "too late" keep coming up again and again. I am looking into a future as a cold human being, without any feelings. Nothing good can come out of this. I don't want to be happy with another man. I have spent many a night in my bed and reproached myself bitterly. Then I decided to write to Hans 'tomorrow' and pour out my heart to you. Mum also told me I should. At that time it would not have been too late. Papa did not once reproach me and mum was always lovely and kind but I know that I have hurt them both very much. Your lovely mum also wrote this in her last letter. Why is everyone so kind to me? I do not deserved it one bit. I cannot comprehend what I have done. My conscience is endlessly tormenting me. I am so grateful for my lovely mum. She consoles me and tries to lead me on the right path, because there are moments when I am totally overwhelmed and incapable of doing anything. A few days ago I sent your large photo from R.A.D.* to your mum. She asked if she could have it. Last year I had already sent a photo from your R.A.D. time to her. I am keeping the small photo of you. It's among your letters which you wrote while in captivity. These are the only treasures I still have of you and I will keep them forever. When I wrote my last letter to your mum it felt like I was losing the ground under my feet. How well we all got on together. I know that your mum loved me like a daughter. She suffered a lot because of me too. I was bitterly upset when I had to give her the bad news. I can do nothing else but constantly beat myself up. I want to write and write but all this makes me more and more upset. I do not know a common path for us. It is not my own, wish to avoid a reunion. On the contrary, I am hoping that I will see you again one day. May it give me all my strength however painful it will be. You were to be the fulfilment of my life and it is my own fault

that you are now unreachable for me.
Now, Hansi, had I received your letter 24 hours earlier, I would have made a different decision. Think of your mum. She needs you and is waiting for you. We thank you for your kind condolences on Papa's passing. We miss him very much. Sometimes I long for inner peace and I want to join all our departed loved ones.I think of my mum too whose only support I am. You are allowed to write if you wish. Do you know anything about Jochen Thormann? His father asked me about him.
Wishing you all the best, I am sending you my love, yours Vera.

* Reich Labour Service

replied 3/11.46   Aschersleben, 29.9.1946
                                            26.10.46

          My dear Hans,
Today we are again sending you very warm Sunday greet-ings. We are keenly awaiting a letter from you. The day be-fore yesterday I received a letter from Vera, in which she sent me your photo. She is deeply upset that she hurt you so badly and she is worried how you will react to the deep disappointment. Hopefully by now you will be a little more at peace about it. My dear boy, I know how much you will be suffering, but just think a little about what I have been through and what I have endured. You will find proper hap-piness again.
Today it is such a lovely late-summer Sunday, that home-sickness really hurts. I am totally alone, Horst went dancing – he deserves some fun, after all, he works so hard every day. Earlier I sorted the potatoes that I had gathered – it's already more than 5 Kg. Tomorrow I'll return to the field again. Some days we go as far as 25 Km. Then, in the evenings, we are dead-tired, but it's wonderful to think that we'll have provisions for the winter.
We are all well and we hope you are too. Have you still not

received any post from us? So far, none of the letters I have written to you have been returned, so I assume you have received them. You must be working really hard on the land and that is good, working helps you to forget your worries. If only we were able to return to our homeland, we would manage to rebuild a home! The main thing is that we are all healthy and together.

Now my dear boy, stay healthy for me and know that your mother always worries about you, and, just like your brother, I am full of longing for the day when we see each other again.

From the bottom of my heart I send warm greetings and a kiss, from your mother and your brother Horst. Looking forward to an early, healthy reunion!

Replied 17/11.46   **Aschersleben 15.10.46**
                           5.11.46

     My dear Hans,
Today, with great joy, we received your dear card of 15.9.1946 and your dear letter of 29.9.1946, for which we thank you from our hearts. From them, we can see that you are well, which we can also say for ourselves. Now the winter is slowly drawing closer. I have now finished gathering potatoes, we have an additional 10Kg, so we do not need to be anxious any more. Horstel and I want to go to Vorpommern at the end of this month, hopefully it will work out. Didn't you get the letter in which I wrote Frau Streese's and Gertrud's address? Frau Streese, Woltersmühlen near Pönitz, (East Holstein)

Many people from Pyritz are no longer here, only Dräger and his family, who you definitely know – he also worked at the Court House . There should still be others in the area: Frau Lehmann, the woman teacher from Stechlin, who was always at Uncle Erich's, is here. We gather potatoes together. I never lose hope that we will see each other again. Without that my whole of life would have no purpose anymore. I have written to you so very often, I hope you get all the letters. You must also write to me really diligently. After all, it is always a day of great joy when post arrives. Do you think you will be able to come to us here this year? Aunt Lina has not yet received any news from Bruno, I wish he would get in touch with her as she now has no-one other than Christel, and has also lost everything. Alas, one cannot allow oneself to dwell on the past.

Now, my dear boy, stay healthy. With greetings and kisses from the heart, from your mother, who is always thinking of you, and from your brother Horst.

To a healthy and soon-to-be reunion!

24.11.46   Aschersleben, 7.11.46

20.11.46

My dear Hans

I thank you from the bottom of my heart for your letter and card dated 6 and 13.10. We were so happy to hear from you. I am sure you have received my letter in the meantime, which I wrote from our trip. We had a good journey and are happy to be back home again now. Trips are more fun in the summer. We visited all our relatives. Uncle Erich has moved. Here is his address:

Erich Bieck

Am Layerhof

bei Grimmen

Vorpommern

Auntie Erna is also there. Everybody is as poor as a pauper. Will things ever get better for us? Auntie Lina has not got a good job, which I feel very sad about, as she has had so much heart ache in her life. But the farmers don't have a heart in their bodies. They are just looking after themselves. Christel works in a nursery, which she likes very much. She will be 19 years old on 19.12. I wished Bruno would write to us! I sent you Auntie Lina's address. She lives in Voddow,3 Post Kröslin, Greifswald, and Grandma Schünemann lives in Altenpleen, Post Niepars via Stralsund c/o Böger. All our family and friends are sending their love to you. Unfortunately, I do not have Heinz' address, but only siblings and parents can send a card to him in any case. He hopes to be discharged soon. It is very sad that you can't come to us. We are longing to see you again, but of course, I am so grateful to know you are well. As Christmas approaches, one feels double the loss with our homelessness. Can you have your photo taken? We would love to get one. Werner sent one to grandma. He looks very well. Now, my dear boy, take care and write back soon. With all my love and kisses from your Mum and brother Horst.

Replied 8.12.46   Aschersleben, 21.6.46

20.11.46

My dear brother Hans!
After a very long time, we have finally received some news from you. You cannot imagine how overwhelmed with happiness we were. We said so often "we wonder where our dear Hans is now"! My dear Hans, I am now working in a Gents and Ladies Hairdressing Salon, and I like it very much. I shall, hopefully, receive my diploma in September . We hope and wish that you will be home by then. We are both fit and well and hope the same from you.
What is your injury? Are you better now? Aschersleben is a very nice little town. Nothing got bombed, everything is still the same here. I have been to the Harz Mountains a few times. It is wonderful there. Are you expecting to be dis-

charged soon? It would be lovely if we could be together again soon, because it seems an eternity since we last saw each other. We don't know where all the years have gone! We went through such a lot, it does not bear thinking about and hope we'll soon get some news from our Papa. I wonder whether Klawitter is still alive. He is supposed to have suffered a lot under the Poles, but there are lots of rumours going around. My dear Hans, we never imagined that we would have to flee from our lovely Pyritz so suddenly. We had to leave our beloved home and everything in it behind. We could'nt think about anything at all except saving our lives. Your dear Vera cannot wait to see her beloved Hansel again. I can only dream of such thoughts, well, the time will come one day. I have already met lots of people since you have been away, and I write to quite a lot of them. Dear Hans, we are now living in a very nice, sunny room, with nice people and lovely surroundings. Only a few minutes from here there is a lovely rose garden. Once a week we go to the big municipal bath. I have still got my tools, but the razors disappeared. I would love to have an electric hair machine but I am sure it will take several years before Ican get hold that kind of thing. My dear Hans, Pyritz is completely burnt down except a few houses which are badly in need of repair. Mr. Drager from your place of work also lives in Aschersleben now. We lost our beloved grandmother ten months ago, it is difficult to comprehend. It would be so lovely if she could live with us now and spend her last few days happily and peacefully. Well, that's life. Once you are here with us, it will take a load off mum's shoulders. She has a lot on her plate.

Now, my dear Hans, I shall have to finish my letter. Please write again soon. Or better still, come home!

Horst

Aschersleben, 20.6.46

24.11.46

My dear boy
Today is your birthday and we are sending you our very best
wishes. As you are 21 today I am constantly thinking of you.
You are now going your own way in your life and I can only
wish, from the bottom of my heart, the very best for your
future. May God guide you into the right direction and may
we not be separated for much longer. Horstel and I are longing for the day when we are reunited. One day, we should be
allowed to settle somewhere which we can call 'our home'.
Now, my dear Hans, I would like to thank you for your lovely
card. Finally, after two long years, I have received some post
from you. I knew at the time when I received the telegram
that you had gone missing, that you were alive, and my feelings did not lie to me, nor did they betray me. We are so
happy to know that you are well, which we can also say

about us. Horstel looks after the two of us financially. He has a good job, otherwise I do not know what would happen to us. It is best not to look back and think of our homeland and lovely home. We have worked all our lives for nothing and are now dependent on the mercy of others. It is so dreadfully hard to be homeless. If only we could get the smallest sign of life from our beloved Papa. I have tried so hard. Auntie Lina has not heard from Bruno. I would love her to receive a message from him. Uncle Otto died of diphtheria and Helmut 3 weeks later of typhus. Now she has only got Christel. Dear Hans, you are asking when we had to leave. We have a terrible time. It was on 3.2.44 when we left Pyritz. We walked for days and nights and under constant stress. We could only take one rucksack and a bag. Our house was completely destroyed as was 99% of the town. Well, we are as poor as beggars, but we still have our health and for that we are grateful. Maybe one day we can rebuild a new life for ourselves. Last year both Horst and I were seriously ill. I did not think we would ever meet again. During our escape, we both spent 6 weeks at the Hallings in Prenzlau. It was very stressful. When we found grandmother, Horst and I immediately went to see her and stayed with her until she closed her lovely eyes. We laid her at rest in Rosow near Greifenhagen. Her inner wish was to die in her homeland, but it was not to be. Her tired body is 3 hours from home. Grandmother thought of you a lot, she asked me to give you all her love when you come back – she never doubted that you would not return.

Auntie Erna is with Uncle Erich. She wanted very badly to stay with us all, but one does not always get what one wants. She is sending her love to you, and also Auntie Lina and Christel, Uncle Gustav and family and Uncle Erich and family. Irmchen is buried in Anklam. We are so glad you found us through Vera! I had already tried to find you with the help of the Red Cross.

I received mail from the Eichhorns. Regilde's first engagement broke down and now she is married and lives in Lauscha. Her little son Willfrid is 3 months old. Did Vera give you the Streese's address? Please don't worry – we might be poor but we will work something out. The main thing is we shall meet again and are all well and fit.

 Hoping to hear from you again very soon, your mum - who is always thinking of you – and your brother Horst are sending all our love.

I hope you have, meanwhile, received my three letters.
See you soon, take care and stay healthy.

replied 2.12.46   **Altenpleen, 29.10.46**

27.11.46

        My dear Hans
Today, I want to send you my very best wishes from the bottom of my heart. We are, at the moment, in Altenpleen near Stralsund, and are visiting Grandma Schünemann and Erna. We already spent a few days at Uncle Gustav's and his family in Tentzerow near Demmin. Tomorrow we are going to see Auntie Lina and Christel in Voddow near Wolgast and then we shall be paying Auntie Erna and Uncle Erich a visit in Gerdeswalde near Grimmen. On Saturday, we are returning to Uncle Gustav's and on Monday we are going back to Aschersleben, which will conclude our journey.

I had intended to write to you earlier, but I was quite busy with the preparations for our trip. Horstel passed his exam in Ladies and Gents Hairdressing on Sunday, 20.10.46 and he is very happy about it. We like Aschersleben better than Altenpleen, even though nothing can replace our homeland. I don't think we shall ever be really happy unless we can go back to our homeland. The main thing is that we will be together again and are all enjoying our health.

Auntie Lina has still not heard from Bruno. It is so hard for her, as she has only got Christel. If possible, I would like you to write to her sometime. Her address is:

Frau
Lina Klein c/o Breitsprecher
Voddow
Post Kröslin
Near Greifswald

It would make her very happy.

Grandma is not very happy here either. People who did not go through what we had to endure, cannot imagine what it was like for us. Little by little, one has to move forward and look to the future again. I have managed to collect a further 10 hundredweights of potatoes, which will see us alright.

I want to care for you, my boy, and for Horst. I managed to get a very nice, warm hat knitted, and I have already got some wool for a warm pullover for you. Things are looking up. We hope there will be some post from you when we get back home. Now, my dear boy, take care and look after yourself. With lots of love and kisses from your mum, who is always thinking of you, and brother Horst. Hoping to see you again very soon. Much love from Grandma, Erna, Uncle Gustav and family.

Replied 2.12   *Aschersleben 10.11.46*

28.11.46

My dear boy

Again, we are sending you loving Sunday greetings. We are well and hope the same from you. We have had some awful weather these last weeks, it rains all day and today we even have snow. I think winter is upon us. Horstel went to a hairdressing show followed by a dance. He loves dancing. He needed a bit of distraction from his job. He works so hard.

Dear Hans, did you not receive my letters in which I gave you the address of the Streeses? I am writing them down again: Frau Marta Streese or Gertrud Schnandke, Woltersmühlen (Ostholstein). When we meet again, we shall have so much to talk about! Today all the hairdressers and apprentices are having a get-together. Everybody contributed something towards it so they had afternoon coffee, and in the evening, potato salad. I bake a cake for ourselves every Sunday – it's not quite as nice as we had at home because not all the ingredients are available. How much we would love to give you some of the cake, I imagine you have not had any for a long time. We are longing to get a message from our beloved Papa, it would make our lives worth living again. I have made our little room nice and warm, it is quite cosy. Christmas is here in six weeks – I would rather not think about it, because it reminds me of what we have lost. We never thought that we would still be separated at Christmas!!! Now, my dear boy, we are sending you our best wishes, stay healthy, and with lots of love and kisses from your mum, who is always thinking of you, and your brother Horst.

Here's to a reunion soon.

Aschersleben 17.11.46

7/12

Replied: 8/12/46

My dear boy

Today on my birthday we are sending you many greetings and are thinking of you with all our hearts, how lovely would it be if only you could be with us. Where might our dear Papa be? If only we had a sign of life from him. I would like to thank you very much for your letter dated 27.10.46, which we very much enjoyed. We have been waiting so long. It would be awful if we had to make do without letters from you, if instead you were having to write to all the relatives. We are so pleased that the post seems to be working, and that our letter only took two weeks to arrive. Your letters to us also take 14 to 15 days to arrive. Now my dear Hans I shall fulfil your wish and enclose a picture, it's not that beautiful, not like the pictures from home, but you have not seen us for three years, we have changed a bit, which is not a surprise, when there is so much worry and anxiety. No doubt things will change once your are back with us. We no longer have much to claim as our own. The worst thing is that we do not have any shoes for winter. Yesterday I received a birthday parcel from Thea, with a few warm underpants, and three handkerchiefs, and a picture of Papa when he was at home six years ago, so I was really happy. Unfortunately all my beautiful pictures have gone, including all our papers.

Our landlord gave me a wonderful pair of slippers, as well as flowers, and Horstel gave me a jewellery box (unfortunately I no longer own jewellery) plus a shopping net, a pair of stockings, a pound of sugar, and some pudding powder, as well as cream.

It sounds like you had a bad injury, let us hope it will heal well. Now my dear boy, please remain well, and write regularly. Lots and lots of love from your ever loving mum and your brother Horst. Here's to a reunion soon

Aschersleben 17.11.46

My dear Hans

At last I get the chance to write you a few lines. My exam is finally over, about time too, as the studying was hard work. I am now qualified as both a hairdresser and a barber. Most of the time I work in the ladies' salon, which I really enjoy. Mum's gets her hair done every day, but she's not too keen on the new styles. Dear Hans, do you know how to dance? I go dancing a lot. Eight days ago we had hairdressers' fun night, including hairdressing demonstrations and then dancing until 2 am. And on Sunday we had a social evening, but only for the upper levels of the professional training college, with coffee and supper. I shall now continue attending the training school in order to catch up with what I have missed out on. I am in a class with thirteen women, the only (male) in the class! I just wish you were with us. Can you not come soon? Our trip to Pomerania is now behind us and it wasn't very exciting, as everything is now very different. How nice it would be if on Sunday afternoon we could all be together having coffee. How do you like our picture? I am closing now, so please write again soon. Stay well and cheerful. Lots of love from your brother Horst.

See you soon!

Aunt Erna's address is:
Erna Bieck
3 Layerhof
Kreis Grimmen

Replied 15/12.46   **Woltersmühlen, 29.11.46**
7.12.46

Dear Hans

Thank you very much for your lovely letter, which made me very happy.

Today, I want to write to you a little letter. I am very pleased to hear that you are well and you have got over the war without any problems. Those are really the main things, and also that you have work. What else can we wish for? Don't you want to come home soon? I am sure your mum is missing you terribly. It is a great shame that we have all been separated and now live so far away from each other. We would love to be nearer you, it is very lonely here. You know how I always loved to live in the country! Hans, we are quite well considering the circumstances, we must not complain. We have got over the escape. Who would have thought that one day we will finish up in Schleswig-Holstein? Fate can deal you a tough card, but we are very pleased that we managed to 'escape' the Russians. It is dreadful what they did to the women, but it was not the same everywhere. At least, here,

we did not have to put up with any personal sufferings, even though we lived below our dignity, it was still bearable. We do not know where our Papa is. We have not heard anything from him, but are not losing hope that, one day, he will be found somewhere. I have not found any work yet. But, there is plenty going on here, though a city dweller like me does not get much satisfaction from living in the country. Can you imagine: I am now a passionate dancer. I go dancing every Saturday. On Sundays, I dance in the next village. I can tell you, there is quite a lot going on! Thank goodness, they don't have any Schnaps. I would stop going there if they did, because there would be fights and beatings going on. The men from the different villages do not get on with each other. Well Hans, things have changed. Years ago one would never have gone to a public dance, and now one is glad to be able to go just anywhere. But, thank God, the morale here out in the country has not steeped too low – not like in the towns. Sometimes, one can feel ashamed to be a German girl. It is dreadful how the women and girls throw themselves at the men for chocolate and cigarettes. You will not recognise Germany when you return.
Well, dear Hans, I now want to bring my letter to an end as I have moaned far too much.

We are sending you our greetings with love, Gertrud and mum.
Write back soon!

Replied: 23/12   Aschersleben 24.11.46

9.12.46

My dear Hans
We thank you from all our hearts for your letter dated

3.11.46 as well as for my birthday greetings. Let us hope that your wish will be granted and that your dear papa and you will finally be reunited during the coming year. Today is Totensonntag, * and one's heart is heavy, thinking about all the graves of our dear relatives we had to leave behind in our homeland, and all the loved-ones who had to leave us over the last few years. I wanted to decorate the grave of our dear grandma, but Aunt Bertha will have done it for me, as I requested, and I have sent her money for a wreath, she lives in Roserov, near Schillersdorf, where you were four years ago. Today we are really pining for you, who knows when the day will arrive when we will be together again? Another four weeks until Christmas, and I am so frightened of being alone, but I shall not complain. It is not as difficult as it is for you, living amongst strangers, and away from home. Dear Hans, did you receive our birthday greetings? So far the letter has not been returned. I sent the photo of us last Sunday, let's hope you receive it soon. Believe me son, it is better for you, now that you have got over Vera, nothing much would have come of it. We should not judge; everybody needs to know what they are doing. I have kept the letter which Frau Halling wrote at the time, and made a copy of my reply for you. Now, my dear boy, we wish you a very merry Christmas and all the very best to you – you are always in our thoughts. Thousands of greetings, love and kisses to you from your mum and your brother Horst.
Here's to a healthy Wiedersehen

* the Sunday of the dead -a religious holiday commemorating the dead.

Replied 23/12   Aschersleben, 30.5.46
14.12
My dear Hans,
I sent you a letter yesterday and want to send you warm

greetings again today. We have heard nothing from you for a long time, (nor you from us). But now that we have your address, I must make sure that you receive post from us. Horst is doing a tour of the Harz today with his boss and his boss's family. I was supposed to go as well, but I was too tired.

Would you write, sometime, to Aunt Lina. Her address is: Lina Klein, c/o Breitsprecher Voddow Post Kröslin, [Kreis] Greifswald.

She, with Christel, is completely alone. Uncle Otto and Helmut were taken from them in October and November 1943. And we placed our dear Grandmother in her last resting place on 1st August 1945. She wanted me to pass her last warm greetings on to you. At Christmas 1945, we had to bury Grandpa Schünemann. So many people have passed away. Uncle Gustav and his family, are with Herwig in Tenzerov, Post Hohenmocker, Kreis, where we were very near to them for eight months,. Uncle Erich (and family), and Aunt Erna are with Müller. Gerderswalde, Kreis Grimmen; Horst visited us a lot. He was buried on exactly the same day that Vera received the first news from you. She hoped that you would be able to come, so that she could explain something important to you. During that time, her father died and just before she had to promise him that she would never leave her mother and that she would marry the father of her child. Because Vera's father assumed that, if you were to forgive her and marry her, later on in the marriage you might rightly reproach her. My dear boy, that must now be the biggest disappointment of your life and it hurts my soul to write about such troubling things. I beg you from my heart to stay strong and overcome your upset. You are still so young and you will find your own good fortune. We are waiting with longing for your release.

We have a room with very nice people, where there is also room for you. Give this address if you get your release. We could only bring very little with us. The main thing is that we should all stay in good health and be able to meet again

We send you our heart felt greetings and kisses, from your mother who always thinks of you and your brother Horst

Replied 23/12   Aschersleben 1.12.46

                                                    17/12

My dear Hans

Once again it is Sunday and I am sending you my best greetings. Unfortunately we did not have mail from you this week, presumably there have been delays, and maybe something will arrive tomorrow. The first Sunday of advent is drawing to a close. Of course at this time of year we are gripped by the longing for our loved ones as well as for our home more than usual, but I have had plenty of work. We have harvested eight hundredweight of sugar beet, and yesterday we made four hundredweight of syrup, the next lot will be done in a fortnight. At least we have something to put onto our bread, and although the work is hard, we do everything possible to survive. Please forgive the bad handwriting, I have such a pain in my right arm. You should have seen us digging the field, loading four hundredweight onto the large wagon and then draging it along for many kilometres, that costs a lot of sweat. But, in the end I manage it and am happy. Otherwise I would not earn anything and would feel completely useless. We both look forward to the day that will bring us a reunion. I hope you have received our picture? When, my dear boy, will you send us a picture of you? Tomorrow evening Horst is insisting on taking me to the theatre, they are showing Mascots, which is supposed to be fun. He got the tickets from a client who works at the Volksbuehne theatre. Tickets are very difficult to come by, but you know that I love best staying at home. If we were all together, things might be different. Healthwise we are doing ok, and we hope the same applies to you. We wish you a healthy Christmas and are sending you lots of love and kisses from your ever thinking of you mum and your brother Horst.

Prenzlau, 16.6.46

11.1/.47

My dear Hans

I want to send you a little letter from your homeland today. I know you are waiting to hear from me and my letters make you happy. Dear Hans, I want to tell you something. The pen seems to go on strike every time I want to write it down. I have to tell you personally but want to spare us a lot of agony. If you then despise me I shall have to accept it and will not try and make you change your mind. Yes, my (dear, little) Hansili, some of the soldiers returning from the war had to experience nothing but disappointments. It depends on whether or not we want to build a life together. You would not understand if I wrote it down and you would not be able to guess. I beg you not to go down this road and please do not ask my mum. She does not know anything. Don't worry too much. I am hoping everything will come right in the end. I know that I have been longing for you all my life and only I am to blame for everything should we not be together one day. Oh Hansili, life is very harsh. If only you could come soon because sometimes the burden is just too much for me. I am so terribly sorry that I have done this to you. If only I could make it up to you. I fear you might not understand me. This letter is a huge mystery to you. Papa is very ill and there is no hope of a recovery. Otherwise, we are all well considering the circumstances. I am sending you my wishes which come straight from the heart, and I hope that my wish will be fulfilled one day .

With lots of love

Yours Vera

Replied 9/2/47   Aschersleben, 15.12.46

21.1.47

My dear Hans

At last, I am managing to write to you. Don't worry, you will now receive more post from me. The exam is behind me, it was not too bad. I had to do such a lot of studying. Now, Christmas is upon us, we are getting busier and busier. It would be so lovely, dear Hans, if you could be here for the Christmas holiday. We hope we do not have to wait much longer. Dear Hans, did you receive my two letters? We have not heard from you for three weeks, I really thought you would be here for Christmas. What are you doing now? Are you still on the farm? Winter is upon us. It has snowed and we have minus 14 ^{o}C. What is the weather with you? We have been busy cooking syrup. Mum has been picking the grain and potatoes all summer and autumn. I have made quite a few acquaintances here. At the moment, I am working in the ladies hairdressing salon. It's a little more interesting. Today I am going dancing again with Berni. She lives in the same house, and also her friend Gretchen. We shall have to teach Berni how to dance first. It would be so lovely, if you and I were together. What is the general mood like where you are? We already had quite a few soldiers coming from England. They had minor injuries. We hope that it will soon be your turn to be discharged. Have you written to Gertrud yet? It was so lovely when we used to spend the long winter evenings at home around the stove, and now everything is gone. It is hard to believe what we had to endure. Papa's lovely suits, the furniture, all had to be left behind. But, slowly, surely, we are starting to rebuild a new home. I have bought mum a standard lamp already and a few other things. But, our one and only wish is to all be together again, healthy and fit. We are longing to hear from our beloved Papa. Mum has written so many letters – hopefully we shall hear something.

My dear Hans, I will finish my letter now, wishing you a healthy and happy Christmas and a good New Year, which hopefully will bring us together again very soon.

With love from your brother Horst and mum.

Sending you our love for Christmas

And all best wishes for a healthy new year

Your Brother

Horst and Mum

2/2.47   Aschersleben, 15.12.46

21.1.47

My dear Hans
Finally, after a long wait, we have received your lovely
letter dated 17.11.46. We were so happy to hear from you
and thank you very much. As we did not hear from you for
three weeks, we thought you might come home for Christmas. However, it does not seem that we shall see you this
year either. It is a great pity because our Christmas, too, will
be very lonely. Our reunion is taking so very long, but one

day, the hour must come. Eight days ago, Thea came with her friend to stay with us for four days. They got a chance to relax a bit. Thea is sending her love to you. Last week I worked very hard making syrup but I have finished now, thank goodness. I am so glad that we now have some spread for our bread, even though it was hard work. I managed to collect nine hundredweight of sugar beet.

Dear Hans, three weeks ago I posted a small parcel to you, with some Christmas cookies, via the Red Cross. I hope it reaches you in time. I wanted you to have a little something for Christmas. A few days ago, it started to get very cold, with the first snowfall and minus 14°C. If only the winter did not get so cold, because we do not have sufficient wood to keep us warm. Dear Hans, Horst has written to you today. He also sent you two letters earlier. Did you not receive them? Sometimes, Horst can get me down a little, because he is constantly saying "if only our Hans would come home". Yes, we are both longing to see you again. I wonder if, in the meantime, you have received my letter in which I talked about our trip through Vorpommern. Please excuse my poor handwriting. I have a lot of rheumatism in my arms. I expect it is due to working such a lot in the cold weather. Oh well, it will get better, I guess. Now, my dear boy, we wish you a Merry Christmas and a very happy, healthy New Year. We hope and pray to meet you again and also see our beloved Papa. With lots of love and kisses from your mum, who is always worrying about you, and from your brother Horst. Hoping to see you very soon.

Replied 9.2.47   Aschersleben, Christmas 1946

29.1.

My dear boy

Today, at Christmas, we are sending you all our love. We are wondering, what kind of a Christmas you are having, so far away from home. We are constantly talking about you, my dear boy, and are sure you are also thinking of us. I baked a lot of cakes. We do not starve, but obviously, it is not how it used to be at home. I have managed to make sure during the summer and autumn, that there will be sufficient food for us all. Did you have some cake for Christmas too? With every bite we take, we are wondering if you have some as well. Now, my dear Hans, I want to thank you from the bottom of my heart, for your letter dated 24.11.46, which reached us a few days ago. I reckon your Christmas mail will reach us some time after the holidays! Yes, it is now the fourth Christmas without you, and the sixth without our beloved Papa. I suppose we have to be grateful that, at least, Horst is still with me. If he had not taken matters into his own hands, I would be completely alone during these hard times. He only remained a few hours in Heringsdorf in April before returning to me in Loitz-Schwinge/ Vorpommern, otherwise, we might never have found each other again. What would have become of me, without money and any kind of support? God has not let us down and rescued us out of hardship and danger, I am confident, he will help us in the future and make our reunion possible.

We both went to church on Christmas Eve. Last night, the manager of the weaving company invited us. He lives in the house upstairs. His eldest daughter celebrated her engagement. Father Christmas was very busy in our house. Horstel made a big effort and gave me an electric blanket, an electric cooker and a big writing set with writing paper. I also got a shopping bag, face toner and cleaning cloths. All these things are hard to come by and can only be obtained via 'someone you know'. I also got some knitting wool from Horstel and some from my landlady. I knitted a gents vest with it. It got finished Christmas Eve. I sometimes knit through the nights because I am so glad when I get more wool in exchange and then I can keep knitting clothes for us all. Horstel got a lovely white woollen scarf, two pairs of warm stockings and a cigarette box, a cigarette holder and also a small machine to roll his own tobacco.

I am so happy that Horstel has not started smoking, because cigarettes are hard to get. Women don't get any and Horst is not 18 yet, and even if he were, they are not easy to come by. Do you get any? We are so sorry that you cannot send us a photo. Have you received ours? Today, we are having real coffee made from real coffee beans, which were given to Horstel. Now, my dear Hans, we send you our love for a happy and healthy new year. Hopefully it will bring us together and our innermost wishes will be fulfilled. The daughter of the Manager of the weaving company gave me a pair of leather shoes. Oh, how poor we have become, but Auntie Lina is even poorer than we are .

I will finish writing for today. Lots of love and kisses from your mum, who is always thinking of you, and your brother Horst.

Here's to a soon and healthy reunion.

Replied 2.2.47

Aschersleben 31.12.46 New Years Eve

29.1.47

My dear boy

We are thinking of you today, the last Eve of the old year, and are sending you our love. In four hours, we shall have a new year. When I think about the past and all that has happened, I know that God has been good to us, he guided us mercifully through our escape and we were spared enormous suffering and misery, even though sometimes we had lost all hope. We want to pray to God and ask him to grant us a reunion in the new year, and I am also praying that I will see our loving Papa again, fit and well. What will you be doing on the last day of the year? Dear Hans, we are longing to receive post from you. 14 days have passed since we last heard from you. Christmas came and went very quickly. I have been busy knitting every day, because we need warm clothes. I have finished a white scarf for Horst. You are getting one as well, and a pair of stockings. I know you have always wanted one. I am longing for the time when you can wear them! Dear Hans, I would like to knit you a jumper with long sleeves, or would you rather have a cardigan with buttons in the front? Please let me know what you would like in your next letter. Horstel has just picked up a gramophone from the lodgers upstairs and the younger daughter of the manager of the weaving company is coming up to see us so we shan't be on our own for a change. I am going to close my letter for today. Please take care and stay healthy.

Hoping to see you very soon, lots of love and kisses from your mum, who is always thinking of you, and your little brother.

Height: 1.73 m

2.2.47   New Year 1947

29.1

My dear son,

Today, on New Year's Day, we are sending you our best wishes.The last day of 1946 lies behind us and a new year has just begun. Will we see you again this year? We shall hope that our wishes come true. I have been knitting last night, Berni, and Horstel played the gramophone to the point of unconsciousness (non-stop), it was a rather cosy evening, we thought about you a lot, how fabulous it would be if you were with us. Berni sends her love too, although you don't know her. Horst is downstairs at the moment, they are dancing a bit now, or else they don't know what to do with themselves, they are bored, as it is a public holiday. At Christmas we had nice mild weather, but from yesterday it started being really frosty again. If only it doesn't turn as cold as 2 weeks ago. How did you my dear Hans spend the holidays? I wonder if you got some cake? With every little bite I'm thinking of you, how much I would like to share it with you. What kind of work are you doing now? Are you cutting wood in the forest? Isn't this the work, the farmers do in winter? I hope you have warm clothes so you don't catch a cold. Here, a few soldiers have returned home from imprisonment over the Christmas period. At some point, the day will come, when you also come back to us. Almost all of Papa's siblings are over there, only Erna and Gerhard with his family are in this area. Are you still together with Gerhard Fenner? At least you would have someone from home with you. Horstel is really looking forward to getting a letter from you. Tomorrow he doesn't need to go to work, the hairdressers are closed. Now I need to come to an end, my dear Hans, keep well and healthy, with lots of love from your Mutti, who is always thinking of you, and your brother Horst. I'm sending you a big New Year's kiss and a healthy re-union very soon.

9.2.47   Aschersleben 2.1.47

31.1.47

My dear Hans,

Today is 2nd of January 1947 and I would like to write to you. The hairdressers are closed today, so it's easy for me. Christmas and New Year are over now. How did you spend the holidays? I hope we can be together really soon, oh, how nice that would be, I can almost not even imagine how it would be. Christmas Eve we went to church, but no feast though, because we didn't have much food. On Christmas day we went to the engagement party. The daughter of the Spinnmeisters got engaged and it was really nice. They had a beautifully laid table. We were talking a lot about you, hoping our wish comes true soon, that you can be with us in the very near future. During the holidays I went to the theatre, and they played "Ein Walzertraum" (A dream waltz) and

"The Silesterbowle" (New Year Punch). Mum is only interested in cinema.

Some people have arrived here from England. We think that it should be your turn now. What do you think? How are you doing, are you still healthy and ok? That's certainly the case for us. Are you still working for the farmer or did you get different work? Before the holidays we were so incredibly busy and the electricity was cut off. At home I got much more tips than here. But some people are "already bent over when they bend down" *. But it's enough anyway. On New Years eve Berni, a neighbour was here and we played the gramophone until midnight. At 12 o'clock we went outside and listened to the ringing of the bells. The war has been over for one and a half years and so many are still missing. If only our Papa would make contact. You probably didn't even have a drop on New Year's Eve, we have been thinking of you so much! Mum has gone out quite a while ago, she is having a good chat. Do you still have really bad weather? Today it snowed a bit again. Tonight I combed my wig again, which I really like. I would really like to have a beautiful wig, but these things are really hard to get. I could make one myself, but you can't get the material, there is a shortage of everything. Dear Hans, what do you think, when you come home, should we stay here or move somewhere else? Perhaps you can get a job in town? Gertrud has sent a picture, she looks quite nice. Did you also get a letter from Gertud? She has already got herself a boyfriend. Now I will finish. Stay well, write soon. We have not heard from you for 2 weeks, My Dear Hans, hope to see you very soon, greetings from your brother Horst and Mum!

*i.e. stingy.

Gertrude Schnandke (nee Stresse)

9/2.47   Aschersleben, 12.1 1947

6.2.47

My dear Hans,

Today is Sunday and we are sending you lots of love! We have not heard anything from you for the last 4 weeks. What's the matter with you? I hope you are not ill? I can't get any rest, I have a terrible headache today. If only there was some news from you. I hope you didn't go back to work too soon after your tonsillitis. Are you not receiving any mail from us either? We have written quite a few letters. Did you get my Christmas parcel with the cookies I sent you via Red Cross in Hannover? The people from the Pub now need to forego another room for the refugees, where shall these poor people a be housed, everybody needs to have a roof over their head. These people have all been expelled from Poland, it is so difficult to be homeless and in a foreign country. Perhaps our fate will turn to positive at some point again. I have just written a letter to Werner, he is in Belgium. How is the weather where you are? Fortunately we have survived the second cold front. I hope the winter is soon coming to an end, firewood is sparse. Horstel just went for a walk, he really needs some fresh air, it's really freezing in his shop . What kind of work are you now doing at the farm, are these farms as big as at home? In a few more months it's going to be better, spring will be here. I hope we will be together then! On February 3rd it will be 2 years since we had to leave our homeland, it doesn't even bear thinking about what we have lost. Even in a lifetime one can't recreate again what we had at home. Now, my dear son, I want to end my letter, please stay well and write as often as you can .Sending much love to you, from your Mum , who is permanently worried about you , and your brother Horst .To a healthy reunion, see you again, very soon .

16.2   Aschersleben, 5.1.1947

12.2

My dear Son,

Unfortunately we have spent the last 3 weeks without mail from you, but nevertheless I want to send you lots of love. It is Sunday again, we had so many public holidays , but that time has gone and we are heading for straight weeks without holidays. How is it possible that the mail system doesn't work well. Horst always thinks that you are already on your way to us. I didn't even have Christmas wishes from you. Last night I dreamt that you were here with us and that we went to the job centre together to look for work. Here it is really cold again, it's better not to leave the house at all. A woman I know just told me that prisoners of war in England are allowed to send parcels to their family. Her husband has already sent one to his parents in the British zone and they then forwarded it to here. I don't know if you have the same rules. It doesn't need to be only for us, because when you are free to come home, there will be a shortage of everything. As I have not heard from you for such a long time, my thoughts are running wild, I hope you are not sick again. The peace negotiations will be in spring and then we will find out, if we will be able to return home, or if our homeland will be lost to us forever. But it can't stay like this forever, all these people are crowded together in one place, more and more transports with refugees are arriving from Pomerania, Silesia and the Sudetenland. Yesterday the regulators were here again, saying even more refugees should be housed here, but I immediately said that we were still waiting for 2 family members. At the end of the day, there has to come the time when you both are back with us again. Now, my dear Hans, I want to finish this letter in the hope of seeing you again soon. Lots of love, with all my heart, Your Mum and brother Horst

Replied 24.2.47   **Aschersleben 31.1.47**   2.2.

Hedwig Schünemann   My dear Hans

I will send you a few lines today. Thank you so much for your letter dated 26.12.46. I am so sad that none of your letters arrived in time for Christmas, but we hope you have received ours. Yesterday we had -28 degrees and today it's -26. It is not very pleasant. There is a little more snow. At least Horst does not have to be in the salon just now. I have read that in the South of England it is also very cold, with lots of snow. I am so glad that you are not in the foreign service. If you are still suffering pain from your original injury, wouldn't it be good if you went to see a doctor. Is your bone damaged? I shall write a letter to Frau Streese today. We are looking into buying a cooker, as our cast-iron one eats up too much fuel, I am using three buckets of coal every day, that's more than I can supply. What a beautiful cooker we had at home! And our beautiful home, such as we'll never have again, but there is no point complaining, what we've lost will never come back. We have struggled all our lives for nothing. We now wish for nothing more than to be together again. Is the young Pfenner in the camp with you? Are there other Pomeranians there with you? Are your comrades the same age as you or older? Tomorrow it will be two years since we have had to leave our beautiful home, and then spend a night at the Streeses, because it was not too near the main road, then there were two nights in the cellar at the dyers Krueger in the Marktstrasse. If you will be with us one day we shall tell you all about it. My dear boy, remain healthy and receive our love and kisses from your mum and your brother Horst.

Here's to a healthy Wiedersehen

Aschersleben 19.1.47

12/2

My dear Hans

We have finally received your dear postcard as well as your letters dated 15.12 and 30.12.46. Many thanks. I have been so worried, but you now have a different job! It being winter, it is probably better for you. I am delighted that you can now undertake long walks, that must be very nice for you. At least you have a change of scenery every now and then. Hopefully the food is good? Did you usually eat at the farmer's? Do you get any tobacco? I know that at home you really used to like smoking. My dear boy, you are telling me that there is little hope of a reunion this year, which has made us very sad. The war has now been over for two years, so the time should soon arrive when you will be able to return to your loved ones. Do we from the East really have to put up with all the hardships of war, having already lost our possessions as well as our homeland, and then have to be separated from our dear ones so long after the end of the war has ended! The people in this area have not had to suffer and cannot put themselves into our shoes. Let us hope that the sun will shine for us one day too. So, you were without mail from us for the holidays. I have not received any Christmas greetings from you either, the mail seems to be stuck somewhere! Did you not receive our letter dated 17.11.46, with our picture ? I have written to you many times, and so has Horst. Please write to Horst as well, he would be so pleased. Well, we have now not seen each other for three years, and what a long and fateful journey we have had to undertake. Before the holiday we have had eight days of grim cold, and the same in the first week of January, but little snow. Stay well, as then we will overcome the long separation more easily. Many dearest greetings and kisses from your always loving and thinking of you mum, and your brother Horst.

Aschersleben 26/1/47

12/2

43

My dear Hans

We are sending you our usual Sunday greetings and thank you very much for your dear letters dated 2.12 and 8.12.46, as well as 5.1.47

Horst also sends his thanks. So you've had to wait for news from us just as we have had to wait from you, for which I am very sorry, because I know how it feels to wait for mail in vain. Both of us are still well and cheerful, and we hope the same applies to you. Who knows where the letters might have been held up for so long. We thank you from all our hearts for your dear Christmas and New Years wishes, if only the New Year may give us a healthy reunion, that is our greatest wish. There is a lot of post coming your way from us, let us hope that slowly slowly it will turn up at yours. So you have received our picture, well it wasn't that great, since then I look a little healthier, I have put on some weight and now weigh 122lbs. Once we are all back together, slowly, slowly we shall acquire everything, because you will be with us for a good while and not want to get married immediately, bearing in mind how young you still are. We are so looking forward to being together once more, and one day that day will come. Provided you have written to all the relatives, you should receive quite a bit of mail. Thea's address remains the same: Thea Rueger Limbach i/Sachsen, Frohnaersstrasse 42. Frau Lehmann sends her best regards, we shall go and visit her this evening. She lives at the other end of town, 20 minutes away from us. Now my dear boy, be healthy and receive love and kisses from your always thinking of you mum and your brother Horst. He will write to you in the next few days.

Replied 16.2.47   Prenzlau, 9.1.47
                              15.2.

Dear Hans

I want to acknowledge receipt of your card dated 17 November 46 and thank you for it. You asked me for Thormann's address. Mr Thormann intended to write to you. Perhaps you have not received his letter yet.

Dear Hans, please don't think of me as a bad person albeit you have every reason for it. I must pour out my heart to you again today. Who else can I trust? I do not know anything about a marriage of unity because both of us have completely different interests. My hands and feet are tied and shall be forever. Sometimes I am finding it very hard. What is my life without any hope of improvement? It is utterly pointless. Oh Hans, it is not right for me to burden you with my misery. I should be writing a proper letter to you. One more thing I would ask you is not to think too badly of me and not to forget me. I know I am not worth worrying about. There is an old saying "you make your bed and lie on it". And that is why I want to try not to cause any more upset. I shall try. In the Spring I shall make an attempt to get over the border and will be staying with my sisters for a while.

We are having unbelievably cold weather at the moment and have no heating or electricity.

Mum is sending her love.

Manfred and Vera

Emil Thormann
Prenzlau Schlenkenberger Strasse
New Pharmacy

Replied 9.3.47
PRISONER OF WAR POST

From: Gerhard Fenner,
PoW No.:   B24237,
Camp: Lodge Moor Camp,
    No. 17 Sheffield,

Yorkshire,
Great Britain.   17.2.47

To: A57285,
                 Johannes Klawitter,
                 PW Camp No. 94 Gaulby Road Camp,
                 WARTNABY, Billesdon,
                 Leicester.
                 GREAT BRITAIN.

This part is for the PoW to write on. Write clearly, only on the lines, and in the Latin alphabet.

Dear Hans   2.2.47

Many thanks for your card, which arrived yesterday. I was very pleased to hear from you. I am still in my old job and am quite well. We still have a lot of snow. It does not look like that I will be discharged soon. When are you leaving? Have you any contact with your loved ones? I am looking forward, with anticipation, to your letter which you promised me. Loving greetings, Gerhard

Replied: 2.3.47   Aschersleben   a/Harz
28/1/47

24.2.47

Horst Klawitter

Dear Hans
I now have time to send you a few lines. Thank you so much for your letter dated 8.12.46. Our salon is closed for six days, as part of the energy saving project. Every hairdresser takes it in turn. Just once, it is very pleasant. It is snowing heavily, we had spring weather for a while, and now winter has returned. Is the weather still really bad where you are? I have been to the theatre several times and have seen the following: 1 Sylvesterbowle (New Year's eve punch), 2. Honey-

mooners and 3. Schwarzwaldmaedel (girls) from the Black Forest. What else can you do, one only lives by air and love. Dear Hans last week I received my final report from the training college, as well as my Master of business administration. It all feels very different when you are holding a piece of paper in your hand. If only you could be with us, it would be so wonderful. How happy I would be to bring you a cake on a Sunday, but unfortunately it is too far. Yesterday I was invited to Gretchen's, she is the friend of Berni who lives in our house. It was very nice. They stuffed me with cake. I ate six pieces of cherry tart, but could easily have eaten a few more, but one mustn't be greedy. It would have been great to see you stuffing yourself with cake too. On February 6th it is Berni's birthday, so there will be lots going on. Dear Hans, we are still all healthy and cheerful and hope you feel the same way. The fact that you are now in the orderly room sounds good, as it will be a bit less demanding? How is your injury – are you still in pain? We have now not seen each other for such a long time, who knows where the time has flown to? Who knows whether we'll ever see our home again??? Let us hope for the best. We did not realise quite how nice it was at home, and now we look back on it with fond memories. The people here who still own their own property cannot understand at all. Very slowly we start from the beginning. Once you can be with us again everything will be easier, because the things we once had no-one is going to give them back to us. So let's not hang down our heads, there are thousands missing in our immediate circle of friends and aquaintances. I am really enjoying my work. The only thing that is missing is a wig which will let me try out various hairstyles. The same applies to tools – there's nothing available. The hair-cutting gadget you gave me has been passed, Mum passed my tools, by employing very clever tricks. Many thanks for your congratulations re my exam, you can't imagine how pleased I was. I worked really hard for it. In the end I did not know where my head was.

Now my dear Hans I would like to send you a picture, it could have been better. Please write soon, bearing in mind that the mail is the only thing to look forward to. Stay well, and may our wish soon be fulfilled. There is no news from Papa. Let us hope we shall all see each other again soon. Lots of love from your brother Horst and your mum

Replied 21/3

    Postage Free

Stamp: Censured Camp 402.   1/3/47

From:	Eichhauer Theodor.
Rank:	Feldwebel (Sergeant).
Identity No.:	1482502.
Squad No.:	20278.
	Depot 402/Thorée/Sarthe/France.
To:	Klawitter, Johannes, Gaulby-Road-Camp No. 94, Camp Wartnaby, Billesdon /Leicester. Great Britain.

_____
_____
This part is reserved for prisoners of war   Write clearly, only on the lines, and in the Latin alphabet.
My dear Hans   Thoree, 10 Feb 1947

I was rather surprised to receive your lovely card dated 23.12.46 and even more so because I expected you to be back home by now. I want to wish you, rather belatedly, a very happy New Year. I am sure we will be discharged soon. Regarding my private life, I have already contacted Washington, but not yet received a reply from a certain department. I shall keep you updated. Yours Theo

20.3

My dear Hans

Today is Sunday and, as usual, I am sending you my Sunday greetings. I had written a letter on Wednesday, but never mind, you won't be cross with me if you receive extra mail. I had also included a photo. It is six weeks today since you wrote your last letter, it arrived four weeks ago. Horst is always in such a bad mood when he returns at lunchtime, and there is no mail from you. I should not forget to thank you for your lovely postcard dated 26th March, which you sent to us in Pyritz just before your departure from America, it was sent to me from the Berlin Post Office, I had given them my address last winter, knowing that this is where all the mail addressed to people on the other side of the river Oder is being sent. If only we were to receive a sign of life from our dear Papa. Yesterday I was very excited and pleased because we had a new cooker delivered, also with an oven, although not quite as big as the one we had had home. The factory owner who is our landlord very kindly delivered it. It cost 132 Mark. Tomorrow I will have to talk to the boss, as I would very much like to pay for it, that way it would be our property and we would have something for our new household and one would not feel quite so poor. How wonderful that we can cook for ourselves. Tomorrow Horstel will be going to a fancy dress party, organised for all the hair artists and you can imagine how much he is looking forward to it. Don't be cross with him for going out dancing, he works so very hard to provide us with the income to live on and he has to have time to enjoy himself too. We are no longer destitute, and have managed to save our first 1000 Mark. Isn't that a wonderful achievement? Now my dear boy, stay well, and let us hope you will soon be with us again. Lots of love and kisses from your mum and your brother Horst, here's to a healthy Wiedersehen soon.

Replied 24.3.47   ## Aschersleben Sunday 2/3/47
22.3.47

My dear Hans

We are sending you our best Sunday greetings and thank you for your letter dated 2.2.47 which made us very happy. It took nearly four weeks. If you've written every Sunday, there must still be a lot of post on its way. Good to know that you have also received some letters from us; believe me, I write as often as you do, and unless I am sending you my Sunday letter, it really is not a Sunday for me. Dear Hans, thank you for sending the address of the Red Cross, I had already written to them 14 days ago, I received the address of the Red Cross in Hamburg and also wrote to them, and they asked me to write to the Red Cross in Moscow, oh if only this was going to be successful!! I have tried everything and spent a lot of money and we don't mind that at all as long as we can find our dear Papa. How lovely it would be if all four of us could be together again. Well, your wish for a jumper I will gladly make come true. Here we still have lots of snow and it is cold. Sometimes it seems as though the thaw will set in, but so far it has not happened. I now have to produce a knitted cardigan and a sleeveless jumper, that way I can earn myself some more wool, so maybe I can knit you a sleeveless jumper for the summer. That way you will have something new to wear. If only it was spring, our lives would be easier then. Well, now you are the same height exactly as your brother Horst – well, if I stand between the two of you I'll be invisible. I think you are both taking after grandpa. Well my dear now I shall finish this letter, stay very well and be loved and kissed from your dear mum and your brother Horst. Please write to Horst every now and then, it will make him very happy. Here's to a happy and healthy Wiedersehen

Replied: 30.3.47   ## Aschersleben 23.2.47

29.3.47

My dear boy
Another week has passed, and we are sending you our very
dear Sunday greetings, and still no news from you. It makes
one downright miserable when you have to wait for mail
every day. We hope you are well as indeed we are. If only
you didn't have to be without mail from us for so long. It
has been absolutely freezing here for so long, if only it would
stop being so cold. Some people no longer know what to
use for cooking their lunch, the older people in particular,
as they are no longer able to collect fuel. Last week I sent
a package to Aunt Emilie in Berlin, that way she can make
herself a nice soup. I feel very sorry for her, all alone. She has
also heard nothing from their Erich. Hilde Rindt also has to
provide for herself, her two boys and her father. Life seems
to be twice as difficult now. My only wish is for us to be reunited in health as soon as possible. Surely one day this day
will arrive. We have been using our new cooker for eight
days now, it makes much better food. I'm not sure if I already
told you, but us women are now receiving ration cards, not
that you can buy much with it, but it is better than nothing.
Are you enjoying your new job? Do you have to go out in the
freezing cold but maybe it is not that cold there? Now my
dear boy stay well, keep your spirits up – the time will surely
be over one day soon. Lots of love and kisses from your always thinking of you mum and your brother Horst. Here's to
a healthy Wiedersehen

Replied: 30/3.47 Aschersleben 26.2.47

Received 29/3

My dear boy
What a pleasure it was to receive your letter dated 20.1.47,
which took five weeks to arrive. We had been waiting for
news from you for such a long time, and every day Horst

was so disappointed when nothing arrived from you. From your letter I can see that you also have not received anything from us for a long time. You can believe me that I write to you every Sunday and sometimes also during the week. In your letter you say that you are sending us five letters a week, but surely you wrote that in error and meant to say that you are writing five letters per month? It means that there is a lot of mail still on the way. If only the letters arrived at regular intervals, the long wait is terrible. It must be hard for you when others get mail and there is nothing for you. We also had a letter from Aunt Edith today – Uncle Gustav has taken over a settlement, near Altentreptow in Vorpommern. He cannot carry on working as a farmhand with six men and without his son. She also told me the story about Herta. He is a right scoundrel, abandoning Herta with little Inge, and such a guy returned home in good health!

I also had mail from Mrs Unger from Pyritz, she is in Itzehoe in Holstein. In January she found her husband, they had been looking for each other for 23 months and have now found each other and they are so happy. Her husband was released in July 1945 and worked on a farm in Bavaria. If only we could finally find our papa. Sometimes one could despair when there is no news. Winter has not yet finished here, if only spring would arrive. But do not worry about us, even this winter will finish eventually. Much love and kisses from your mum and your brother Horst – here's to a speedy Wiedersehen

Replied: 6/4.47   Aschersleben 26.2.47

29.3

Dear Hans

As I have some time today I would like to send you my greetings from afar. After a long period of cold today finally everything is melting and when the sun smiles everything looks brighter and more cheerful. I am finding it difficult to write because, just imagine it, we are both suffering from full stomachs, me having eaten ten potato pancakes for supper and mum has eaten nine, but of course made without fat. Do you still have such terrible weather? If only spring were here, so we could go for walks in the evening. What are your thoughts about your release? Hopefully the day of seeing each other again will arrive soon. On Sunday I went sledging at the castle, but I sat more in the snow than on my toboggan! Eight days ago last Monday we had our hairdressers fun evening, hair styling and fancy dress show, it was really interesting, but very crowded. And all the drunk women!!!!! I had borrowed a black tie outfit but looked as though I was about to get married, the suit fitted me like a glove. The do started at 7 in the evening and ended at 3 am. I went home at 1 am as there was no more room to dance. Edith has written today, they are planning to settle in Altentreptow, they have been farmhands for so long without really earning anything. Herta also has a tough deal, who would have thought that Heinz Ludwig is such a bastard to abandon her like that. We have expanded our shop and employed a helper and another hairdresser, but in this freezing weather we are sitting around without much to do. I am based in the ladies' salon, but also work in the barbers section. If only there were more tools available, you can't buy any combs, and it's the same with other tools too. Gertrud also wrote, she had a sweetheart, but has now sent him on his way. But how are you, my dear Hans? The long wait for mail is terrible and the bad weather causes even more delays. I have written several times. Have you been spending time outside? The fact that you are allowed time outside is clearly worth a lot, but my biggest wish is that we shall all be together again, build up a new future together and be able to call something our own. Some things we have already acquired, now we're about to buy a small cooker and a hand cart, one has to start somewhere. Today we received your letter dated 20 January – what delight and excitement to receive a letter from our Hansell! Are you still working in the writing room? Hopefully your leg is not giving you too much pain? It has been such a long time but it does not seem to want to heal? What are the people like? I am now used to going to bed early – not much to do when you are lonely. Mum also wrote to you today, let's hope it won't take too long to reach you. I have grown a lot, Hans, I am now 1.76, so quite tall. How tall are you? Now I shall stop as there is nothing more to say for now. Stay well and write soon

All the best from your brother Horst and mum. Here's to a healthy Wiedersehen

Replied 30.3.47 **Aschersleben 5.3.47**

29.3.

My dear Hans

I thank you very much, from the bottom of my heart, for your lovely letter dated 12.1. and card 26.1.47. Slowly, the mail is starting to get through again. Well, you can listen to the radio, that's great. At least it will give you some other interest.

We are looking forward to receiving your photo soon. It would make us really happy. Ice and snow are showing signs of thawing.. We shall all be very relieved when spring comes in a few weeks, and winter is gone. I would love to have a suit made for Horstel, which he badly needs, but we cannot get any sewing cotton, in spite of having had the ration voucher since October. Horst has outgrown all his clothes and it is very difficult to get anything at all. If only we did not have to leave everything behind and now we have nothing. Papa's lovely clothes! Horst only salvaged Papa's winter coat. It was a good job he wore it when we escaped, otherwise he would not have anything. I was not able to take anything apart from my skirt which was part of a suit. I had to leave all my coats behind. Later on I managed to have grandma's winter coat altered for myself. We often talk about the home we used to have and can still not believe that we have lost everything! If only it were a bad dream, from which we would awaken, and we are back home again.

Horstel is already asleep. It is 10 o'clock, and I shall also go to bed soon.

Easter is here in 4 weeks' time. Looking back at the last winter, it was very harsh but it had gone quite quickly again. I am sending you lots of love and kisses, your mum and brother Horst. Looking forward to a healthy reunion.

Replied 30.3.1947   Aschersleben, 14.3.1947

29.3.1947

My dear boy

Today it's already Thursday again and we are still waiting in vain for post from you. If only letters would start to be delivered regularly again ! Today we want to give you a little pleasure, we have had our photos taken again. The photo of Horst is a good likeness, but mine is not especially good. On the photo my mouth looks so wide, as if I could eat asparagus side-ways on! But at any rate you will notice that I look in better condition than in the photo taken in August.

I received post from Aunt Erna and Aunt Grete. They send you hearty greetings. In August, Herta was in hospital with diphtheria, for a long time. Meanwhile her husband (Heinz Ludwig) got involved with someone else. That is surely wickedness without compare! I feel really sorry for Herta. She waited for him for such a long time and has been living a totally blameless life. All one can say is … "Ugh !"

The farmer where Uncle Gustav is living is now selling his business. He wants to better himself. For two years now, Uncle Gustav, with 6 people, has been doing his work for him for nothing and now they have no idea where they can go! Everywhere, the refugees are simply exploited and they certainly weren't to blame for the war, yet had to leave their homeland and lose all their goods and possessions. People who have never had that experience are completely unable to 'put themselves into our shoes'.

Now, dear boy, I must finish this letter. Stay healthy and write as often as you can. From your ever-caring mother, with hearty greetings and kisses, also from your brother Horst.

Replied:14/4.47 Aschersleben 9.2.47
9/4.47

My dear Hans

We are sending you our very best Sunday greetings. The post is terrible. The last letter we received was dated 5.1.47 and it reached us three weeks ago. Probably the fault of the long, fierce winter. This winter really has it in for us! Some people really must suffer from this extreme cold. I am so glad that you are keeping warm! I only go outside if it is unavoidable. Aunt Lina and Uncle Erich have written this week, they send their best regards. They had received your mail and were very happy, and will reply soon. They think that in the New Year we shall all be back home, but I don't really believe it yet. Who knows whether the time will come that soon, but it would of course be lovely as one does not want to carry on living in foreign parts forever. The main thing however would be for you and Papa to be back with us. Last night in my dreams, as so often, I was back in Pyritz. If only everything hard was only a bad dream, and we could call our lovely home our own again, and we would not be so poor and without our homeland. We have heard that in April they are releasing the soldiers who were fighting in Africa, so maybe after that it might be our turn soon – let us hope. We also heard from Gertrud this week – she no longer has her boyfriend, they had a fight. Now my dear boy, I shall close this letter. Horstel is already in bed. Stay well and write as often as possible. Much love and kisses from your always thinking of you mum and your brother Horst. Here's to a healthy Wiedersehen. Hopefully we shall receive post from you tomorrow.

Replied 2/.4.47 **Aschersleben, 9.3.47**

9/4.47

My dear Hans
We are sending you our love today, Sunday. We are sorry to say that we have not received any post from you yet, but we are hoping something will arrive next week. Mrs. Höhl, who lives downstairs, has just brought us two lovely rabbit joints for our lunch. We were so happy about it because otherwise our lunch would have been completely without meat and fat. This is the fourth time we have been given meat for our lunch. Do you think our lives will ever be as good as they were before?

Only four more weeks till Easter. We are sending you our love for Easter and hope you will have a healthy holiday period. It seems one holiday follows another and we are still separated. Please would you write to grandma? Her birthday is on 8.4. She is staying at Erna's in Altenpleen, near Stralsund, c/o Böger. They would all be very happy to hear from you. I had a letter from them during the week and they are saying 'hello' to you. They were asking after you and would like to know how you are getting on. Grandma has a very bad heart. She worries a lot about Werner. You see, everybody has their own worries. It was very hard for her that grandpa had to leave so early. I would have loved to have both of them here with me, but I cannot obtain a permit for their relocation. Horstel has gone out for a while. He badly needs it as he spends all day standing up in the salon and the bad air in the salon is not good for anybody. There is no fresh air which leads to germs breeding and results in staff getting sick. He is trying to find another job, as his boss is a terribly nervous man. He is always trying to get one over on this staff. It would be good if he could find something else. , Today I went to the hairdresser's. They made a fantastic job. Now, my dear boy take care, look after yourself, and stay healthy. I am sending you lots of love and kisses. Your mum and brother Horst.

Replied 14/4.47   **Aschersleben 16.3.47**
                                              13.4

My dear Hans

We are sending you lots of love today, Sunday. We are so sad not to have received any post this week again. This constant waiting and hoping for post is very upsetting for us. We received a letter from Werner this week. He wanted to know how you are and is sending his best wishes. Winter has not left us yet, today it is freezing again. Right next to the house in which we live, flows the Eine, a small, calm river. It has an ice cover of 80cm thick and normally it has to be blasted. Well, two days ago we had 8°C which caused the ice to melt resulting in a terrible flood never seen before. An entire part of the town was flooded. The water came so quickly killing cows, horses and also smaller animals. The water came up to 2 metres high. We were lucky. The entrance to our yard was blocked, which stopped the water from gushing in. The house we live in is standing practically on its own, which is better than being in the middle of town with narrow roads. If we get a repeat of the melting snow and ice, it will start all over again and also we shall be getting water from the Harz mountains. It is a completely different landscape from what we had at home. I told you in my last letter that Horst would like to change jobs. Well, this morning his boss came to him and begged him to stay. He offered him more money as well. He knows that Horst is a good worker and if Horst left him, all his regular clients would be following him too. He said that he made a good impression on his boss from the minute he saw him. 'He recognised that he was upright, righteous and vigorous, and he has great respect for him'. Well, I would not put up with too much nonsense. One has to stand up for oneself in life, otherwise they do what they want with you. Horst is still working in town. He has a few private clients, who want their hair done.

My dear Hans, please stay well. I am sending you lots of love and kisses, your mum and your brother Horst.

To a healthy reunion

Replied 14/4.47   Aschersleben 26.3.47

12/4.

My dear Hans

Thank you very much for your two letters dated 16.2.and 24.2.47. We were very happy to hear from you. Well, finally, you have now also received our mail. I am sending you our first Spring Greetings. The snow has only just disappeared and the first snowdrops are coming through. Spring has truly begun and we are enjoying the better weather. The starlings have arrived too. You know, Hans, it is quite impertinent of Vera to write to you. She should really give you some peace. Her mother wrote to me in January and mentioned that Vera is not happy in her marriage. She did not think the young man would behave the way he does. He does not do any repairs in the house. Frau Halling wrote 'if my husband knew about it, he would turn in his grave'. Well, they cannot blame anybody, only themselves. She wanted it that way. I was supposed to send you her best wishes, but I intentionally did not want to, because I am happy now that you have got over her. I don't wish to keep reminding you. Believe me, it would not have been the ideal marriage for you. And it would have upset me if we had not been able to see you anymore and I should have to be in this world all on my own with Horst. I would have been very happy for you had you settled in a nice home all of your own, but we are also very happy and looking forward to being together again. What will be will be. Horst did Köhl's two daughters hair again, and he came back with 1.5 lbs. of butter. Last week, he came back with 1.5 lbs. of bacon and four eggs. We were so happy about the food. It all goes towards our Easter meals. You are asking if we have sufficient fire wood. If we did not help ourselves, it would have been quite bad. Horst has gone out again today to try and get what he can find. There are usually hundreds of people doing the same thing, some are better off than we are. Necessity is the mother of invention. We are finding it very difficult, but what else can we do? Mrs. Lehmann has already got some good food reserves. She is sending her regards to you. She has not got it easy with her four children. She doesn't know anything about her husband. Do look after your leg. I am always worried about you. Now, my dear Hans, stay healthy. We are sending you our love and kisses. Your mum and Horst.

Me with my grandchildren Udo and Ursula Waldeck.
The smaller one is Lutz-Werner Pöppen , Johannes' youngest.

I wish you a very happy birthday, with my love..

Mum Halling

Replied 20.4.47   Gross Rhüden, 31.3.47
                                    14.4.47

Dear Hans

You will be surprised to receive post from me. I have carried
a heavy load on my shoulders for a long time and I intended

61

to write to you long before now. Werner and Erna and Gerhard have brought me here so that I can regain some of my inner peace. The last two years were just too much for me. And you, my dear boy, have not been spared any agony either. Although we have not seen each other, for some time I hold you in the highest esteem along with your with your lovely mum, with whom I am also corresponding.

Dear Hans, I want to reproach Vera and myself every day for our feelings. Fate dealt us a big blow. If only Vera had received your lovely letter of forgiveness one day earlier, everything would have turned out better and Vera would still be free today. The wedding application at the Registry Office was made only one day before your letter arrived. Both Vera and I cried our hearts out when we read it. It is a big weakness on behalf of Vera and myself, that we were so frightened of this scandal becoming public, and now we have to live with the consequences. I am reproaching her to a large extent because she did not trust me completely and caused Papa and me terrific pain. In spite of her big mistake, we did not judge her. We loved her pretty, happy little girl and were heartbroken when we had to bury Helga on Christmas Eve 45. Her parting is still today incomprehensible to me. We were left with despair and the fact that my dear husband was quite ill at that time added to our agony. When Marga and her husbands family went to the West, our lives seemed desolate and empty. AND: one of Papa's fellow soldiers sought refuge in our house as he was unable to find any of his relatives after his discharge, he died a few weeks later in our house. He was in Russian captivity. Our house is also badly damaged. Some parts are almost in ruins and badly need our attention. Our Papa was unable to do anything, he was so ill. I have now opened a dressmaking business. After my dear husband was very sick at home in bed for weeks, he then had to spend another thirteen weeks in hospital. I went to see him every morning and every afternoon. He begged me to take him home, which I did of course, and on the third day I closed his eyes. In the meantime Otto arrived. He promised Papa he would look after Vera and me as best he can. His promise eased my husband's parting. He, who only cared for others all his life, worried until the end of his dying days about his loved ones. We postponed the wedding by

three weeks and all the time we were waiting to receive a letter from you with your decision. Unfortunately it arrived one day after Vera had submitted the application. Vera cried bitterly half the evening. The wedding was a very miserable event. Vera still lives with us because her husband lives with his mother, his three sisters, their husbands and nine nieces together in one house. There are constant arguments among those women, they are always fighting. I was there once and never again. Otto makes lots of promises but does not keep any. I am not going to take him seriously any more. Fate will take its course. I do not expect a good outcome of Vera's marriage. I am very happy at the moment where I am, with my child, because I was at the end of my tether. All is well here. We are enjoying peace and quiet. Dear Hans, I wish you the very best in life, it is coming from the bottom of my heart.
Mum Halling

Replied 27/4.47   Aschersleben, 23.3.47

14.4.47

My dear Hans
Today is Sunday, the first day in spring, and we are sending you lots of love. The weather is gorgeous, warm air and – yes – immediately one is in a completely different mood. I have already spent all morning hanging up the washing for Mrs. Bode. She gave me two eggs and a bucket full of firewood. That's how we have to help ourselves.

I have just had a visitor. A woman from our homeland, from Soldin, came to see me. She lives in Aschersleben too. We see each other now and then and it makes us very happy when we can chat about our homeland. It is evening now. Horst went to the theatre. He begged me to go with him, but I did not feel like it. They are playing ' Maske in Blau' ('The blue Mask'). It is supposed to be very good, but never mind, my thoughts are always with you and our Papa. You, too, have to cope with all this, so I have to make an effort to do the same. I am busy knitting, having just delivered another jumper.

Horstel's new suit is finished and I have nearly finished your sleeveless top. I shall soon be able to start on a short sleeved jumper for myself, which I shall wear with my skirt. It is the only garment which I was able to rescue and is part of a suit, which Papa tailored. I am sad that I don't have the lovely suit jacket to go with it. I had nothing but the winter coat from grandma! Easter will be here in two weeks' time. How will you be celebrating the Easter period? We hope you will have a lovely Easter. Make it as nice and pleasant for yourself as possible. My dear boy. Please stay healthy, and we are sending you our love and kisses. Your mum and Horst.
Hoping to see you again very soon. We are longing to receive some news from you.

Replied 27/4.47   Aschersleben, 19.3.47

16.4.47

My dear Hans

I received your lovely letter dated 9.2.47 today and thank you from the bottom of my heart, and the same for Horstel's letter dated 9.2.47. It was so lovely to get some news from you. The constant wait for post is awful. I think there must be some post from you, which you wrote in January, still outstanding. I am quite upset that you still have not received my Christmas parcel. I made the cake especially for you because I know how much you love cake. I hope it will get there one day!! I would love to send you more parcels more often, if I knew they would reach you. Please don't think that we have to suffer because we are sending you food parcels. We shall always have some cake for you. I bake a cake every Sunday for the two of us and we always think of you when we enjoy it. How we would love to share the cake with you. It's a nice day today, much milder. Perhaps winter has finally left us now. When I think back about our home and lovely garden – we would be able to almost start with some gardening work now- my thoughts are make me very sad and my longing for our homeland gets greater and greater. Sometimes, I get so sad that I could cry forever. I know I must not let Horst see me like that because it makes him sad also. When I have finished my letter tonight, we are intending to walk out a little. I have a bad headache which comes from all the knitting I do. Our one and only electric lamp only has a 15 Watt bulb. The 60 Watt has broken and we are unable to replace it. The poor light makes my eyes sore. If only you could come out for a walk with us!! This day must surely come sometime!! Horstel sits by my side and is trying to smoke a cigarette. He looks rather clumsy. When you were his age you had a lot more experience in that respect. Horst thanks you very much for your letter. He will write back soon. Lots of love and kisses from your mum and brother Horst. Here's to a very special reunion.

Replied 4/5.47   Aschersleben, 30.3.47

19.4.47

Horst Klawitter

My dear Hans

Many thanks for your lovely letters dated 9.2.47 and 2.3.47. It always makes us very happy to hear from you. It is nice to know that you are now in the office. It must be better for you and more peaceful. How do the people behave towards you? Why are you not hopeful that you will be discharged soon? It will be wonderful when we are all together again. We are almost like strangers now as we have not seen each other for so long. Now spring has come it gives us more opportunities to get out of the house. I wish you had a bit more variety to take your mind off things. Your camp sounds rather small, but I would imagine that is nicer than being in a huge camp. I went to the theatre recently and saw 'Maske in Blau' (Mask in blue). It was wonderful, it went on for 3.5 hours. Two days ago I took mum to the cinema. We saw 'Foundling', a Russian film. It was such rubbish we felt like leaving the cinema. Our films are much better and they are always fun to watch. I want to go dancing this afternoon. I have not been for a long time, because I don't have the shoes I need. Dear Hans, when you switch on the radio, you are not far away from us. We are missing our lovely radio a lot because when you listen to music, it puts you into a different mood.

When we have our coffee on Sunday afternoons, we always say that we would love to offer you some cake, but you are too far away for that. The post takes so long and you have still not received the parcel with the cake from us. Who knows where it got stuck. We were given the envelopes from Eichhorn as a gift after our examination. Yes, my dear Hans, where have all the years gone? I will be 18 years old soon and I really don't feel like it. And I don't have much to do with girls. They are usually all the same. It would appear that Vera made a big mistake. Oh well, we don't know whether it will do any good. She is not like my little Berni. I am only her hairdresser and nothing else. My new suit which I should have had for Easter, is still not finished, but it should be ready after Easter. I have quite a lot of female clients. They all want their hair combed every Sunday. It's very busy at the moment because Easter is approaching. I am doing one perm after another. Everybody wants to look smart for Easter. You say that you will not be with us in the foreseeable future. You are now in the Office and as such, you can write out your own holiday permission; that should be very easy! But easier said than done I suppose. Today is Confirmation Day. I always think back to our Confirmation. How lovely it was back in our home country, and now there is a dark shadow over it all. We had a terrible flood caused by the river Oder. The river rolled slowly on the ground for over 50 km. Over 20.000 people lost their homes. It seems the war has not taken enough victims. Only the very tops of the roofs are visible, everything else is under water.

After Easter I want to look around for another job. I want to better myself and gain more experience. I have been in the current salon since April last year, almost one year now. Dear Hans, I cannot think of anything else to write at the moment. Please write back soon. We are sending you lots of love and kisses, from Horst and mum. Here's to our reunion. Take care and stay healthy.

Prisoner of War Service

From: Hans Klawitter.
Prisoner's No.:   A572859.
                    Gaulby-Road Camp No. 94 (Wartnaby).
                    Billesdon/Leicester – Great Britain.

To: Mrs. A Halling c/o Waldeck.
                    Gross-Rhüden am Harz.
                    Schlackenstrasse 179.
                    Germany – ~~Russ~~ British Zone.

My dear mum Halling   England, 20 April 1947

I received your letter dated 14.4.and thank you very much. Obviously, I was rather surprised but, of course, very pleased to know that you are still thinking of me. I was interested to read the contents of your letter. I did not see very clearly at the time. Please don't worry about me, because it is easier for me to be on my own than it is for Vera. Her letter was the first one among the post which I received after two years of living in England. You can imagine how happy I was to receive it but as I had read on, I got more and more upset. The pain and the disappointment became too much for me. I was suddenly confronted with an irreversible situation. I loved Vera very much and would have done everything for her. But one can be wrong. Before I got discharged I had to state my address in Germany and I put down Prenzlau (Vera's). Therefore, all the other documents were issued with her address. My only wish is that she will have a very happy life and that all her worries and sorrows, with which she is now burdened, will soon be taken from her. I am also looking forward to seeing you and having a nice chat. May you find calm and relaxation. Please give my regards to everyone and pass on my congratulations to Marga on the birth of her Ursula. I would be very happy to hear from you again soon. I must close for today, with love, yours Hans.

Replied 27/4.47 **Aschersleben, Good Friday 1947**

21.4.47

My dear Hans

Thank you very much for your lovely letter dated 2.3.47, which reached us in good health. It is very strange that you have to wait such a long time before you receive our letters and, of course, vice versa. We always write back to you soon after receipt of your letter. Now the bad weather has taken a turn for the better, mail deliveries should be much easier. Horst worked very hard before Easter and is still busy doing ladies' hair. He has to keep all his private clients happy. I had my hair done very early this morning. I have prepared his favourite meal today: dumplings made with yeast and pears which I had preserved. He does not know it yet. I know he will be very pleased. How I would love to share it with you! Two days ago we bought a hand-drawn cart. It is a very strong one, but not as good as the one we had at home, and it has metal wheels. I was in real need of one. I will use it to get the coal home, and also – if I stay healthy – to transport the potatoes which I hope to glean again later in the year. It would be too difficult for me to carry such loads long distances. We had to pay DM 110. It is a lot of money but needs must. We are managing to build up a few possessions again little by little. If ever we have to move or go back to our homeland, we shall have quite a few belongings to take with us. For Whitsun Tide we have been invited to Eilsleben. The Gogolins have invited us. You don't know them, but it is your Aunt. The last time they came to us, you were only 6 months old. I knew that they then lived in Eilsleben near Magdeburg. I wrote to the Citizens Registration Office to enquire about their address. They wrote straight back to me and I subsequently sent the Gogolins a letter. They said they often talked about us but did not know where we lived. They are sending their best wishes to you. Of course, I would not have accepted their invitation if they had any connection with Klawitter but they don't know anything about him. They never really had a good opinion of him. They would love to know why we went our different ways at the time. Uncle Karl Klawitter in Berlin, Auntie Marta and their son Gerhard have all died. The Gogolins also had to make many sacrifices during the war. It will make a change for us to go there and they are looking forward to seeing us again. Leopold and his family from West Prussia will be there too.

Now, my dear boy, we are hoping you will enjoy a good Bank Holiday. Stay healthy, and we are sending you lots of love and kisses. Your mum and your brother Horst.

We are looking forward to a healthy reunion.

Mrs. Lehmann wishes to be remembered to you.

4 /5.47   ## Aschersleben Easter 1947
28.4.47

.

My dear Hans,

We send you sincere Easter greetings, the weather today is very uncomfortable. Rainy and stormy which makes my heart feel very heavy. 6 years ago, I was with Papa in Schlesien and it was much nicer. I wonder where our Papa is? The thought never leaves my mind, how happy I would be if I would have a nice life. I am waiting desperately for it every day. Last night I dreamt Papa was with us, wouldn't it be nice if the dream came true!!! I haven't received any Easter wishes from you yet, I guess it will arrive later. What would you be doing today? I am sure you will be having a nice walk. When I finish with this letter, I will write to Thea. We received post from her today and she sends regards to you. She received your Card and she was very happy, but she wonders if she can write letters to you or if you're only allowed cards. We received a letter from Aunt Lina the day before yesterday, she

69

misses the homeland . Her hosts are not nice people. I am so sorry for her, because she had to endure so much in her life. We don't have much, but Aunt Lina has even less. She wrote about her frozen feet which won't heal.

She didn't have any felt slippers for the winter, so she had to walk with her socks on. I sent her 100g Wool for Christmas, so she could at least fix her socks. If you think about it, she had such a good life at home. I thought that everything was OK until I read something in a store window. "Forget what was yesterday, don't think about what was. It is not going to come again, even if you cry very much." Horstel sends you his kind regards, he has just gone out. He didn't want to leave because he thinks that I ponder too much when I am alone. It is so good for him to get some fresh air as he worked the whole afternoon. Dear Hans, don't worry too much about us, we are both healthy and hope you too. Horst`s salary is quite good, he gets about 50 M. including tips per week. He is very economical. You remember we told you to be economical when you grew up. When you read this letter you might think that I am very melancholic today, but hopefully these cloudy days should be over soon and the sun will shine for us again. So, my lovely boy I hope that you will stay healthy. My thoughts are always with you. Kind regards and kisses from your Mum and your brother Horst. So long and good-bye. Frau Lehmann sends her regards.

4/ 5.47   Archersleben, 9.4.47

28.4.47

Dearest Hans,

I wanted to write you a few lines today. The Easter festival is over now. The weather is not very nice at the moment, mostly rain. April does what it wants. * I went to the cinema on the 1st and 2nd holiday with mum. "Der Flo im Ohr" (The flea in the ear) and "Tanz mit dem Kaiser" (Dance with the Emperor) were on. Mum needs a bit of a distraction or she thinks about things too much. There was a nice Easter meadow near the Castle for the festival, the kids were rolling the Easter eggs down it. They also had three carousels there. We were so busy before the festival, everyone wanted to perm their hair and the air was very bad, I was glad that I could breathe fresh air at the end of a working day. Now I am working at the men's hairdresser. I really enjoy it. There was a 25th anniversary party in our house and we were invited. It was really nice, above all they had "Friedenskuchen" which melted in the mouth like butter. I wished you were here, then it would have been very cosy. Our biggest wish is that we could be together again soon. Mrs. Lehmann visited us on the 2nd holiday with her kids, the lounge looked very messy afterwards. Dearest Hans how are you? I need to try on my new suit, hopefully I will still have it when you come, so I can show it to you myself. Don't think I don't have time to write because I go dancing, that would be very sad, I always have time for you. So, dearest Hans the next time I will write a bit more because I don't know what to write anymore. Write back.

Best greetings and kisses from Horst and Mutti. Hopefully see you soon and healthy. Come back to us soon.

- a german saying

Replied: 4/5.1947   **Aschersleben 30.3.1947**
                                   30.4

My dear Hans,

Today I want to send you my usual Sunday greetings again.

It is Palm Sunday and today those who have been confirmed are going to be blessed. Eight years ago we celebrated your confirmation and yet it seems as if it happened only yesterday. Horst's confirmation was 4 years ago. Time just flies by. Last year we were invited to Uncle Gustav's, when his three boys were confirmed, that was also a wonderful day.

I had already replied to your letter last Wednesday, then yesterday Horst received your mail of 2.3.1947. He was very pleased and will write back to you later today. At the moment he is out again, working for his private clients.

Tomorrow is my washing day. Hopefully it will be good weather for drying. I have already finished a major cleaning of our room, so now we are ready for Easter. Recently we received mail from Aunt Grete. She writes that Hilde Rindt (from Berlin) - who visits her with Jürgen every three weeks - wants to come again at Easter. I can only think that it is a pure nuisance for her.

Everyone, of course, has to look out for themselves as best they can. Anyway, Berliners get more allocation than anyone else – they get [Ration] Card 3 whereas we get [Ration] Card 4. But then, they always had it so much worse. Hilde has written several times to ask me if I could get hold of butter, flour and potatoes for her. That is impossible for me to do, as we live in town as well and are glad if ever we can wangle something for ourselves. Those who own gardens are busy working strenuously to grow food, if only we could be at home and working in our own beautiful garden. It is so sad! Will we ever get back to our own garden again?

Who would have thought that fate would force us to come to the Harz region! If, in spite of everything, we manage to stay healthy, we'll take a few trips there in the summer. Maybe you'll be back here by then, that would be wonderful. Now my dear boy I will finish for now. Stay in good health for me! With warm affection and kisses from your mother and from your brother Horst.

With hopes that we'll see you again very soon!

Mrs. Lehmann sends you her best wishes.

Replied 4/5.1947   Aschersleben. 13/4/1947

30.4.

My dear Hans,

It is already Sunday again and we send you many greetings. Sadly we have received no post from you this week. It is really peculiar how mail from you never arrives in time for any festive event. Your last letter was dated 9.3.47. Never mind, we have hopes that the new week will bring something.

We have wonderful spring weather now. The bushes are turning green and soon the shoots will be out. Life will be very different compared to the biting cold we have had. Yesterday I had another letter from Frau Halling. She is now in the west at Marga and Ernst's place and wants to stay there for the time being and recover. She writes that she also wrote to you the same day and that you have written to her more than once. But none of this has any purpose any more and only reminds you of what happened again and again. I think Vera would prefer to get a divorce and then marry you. Well anyway, I hope you would never be so stupid, would you! Because there are many other girls, besides Vera, so you still have plenty of choice. She should have thought about it earlier. The good thing is that it happened in this way, before you married each other, because what would have happened if you had already been married to her!

Aunt Else and family asked me to pass on their best wishes to you. They have already settled in. For nearly two years all six of them have worked at Herrwigs for nothing and are just as they were when they arrived. They gave each one of them a room, together with 6 eggs, ¾ butter, 2 Ltr. of potatoes and 1 ½ Ltr. dehydrated food for horses. They have worked strenuously day in, day out, wearing themselves to the bone. But that is the fate of refugees, they are exploited like working slaves.

Aunt Erna also sends you warm greetings. I always feel very sorry for her, because whenever Aunt Grete barters anything, there is never anything left over for Aunt Erna. From time to time she gets a small packet of something and a little bit of money, so that she can get something she wants. She doesn't have any cash left now. Just like I have used up every bit of the money I had. In spite of everything though, we aren't in dire need in that respect.

Well, my dear Hans, I must end my letter now. Stay in great health, with warm greetings and kisses from your mother and your brother Horst.

Prenzlau 6.4.47
30/4

Dear Hansi

Thank you very much for your card dated 16.2., which I received a while ago. You have agreed to stand by me, to be my confidant. I did not really want to burden you with all my problems, but I know that you understand me completely. I do not intend to embellish anything. I am still angry. Erna and Werner collected mum on 23.5. and took her to the West so that she can have some rest and find a new lease of life from being with the children. I am attaching a small photo of us. You can see by the picture how mum is. I am all alone in the house and sometimes even half the night. Manfred cannot get enough pleasures! The reproaches he gets from mum and me do not help, they only cause more trouble. We mean well and only want to help him. He also has some strong political opinions and participates in political activities far too much. With mum not here at the moment and he does not listen to me. I attended a cutting-out-course in January/February and am now working independently as a self-employed person. I manage to have sufficient money to live on for myself and Fredi. I don't know how long I can continue like this. I quite like this situation and am satisfied if Otto, my husband, does not ask me to move into his house. I am fighting against it as long as his sisters are living in his house.

There are six women in the house: three are married between 36 and 50, the men were all in captivity and have already two grown-up daughters. His 70-year-old mother also lives with them. It is just impossible. I go there rarely and then I have to hold my tongue not to say the wrong thing. I am not allowed to voice my opinion. Otto is 27 and he has obviously been spoilt as the youngest child. I do not want to say anything against him and would ask you, please, not to get me wrong. He took over the farm. He is not a bad man but had expected more from our marriage. Because of his work he has no time for us. We live five kilometres apart and sometimes don't see each other for a fortnight. I objected to this separation in the beginning but I now don't care about it anymore. On our wedding day there were already unpleasant arguments between my mum and his sisters. I want to tell you that it was the most difficult and saddest and day of my life and ......something .... will come true. I shall never find inner peace and do not want to be happy with another man. I am sure there are not many brides who shed the amount of desperate tears the night before their wedding and on the actual wedding day. I should not have written this. I shall have to follow my path, without happiness or purpose. I used to be full of hope and optimism for my life. I have to pay my debt. Had I been able to keep the little girl, everything would have turned out better. Only mum and I are mourning her death. Sometimes I think that Otto has no heart at all. Any kind of emotions are completely alien to him and he has never been taught to say 'thank you'. I have just realized that I have written more than I intended to. Only fate decides whether you will receive this letter. Thank you for allowing me to write to you. All my wishes and thoughts are about you. I hope that you will always be happy on this earth.

I only had two copies of the enclosed photo, mum has one and you have one. I had a copy made for you to keep as a souvenir. Hansi, please I would like a photo of you now if possible, or later on when you are back home, will you have one made? I would very much have and keep a photo of you. I have still got a small one and sent the big one to your mum, with a heavy heart. She asked me for it and has a right to have it. Will we ever meet again?

I want to finish my little letter for today. I am wishing you only the very best in life and a safe journey home. My best wishes are coming from the bottom of my heart. Yours Vera.

Vera taken in 1943

During my time as PoW, England, 1.5.47

My thoughts in relation to Vera's letter dated 6.4.47

I was quite surprised when I saw a familiar hand writing among the post, in fact too familiar, because at one time it meant everything to me. If anyone had ever told me that things would turn out this way I would have laughed him in the face. But, one can be wrong. When I received Vera's first letter I was overwhelmed with happiness. Reading her second letter gave me such a shock – the unbelievable became reality. I think everyone would sympathise with me. It caused me so much pain and took a long time to get over it. I just could not wipe it out of my memory and shed many bitter tears. It sounds unbelievable, but I went to absolute pieces. It seemed the whole world had collapsed on top of me. I wrote to Vera that she can tell me everything when something is bothering her. I want to give her advice if I can and stand by her. Little by little, I managed to calm down somewhat. I do have bad days but I am able to put this experience into an illusion, a dream. Sometimes one is able to let everything go and almost accept it. I am telling myself: you cannot change anything. Everything runs its course. It will take years to forget all this. I have now received a letter with a photo. In spite of everything I was very pleased. I hoped she will be very happy with her husband. But what I read in her letters points to the complete opposite, and this is why I feel so dreadfully sorry for her. I feel like beating her husband up because he does not know what a good woman his wife is. I like the photo very much and hung it up over my bed. I could not help it. I want to see her all the time and have her by my side. She was everything to me. I loved and valued her. Will we ever meet again? If I ever get home, I shall tell her and I know that it won't be long then until she is with me again. It will all be very painful for me but I want to see her and speak to her one more time. Who knows what our lives have in store for us? Fate runs its course and one must not fight against it.

Replied 4/5.1947   **Aschersleben 20.4.1947**
                                        3/5

Hedwig Schünemann

My dear Hans,

We received your lovely card of 16.3 with great joy, and also your letters dated 24.3. and 22.2.47. which your aquaintence sent. Thank you very much. Yesterday, as I read the name "Helmut Klinger" (a name unknown to me) on the envelope*, my knees trembled, as I assumed it was about Dad, - but then I saw your writing.
We are so pleased you sent such a detailed letter this time and are so happy that you are well, which, after all, is the

most important thing. I do think that the day of your home-coming will be soon. We still have enough food to feed our-selves, - different from 1945, in Rosow an der Oder, where we were three-quarters starved and could only just drag our-selves forward.

You don't get as many cigarettes a month here, but we have been saving some tobacco for you already, but all this is not really important and you are certain to be content with what we have: I can't wait for you to be here! You had to wait so long for post from us again, but please don't be so concerned, if I had been sick, then, of course, Horst would have written to you. I sent you the letter with our photo on 13.2.47, and hopefully you have received it in the mean-time. From what you write, you have already written to Papa. You probably don't have his last military mail number, do you? It's a stupid thing, that I am not able to give it to you.

 You know, dear Hans, the best thing is for you not to write to Prenzlau any more, then they will have to stop too. Be-lieve me, you will find the right woman at the right time and will be happier. Just remember, in August you were missing and, in November, I received the first signs of life from you and Vera was already 'involved' with someone else and was 'in other circumstances'. As we were together at Christmas, it was a very ugly situation because I was totally unaware of all that. She's now very unhappy that she treated you this way. Now think about it, if you always answer her letters again and again, then she will be going behind her husband's back and they will live in conflict with each other. It is all so pointless.Today we want to go to Nachterstedt again, to visit the Kahns, who came from Pyritz. Frau Kahn was so pleased to see us when we got there last Sunday, although she didn't recognise me at first. Her husband was not there, he had gone to Tantow, where they are moving to next week. It is a 4km distance from Rosow, where our dear Oma (Grandma) lies. It was there that they always used to rent the avenues of fruit and now they are getting them back again. Their lives will then improve again quickly, currently they have almost nothing left any more, and hardly anything to wear. Back then, in Pyritz, Frau Kahn was so severely wounded, her lower right leg was completely shattered. She had 7 months in Halle lying in plaster. Now she can walk again, only her leg is 2cm shorter. The Kahns knew about many people from Pyritz. Gutmann and Klawitter were said to have come back through Poland and the Poles are said to have captured them. The Kahns reckon that the two of them are no longer alive, as Semrau was beaten for so long, by the time he died, he was as emaciated as a skeleton, Erwin Kahn saw him in Pyritz. Many Pyritzers are dead.

Now dear Hans, we send you warm Sunday greetings. Stay healthy. While I am writing this letter, Horst is drying my hair with a hair-dryer. He's wearing his new suit today for the first time and so he is very proud. If only I had some material for you! Horstel's suit fits him very well. With hearty greetings and kisses from your mother, who is always thinking of you, and also from your brother Horst. Looking forward to seeing you again. The Kahns also send their greetings.

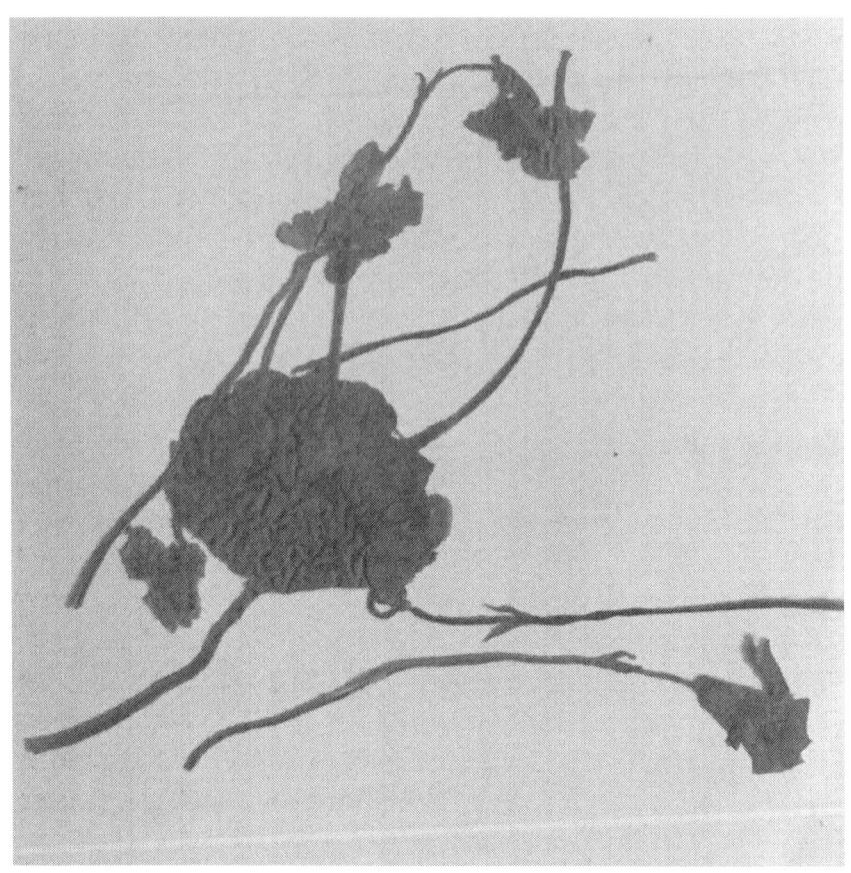

Pressed flower enclosed with the letter

Replied 11/05.47   Aschersleben, 23.4.1947
                                        10/5.47

My dear Hans,
We thank you greatly for your lovely letter of 10.3.1947
which we were very pleased to get. So, you received a lot of
post all in one go, then. I can well believe that you were delighted with that.

We received post from the Gogolins again today and they send you their best wishes. They are already looking forward to us coming at Whitsun. We were hoping so much for a photo of you, but sadly none has come.

Now my dear boy, I must first tell you some news: We shall be moving at the beginning of May. You'll no doubt be astonished. Because these are workers' flats where we are living now and workers from the factory will be moving in here. At first, we were really quite upset as we are loving living here in the countryside, where everything is now getting so beautifully green, but after all, we're only refugees and can be evicted and moved anywhere again and again. The men from the Housing Office requested me to go with them to have a look at the flat. It is more in the town centre, at a Master Decorators: two attic rooms. The flat will be completely renovated first, and the furniture and the floor will also be painted. Then it should be lovely. The main thing is that we will have the flat to ourselves and that will be wonderful as it is not comfortable always having to go through someone else's room, as we do here. And then at least we'll be able to have visitors and when you come, we'll have enough room. The Master Decorator has put furniture in for us. We must hope that all four of us can be together in our new home. Now I must finish this letter for today. Stay in perfect health! With greetings and kisses from your mum and from your brother Horst.

Looking forward to seeing you soon.

The new address:

H. Schünemann, Aschersleben / Harz

Hinterbreite 24, c/o Malermeister Brandt

11/5.47   Aschersleben, 27.4.1947

10/5.47

My dear Hans,

81

It's Sunday and we are sending you all our love. The weather is wonderful. I have not been feeling well for a few days, but I'm on the mend now. Yesterday we even got butter for 2 food vouchers, so I made fresh rolls, it was just wonderful! Perhaps we might even get our hands on meat tomorrow, it would have been even nicer to get it for Sunday, at least one would know what to put on the table. Now we have potato salad, yesterday they even had beetroot and sour gherkins at the potato shop and I will mix it all together. The decorator has started working in our flat, it's already looking very different, so homely. Perhaps we can move in in 8 days. Well, we will do our best to make it as cosy as possible. Horst got your letter, he was so pleased to hear from you. It is amazing how all of a sudden the buds and flowers are coming out, only a few weeks ago there was snow everywhere and now everything is in bloom. If the weather stays like this, the lilac will be blooming in about 8 days. And soon the long and hard winter will be forgotten. If the summer turns out to be as hot as the winter had been cold, then we won't know how to deal with it, many will collapse after having survived the cold. The body has been weakened and isn't as resistant as some years ago. Hope you are healthy and try and go for walks when you have time off. Lots of love from your Mum, who is thinking of you all the time and your brother Horst. Hope to see you soon again, happy and healthy.

18/5.47   Aschersleben, 27.4.1947

12.5.47

Dear Hans,

I am very pleased and grateful to have received your letter from April 6, 1947. I am now doing some ladies' hair on Sunday mornings and have just returned home. Today the weather is just magnificent, it's green everywhere and the cherry blossom's in full beauty. How are you doing? I would like to go to a dance this afternoon. We are moving in May, and at least then we have 2 rooms, so when you and Papa return home, we will have space and just the family together without disturbing others. Oh Hans, if only you were already here, we could have such a good time. If only our dear Papa would give us some news, who knows where he is wandering around and looking for us, it would have been so much easier for him if we had relatives in the area, then he could have sent a message to them. When you are back with us, you will also be able to eat your much longed for potato pancakes. How is the food there, what do you get to eat? The food is supposed to be fabulous. Dear Hans, I would be so happy if you could bring a stalk comb for me, because you can't get your hands on things like that, we are still very backwards here. Look after your leg, you can't afford it getting worse. My birthday is approaching fast, 18 years, one is getting older. When will it be your turn to be released? Some here have already returned home. I am going to buy a beautiful picture and I have already had two painted in order to make our home more beautiful. I do hope that this letter isn't going to take too long and you will have it soon. Dear Hans, please write to me very soon, because your letters are the most interesting. I have to finish now, bye for now, sending love and kisses from Horst and Mum. To a healthy and happy reunion in the very near future.

Replied 18/5.47   **Postage free**

To: Johannes Klawitter.
        A572859.
        Gaulby Road, Camp No. 94.
        Warnaby.
        Billesdon/Leicester.
        Great Britain.

From: Eichhauer
        Theodor.
Squad: Kdo. No. 20278.
Identity No.:   1482502.

Address Depot 402.
      Thorée/Sarthe/France.

My dear Hans   Thoree 15 April 47
    15/5

I want to write to you today and thank you very much for your lovely letter. I was very pleased to hear from you. Concerning your question, only Erwin Halter came with me. But he works somewhere else and also lives in a different depot. When I am able to write another letter, I will tell you more. Until then, with old loyalty, Yours Theodor.

25/5.47   **Aschersleben, May 1st, 1947**

                17/5.47

Dear Hans

I want to send you my best regards today. Horst has just returned from the 1st of May march. We have quite unpleasant weather now, lots of storms and rain, so it's best to stay near the warm oven. Yesterday I had to queue for 6 hours for our food rations, and in the afternoon also for meat, and I'm exhausted today. The day before yesterday I cleaned our new flat, also all the windows. I'm sure it is going to be very beautiful, it is bright and friendly. The old painter and decorator is really working hard in order to get it all in good shape, despite the fact that he is 73 years old. I am really excited and so is Horst. We will be able to be together here, all 4 of us, how happy would we be! We had a letter from Gertrud yesterday, she has met Irmchen Hoffmann, who is in Lübeck. Gertrud lives nearby and was looking for her for a long time, and by sheer coincidence found her. That's life sometimes, one is searching for years, and then all of a sudden you find the person. May it be the same for us! Now, my dear son, stay healthy and well , sending all our love and kisses, from your Mum who is always thinking of you and your brother Horst. May we see you again very soon.

Aschersleben 4.5.1947

24.5.47

My dear boy

Despite the fact that we are not receiving any mail from you, I won't give up writing my Sunday letters to you and sending you my love. Horst has also written you a letter today, now he has gone for a walk. The weather here is really unpleasant, with an awful wind and it's so cold, we really had more than enough freezing weather in the winter and it would be nice if finally it improves I have spent all day today with my curtains, I have been given a few pieces for free and now I am making new net curtains for our windows to make it more homely. Aunt Emilie from Berlin has sent us a tablecloth, a cover for the washstand and two curtains, all very welcome gifts. If I think of all the nice things we had at home.... I don't even want to think about it. We also had a letter from Aunt Lina the day before yesterday, she writes that an acquaintance from Zimmermannshorst in Anklam (Western Pomerania) lives nearby, whose son in law works at the power station. He was working in a village near Tantow (Western Pomerania) and there people were talking about a "Klein" from Zimmermannshorst , who can't find his parents. This can only be Bruno. Now Aunt Lina is full of hope, I wish for her from the bottom of my heart that it is him, Aunt Lina has gone through so much. That's what happens, people are wandering around and cannot find their families. I think, if I had such news from Papa, I would not hesitate one minute, but would make my way there and bring him home. But who knows when this happy day will come for us. I have been restless all day, I wonder what we will have to endure next. My dear Hans, now I will bring this letter to an end, stay well. Sending lots of love and kisses from your Mum and your brother Horst. Hoping to see each other again soon.

Aschersleben , 4.5.1947

28/5.47

Horst Klawitter

Dear Hans,

As I have not received any letter from you this week , I would like to send you Sunday greetings. I hope that we will receive some mail from you this week. We have just finished our lunch, we had potatoes, meat and white sauce and it tasted really nice. First of May is over again, there was a lot going on. Gathering at 8 am for the march, but at 9.30 we were all still standing at the same spot. Then all the way through town and at 11.30 am the Mayor held his speech, and he talked, lots of people left , no one wants to listen to him. In the afternoon there were dances in all the ballrooms. In the evening the Kaiserhof held a social evening to which I also went, followed by a dance, but they only played old tunes and it was so full that I was home by 11 PM. How are you my dear Hans? Any news about being sent home soon? We had someone in our shop, whose brother in law came from America to England and he wrote that he would be dismissed in July, he is in Camp 73. I have been to see our new flat again today, the landlord is a painter and decorator and he did a really great job. It looks as though we can move in on Friday, it should have dried by then. Then you and Papa can come home and we will be all together without other people around. If only the day of your return would come and we could all be together. We still have not heard from our dear Papa. Mum is tidying up quickly so that she can enjoy the rest of the Sunday, she was busy doing the net curtains all morning. And I want to go out a bit now in order to get some fresh air. The cherry blossom is over, and now the apple trees are in full bloom, it looks absolutely amazing , the only thing that is missing is our beautiful home, but who knows how run down it is now. My dear Hans, I'm finishing now, let us hear from you soon, getting letters is just the best! Please stay well and healthy. Sending lots of love and kisses from your brother Horst and Mum

Hoping to see you happy and healthy very soon.

Replied 1 / 6   Aschersleben. 7.5.1947

My dear Hans,

We are thankfully confirming the receipt of your letter from 14 April, 47, and we thank you very much for it. At the same time we would like to wish you very healthy Whitsun holidays. One holiday after the other goes by and we still can't celebrate them together, but sometime the day of our reunion must come. Since yesterday we have had some mild air, it's about time now, because we really can do with some warmth. Today our last day in the flat has arrived, tomorrow we will move. May our Lord make sure that we will all soon be able to spend many happy hours in our new home together. We have already moved some of our things, slowly but surely we are gathering some possessions again, which you only realise when packing up. I can imagine that there are so many floods over there, there is more than enough water anyway. I'll send you Werner's address next time as I have already packed everything up, he seems to be working in mining. Horst is still fast asleep, I'm writing early in the morning today, because I won't find time during the day, as I still have lots to do. From 4.45 am the birds are holding their concerts and waking me up. Now is the best time where everything is green and blooming. My dear Hans, now I will end my letter, it is time to prepare breakfast. From Sunday the clocks will go forward an hour, which means that the sun will still shine at 10 PM. Keep well, lots of love and kisses from your Mum and brother Horst. The clock has just struck 6 am. Hoping to see you healthy and happy again soon.

Replied 1/6.47   Aschersleben, 11.5.47

     My dear Hans

Today is Mother's Day and I am sending you my love. Your thoughts too are with me today. The weather is beautiful. Horstel brought me lots of flowers, which were also from you. We moved to our new home three days ago. It is truly lovely to be on our own again. We have beautiful, wide beds with soft mattresses, we had almost forgotten how lovely they can be. We thank you from the bottom of our hearts for your lovely card dated 21.4.47. The post does not take quite so long any more. That means a lot to me. We had a letter from Aunty Else and Herta during the week. She now lives with her little girl Inge at Gustav's. I would imagine she will start divorce proceedings. There does not seem any point for her to stay in the marriage. The Ludwigs are setting him up against Herta and that's sad. They don't have any understanding or compassion for her. I don't think she should put up with this villain any longer. Auntie Else likes living on the estate. It's much better than it used to be at Herwigs. Now they know who they are working for. Edith now sews for other people. Günter helps Uncle Gustav. Reinhard works for a lady whose husband has not come home yet and Horst works for a gardener. That's how everybody earns a living. I am sure they will get through these difficult times. Who knows whether and when we might go back to our beloved homeland. We are not even allowed to put a few flowers on our grandma's grave on Mother's Day. She was always there for everybody!! We are now getting sugar instead of fat for 20 days. For 100g fat 200g sugar, which means we have to live fat free for 20 days. That's not very good!! My dear Hans, we wish you a happy Whitsun Tide, which we shall spend in Eilsleben with the Gogolin family. They wrote again this week and said they are looking forward to seeing us very much. They wish to be remembered to you and also Auntie Erna, Grandmother, Erna (twice), the family of Uncle Gustav and the family of Uncle Erich Now my dear boy, we are sending you our love, your mum who is always thinking about you, and your brother Horst.

We hope soon we will have a happy reunion.

What did Mrs. Halling want?

Prenzlau 27.4.47

31.5.47

Dear Hansi!

My will tells me not to write to you today but the urge to write is so strong. I am ill with pleurisy at the moment and therefore have more time to let life pass me by and reminisce. I am thinking and thinking, as so often happens. I read your letters and also your mum's. The nicest thing was that I came across the many letters from you which were in a separate file. They had arrived whilst I was not here and mum had put them away without ever giving them to me. She meant well. In these letters you talk about your work assignment on the farms in July/August. Please forgive me for bothering you again with my post. I cannot help it. Hansi, I am at the end of my tether. Can you imagine, I am still the person I used to be, exactly how you know me and I have betrayed you, it is incomprehensible to me. I am being eaten up by my own guilty, tormented conscience. I feel physically sick when I think about what I have done. If only I knew what you think about me. Today is Sunday and I somehow get the feeling that you are thinking of me at this moment. When you get home, please, please dear Hansi, promise me that you will let me know when we can meet up. I would love to see you again. Of course, if you would rather not see me I shall accept your decision. I have so many wishes and must not ask for any more.

You have such a big heart and are a very lovely person, and now we have to just follow our separate paths, but mine is very hard. I am missing my mum a lot. Every day I have to get out of bed and cook for Manfred and myself. Mum is still in the West and now also very sick. If only she would get better, I am so worried about her.

I am sending you my love.
Yours Vera

Aschersleben, 15.5.47

4.6

    My dear Hans

I am sending you my love today, on Ascension Day. We are having the usual thunder storms all around us. We badly needed the rain, in order to avoid a catastrophe at harvest time. We are hoping for a good harvest, otherwise we shall have even less food to eat than now. But we mustn't complain though, the people in the cities are even worse off than we are. Last night I dreamt that our Papa was here and Horst had the same dream. It was so real. If only it became reality! How happy we would all be!! Yesterday we went to see the Schmetzges in Güsten, who used to live in Pyritz. Güsten is a small town, half an hour away from here by train. Mr. Schmetzke used to be the tenant in charge of the orchards and used to live in one of the town houses in the Stargarter Road. They were very pleased to see us again. We met them at the Kahns in Nachterstedt. I managed to get some onions to take home. Mr. Schmetzke works in a large building firm as a carpenter. They are doing quite well. They intend to visit us after Whitsum Tide. One is always very happy to meet someone from the homeland. Mrs. Rotsprach also lives in a village nearby. Her husband has died and her son is a Prisoner of War. The Zischels, who used to live on the Weinberg estate now live in a different village, also on an estate. You can see that everybody is here, there and everywhere.

We are keeping well and hope the same from you. Horst has also written to you today. My dear boy, should Vera write to you again, it would be best if you did not reply to her, because she has decided to be the wife of another man and has to be true to her marriage. She should not write letters to other men, and keep her conscience clear towards her husband.

Take care and stay fit and well. I am sending you all my love

90

and kisses, from your mum and brother Horst.
We hope to see you healthy and fit again soon.
Looking forward to receiving a letter from you very soon.

Replied 15/6 **Aschersleben 18.5.47**

9.6.47

My dear Hans

Thank you very much for your lovely letter dated 27.4.47 and the card you sent to Horstel dated 27.4.47. We were very happy to receive both and are sending you our loving Sunday greetings. I am beginning to believe that my Christmas parcel to you has gone astray! I wonder who has enjoyed the contents. What impertinence! And I really wanted to make you happy with something home-made, and you have been waiting in vain. Horst does not smoke properly yet. He tries it now and then but he still looks rather clumsy. I do sometimes try to stop him from smoking because he has to be careful as he has grown such a lot. The nutrition is not what it should be. A young body needs more fat, and the tobacco is not what it used to be either. Last night we went to the theatre and saw 'Hurray it's a boy'. It was quite nice but this sort of thing does not interest me. I was so tired that my eyes closed towards the end. I much prefer to stay at home or take a short walk through the lovely countryside. We do not get enough sleep now, that the clocks have been put forward by two hours. In the evenings it does not get dark until 11 pm and in the mornings we get up very early.

Two days ago we went to the aid organisation and obtained a wardrobe. This is now our own property. I used to have a soldiers' wardrobe, which I had painted. Unfortunately, it was so tall that it did not fit into the room. We managed to exchange it with the 'new' wardrobe. I have also applied for a table and one chair. This morning we built our own chaise longue. I managed to obtain a bed from an air raid, Höhl got me the wool for the stuffing, then we covered it and put a blanket on top, et voila! – it is ready to use as a bed. We have to be inventive. It is very cosy in our home now. If only I knew Papa's army number. I have racked my brain but I just cannot remember it. This Wednesday is Horstel's birthday. It would be so lovely if you could be here too. I have to bake a cake for him. He has invited a few guests. We have always been invited to the Köhls and the Bodes for their birthday celebrations. On Friday he went to a Social Evening at the Marjoram Works. He is always looking forward to these evenings but when he comes home he says to me: "I can't really enjoy anything because I keep thinking of Papa and Hans so much".

Well, my dear boy, please stay healthy. I am sending you all my love and kisses, your mum and your brother Horst.

We hope to see you very soon!

Replied 15/6   **Aschersleben, 24.5.47**

9.6.47

My dear Hans

Thank you very much for your lovely letter 4.5.47. It made us very happy. Horst thanks you for his birthday card. He will write to you as soon as he can. He is already in bed. It is almost 11 o'clock and I shall go to bed soon as well. We have to get up in the morning at 4 o'clock because we are going to Eilsleben. Horst had a bit of bother with his boss. He did not want to allow him to take a day off after Whitsun Tide. We now have to come home a day earlier. The trip costs us 28 Mark! I was really angry and gave him my piece of mind. They are just slave-drivers and get rich at our expense. I get too angry these days!

I shall go to the Trade Union and also register with the Employment Agency after Whitsun Tide. Horst's boss came to see us before Easter and begged him to stay, and now he is getting very rude again. Well, there are other opportunities for Horst. Since I have been very ill, I am finding it very hard to cope with this kind of upset. Are you trying to console us by saying that you are not coming home before January? This means that we have to wait for much longer than we thought!! Now, my dear boy, I have to finish my letter. I can't write any more because I am so very tired. I hope you will stay healthy and am sending you all my love and kisses, from your mum, who is always thinking of you, and your brother Horst.

Here's to a happy and healthy reunion.

I shall write again when we return from our trip.

Replied 29.6.

Aschersleben, 15.4.1947

9.6.1947

Dear Hans,

Today, on Father's Day, I want to send you a few lines. Since we moved here, into the new flat, we have had no post from you. We've now been here for eight days and feel as if we've been born again. Above all, we have everything to ourselves and everything around us is new.

How are you? Are you still healthy and chipper - which is what I can report about ourselves. I wanted to go dancing this afternoon. Moum is going to the garden of the house where we lived previously to see the people who live there and to think of other things. Tomorrow evening I have been invited to the Majorenwerken for a company celebration. It will be wonderful, it starts at 8pm and goes on until 2 a.m.

Our clocks here have been put forward by 2 hours. It is awful! At 10p.m. the sun is still shining, so one can hardly go to bed, then in the mornings, it's hard to get up!

This coming Wednesday it'll be my birthday* – how great it

would be if you could be here and we could enjoy a cosy cup of coffee together. Maybe you'll be able to spend your birthday here. We feel as if we ought to receive a letter from Papa – it would make us all so happy if, after all these years, we received a sign of life from him.

Things have improved a lot for us, with the move to the new flat. We now have two rooms and everything is newly painted, so that we all have enough comfortable space. Now it all depends on your return ! Dear Hans, do you still listen to the radio? How is your wound doing? Is it better yet ?

So, now I'm going to carry on writing, - in the meantime, I stopped for lunch. We had grated potatoes. Most people haven't had any potatoes since Christmas, but mother took care of that for us by spending long hours digging potatoes up, and going quite a long way away.

The weather here is glorious again, only we need a considerable amount of rain as everything has badly dried out. How is the weather where you are? Now dear Hans, I will finish. With love and kisses from me and Mum. Hope to see you soon!

Replied 22/6.47

Aschersleben, 27.5.47
14/6

My dear Hans

We have come home today from our trip to Eilsleben, where we spent the Whitsun holidays. We had a very nice time!

The Gogolins, Uncle Leopold and family were all so very welcoming and looked after us splendidly. They were all very pleased to see us and said that we should come back soon. I have to say that we felt very comfortable in their company. They are all sending their best wishes to you and would like to see you when you come home. If you get a good connection, it takes 3 hours to reach Eilsleben, only the trains usually arrive late. The outbound journey took us via Magdeburg and the return journey via Halberstadt. But don't ask me how crowded the trains are. The passengers sat on the steps and on the roofs. We were lucky to get inside a carriage where we had to stand so close to each other like sardines in a tin. We took some food with us but brought it back home again. The Gogolins cooked a rabbit dish and at Uncle Leopold's we had pork. In the afternoon, we had coffee, gateau and a tasty cake with whipped cream, which was quite new to us. It would have been lovely if you could have been with us. They also offered us a selection of liqueurs. Leopold owns five Morgen land * and he uses his horses to transport beet to the sugar factory. They pay him 300 Marks a month for that. He also keeps pigs and poultry. They were able to bring quite a few possessions out of west Prussia, but in the end they could not get rid of any. The Gogolins flat is very nice. Uncle used to be a railway official but he retired 10 years ago. When Horst got back to work today, his boss did not say a word. It looked like he was pleased to see him back. I want to finish my letter now, I am going to bed soon. We left Eilsleben this morning at 4 o'clock. We are wishing you good health and sending you our love and kisses, your mum and brother Horst.

Here's to a healthy reunion.

*one Morgen is anywhere from 1,906 to 11,789 square meters. It was approximately the amount of land tillable in the morning by one man behind an ox or horse dragging a single bladed plough

Aschersleben, 1.6.47

Dear Hans

Thank you very much indeed for your lovely birthday
wishes. You worked the posting of the card out very accur-
ately: it arrived on 21 May.
Happy birthday to you too and let's hope that you come
home very soon, so that we can all be together, fit and
healthy! The years go past us and before we know it, we are
all getting older! I want to tell you what presents I received
for my birthday: Mum gave me a writing set, a cigarette
box, a silver tie pin, trouser braces, Twenty Deutsch Marks
and flowers. From my guests I received: three balls of white
wool, a tie, gooseberries and several bunches of lilies of the
valley. The gifts were plenty – considering one cannot buy
very much here. What kind of weather have you got? We are
enduring a dreadful heatwave. Yesterday, the thermometer
went up to 45⁰C. Dear Hans, tell me how you are. Have you
moved to a different camp now? I hope it is the Discharge
Camp. We spent Whitsun Tide in Eilsleben at the Gogolins.
It was very nice there. I did not realize I have such kind
cousins! We might go back when I get my next holiday. They
badly wanted us to stay longer but my boss did not give me
an hour longer! I am starting my new job on 16.6. I just had
to find another Salon. I am surprised I managed to last there
over one year. We lost four hairdressers and two apprentices
in one year! You can imagine what kind of a boss we have. My
new post has lots of clients and the boss seems very calm.
Tomorrow morning I have to start with my assignment of
dismantling the Munition factory in Aschersleben. The job
will take 2-3 days. I don't mind doing this job because – as
you know – 'he who knows the job and has no aversion to
work.........'

Oh Hans, if you were here with us today, we would be going swimming together. I will go this afternoon. Now, dear Hans, I am sending you, from far away, my love again and hope you will have a happy birthday. Please write back very soon!

Yours Horst and Mum. As I write, mum is also writing a letter to you.

Let's hope we shall all have our health when we meet again and we do not have to wait too long.

Replied 22.6.47   Aschersleben, 1.6.47

14/6

My dear Hans

Happy birthday to you, lots of luck and blessings, all the best for the future and a healthy reunion. These are our wishes. You are already celebrating your fourth birthday away from us. We hope very much, that you wil celebrate your 23rd birthday with your family. Thank you very much for your lovely letter dated 11.5. We are enjoying good health. I see that you are moving to a different camp again. I hope it is your Discharge Camp! Will they be forwarding your mail to your new address? It means you will be yet in another, strange environment. Will you have to go back into agricultural labour on the farms again? We are seeing a lot of ex-Prisoners of War here now. One day your day must surely come too! We are having a real heatwave at the moment. Everyone is longing for some rain. It's bad for the crops, nothing is growing. We wanted to go to Vorpommern again during Horstels' holiday but we cannot go now, because he only gets six days holiday. When they closed in the winter, those days were taken off his holiday. We cannot plan such a long journey for just a few days. It now takes two days to get there and then another two days for the return journey. Horst is starting his new job on 15.6.47. I hope he will like it there and earn good money. This is a Gents Salon only. He will be working in a much healthier atmosphere than in the Ladies Salon because of the amount of perms they do there. In these times, where nutrition is not what it should be, one has to really take care of oneself. Thea has not written to me for several weeks. Perhaps she is too busy. She works from home for the business. Now my dear boy, I will have to finish my letter. I wish you good health and send you all my love and kisses from your mum, who is always thinking of you, and brother Horst.

Here's to a soon, and healthy reunion, and we hope we don't have to wait very much longer.

Replied 29/6

Aschersleben, 8.6.47

21.6

Dear Hans

Thank you for your letter dated 18.5.47. I was very pleased to hear from you.

I am well and we hope the same from you. We are having very changeable weather at the moment, it goes from rain to shine. Well, we have to take it as it comes. I am currently involved in a special operation at the Muna factory in Aschersleben. I am finding it too heavy to throw 15 kg from one person to another. I am sure you agree. It will all be melted down. I weighed myself yesterday and also measured my height. I am 1.78 m tall and weigh 55 kg. I hope you had a photographer over Whitsun Tide. We would be ever so happy to get a photo from you. Three years have passed since we last saw each other, and we have not seen our Papa for nearly six years now. If only we could get some news from him, we will not give up hope. Today is Mission Day and mum and I went to church. We enjoyed it. We hope your day of discharge will not be in the too distant future. This afternoon we are going to the Guts-Muts Square to take part in a folk festival, and tonight we are probably going to the cinema. Mum never really feels like coming, but I nag so much that she finally gives in, because if she stays at home, she dwells on the past too much. Last Sunday, Frau Lessin from Pyritz came to visit us. She was very keen to see us again. When we meet people from Pyritz, it feels like being with family. They are all such lovely people from our homeland. Who knows if we will ever see our lovely Pomerania again. What did you do on your birthday? I have to close my letter for now. I am sending you my love, your Horst and Mum. Please write again soon.

Replied 6/7

Aschersleben/Harz the 16.6.47

3/7

My dearest Hans,

We thank you very much for your letter from 1.6.1947, which we received today in good health. And we are happy to hear that you are in good health as well. I couldn't send you Sunday greeting yesterday because we only got back from our Journey yesterday. We drove to Eilsleben on Tuesday morning and we enjoyed a nice couple of days there. Everyone was happy to see us, but unfortunately the days went past very quickly. Family Gogolin and Family Klawitter send warmest regards to you and hope to get to know you soon. We went to Uncle Leopold`s Field to collect potatoes on Sunday. That was fun! After we finished, we had cake and a bottle of Schnapps. We were so busy, we also had to plug rabbit food. Herta, your cousin made us a big bag of Bonbon for the trip home. We dined very well, sometimes at Family Gogolin`s and sometimes at Uncle Leopold`s, and we also had our rations with us. We can visit them together, when you are here. Herta is 28 years old, not married and she has a cute little boy who is 6 Months old. Hildchen is 26 years old and soon to be engaged. Uncle Leopold and Aunty Selma are in their late 50`s . Uncle Gogolin is 73 years old, but looks much younger. Aunty Hedwig is 68 years. Helga is 32 years old, and lives with small Peter and small Heidi with her parents. They have a nice Flat. Everyone is very nice. Everyone is breeding rabbits, Gogolin`s have 18 and Klawitter`s over 20. We really felt very comfortable again. It was Horst`s first day on his new job, he likes it very much. At least the Boss is not nervous like the last one! You know Hans, I am so happy that you are doing so well and that I know where you are. Sometimes I live with worry. I wish Horst can always stay with me, it would be too hard for me to be alone. I hope for the best! So, are you in a different place, a Warehouse now, I hope you may be fine there. You probably can't listen to the radio there? Hopefully we will get your Picture soon, we are looking forward to it. Well, my dear boy, I hope you stay healthy. I send you my warmest greetings and kisses. Always thinking of you, your mum and your brother Horst. Again, best wishes for your birthday and a happy healthy reunion.

Replied 29/6   Aschersleben   8.6.1947

    My dearest Hans,   26/6
We send you lovely Sunday greetings. Horst already wrote to you today. The heatwave is over at last, it was nearly worse than the cold winter. We didn't know where to go anymore, it was nearly 50 Degree Celsius. We were glad that we had supplies but we are approaching the end of them. Hopefully I can go out to work this year, only Horst works, he shouldn't be the only one to work. I had such bad pain in my heart for a few days, today things are a little bit better. I just worry

too much about everything. Horst always worries about me if I feel unwell. He wants to go to the folk festival with me this afternoon and to the cinema in the evening, but I am not very interested in these things. My thoughts are only with you and our Papa. If only there could be a day where we could be together again. It is your birthday soon. I already wrote a birthday letter to you last Sunday. Hopefully the letter will arrive on time. We both went to church this morning and it was nice. I think the pastor was certainly also a refugee, he spoke very well. Mrs. Lehmann went to Artern near Sangerhausen, where her parents and siblings are in a camp. Until now they used to live in Schloessin near Maigard. They are finally out from Flen, and surely they will be safely housed in Saxony Anhalt. She is happy that she has her relatives nearby. I hope we will receive some good news from you this week. We haven't had any post from Thea for a long time, hopefully she is not ill. My dear Hans I have to finish, stay healthy. We are waiting for the promised photo. Warm greetings and kisses from your mum who always thinks of you and your brother Horst. To a happy and healthy reunion.

Saltby, 15 June 1947

My dearest mum and Horst,

Thank you very much for your letters form 15.5, 18.5. and 24.5. which I received last week. Our first forwarded post has arrived. Let's hope that Dad will come home very soon and before me. I also met a pyritzer here when I arrived, in fact his name is Guenter Lascho. It is always a pleasure to meet someone you know. We also had theatre on our campstage last week. I liked it very much, of course it was only just a kind of colourful evening. Have you already bought a wardrobe yet? Slowly my clothes accumulate, one by one. The weather is good at the moment. But you never know how long it will stay like this. You know you shouldn't get angry,

because in the end you can't change things and you lose cal-
ories. So take everything lightly. I am very fine, which I hope
from you as well. I don't have my pictures yet, but I wait for
them every day. Greetings from your Hans for today.

Replied 13/7.47   Aschersleben, 20.6.47

My dear Hans,

Today on your birthday we are thinking of you and we send
you heartfelt greetings. I bought you a beautiful flower bouquet and I bought you a nice little box for your cigarettes,
too bad that you can't pick it up yourself. Well, next time
you come back to us. At the same time we would like to
thank you for your lovely letters from 25.5. and 1.6.1947.
We were very happy to receive such a long letter from you.
So, you have already moved. I am happy that you like it
there. Are you working on the farm again? Take care of your
leg, so you don't harm it. It will be sad if some are released
and it is still not your turn. Don't lose faith my boy, it will be
your turn soon. How we would love to have you with us. But
dear Hans, I don't think it is right to meddle with destiny. It
will come to us, as dear god intended. He has protected us so
far from all the dangers. If only we were 14 days ahead, the
air is thick with rumours. I am really happy and reassured
knowing that you are there and that you are healthy and
fine. Everything will be different when you return! We will
just wait and see. Aunt Lina's joy was for nothing because
she didn't find Bruno after all. I would have been so pleased
for her from the bottom of my heart. Once you are here,
there will be work for you so don't worry. If the situation
is clarified, I will try to apply for you. We are so longing to
have you home. We just have to wait and see, I only want
what's best for you. We also received post from Thea, she is
also very hungry and has little to eat. It would have been
terrible if you had lost your leg, there are already so many
poor wounded guys around here, everyone should be happy
when they still have their healthy limbs. The harvest is very
good so we won't starve yet. I will write to you again on
Sunday. Stay healthy. Warm greetings and kisses from your
mum who always thinks of you and your brother Horst. To a
happy and healthy reunion.

Ascherlsleben, 22.6.1947

My dearest Hans,

Today, we send you many lovely Sunday greetings. Frau Lessin from Pyritz who lives in Güsten came to visit us today. We just took her to the station. We are very close to the train station, only 5 minutes. She sends kind regards to you. We are always happy to see someone from our homeland. Tomorrow is wash day, I'm glad when I am finished with it. It is always a problem with the little washing powder I have. It rained really bad today, so everything will grow nicely! I also wrote you a letter on the day before yesterday, on your birthday. Horst will write to you in the next few days. He completed the first week with his new boss, he likes it. He earns a few Marks more, than in his previous Job. On Thursday I went to Quenstedt with Frau Lehmann, it was 14 km there and back. We left early at 5.30 am queued up for 5 1/2 hours. Then we were very happy to receive 1 pound of curd cheese, which the dairy passes on, but we don't go there very often. There were already over 250 people in front of us and over 100 people behind us. And there were as many at the second gate. You can't imagine how busy it was. Hopefully this year we can forage in the fields again, otherwise it will look sad! We want to hope for the best!! Times were hard if you had no supplies. Everything will be fine again, just wait and see. If only the shoe situation would improve, Horst has no proper shoes and he stands all day and evening, his feet hurt so much. Horst was recently measured at the doctors. He is now 1.78m tall, he can stop growing now and maybe grow sideways. He only weighs 110lbs. That is not enough for his height. How much do you weigh? With this my dear boy I want to end my letter. Stay healthy and warm greetings and kisses from your mum and your brother Horst. To a happy and healthy reunion.

Pressed flower enclosed with the letter

Replied 20 7.47 Aschersleben, 29.6.1947

17.7.47

My dear Hans, many thanks for your lovely letter from the 8.6.47 and we are sending you all our love on this Sunday. Tuesday and Thursday I went with Mrs Lehmann to pick blueberries in The Harz, it is an hour by train and then another hours walk. We started at 4.30AM. On Tuesday the train had an hour and a half delay in the evening and we got home after 10 PM. The picking is a laborious task, as there are not too many blueberries due to the very dry weather, but I managed to collect 8 litres each time, so it was well worth it. We want to go there again. You cannot imagine how many people were heading to this area, there wasn't even enough space for everybody on the train. Travelling is a huge problem at the moment, people are sitting on the steps, roofs, even on the bumpers. It is incredibly hot again, we really don't know how to cope with this heat. If only we could have some rain soon. We have been told that this year we are not even allowed to collect the leftover potatoes from the fields, we will have to wait and see but without that - it doesn't bear thinking about, one cannot survive from the little we get with the coupons. Horst just brought me a glass of beer, he always means so well, he has also written a letter to you today. So you are back again at the typing room, no job for you at the farm? Have you still not received any news from Thea? I will have to go and ask why she still has not written to you.

Pressed flower enclosed with the letter

Pass the time as well as you can, it must be very boring for you there. People talk about lots of things going on here but who knows what you can believe to be true. I hope you received all the letters that I sent to the old camp, I did write to you regularly. Lots of prisoners of war are arriving from the east now, if only Papa was one of them! I have written a letter to Frankfurt/Oder again today, no one can give us any news, the fruitless waiting is becoming more and more painful. Now my lovely boy, I carry on wishing you all the best, and that we will be able to see you again soon. Stay healthy. Sending you all my love and kisses to you, from Mum and your brother Horst. To a healthy reunion in the very near future. Mrs Lehmann sends her regards. Elfriede had her little Renate in the spring, but she only lived for 8 weeks. Her husband is also still in England, he will be very sad too.

Replied 3 /8.47

Aschersleben, 29.6.1947

17.7.47

Dear Hans,

Today I would like to drop you a few lines. It is a very hot Sunday today, almost fading away, if only it would start raining soon, everything is very dry again. How are you doing anyway? We are all good and healthy and I hope the same goes for you. I have been busy again, this morning I combed the hair of seven ladies, shaved one man and cut his hair, and soon I'm off to set a young lady's hair. One feels a bit stupid to spend the Sunday doing things like that. If you are honest you are not gaining anything. I'm just doing it for my love of hairdressing. Mum and I went to the Varité yesterday evening, and there were lots of well known radio presenters there, like Lotte Werkmeister and Udo Vietz, it was quite nice but it was so hot. Mum never wants to join me but I'm always pushing her to come with me. I really like my new workplace, it is a barber not a salon, but I am having enough ladies as private clients. In the summer it really is awful working in a salon, as the heat from the hairdryers and the perms is terrible. Dear Hans, it seems that you quite like the camp you are in. Try and look after your leg as well as you can. Are you still in contact with the farmer you worked for before? Today I received another address in Frankfurt/Oder where the transports from Russia are arriving. Oh, if only our Papa would get in contact. How nice it would be for us to all be together, I hope it won't be too long now. We are longing to see you again. If only you were released this year. I will keep my fingers crossed. Today we had peas and beans for lunch, which was really nice. Finally now the clocks have gone back again an hour, we were really tired in the evening, but couldn't go to bed before 11PM and couldn't get out of bed in the morning. Mum is not happy that I also work Sundays all day. My dear Hans, write again soon, we are really looking forward to your letters. Papa's birthday is fast approaching on July 4th. In our bedroom we have three nice bunches of carnations , all for you and your pictures are nicely decorated. I want to finish now, sending lots of love to you my dear Hans, from Horst and Mum. Hoping to see you happy and healthy very soon.

Replied 22/7   Aschersleben, 3.7.1947
                                                    23.7.47

    My dear Hans,

Many thanks for the letter from the 15.6.47. We were once again delighted to hear from you. So, you once again met someone from Pyritz, I can imagine what a pleasure it was. You write that we don't have to get upset, that it causes white hair. Well, I have enough of that already, it won't start now. We are eagerly awaiting your picture, I hope it arrives soon. You are even typing with a typewriter! There are some advances there, aren't there? That's good. Here we have nice weather again after rain. Yesterday I finally managed to get hold of a raincoat for Horst, I have been trying endlessly to find one for him. Horst is as happy as I am, he doesn't need to mess up his clothes in the rain any longer. We were living in hope that things would change here, but it seems that R will stay here. We cannot take seriously what people are talking about, but we will see. Already it is July now, time goes by so quickly. The time will come soon when you will be with us again. It is our dear Papa's birthday tomorrow, how will he spend the day, and where will he be? Lots of men are coming from Russia now, a large number of them are in the camps, and cannot find their families. I have already written to 7 places, if only I was successful soon. When I am finished with this letter I will go to the cobbler and pick up Horst's shoes, they should be ready, they have been there for months. The issue with the shoes is a story all to itself. Try and get a decent pair of shoes for your feet if you can. Because there is no chance of getting shoes here. Tomorrow we will be able to get a bottle of Schnaps from the merchant, it is very expensive, 34.50, but perhaps we can swap it for some food at a later date, that's how we are helping ourselves. Tomorrow we are going to Mrs Höhl to celebrate her birthday and on Monday to Mrs Lehmann, yesterday it was Mrs Streese's birthday. How long will it be and I too will be another year older, I will then be 43, the last time Papa was here, I had been just 36. Do you think he will recognise us all? Now , my lovely boy I will finish my letter, stay healthy, sending lots of love and kisses from your Mum and your brother Horst. Hoping for a healthy see you again in the very near future.

Replied 27/7   ## Aschersleben, 6.7.1947
                                            23/7

          My dear Hans,
It is Sunday again and we are sending you lots and lots of love. Last night we went to the refugee camp, a new transport had arrived, also many from Pomerania, from the Stolpe(Mecklenburg Vorpommern) and the area around Flatower, it is a heart-breaking picture. The poor people were in a very big camp near Bromberg for 2 years, all together over 30 thousand people imprisoned. Such inhumane treatment, no one can imagine what it must have been like, the women all with their heads shaved. How can this even be possible in our world. We are so thankful that we have escaped this terrible fate. They are left with absolutely nothing! Even though our possessions are very little, we have our health. I couldn't get any rest last night with these pictures in my head. If only we could help them somehow. I am feeling so incredibly sorry for those people. On Tuesday we want to go back to the forest to pick raspberries and I hope we will be very successful. I hope we will get your letter with the picture; we are so much looking forward to seeing it! Aunt Lina is sending her love and also Christel. Otherwise there is no news. It won't be long and July will be over again. I am really

afraid of this coming winter, as we won't have much coal or wood for the heating. I just hope it's not going to be as cold as last year. I don't even want to think about it. Horst has gone to Mrs Lehmann's, I should have gone with him, but I wanted to finish the letter first. Because during the week I am busy queuing for things. Now my lovely Hans, stay well, one day after the other has to go by and then the day of our reunion will come for us too. Sending you lots of love and kisses from your Mum who is thinking about you all the time and your brother Horst. Hoping to see you again healthy very soon

Replied 27.7

Prenzlau, 29.6.47

/ 23/7

Dear Hansi!

I cannot stop myself from wanting to write to you and thank you for your lovely mail. Your card arrived on 1.6. I waited with some restlessness to hear from you. Dear Hansi, don't torture yourself with my problems. I have done some terrible things to you and to myself, I have to follow my difficult path and I must pay for my sins. You promised to meet up with me and this is what I live for. I do not harbour any hopes, please believe me. I want to be open with you all the time and admit everything. All I want is to see you again. These thoughts are constantly on my mind. When I work on the fields in 35°C harvesting the sugar beet, I can think of nothing else. Whatever follows will be even harder to bear. Your mum won't be very happy about this. If she wants to deter you, she only wants what's best for you, I am sure. Everything is my fault and I have no right to ask for anything. I am constantly thinking of the fact that I have destroyed our happiness, and I am getting more and more desperate. I am shedding bitter tears. If I knew that you have accepted it, I would be a little calmer. Please forgive me that my letters do not bring you any pleasant news. If my letters make you feel uncomfortable, please let me know. I do not want to annoy you. Even if we never hear anything from each other again, in my heart I will always be yours and yours only.

I am wishing you a very happy birthday and only the best. I am sure your life will be a happy one in spite of the sad news I had to bring you. It was on your 18th when I first wished you a happy birthday. How happy we were then.

> Although my aims were sometimes very high
> I managed to get through joy and pain
> But how the dice has rolled for life
> I can never forget you

Replied 27.7.47

Prenzlau, 30.6.47

23/7.

Dear Hans

I arrived back in Prenzlau one day after Maundy Thursday. Marga and Udo brought me home. I intended to stay until after Whitsun but when I heard that Vera had been taken ill, I left immediately and surprised everyone with my arrival. I had a relaxing time and also put on some weight, but now everything is back to its old self. I seem to get thinner by the day and feel I am getting nearer to joining my departed loved ones. My dear husband died on Saturday (5.7.) a year ago. I am fighting to keep my head above water. If our Papa saw me, he would turn in his grave. Vera's life is just the same. How on earth did she get where she is now! Lots of lovely promises were made. Vera said to me yesterday that her husband is so lazy and relies on other people to work their fingers to the bone and slave away in the fields. She only gets very small portions of food, the three sisters rule the roost and inside, the mother-in-law joins the sisters in their controlling ways. Vera is the factotum – Girl Friday, the girl who does everything......... She cries such a lot, I cannot help her and don't wish to interfere. She will have to cope with it on her own. Manfred is not too bad but he is always hungry and looks very poorly. His second apprentice year is nearly over.

Dear Hans, I have done enough moaning and it is time to ask how you are. We hope you are fit and healthy. I am sending you my best wishes for a happy birthday. May all your wishes come true. Vera is also sending you her best wishes. May the day come when you have your freedom again. It should not be much longer now. We can only hope for better times. Stay well and write back soon. It is very hot here. We are longing for more food and drink. What are you up to? Thank you for your nice letter which I received when I was still at Marga's. I had a lovely time there and also at Werner and Eva's in Hanover.

I am sending you loving greetings and wishing you all the best.

Your mum Halling

To: Miss Vera Halling.
             (2)   Prenzlau/Uckermark.
             Neubrandenburger Strasse 7b.
             Germany, Russian Zone.

From: Johannes Klawitter.
Prisoners' No.: 872859.
             262(G) PoW Camp Langar near Barnstone.
             Nott's, Great Britain.

Saltby, 27 July 1947

Dear Vera

Thank you very much indeed for your letter dated 29.6. First of all I need to say; if there is something, anything at all, that bothers you, just write it down for me. I have accepted everything and you should now calm down a bit. I will also write to you and you must not get restless. But I do not want to cause any problems you might get because of my letters. We are connected by an old friendship from our youth, aren't we? I know all about working in the fields, because I have been working on them for a long time. Should my mother not agree, I am old enough to know how far I can go.

111

Please stop talking about the blame you have to bear. It has happened and nothing can be done about it now. Put a bit of pleasure into your letters, in the same way as I used to know you. I do not feel annoyed by your letters. Thank you very much for your birthday wishes. Yes, it is four years ago since the first. May your secret wishes also come true! Our lives have somewhat changed and not for the better. Otherwise, I am well, and I hope the same of you. Please pass on my best regards to your lovely mum and Manfred. Write back soon and stay healthy. I am sending you my very best wishes today. Hans

Replied 10.8.47   **Aschersleben , 13.7.1947**
                                                        8.8.47

     My dear Hans,
We have gratefully received your letter from the 22.6.1947 and we were so pleased to hear from you. Sending you much love on this Sunday. I am so tired; I have to force my eyes to stay open, because today we went together with Mrs Lehmann, her children and a few other acquaintances to pick raspberries in the Harz. It was fun and well worth it. It is wonderful in the Harz, I have already been twice this week, one has to get some "butter" to go on the bread. There are so many raspberry fields, but they are laced with brambles and they rip all our things apart. Health wise we are still ok, hope you are ok too. On Tuesday I will once again go and pick berries. I always have to get up at 2 AM and in the evening I am totally finished. But what can we do, we have to try and get food on the table.

Pressed flower enclosed with the letter

I will give you Gogolin's address, and you can also write a card to Uncle Leopold and Aunt Selma, otherwise they will be upset if you write to Gogolin and not to them.

Mr Hermann Gogolin , 19 Eisleben, county Magdeburg, Kleine Bergstr.3

Leopold Klawitter, 19 Eisleben, county Magdeburg.

I don't know the street, but it will arrive anyway. I want to finish my letter now, I can't keep my eyes open any more, I'm dead tired. Sending all my love and kisses from your mum who is always keeping you in her thoughts, and your brother Horst. Hoping for a healthy reunion very soon. Mrs Lehmann sends her love to you.

10.8.47   Aschersleben, 20.7.1947
                              8.8.47

My dear Hans,

Many thanks for your lovely civilian letter from the 29.6.1947. Horst's letter from 29.6 has also arrived and he

113

will respond later today, but he has gone away with Berni. They are on a bicycle trip, it makes him happy, and perhaps they can get their hands on some food too. The food situation looks very dire at the moment, we only have potatoes for 3 days now, and we hope we can get some more after that. A few times we went and collected some winter barley, we already have 25 pounds, we had to walk for 30 km, but what can we do, hunger is painful. We have a few exhausting weeks ahead of us, but even those will pass. If only you were to come home this winter, I don't want you to suffer from hunger. The main thing is to stay healthy, but I do not have the same strength as last year. Yesterday the police controlled our backpacks, I don't mind really, they have to do some work for their money. Recently they caught some people stealing potatoes, and they locked them away for a few years. I know it's not allowed, but if a person has nothing to eat despair drives you to do these things. But when the big bosses mishandle tons of food, nothing happens. Is this justice? Honestly, the little bit of collecting that we do, I want to see if anyone can catch us and take it from us, it won't be that easy. When your letter arrived, I quickly opened it, but again no picture, what a shame. How nice that you had a little birthday party, I bet you were happy. I'm sure food wise you are not worse off than we are. Thea is not married, but she is engaged, she is very busy, she does homework for shops. On average it seems that we will have a good harvest. If we could keep all the food here, we should not have to suffer as much. I am feeling ok, if only the hours and hours of queuing would stop. I get up before 5AM in order to do the housework and prepare the food, because if the weather is good, I want to go and search for food in the fields. Now, my dear Hans I want to come to an end, , stay healthy, sending much love and kisses from your Mum and brother Horst. Hoping to see you soon.

Aschersleben, 21.7.1947

My dear Hans,

I have gratefully and with huge pleasure received your card and letter from 22.6 and 29.6.1947. We are both healthy and content and I hope the same is true for you. When you receive this letter you hopefully will have already sent your picture, we are so incredibly curious! Yesterday I went with Berni to Bräunrode, which is 16km from here and we brought twine to a farmer, I only joined him for the food. The trip there was a real adventure, we left at 10.30AM with our bicycles and arrived at 4.30 in the afternoon, we were caught up in a proper "Harz" thunderstorm and we had to take shelter in a barn for three hours. It was a real deluge. We left from there at 6.30PM and were back home by 7.30PM. Berni's Mum again gave me a litre of beautiful full fat milk from the farmer, a small piece of bacon, a fried rabbit leg and a few pieces of sugar. Mum was very happy, it's been a long time since we have seen milk. At 8 o'clock I want to go to the employee committee election for hairdressers. And tomorrow I want to go to Winnigen and try and get some carrots, we also want to dry some. Mum went out to glean corn this lunchtime and now it's 7.30PM and she still isn't back. I really feel sorry for her that she has to work so hard. We are both trying to make provisions for the winter when you will arrive. This winter will be very cold once again and no fuel will be available for heating. I hope that this is your last camp!! I like my new workplace and the boss has already organised vegetables for me a few times. At the moment we have an existence full of deprivation and it's a disgrace. The harvest will start soon. I have not been out for a dance for ages, as that's not the priority now, I'd rather go and pick leftover potatoes from the fields, that's more important for us. Hopefully we won't have to wait too long for your return, we are longing to see you, still no news from our dear Papa, but I'm sure he will come soon. I want to finish now.

Write again very soon. Lots of heartfelt greetings from your brother Horst and Mum . Hoping for a healthy reunion in the near future. Be safe, look after your leg- see you soon!!!

Replied 17/8.47   **Aschersleben 27/7/47**

15 AUGUST 1947

My dear Hans

Unfortunately this week we have not received any mail from you, but I am sending you our dearest Sunday greetings. We went digging again today, Horst came too. We hdid our 18 km as usual. You end up not feeling your feet anymore, but it has to be done. This year the whole process of digging does not look too rosy. About a quarter of the population has been issued with permits to dig and those who do not have any are not allowed to collect anything. I had a permit, and so did Horst, from his business. And Mrs Lehmann had one from Social Services. But near town there is nothing to collect, which is why we have to travel about 18-20 km every day. Those who cannot collect anything for the winter are in a sad state. Let's hope we will be as lucky as the previous year. I cannot let you starve once you are with us. Crossed fingers that it will work out. The whole week we walked around unsuccessfully, but it is only this week that the harvest really starts. I now cook the food in the evening for the next day in order to be able to leave by 6am. That way we are home by the evening. Otherwise we are both healthy and cheerful, and we hope that the same applies to you. On Thursday we went to a pea field which had been opened to the public, but don't ask, there were about 2000 people, so we went back home, you don't want your ears to be trampled upon. We then took the train and went to Frohse to pick up a few pounds of carrots. I had to pull 50 Mark from my purse, I got very cross, but that doesn't get you anything back. Now my dear Hans, lots of love from your always thinking of you mum and your brother Horst. Here's to a speedy, healthy Wiedersehen

Replied 24/8   Aschersleben 3/8/47
                                                    20.8

My dear Hans

Many thanks for your dear letter dated 13.7.47, and many dear Sunday greetings. Healthwise we are still doing well and we hope the same applies to you. Now is a difficult time for us, we would so much like to collect provisions for winter, and this year it is so hard – the people are forced to go out to the fields, as hunger is painful. It is not exactly very pleasant to go out and walk about 20 km in this scorching sun every day, and to be bending down continuously, I leave at 6am and return between eight and nine in the evening, even if you take a few slices of toasted bread along, it's nothing much to sustain you, one never manages more than 10 pounds of grain. Three weeks from now this torture will end. Horst's working hours have changed, he now works from 12 o'clock until 19.00 hours – it is also very exhausting for him to stand for seven hours. In the mornings he cleans the apartment and does the shopping, which is a great help to me. On Sundays and Thursdays he comes with me into the fields. Yesterday he baked us a cake, it turned out beautifully and of course he was very proud. In the evenings I am busy preparing next days' food until about 11pm, and by 4.30am I am out of bed. If only one had a bicycle one could go further afield. Dear Hans, how good to hear that you are in such good form, a rarity here, as there are only haggard creatures around. Believe you me, we would much rather have you here sooner than later and I am doing everything in my power to provide us with enough provisions for the winter. In the meantime you will have received Thea's letter? So you have laundry day once a week? Amazing what one has to learn. Today I was thinking so much about our dear grandma, it is two years ago that we laid her to her eternal rest at 6pm, and we can not even visit her grave. Life is so bitter. Now my dear boy please stay well and return home soon to us. Much love and kisses from your mum and your brother Horst

Replied 31/8.47   Aschersleben 10/8/47
                                          30/8
          My dear Hans
Today again I am sending you many dear Sunday greetings, unfortunately we have not had any mail from you this week, but let us hope for the next week. We are not doing too badly health-wise, and hope the same applies to you. I am very low physically, but why would it be any different, bearing in mind the terrible strain. Today we walked over 25 km, and then returned with the load, Horst was with us. During the week I had collected quite a bit, got up at 4am and went a few stops on the train, and returned at about 8pm, but once it was already 11pm when we returned, we had missed our train and had to wait for the last one. That meant only four hours sleep. I have to bring in provisions for winter, otherwise what will become of us? Here in this area there is no point, because there are a few thousand people and everyone is hungry. At least I will be pleased when this time is over and I have been successful. Let us hope for the best. It is becoming quite dark now whilst I am writing, the days are getting shorter. For three days we have had rather cold weather, so we were freezing in the fields, I had collected eight pounds of peas, which were very much needed. Now my dear boy, please forgive me if I do conclude this letter, I am ready to fall down from tiredness, more another time. Love and kisses from your always thinking of you mum and your brother Horst. Here's to a speedy Wiedersehen

Replied 11/9.47   Aschersleben 24/8/47
                                          10.9.47

My dear Hans

Many thanks for your letter dated 27.7.47 and for your civilian letter with the picture, which we so enjoyed. The picture really is not too bad, maybe it should have been taken more from the side, but at least it is good to know that you are still your mother's son. The similarity is still there, and you are looking really well, which makes me so happy. I no longer look the same, the last few weeks have really taken it out of me, but at least the result is not too bad, we haven't been doing any threshing. I have done my absolute best to get things done. As far as the potatoes are concerned, it looks rather grim, due to the drought. On some days the heat was unbearable, plus we were so incredibly thirsty. We have of course made the most incredible treks, but had we not been doing that, the results would have been rather sad. The time has now come that we can finally rest a little. Dear Hans, we are happy that you have done some shopping for us. Maybe you can buy white as well as brown twisted yarn? We have not been able to get hold of anything, I cannot mend any of our things, especially as we own practically nothing. Not a single sewing thread, no soap, so that one can have a proper wash. I have heard that over there you can even get coffee, the husband of an acquaintance has sent some. But where would the money come from, considering what you are earning? If only we could send you some, but that is also out of the question. You are asking me about Elfriede, but you know her very well, she worked in the office of Uncle Erich in Stechlin. I am really pleased that you have now more freedom to move, just go to the café and the cinema, you have had to put up without these things for too long, and life is hard enough. Horst is going to the cinema this evening, he really wanted me to join him, but I am far too exhausted and would just fall asleep. Please stay very well my boy, one day the day will come when we shall see each other again. Much love and kisses from your mum and your brother Horst. Here's to a speedy Wiedersehen

Dear Hans

Thank you very much for your lovely letter 27.7. You are saying 'I hope you won't have any problems because I am writing to you'! Dear Hansi, please don't worry about it. I am so happy that I am allowed to write to you, and I am determined to hold on to this, my only happiness. Please Hansi, forgive me if I was unable to write to you in a calm manner. I want to try very hard and get better in the future. I do want to write some cheerful letters and I want to write every time when life gets a bit too much for me. But, I can't possibly write to you what I really want to write. Please Hans, I want to ask you once more – I know it is not necessary – because you know what you must do. Please answer my letters straightforward. The fact that I will never forget you and that Otto disappoints me again and again will not change. I am so much looking forward to seeing you again so that I can pour my heart out to you. I want to tell you about my worries and also about my inner feelings. I will remain patient. The main thing is you are coming. I want to spend a whole day with you somewhere, anywhere, where nobody knows us, but – who knows – whether my life will then become easier to cope with. If I should turn my back on the family to whom I am supposed to belong, I shall be a completely different person. I attended a fashion school which came to our town from Berlin and had a really nice time in the company of all the other students. I am also quite happy with my report. They promoted me to an apprentice supervisor of future female tailors. Currently I am practising folk and modern dance with the girls which we shall perform on 8 September on the occasion of the tailor's' ball. Unfortunately I am pressed for time at the moment and am rushing around in order to get to the classes on time, which I have set up myself. But I enjoy it all and it reminds me of the lovely times I once had.

On the side:
Dear Hans, I want to close my letter for today. I am very tired and intend to write to you more often. I wish you all the

best. Stay healthy and happy and think of me a little, when you have the time. With love. Yours Vera

What's happened to Jochen Thormann?

Pressed ear of corn enclosed with the letter

Aschersleben 24.8.47

My dear Hans

I have received your dear letter dated 3.8.47 with thanks and delight. We so liked your picture, you look quite chubby. Just keep eating lots and you will have something to fall back on. I have lost 6 pounds in weight and only weigh 114 pounds, slim like a fir tree. But this is due to the amount of time we go digging, sometimes travelling 25km, plus the queuing, we are totally worn out Mum is totally k.o'd. I would not have coped with it for more than three days. Now the difficult time is finally over, and about time too. We have brought in our harvest bouquet, it is standing on the wash table. How are you anyway? Are you happy and well? Which is what I can report from us. Please do look after your leg, I am so sorry that you have such pain. After a long, long time it finally rained last night, the drought was terrible, everything has dried up and it looks bad with the potatoes, at the moment we cannot afford ordinary potatoes, only grated or mixed in, this situation cannot continue, it is just terrible. Mum has lost 13 pounds in three weeks. Today mum has eaten too much, there were peas and beet in abundance plus a few plums with artificial cream, now she cannot move and is lying on our homemade chaise longue and snores like a bear. I am really pleased that you have thought of me and so is mum, as you cannot get such items here at all. Dear Hans when you are released please be careful when you cross the border, and the quarantine, make sure that you hold on to your belongings, because much gets pinched, which would be a real shame, so please consider whether you might want to send some of your stuff, as many parcels arrive from England. Good to know that you have a bit more freedom and you can enjoy yourself a bit more. Me and mum cannot wait for the time until you are with us again. Eight km to the next town is quite a way. Are the shops open on Sunday where you are? Now my dear Hans please write again soon and lots of love from your brother Horst and mum. Here's to a healthy and speedy Wiedersehen.

Aschersleben 31.8.47
25/9

My dear Hans

Already it is Sunday again and I want to send you dearest Sunday greetings. Thank you also for your dear letter dated 10.8.47 August has now finished and tomorrow is our dear grandma's birthday. How much we always enjoyed going to see her, and now she is resting all lonely and abandoned – it really does not bear thinking about. Good to hear that you can eat so many blackberries – here they have all but dried up. No, Horst has not as yet got his own bike, he borrowed it from friends. This year it really looks bad with the potatoes, who knows how it will end, I shall try my best to dig as much as possible, but I do not think it will yield much. We finished harvesting our grain the day before yesterday, it really was a torturous time, but even that has finished and we are content. For four and a half weeks I have been on the road from morning to evening, and some of the time was on my last legs, despite everything we achieved our aims, but I no longer have a single dress. Since yesterday afternoon and today from 7am in the morning until 1pm, I have been threshing. My hands are very painful, but it has yielded 1 hundredweight of rye. Tomorrow we carry on. You have to have a milling permit – let us hope they do not have the cheek to deduct this from our ration. Everything is possible!!! Once I have finished threshing I will tell you the full result. You can of course also buy cereals, Wheat is 800 Mark, rye is 700 and white beans 600 Mark. All completely impossible for us. On Tuesday we are planning to go to the fields again, to see what we can dig up in terms of beans and onions. Here it is forbidden, so it is better if the sheep are being driven across the fields. I am sure that the Gogolins and Uncle Leopold will write to you eventually. My dear boy remain healthy, perhaps you will be with us by Christmas. How wonderful that would be. Lots of love and kisses from your mum and your brother Horst Here's to a healthy Wiedersehen

Replied: 21/9.47   Aschersleben 7.9.47
                                        21/9.47

        My dear Hans

Thank you so much for your dear letter dated 17.8.47. We are always so happy when receiving post from you. We are sending you many dear Sunday greetings. I have just returned from the Harz, we had hoped to find blackberries, but unfortunately we only collected rose hips – they also make a good jam. We are on the road nearly every day of the week. This week we were traveling for two hours in the countryside looking for left-overs, found enough grain for three loaves of bread, some onions and a few beans. Although the fares are over three Mark, let's face it, you can't eat money. I have been threshing our corn for several days now, I am almost done, except for threshing the five sacks of wheat, that's a big problem. There is much hard work to be done before one can eat. But I have more or less the same amount as the year before, which makes me very happy. The days are still quite warm, and the nights are noticeably chilly. If only it would work out with the potatoes. Now we're already in September, so hopefully it will not be too long until you come home. Maybe even before Christmas? It would be too good to be true. On Thursday and Friday Horstel has to dress two women's hair for their weddings, he is so looking forward to it.

Tell me, Hans, do you have soap and elastic thread where you are? These are things we can't even think about here, as we do not even have any sewing thread or twist in order to mend the few items we still own, it really is miserable. I was hoping to have something made to wear this winter from some old woollen blankets, but there is no thread. Unfortunately, it is not possible, if only there was some form of support. Well, maybe even for us things will get better one day. Now my dear Hans, please stay well and write as often as possible, we are always awaiting your mail. Much love and kisses from your always thinking of you mum and your brother Horst. Here's to a speedy Wiedersehen

Replied 23/9.47   Aschersleben 9.9.47

22/9.47

My dear Hans

Yesterday we received a 'Civilian' letter from you. The fact that you are now driving is really grand – you really have learnt a lot. Mum has been out since 5am collecting onions, she really puts in an enormous amount of effort but she looks emaciated and I am really worried about her. She no longer has any shoes, the last pair split in two when she went digging. And there are no shoes for the winter. Our situation really makes us despair. The woman with whom mum goes digging received two large packages from her husband in England yesterday, it is amazing the things we have forgotten we know, one is just surprised about what's available in other countries and not here. In your letter you write that you have been seeing a young lady !!!!!! Well, we do of course not know whether the English women are any more faithful, something we can say here only rarely. How are you otherwise? Is your leg getting better? On September 28th we have a big hairdressing competition here in Aschersleben, with top professionals from Berlin, Dresden, Halle and some other towns. It starts at 2pm and finishes at 5am the next morning. The evening costs 5000 Mark, everything included. I would love to take mum along, but she never wants to go. My boss said that if she does not come, she will go and fetch her herself. This is a unique event and I would like her to have some distraction as otherwise she broods too much. My dear Hans if only you could be back with us, and if our papa came back we could all be together again, and everything would be easier to bear. Mum has provided well for us. People are always amazed at her staying power. I just feel sorry to see how she torments herself. On Thursday and Friday I have to dress two brides' hair, Friday is Berni's sister's wedding, and we are hoping to be invited for the afternoon event. You just have to make sure that every now and then you partake in a tasty morsel! Please dear Hans write again soon, Lots of love dear Hans from your Horst and mum
In the margin: Here's to a healthy and speedy Wiedersehen

Postage paid

Stamp: Censured Camp 402,

To: Johannes Klawitter.
A 572859.
262. G.P.W.W. Camp.   25/9.47 JK.
Langar near Braunstone Notts.
Great Britain.

From: Theodor Eichhauer.
PoW No.:   1482502.
Address: Thorée 402/Sarthe/France.
Squad No: 20292.

My dear Hans   26.8.47

Many thanks for your letter 3.8. As you can see I am still alive and I have already made a note of your address. There is nothing much to report. Nothing has changed here. I expect I shall lose my job in the Spring 48! My brother was discharged from England a few days ago and is now at home with us. I, for myself, am waiting for a few important replies.
Best wishes
Yours Theo.

Aschersleben 14.9.47

29/9

My dear Hans

Today we are sending you our usual Sunday greetings and thank you for your civilian letter dated 24/8/47. It arrived a few days earlier than your usual letters. But you earn so little and have got to buy the stamps as well. We are so happy that you are now able to write as many letters as you want. Healthwise I am not doing too well – Horst is really worried about me, but as long as I get a bit of peace and quiet, I am sure things will improve. My heart is really troubling me.

The last weeks have also been really tough. I have brought in more than five hundredweight of grain and am delighted with it. I am hoping that we can share it together in good health. But I am worried about the potatoes – they are the most important. If only I was fit, as this is most exhausting, especially carrying it all. How do you feel being a driver? You used to love driving the motorbike at home. It is not very good to know that the post has reverted to being bad. Let us hope it will soon change. Who is the person who you have been seeing? Don't fall in love too quickly, as you will have to leave eventually. It sounds as though during the harvest you also have long working hours. Well Horstel has been doing all the housework beautifully, it is not easy for him, he does everything he can possibly do for me. In the meantime you will have had the confirmation that we have received your picture, you are recognisable and look very well. It's only two and a half months until December, and maybe you will be with us by then. It is hard to imagine a reunion after such a long separation. I would much prefer to meet you in the other zone, they say that life is totally different there. They even receive milk, something we do not know here. They also have cheese and fish – and here? I am pleased to know that you can buy a few things for yourself, as here we have nothing. One thing after another tears, and we have nothing to mend it with, as everything is missing. I had a letter from Mrs Unger from Winselsdorf by Itzehoe, (Holstein) - she writes that Dr Rocke's wife has left him with the four children and has gone off with an E. Losgeganen Preck and his wife are divorcing, so everything is in disarray. You can only shake your head at what's going on. Now my dear boy I shall close my letter, stay very well and write soon. Lots of love and kisses from your mum and your brother Horst. Mrs Lehmann sends her regards. Here's to a speedy Wiedersehen

Aschersleben 21.9.47

                                    3/10

My dear Hans

I received your letter dated 24.8.47 with thanks and much joy. The hot weather does not seem to want to end, everything has dried up and there is no rain. Mum has worked like a hamster this year and really has fulfilled the target she had set herself, but please do not ask about the strain she has been under, I would not have lasted more than a week! I Hope you are healthy and cheerful, which we can now report from our side as well. Mum has been so exhausted, she has had stabbing pains in her chest, but now she is not too bad. In eight days from now us hairdressers have a big event, The hairdressing competition to decide who wins the prize as top hairdresser in the Harz. We already have the tickets. Mum is coming too, she was humming and harring but she has no choice. The entrance fee is terribly expensive, 8 Mark, but she can't not go as it's just this once. Oh dear Hans, hopefully this Christmas you will be with us, as it will be now four years since we have been alone. If only the time would come! Today people are queuing for potatoes. Thank god mum got ours yesterday, so she did not have to queue. I have heard that you are now a driver, sounds like you can learn all kinds of things whilst in captivity. That will always come in useful. Hans, what's with your leg, do you still have pain? Hans, please don't exert yourself. Now the digging for potatoes starts again, hopefully it will be permitted, as mum is feeling better. This afternoon I hope to be going dancing at the baker's mill under the castle, they have a cool band, which of course is the main thing. Dear Hans, have you learnt to dance yet? Now I just wanted to fill you in about the wedding, just fantastic. I was there by 9am, getting the bride ready for the registry office, but in between times I was in the kitchen, helping Berni peel potatoes, as well as preparing lunch, and at the same time I was also able to eat. The ceremony took place at 3pm, but before that I dressed her hair, and I was also present at the church. After the church ceremony there was coffee, but I stayed in the kitchen, where there were the most delicious cakes. For dinner I was the only one who prepared the platters of egg and the sa-lami-ones, but don't ask, it was just all fat. Yuck! I took mum with me, but we could not take in all the flowers and pre-sents. I think I have been eating, smoking and drinking from 9am until 10.30 at night, In any event, it was great, Now I will close and am sending you many greetings from Horst and mum

Flower enclosed with the letter

Replied 12/10   Gross-Rhüden, 2.10.47

11/10

Dear Hänschen!

At the moment I am in Gross-Rhüden and am finding the time, finally, to thank you for your letter dated 10.9, which I received just one day before my departure to my sisters, and it made me very happy. Unfortunately, it seems the pages

read more quickly than ever. What are we going to do with you? I don't know. Now, dear Hansi, I have just arrived at Marga's. I left Prenzlau on the 23rd. The journey was quite quick but not very pleasant. Crossing the border went really smoothly. I can honestly say that I was extremely lucky this time. I can't remember the last time I had so much luck. You should have seen how surprised Marga was when I got everyone out of bed the next morning, on the 25th. Needless to say I came unannounced. I love being here. Oh the beautiful Harz Mountains! Unfortunately the weather is rather unsettled. It is fairly wet and quite cold already. But I want to thoroughly enjoy my time here. Marga's children are so well behaved and affectionate. They take up their auntie's time all day long. Udo, now six years old, has grown into a sensible young boy. Ursula is ten months old. She knows me already. It is rare for such a young baby to be so pleasant and friendly. I am sure you are smiling, Hans, but it is true, and this is tremendous happiness. The children are the only happiness the parents get, without them their lives would just be very sad. It is dreadful to watch Ernst how he crawls on the floor without legs, and he cannot even support himself with both hands either. In spite of all this, they are both contented and understand each other. One can only be full of respect for them. Marga is very homesick and was overwhelmed to have me here. Eva came on Sunday so all three of us were together again after a long time. On Saturday I am going to Hanover. They want to see Auntie Vera as well. I shall stay there for one week and come back here again for a few days. Unfortunately my stay is not very long. I shall have to return soon. I am sure I will find it very difficult to get back into my old routine. It's not really that great to go away because on returning back home it takes a while to get acclimatised again. It's Marga's choir night today, she sings in a church choir. Ernst is next door. The children are peacefully asleep here in the same room where I am sleeping. I can think of you and write to you without being disturbed. I cannot imagine what you are up to there. There must come a day when you can go home. I shall see you then. You made a promise to me and I know I can rely on you with the uttermost certainty. I must see you again one more time. Here in Rhüden there are rumours going around that Commando 21 is being discharged. I don't know whether it is a fact.

I wanted to write such a lot to you and, suddenly, things seem a bit muddled. I would love to tell you what depresses me. I am not shy with you, Hansi, you must be misinformed, but you don't want to hear it. My sub-conscience is all confused, it cannot settle. I cannot enjoy the ordinary daily pleasures. And my heart is still ticking away. I cannot control it and it cannot be fooled. Sometimes I am so utterly unhappy. I thought it might get better while I am here. I would have loved to find my inner peace again. But I fear my turmoil will stay with me forever. I am hanging on to the belief that I will see you again. Only then will I be humble and quiet, I promise you. If afterwards it is your wish, then you shall never hear from me again. And then my only ray of hope will be destroyed. I think I am going mad. I must not think about what I have done to myself. How am I supposed to get over my burdened life. I always get back to where I started: whose fault is it? But there is no point to it, I am only getting more and more worked up.

I told you that my mum married again. Well, my sisters are just as shocked as I am. It means that even my home will become strange to me. Whilst I do not understand mum, I have no right to tell her what to do, but it does hurt. My dad cannot be replaced and I miss him dreadfully. He would have given me some advice and found a way out. I am sure he would have avoided my getting involved in such an undesirable relationship and then live a life of misery. Everything good in my life is now gone. Hansi, don't get annoyed about anything I am writing to you – I cannot help myself.

Take care and write back soon.

With love Your Vera

Replied 12/10   Aschersleben 29.9.47
                                11.10

          My dear Hans

Thank you so much for your civilian letter dated 31/8/47 – many Sunday greetings. It seems that my letter took ages to get to you – sometimes it's fast and the next time you wait for weeks. It sounds as though your life is a bit more interesting, which is to be welcomed, as it makes it less tough being a prisoner of war and so far from your homeland. I was going to write to you a few days ago, but I had to do the washing, which is always a problem when there is no washing powder, so I made jam from the rosehips instead. I was amazed what delicious, tasty jam they produced – it made over 12 lbs, so we have something for winter. I have been feeling a little better since yesterday, and although the pains have not gone, they are not as bad as before. Soon we will go and dig for potatoes, until now it has been forbidden. We have such an unnatural heat. If only we could save some of this heat for winter! Here in this area there are lots of coal mines, so people could get lots of coal delivered, but there is nothing for the refugees if you have nothing to offer in return. I cannot give away any of our grain, bearing in mind how hard I have struggled for it, we desperately need it to support us. On Friday I went to the Provisional Office to enquire about sewing and mending stuff, but, as usual, to no avail. We just get told that nothing is available. In the end we shall no longer have a single scrap of cloth to wear. If I were able to send you the money, perhaps you could buy such things? More than anything, what is needed is black and white thread, and silky thread. Twist, white, black, brown, light blue, pink, light green and grey. If there is nothing more available I don't know what shall be, as one would of course like to at least keep the few things that we still possess, as there is no way of even considering new ones. Enough already! Horst has been given a pair of very solid shoes from America by the Protestant Support Agency, but they are too heavy for him. They are really tough and with a leather sole. I shall have to try to get hold of a dress for every day, digging ruins everything. Are you able to get felt slippers? You can't walk around in socks in your room and there is no way you can get anything like that here. The day before yesterday after a very long time I received a letter from Mrs Halling in Prenzlau, telling me that she got married on 30th of August,

She married a widower with two sons aged 27 and 22. She was explaining that she can no longer manage everything on her own and spends all night at the sewing machine, so she decided to get married again, and has found a good soul of a man. I was speechless. Halling has been dead a year in July. But what can you say – the children have got their own lives to lead and Manfred is not very motivated and Vera's husband does not care about anything and it's all too much for her. Everyone needs to do what they feel is best for them. Marga brought her back here from the West, but she was not able to stay long because of the shortage of food, it is better on the other side. In her letter Mrs Halling mentioned that she often worries about Manfred, it is sometimes terrible. Once he has finished his training he will be going back to Marga's. Now my dear Hans please write soon and cross your fingers that I will be lucky with the potato digging. Please stay well - every Sunday brings us closer to a Wiedersehen. Lots of love and kisses from your always thinking of you mum and your brother Horst. Here's to a speedy, healthy Wiedersehen

Replied 13/11

1

Correspondence of a Prisoner of War
Foreigner
POST CARD   **POSTAGE FREE**

To	Johannes Klawitter.	25/10
No.	A572858.	
Camp:	No. 262 G P.W.W.	
	LANGAR.	
	nr Braunstone.	
	Notts.	
	Great Britain.	
From:	Heinz Bieck.	
Prisoner's No.:	1687.	

Camp No.:	14.
Squad No.:	10 (Kdo).
Address:	Douai (North).

6.8.47

DearHans!

Thank you very much for your lovely card. I didn't know
that you are in England. What do you do for a living over
there? I am sweating every night in a black hole, crawling
through the coal 500 m underground. I hope you have a better job than this. Discharge? How are things with you? Have
the Africans in your camp already left? Whenever this happens (to me) I intend to go home. Sending you my very best
wishes coming from the heart. Heinz

Replied 25/10   Aschersleben 24.9.47
                                    25/10

    My dear Hans

We thank you very much for your dear letter dated 11.9.47,
it took 12 days to arrive, We are always so happy to receive
mail from you. I am so delighted that you have bought sewing stuff for me. Maybe it will be better if you send it. You
can imagine Horst's smug little grin when coffee and cocoa
are mentioned. Just now a work colleague of Horst's is here
with us, she told us that her brother in law has also returned
from there. They were allowed to bring two pounds of coffee
and two pounds of cocoa, but it ended up more than double,
including powdered milk. One has forgotten what real milk
looks like. As well as all types of sewing thread and all kinds
of other good things. Together with many other comrades
he got out of the car, and came here to deliver the goods as so
often things disappear in the camp. He then went into quarantine for two weeks. I am assuming that you will return
to the same area. You are writing about the things you have
lost in the past.The newspapers have reported many times

that all those who have returned from captivity should let the authorities know, in order that their belongings can be sent on, is it the same for you? Yesterday we had a postcard from Werner from Parchim in Mecklembürg, he was released in Belgium on 9/9/47, and was in Parchim in quarantine. By Sunday he will hopefully be at grandma's. Well, they will be so pleased. Who knows when you will arrive in that way. Yesterday we went with our hand cart to the next village to get our wheat threshed, we are so happy that all the work is finished because it was impossible for me to thresh everything by hand. There is a total of 175 lbs. Isn't that wonderful ? I was at the mill today and have collected some of the flour. Despite this we have to plan carefully, as it is a long time until we can get something new. If only it would work out with the potatoes, and that I was feeling well again, Now my dear boy please remain in good health and be loved and kissed from your mum and your brother Horst. Here's to a speedy Wiedersehen

Replied 25 /10   Aschersleben 28/9/47
                                              25/10

     My dear Hans
Today we thank you for your dear letter dated 7.9.47. It arrived eight days after your civilian letter dated 11.9, which I already replied to on Wednesday. At the same time we are sending you many many Sunday greetings. Today the big day of the hairdressing competition has arrived. You can imagine how excited our Host is, he has been begging me for so long that in the end I have decided to go along. I do of course understand him, he only wants the very best for me, but I really do feel most comfortable in my own four walls. Especially as my health is not too good, last night I was in terrible pain, so that I did not think I could join him, but I did not want to spoil his enjoyment. After all the exhausting work recently my health has really gone downhill. The absence of

fat makes it impossible to recuperate. So you still have to wait so long for mail? As you know I am writing every Sunday and sometimes even during the week, and Horst also writes regularly. We are hoping and wondering whether you will be with us for Christmas. Surely you listen to the radio? It stinks and what will happen to the two of you? Then I'll be worried about you both. And what will happen to Papa? Best not to think about it. Today we also received a letter from Mrs Riborth from Pyritz, they are living in Singen on the river Ems. Kurt used to be at the townhall and is now reemployed at their offices. They are very well, they have a bit of land, and have lots of potatoes and vegetables, and are going to slaughter a pig for winter, she wrote to me that all of the Pyritzers are doing well, Solicitor Gabbert occupies a whole floor in a villa, his wife works at the E. How nice would it be if you could also be over there, being employed by E. But we did not get a permit to move. Aunt Else's nephew has also remained in the West, he does not seem to want to return to be with his mother. Maybe he will fetch her over eventually. Hans, do you manage to get sweetener over there? The amount of sugar we get does not go very far. You probably think that your mum is in need of everything, please don't be cross, but such things can only be got here on the black market, and we cannot afford such prices. Now I shall finish my letter, dear Hans. The wife of Horst's boss is about to arrive to pick me up. Stay well. Love and kisses from your mum and your brother Horst. Here's to a speedy Wiedersehen.

Replied 13/11   Aschersleben 2.10.47
                              21/10
        My dear Hans
I have received your dear letter dated 14.9.47 with great pleasure and send you many thanks. We are relatively well bearing in mind the times we live in and hope the same applies to you. Today we have experienced a small adven-

ture; we went digging for potatoes, but it was only permitted to start on October 4th – well we are digging away and finding beautiful potatoes, when suddenly the field police arrive and we have to pay a three Mark fine, but it was ok, because at first he wanted five Mark. We harvested about 16 pounds. This morning mum and I went to the mill and got the wheat exchanged, mum worked so very hard. I am not at work today – the salon is shut every Thursday in order to save electricity. Today we have received our large piece of meat. Aunt Else has also sent us two packets of potatoes, she is doing really well, which we grant her with all our hearts. They even reached their quota of sugar beet, something many new farmers do not manage to do. Hopefully later on she will be able to slaughter her pig, and it won't be confiscated.

The Busch circus was in Aschersleben for five days, the performances were much better than the year before, we really enjoyed it. However, how much better it would be if all four of us were able to watch together. Let us hope it won't be too long. Dear Hans, I have a big request. As you know I would like to become a master of my trade, and that needs practice. Do you think you might manage to get hold of a lady's wig for me? When I can't practice it makes me feel ill. The shade doesn't much matter, but preferably blond or white or a gold-blond or reddish-blond and possibly longish hair for cutting. Please please can you try! Our great event has now been and gone, and it was wonderful. It started at 2pm and finished at 1am. I was very restless because I would very much have liked to take part, but I don't have what is needed to make it possible. Mum also enjoyed it very much. I see you even have a little cat – that must be the guardian of your house? Hopefully your return will not be too long. It is only three months, fingers crossed. Now my dear Hans, please write again soon, all the best from your brother Horst and mum – we have heard nothing from our Papa, but are hoping every day.

In the margin: Here's to a speedy and healthy Wiedersehen – How is your leg?

Replied 22/10   Aschersleben 5.10.47
                                                        21.10

      Dear Hans

We are sending you best Sunday greetings, although this week I have not received anything from you, just a letter to Horst, which he has already replied to this week. Healthwise I am doing a bit better, which is just as well, because as of yesterday digging the stubble for potatoes commenced, as it is now permitted. I have collected one and a quarter hundredweight, but I was digging until the sweat was pouring down my back. If only it would continue to work out so well, I shall be so happy. Just now, many packages are arriving from England, it would be better if you sent one too. This week a few returnees arrived, they had enormous rucksacks, but had to leave quite a few things behind in the camp, isn't that so mean? The husband of the woman I go digging with wrote yesterday that each prisoner is allowed to apply for a care package, it comes from Canada and gets sent immediately to the relatives in Germany. It weighs over 12 1/2 pounds and contains all kinds of food supplies, but it can only be sent to the E. zone*. So please give either Mrs Unger's or Mrs Streese's address. They will no doubt sort it out immediately, they will send the stuff in two pound parcels. Best to Mrs Unger, as she will get down to it immediately, and they live near town and will therefore find it easy to send it. Her address is as follows: Mrs Auguste Unger in Winseldorf nr Itzehoe (Holstein) 24. The husband of the acquaintance sends it to her friend. I was hoping to have Horst's shoes re-soled, but unless you bring along soles and Tekse** they will do nothing. Where should it all come from? In the end we would end up walking around in our socks. How come you have a new address, have you changed to a different camp? Now my dear Hans I shall close my letter –

it is 5am and soon I'll be on my way to the field. Please stay well. Much love and kisses from your mum and your brother Horst. Here's to a speedy and healthy Wiedersehen

*English zone

**wooden nails for clogs

Replied 17/11   Aschersleben 12.10.47
                                                    17/.11

          My dear Hans

Thanks you so much for your dear letters dated 21.9, 2./9, as well as Horstel's letter, also dated 21.9.47. We were so very happy to have mail from you, and Horstel also thanks you very much and he will write to you soon. At the same time we are sending our best Sunday greetings. Today is a beautiful sunny autumn day. During the past week I have been digging for potatoes, but it is so very exhausting, I collected four and a quarter hundredweight, which made me very happy, but of course that's not enough for the three of us. In the area near town there is nothing, so we have to take the local train further out. Yesterday they allowed only small hand carts on the train, so you have to carry everything on your back, which is not something I will be able to do for much longer. Yesterday I carried 60 pounds on my back for a whole hour, and am totally exhausted today, my heart gives me a lot of trouble. Horst carried the sack from the station to home, then he could do no more, but what can you do, at least it stops us from going hungry. I will carry on for another eight days, and hopefully that will be the end of the torture. After that there will be a few trips to the Harz to collect wood, and possibly a bit of sugar beet, but there won't be much, as there is not a large yield this year. I wonder how you might be spending your Sunday? Might you have visitors? The day of your homecoming is approaching, wouldn't it be wonderful if it happened before Christmas.

Well, I'm sure you ate quite a few plums when you were picking plums. How wonderful would it be to once again eat a yummy piece of bread with plum puree. It's a great shame that you are not able to send us anything, I was forced to buy 1000m of white yarn on the black market which cost me 75 Mark, worth three weeks of Horstel's salary, but what can you do, I couldn't sew on a single button anymore. We really notice that the money doesn't go very far anymore. I was very happy about the elastic tape. Well well, you have commissioned someone to knit us a woollen scarf, that is very nice. Were you able to buy wool? Here we have had our first night of frost, the potatoes which were on top of the pile have gone all soft. This afternoon I will have to really get busy, I have eight letters to write. Now my dear Hans please stay well and we send you our love and kisses, from your always thinking of you mum and your brother Horst. Here's to a healthy Wiedersehen.

Replied 17/11   Aschersleben 16.10.47
17/11

My dear Hans

I have received your dear letter dated 23.9.47 with great joy and thanks. We are still reasonably healthy and lively and I hope the same applies to you. Today is Thursday again, and the business is closed. Mum has been extremely busy digging potatoes and she managed to bring in seven hundredweight, but under such duress. Yesterday she missed her train and didn't get home until 21.45, and she left again at 7.30 in the morning. She tortures herself, she always says we must not go hungry when you return. Mum has completely ruined her feet and the worst is that she does not have any shoes for winter. This morning I queued for meat and managed to get a nice piece of mutton. We get two and a half hundredweight of potatoes for storing per person. It would of course be nicer to be in the Western zone, you hear many things.

It has been a few days since we last had mail from you, but we received your civilian letter, which made us very happy. Mum and I were practically sick from laughing so much, but of course the main thing is that Jean is a good girl. We are happy that because of her you have a bit of diversity and distraction. I have a request: Couldn't you send me a nice little English girl via express delivery, could you? The girls here are not very exciting. Perhaps you could send us a picture of her, as we are of course curious. Dear Hans please stick to it, so that something will come out of it. How is the weather? Here it alternates between spring and autumn. Once I have finished this letter I shall be making hair pieces, which for me is the most beautiful task. Fabulous that you are now driving a car regularly, it will stand you in good stead. Your boss seems to be a great guy seeing he always invites you. Eight days ago I went to Halle to buy goods for the business, but there is very little to be had, and what's for sale is rubbish. If only our Papa had sent word, at least mum would no longer have to worry, we are hoping every day, as transports from Russia arrive daily. Mum was going to go digging for the last time today, but she just cannot bear to carry the heavy loads anymore. The other day she came home carrying 40 pounds on her back, so I got cross with her, as she is not meant to carry such heavy loads. I will now end my letter, much love from your Horst and mum. Regards to Miss Jean.

Here's to a speedy and healthy Wiedersehen – Horst and mum

Replied 22.11. Aschersleben 19.10.47

22.11

My dear Hans

We thank you very much for your dear letter dated 29.9.47 and are sending you our Sunday greetings. The weather is very nice, but the nights are remarkably cold. Horst says to thank you very much for your letter dated 5.10.47 – he will write to you in the next few days, on Thursday he sent you a letter, when mail arrives from you, he has to go out for a bit, whereas I always have to write letters, this is my Sunday task. I have now given up digging, in fact it is now forbidden because of the beet harvest. I have struggled enough and am so happy that I managed to bring in seven hundredweight and 80 pounds. Last Tuesday Mrs Lehmann and I carried 80 pounds for a whole hour on our backs, we were totally worn out. On Thursday we had a massive downpour, plus the train was delayed by one and a half hours, so we arrived frozen and wet through, but at least all three of us can eat our proper fill. I have shed the little bit of weight I had put on during all that hard work, but I am always hungry now, so I will surely recover. It sounds as though you have been driving a fair bit with your car, but please be careful. So, you have fallen in love – you might find it difficult to leave! But I don't think that Jean would like it here, nothing is like it used to be when we were at home. But you are old enough and must know what you are doing. We are pleased that she takes an interest in what is happening to us, please send her our best regards. Next week Mrs Lehmann and I are planning to go to the Harz to collect wood. What kind of job does Jean do, if she phones you every day, and are her parents still alive? We would be so happy if you could be with us for Christmas, we wouldn't be so lonely then. My birthday is in four weeks tomorrow, what a shame you cannot be with us. I shall be 43 already, hard to believe. We've not heard anything from Gertrud for a long time. Now my dear boy stay healthy. Tell me, how do you and Jean communicate, in German or English ? Much love and kisses from mum and your brother Horst.

Replied 13/11   Aschersleben 26/10/47
12.11

My dear Hans

I was delighted to receive your dear letter dated 5.10.47. Many thanks. We are still well and cheerful, which we hope you are too. A few days ago we had the first frost, let us hope that the winter will not be too severe. This afternoon I went

142

dancing at the Baeckersmuehle again, the only place that is relatively decent, the others are terrible. We have just had supper, and, as usual, mum has eaten too much, and she is now lying on our homemade chaise lougue and …. One eye does not see the other. The day of your return is approaching, and we are so looking forward to seeing each other again after so many years. How is Miss Jean? Good to know that she manages to distract you from your time as a prisoner. Unfortunately I was not able to take part in the hairdressers' competition as I had nothing to contribute. I very much hope that I will be able to take part next time though. I just need to practice very very hard. It's a great challenge to become a really good hairdresser. As long as everything works out ok.!!! The entrance fee for the evening was very expensive, but one's eyes are able to take in a lot and use it. I am prepared to give everything for my job, even if it is the last thing I do. I just hope that we can look forward to a positive future. It really would be the best present if you could be with us for Christmas. I am surprised that you have learned to dance, but you are absolutely right, it is not the most important thing these days, and when I come back from dancing I always think that it is more or less the same. You turn around a few times, and then it's time to go home. You seem to have quite a few things in your camp, even a band, that is wonderful. We are very happy that you have organised for us to have two scarves knitted, who has knitted them??? Jean? Now it gets dark so soon. In eight weeks from today Christmas will already be over. Time flies ! Mum now sports a nice hair style, an outward turning wave, sides folded under, and large curls on top. I will now finish my letter. Lots of love my dear Hans from your brother Horst and mum. Here's to a speedy and healthy Wiedersehen

Write again soon !

Replied 13/11   Aschersleben 26.10.47
                                        12.11
        My dear Hans
We are sending you our very best Sunday greetings. Unfortunately we did not receive any mail from you last week. Hopefully we will hear from you the following week. Winter

seems to have arrived early. Today there was frost already. It would be good if the weather stayed nice for a while, as we are hoping to collect sugar beet. At the moment it is still forbidden. On Thursday and Friday I went to the Harz with Mrs Lehmann to collect wood, it is always 30 km on foot. Horst came along on Thursday, his muscles were aching so much. If the weather holds we will go again and pick up a wagonload for each of us, it's not very easy, but what can you do if you don't want to freeze in the winter. If only it will work out with the sugar beet. I have had mail from Mrs Streese, she has also heard nothing from her husband. Gertrud is working in a library in Lübeck This week Horst and I have consulted a card reader and we were told that Papa is definitely alive and will return to us at the beginning of 1948. 1947-48 will see a change in our fate for all four of us will reunite. Papa cannot write, but he is very strong-willed and wants to come home to us. There could be no greater joy for us. Has group no 20 been released yet? How nice it would be if you were here for Christmas. But do come to us and bring your stuff before you go into quarantine. That's what someone did last week. Now my dear boy stay well, lots of love and kisses from your mum and Horst. All the best to Jean. Here's to a speedy Wiedersehen

Replied 13.11.

From: Heinz Bieck.
PoW No: 1687.
Squad: 14 Kdo 10.
               Douai (North).

To: Johannes Klawitter.
               A572859.
               262 GOWW.
               Langar near Braunstone.
               Notts.
               Great Britain.

Dear Hans Thank you very much for your card. You know now that your discharge date will be in December. It must be a lovely feeling to know this. We are in a different position. We don't know anything yet. You also have a suitable job. Are you thinking of going into the East Zone? I intend to go there. Have you been to the USA? Please write a bit more detailed next time. My very best wishes and get home safely. Heinz.

Replied 22/11   Aschersleben 28.10.47

20/11

   My dear Hans

Your dear letter dated 12 October reached us yesterday, and we thank you very much for it. I will write back immediately so as not to make you wait too long for mail. I really believe that you often feel homesick, but hopefully the day of your return will arrive soon. I have finished my washing today, without soap and so little soap powder. I need to mend linen as and when it needs to be done, but there is nothing to do it with, some support should really be made available. I am very pleased that you have done quite a bit of shopping, these are such important things when you have nothing. There are no aprons anywhere. Aunt Emilie sent me a sheet from Berlin, I had sent her something and asked, because when you come back you need a sheet. We just have one each. Dear Hans, if you have enough money please buy what you can get, once you return I will reimburse you. Especially sewing thread, twisted thread and saccharine, a packet containing 100 tablets, which here costs 25 Marks, and there is never enough sugar. The day after tomorrow I will return to the Harz to collect wood. Horst will join me as it is his day off. Tomorrow morning I will queue for meat, so every day there is a task to be done, and before you know it another week has gone by, but that way the day of our Wiedersehen will approach more quickly. Now I shall finish my letter, it is 9pm and time for bed. Good night. Lots of love and kisses from your mum and your brother Horst Here's to a speedy Wiedersehen

Replied 22/11   Aschersleben 2.11.47
                                          22.11

      My dear Hans
We are sending you our Sunday greetings as usual. I have replied to your letter during last week. Our trips to the Harz on Thursday and Friday have been successful. We now have a good collection of wood for the winter and are delighted . Equally we have some people in the house who are envious, including about the stuff we have dug up. I really cannot understand it, but cannot be bothered, because it is open to everyone to help themselves, but some of them do not care, and they do not know just how much effort is needed. As long as a refugee suffers, it's okay, but as soon as you worry and struggle in order not to be cold and starving, envy and resentment are round the corner. Our landlord is also no longer as friendly as he used to be. Yesterday he tried to pick a fight with me about the amount of wood and potatoes I brought in, but I told him where to go, and I told him immediately that I would bring in another load of wood as well as potatoes.His place is warm, and we will make sure that we have it warm too. It is very sad – being refugees they do not grant us the air we breathe and they do not understand the difficult burden we have to carry. But you can rely on the fact that I will never let anybody step on my toes – we have had to put up with too much. People ought to be ashamed of themselves seeing how the women have to struggle, with-

out their men around. Now I have to chop all the wood into short pieces, I have worked really hard this morning, Horst is not able to help me. Today he went into the country, and as from tomorrow his working hours are changing, from 9am to 11 and from 12 – 6pm, they really are quite mad, and the free Thursday has been cancelled, so I have to do everything by myself. When Horst came with us last Thursday to collect wood, we had to negotiate a very narrow path, and we were loaded to the hilt, high up and with two lots of wood, and before we knew it we thought the wagon had fallen apart, but it was ok, otherwise we would have been sitting there, having been let down by our cleverness. Hopefully soon there will be some rain. If only we could dig up a few more hundredweight of sugar beet. The beet this year have a very high sugar content. What is happening about your return home? Will you be back with us for Christmas? Stay well and many greetings, love and kisses from your mum and your brother Horst. Here's to a healthy Wiedersehen

Replied 19/12   **Aschersleben 9.11.47**
                                          27.11.

My dear Hans

Today I will take up my pen and send you a few lines. It is more than a fortnight since I have heard from you, there seems to be a problem with the post being sent. Both of us are still healthy and lively, which is what we hope you are too. The time of your discharge is approaching, if only it was time as we are pining for you, as I am sure you are pining for us. No doubt the day when we are all together again will come. Dear Hans, do you shave already and do you have a proper beard? The harvest has finally finished. Next week mum and Mrs Lehmann will go digging for sugar beet, after that mum will finally have some peace, the effort is just too much. Our wood-gathering has also finished, it was worse than slave work. Had we stayed at home we would not have needed to do this, but the past will not repeat itself. Dear Hans, how is Miss Jean? Does she come and visit you on Sundays? At least that takes your mind off things. I went dancing at the Baeckermuehle yesterday, but one can really lose the will to dance as all they play is American jazz, which makes you want to run away. Yesterday we received your dear letter dated 21.10.47, in which you mentioned the parcel you have sent. We are looking forward to it immensely and hope it will arrive soon. This lunchtime we had potatoes, dumplings, gravy and with pork and beef chops, but you can imagine how big they were and this evening there is yeast dumplings with apple soup and a cheese sandwich, unfortunately eating it takes rather a short time. I have already bought a birthday present for mum, it's a beautiful lamp for our living room, beautifully decorated. The electrician has already fixed it but without the bulb, which you can't get hold of, it cost 92.50 Mark. Once you are here again we shall have to set everything in motion in order to get a radio. Apart from mum and Mrs Guenther I have dressed most of my clients' hair, but it takes up most of Sunday morning. Now my dear Hans I will conclude my letter and please receive my best wishes from your brother Horst and your mum. Many regards to Miss Jean

Replied: 2/12 Ascherleben 9.11.47

Aschersleben 9.11.47
1/12

My dear Han

We thank you very much for your letter dated 21.10, we had not received anything for a nearly a fortnight and were beginning to worry. We are really looking forward to the parcel that's on its way, let us hope that everything arrives alright, but why shouldn't it, as so many people receive parcels from there. I am just so pleased if you have a bit of Waesche * as here there is nothing like that to be had. Horst just owns one shirt for winter, in the other one not even 10 cats could catch a mouse, it's so sad that we are losing one after another of our things, it is now nearly three years since we have left home, and when you have to wear the same clothes every day nothing much can remain of them, especially as you have nothing to mend things with. It is just too sad for us refugees, and when our Papa returns he will own absolutely nothing. But the main thing of course will be that we are together again. Your parcel might be here in a fortnight, it has been en route for three weeks now, it would be great if you could try to get soles and Teske** Dear Hans if you could get black sewing thread it would be great too, because once you and Papa are here, I am counting on the fact that each of you will be allocated some material for a suit, but there is no sewing thread, nor lining or interlining canvas, which are all needed for a suit. We need about 700 m yarn for a whole suit. The large rolls always have 1000 m of yarn, but over there they seem to come in rolls of 500 m. I will pay you back. Unfortunately we have had to dig into our thousand Mark bills, as everything is so expensive. And of course one has no idea as to how things will turn out. If so many are to be discharged soon, maybe it will be your turn too? If only it was for Christmas! This week I have cut up all our wood, and stacked it all, unfortunately Horstel cannot help as he no longer has a day off. Now my dear boy please remain well, and return home soon. Many Sunday greetings and kisses from your mother and your brother Horst. Here's to a speedy Wiedersehen

*(generic word for everything from linen, to underwear, general clothes, bed clothes, etc)

** wooden nails

Replied 5/12   Aschersleben 13.11.47
                                          3/12

          My dear Hans,
We thank you from the bottom of our hearts for your lovely letter from 25.10.47, which arrived the day before yesterday. Horst has been waiting 3 weeks for a letter from you and he is very sad. In the meantime he has written to you 3 times. It is now raining every day. We planned to leave at 5

am this morning by train to glean sugar beets, but with this terrible weather we could not leave the house. I'm already afraid of the heavy carrying, I wish the task was already behind us.

I'm so happy to hear that you could buy yourself some shoes. Then at least you have something to wear. It makes us both very sad that yet again we must spend Christmas without you. We were already imagining what our reunion would be like after 4 years.

Yesterday I queued from 5am to 9am for thread, yarn, a dress, a petticoat or an apron, but of course without success. As usual there was nothing. The ones that already have enough always get more. Where should this all lead to? Soon we'll walk around ragged like a vagabond, good enough for us they think!!

I'm sure you've already made a lot of acquaintances over there. We would be very happy to receive a parcel from you. Why did you choose a woman older than you? She could be your auntie, even though those are not to be despised.

Great that you have milk powder and sweetener, Mrs Schulz's husband recently sent some to her. Then maybe we can eat a milk soup soon.

Werner sends his regards, I received a letter yesterday, he's got a sick note until 31.12. Why should one be ashamed of eating gleaned sugar beets? You know that I like to do it for you.

Now my dear boy, stay healthy and keep enjoying life. Drive carefully with the car in bad weather. Be greeted from the bottom of our hearts , we're sending kisses. Your Mum and your brother Horst.

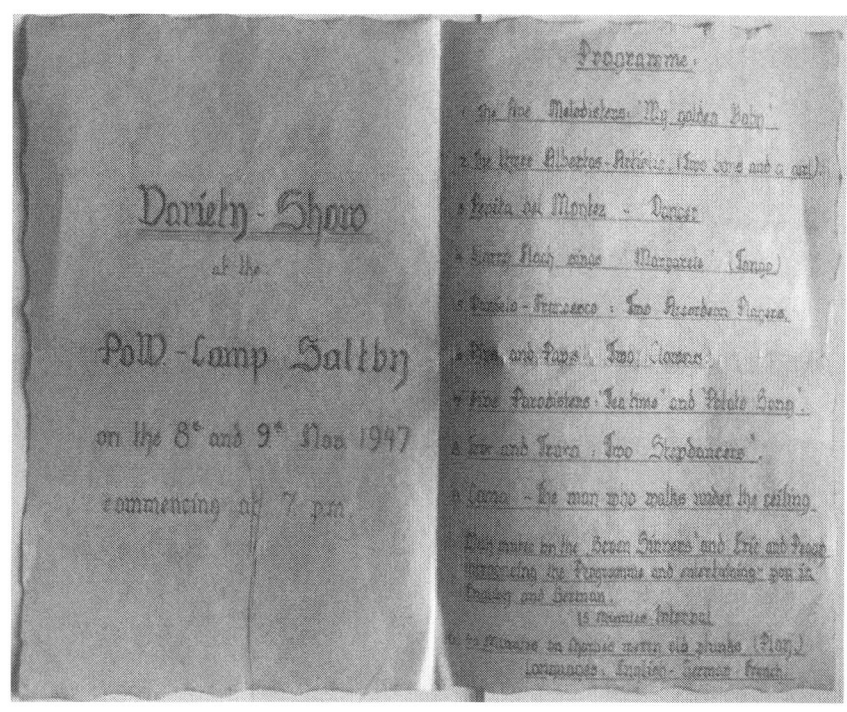

1

Hans Klawitter
LWAEC Hostel Stathern
near Melton Mowbray
4th December 1947

My dearest Jean,

I am here now I arrived by 6 p.m. last night and I have settled already. I like this place because it is more comfortable than Saltby anyway. My room is a very nice one and also better than in Saltby for a comfortable bed makes a bit of a difference. I have the room on my own and I'm quite satisfied. I was waiting for you to come back after the call yesterday afternoon but I've had it. I really was annoyed because it was the very last call from Saltby. But don't worry I hope you'll get this letter soon so you need not to wait too long. All the people around here are very friendly so it makes a comfortable change for me. I am sorry you are not coming on Boxing

Day, I always hoped that it would be possible. We are going to close the hostel for 4 days 24th of December to the 28th of December and so I'll be able to go to Mr Edwards place driving this time and spend my first holidays there. I would have been glad if you could have come. You should have seen my first breakfast this morning. I enjoyed it myself really. Now I want to close because I have to make things ready for lunch hoping that you'll write very soon I remain

always yours
Hans.

PS

<u>I have had it</u>

* Leicester War Agricultural Executive Committee, aka "the War Ag"

<u>2</u>

> Hans Klawitter A 572 859 POW. Camp
> Saltby,
> Saltby Aerodrome,
> near Melton Mowbray Leicestershire.

My dearest darling Jean

I am very quick in answering your dear letters aren't I? At first I want to thank you very much for your prompt answer. I was looking out for the mail car this morning for I knew you'd posted your letter. You are wrong in one case I did not say you are lazy, did I. But there is a little bit of difference. Look this writing makes me happy because there really is something I am waiting for. Don't mind darling you'll learn it very soon. You know I take every opportunity to improve my knowledge of your language and this letter writing is one.
I was expecting your call this afternoon but I know you are so busy sometimes. Did you ring last night? Mr Edwards was

still here. I only heard him saying "what's the matter with Leicester they don't want me now" I couldn't help laughing. What is Lucy like? As you know I don't know her but in spite of all tell her my compliments and she may not be so curious. It is rather a difficult thing to find out who I am. A mysterious person anyway.

I am glad you get your holidays next week. It is good to have 8 holidays during a fortnight's time. What are you going to do all these days? Spend half a day in bed and see a nice picture at night or go dancing? But take all enjoyments you can get hold of. I would do so if I would be able. There is a picture show here tonight in the camp. I don't know the title yet.

Our boss told me this morning they'll be a party in Melton the next week for all the officers of the Melton District. He also has got an invitation for it. We are doing the work but nobody invites us. It is always the same isn't it .

And now about you coming on Sunday. It'll be a long time to wait, as you know. Will it be possible for you to come on Sunday before Christmas and on Sunday after as well?I would be glad if you could arrange it that way so you can take that bag for your mother on Sunday before Christmas. As you know I like you to come as often as possible but I agree you have to take your own affairs into consideration. I'll stay in then the coming Sunday and wait another week.

Your Christmas is not quite the same as we know it at home. We get our presents on Christmas Eve when all the family is together around the Christmas tree. You've a special day the boxing day. I better like a Christmas party only with the members of the own family. I hope you'll have your badly needed rest this year for you are overworked really!

Mr Edwards has got a letter from Fritz yesterday. He arrived at home 6 weeks after leaving Saltby. Rather a long time isn't it. I don't worry about it because....... you know what I mean. It'll be better when I go home. In his letter he says that conditions are very bad and he didn't get his old job back. You are not wanted now was the answer as he asked for. That shows how it is going on now. I signed here for another year. I received a letter from my mother yesterday but she didn't mention this case. She only told me that my first parcel has arrived home safely in a months time. About a dozen times she wrote, I thank you so much for it. so you can see how the situation is. I am glad I sent two Christmas parcels last month and I'm going to send parcels as often as possible.

The Tailor will fix my jacket the first days next week. So it'll be alright when you come Sunday before Christmas. I better say cheerio now for my second breakfast is waiting for me. Give my kindest regards to your dear mother and be good yourself.

I would be very glad to find your letter on Monday or Tuesday morning.

And now darling I wish a nice weekend

    All my love

       always yours Hans.

Replied 9/12.47
                            92 Wharf Street,
                            Leicester.
                            December 6th 1947.

                            9.12.47

My dear Hans.

Here is the letter you made me promise to write. It's getting late to start writing so it will be only a short one.

Hans, are you allowed to have private calls at night? I do hope so after the first time I picked up and that operator cut us off. Did you hear what he said "they're not allowed to have calls". I was so annoyed I called the operated back, and got a different one. He told me to hold the line while he found the ticket, after about 10 minutes I got fed up with waiting. Dialled it again, told another what had happened, he put me through to enquiries, I told him, he told me to replace my receiver as the operator would be trying to get back to me. I waited 5 minutes, still nothing happened so I dialed again and got still another operator. I explained to him what happened. He said it sounded Dutch that the operators should cut me off before my 3 minutes were up. So I told him, to put it plainly, I was speaking to a German and it annoyed the operator. With that he put me through to you again. I do hope you can have calls. I am so very glad you are going to Mr Edwards for Christmas. We still don't know what is going to happen here. My sister can't make up her mind whether to come here or not. I somehow don't think she will be coming, so my mother and I look like going next door. At the moment I couldn't care less what I do. You know that it's not that I don't want to see you Boxing Day, because I would love to see you very much, it would mean breaking your holiday and it wouldn't be worth it for one day. It's getting late so I will say goodnight and God bless

All my love

Always

Jean

P.S. Don't worry if you can't read it I won't be surprised

Jean

23

H. K. L. W. A.E.C. Labour Office,

Saltby Aerodrome Saltby Satellite Camp,

near Melton Mowbray.

December 9th 1947.

My dearest Jean,

I thank you so much for your letter I received this morning. I like to answer at once. I got up by 7o'clock and found your letter already waiting for me for the mail is coming before 7.00 hours. I am well and I hope so from you and your dear mother.

And now about that call. We are allowed to have private calls at any time somebody is calling us. I think it was only jealousy of that operator. I know you were annoyed. There is a difference in your voice.You know I am glad when I get your calls and therefore I also was in rage. Telling Alfred about it he was speechless too. Things like this never happened before. Look! There are always a few people who think there may be something wrong in speaking to us. Time is over we were forbidden to talk to civilians. And just these people won't understand that. But they have to because there'll be more difference when we are civilians ourselves. Please don't worry about other people. I think we know what to do, both of us, don't we?

I was away this morning to get some coal or coke for our office. I had a little talk to the chap in the coal yard. He wouldn't give us any so he came just to the right address. He didn't expect me speaking your language. After calling the chief he was satisfied and kindness himself. So we got our stuff at least and after all more than expected.

I spoke to you already about Christmas. There'll be another Variety Show Sunday after Christmas. If you want me to go to Mr Edwards it will be alright. I also don't want to disturb your Christmas holidays. At my home it always was the only day of the year which saw all the members of the family together. I'm sorry there is nothing settled yet about these days. In spite of all I hope you'll enjoy the holidays. What shall I do about this bag for your mother? Do you like to take it along next Sunday or shall I post it? We better have a word about that. I don't know yet whether we are working on the Saturday after Christmas or not. If not it would mean 4 days off for us.

I won't forget to thank you very much for the two Snaps you sent me. I was waiting a long time I'm at an old proverb says. "Good think need a while think"

I haven't heard from my mother yet, but I am hoping for the next week. Last night there was an announcement about the Russian zone. I'll tell you about it on Sunday. It really is not worth going back home. I hope my mother will agree in this case.

I will close now for I have to bring one of our lorries to Melton this afternoon. I could (not) read your writing easy because I have some practice, however, don't think the wrong reason!!

Please say my kindest regards to your dear mother. Hoping that I will get your answer before Sunday I would like to say "be good" and God bless

  All my love
  Always yours
 Hans.

Jeans family.

Rolland. Hilda. Frank. Fred.Silvia.Jim.

Miriam. Beatrice (Mamma). Grandpa Charles. Grandma Anne. Cissy. Jessie.

Replied 12/12 Aschersleben 22.11.47

11.12

Dear Hans,
I can confirm the safe arrival of your lovely parcel. We are
all so grateful and thank you from the bottom of our hearts.
The tins are wonderful and I can't tell you how happy we
are. Thank God we are finally out of distress. Would you be
able to get hold of dark brown, dark blue and pink sock yarn?
You'll say "Mum and her constant wishes..." my little one,
don't be angry with me, I shall make it up to you. Horst is
very happy with the combs and beautiful white flower. Once
again, thank you very, very much. Unfortunately we haven't
heard from you in 11 days. We are all very sad, please also
write to Horst. He is waiting so excitedly. I've had to work
so hard for the sugar beets and have only 125 kilo's so far,
hopefully I can get a bit more. The ground has been frozen

solid for the past few days making it impossible to hoe the earth. I had some difficulty opening the large tin from you, but everything was undamaged. You simply don't know how happy we are. This evening we are going to have pearl barley with cinnamon. Also, Uncle Gustav and the family send their regards, you most likely haven't written to them for a long time. Tomorrow is Corpus Christi and we can't even afford a wreath for your lovely grandmother's grave, which leaves me deeply disturbed. It is now four and a half weeks until Christmas, I still can't believe you won't be with us, what a pity! Now my dear boy, stay healthy and write us again soon. Lots of love and kisses and always thinking about you, Mummy and your brother Horst. To a healthy re-union soon.

Replied 12/12.47   92 Wharf St.
                December 11th 1947.

                                        12.12.47

My dear Hans
It was very nice to get up this morning and find a letter from you, but it's not so nice when I have to reply which is as you say why I am very lazy and there does not seem any hope of me changing.
Were you expecting me to ring you this afternoon I was going to call you at about 5.00 but Lucy came in to talk to me and you know what Lucy is, she is always trying to find out to whom I speak and gets quite annoyed because I won't tell her. You should hear what she says when she hears me talking to you. Somehow she can always tell.
We had some good news today about the Christmas holiday. We are going to leave off at Wednesday lunchtime. I told you I had 4 days holiday to come, I think I will have them next week probably December the 15th 16th 17th 18th. I will have to have them then or not at all.
By the way the CSCA (that is our union) is having a Christ-

mas party on the 18th I think it will be a proper hen party, Lucy and I are going for a laugh. I told Lucy if things get too boring we can always argue about Ireland and liven things up, but I don't think the party will be the same as when the war Ag had one last year. I went with Gwenn and you know Gwenn, she makes any party.

Look darling I hate saying this but would you mind and if I did not come this Sunday. I know it will make it a long time.You see I have to go to Dora's for tea either this Sunday or next, so if I come this I will not be able to come the Sunday before Xmas. If you would rather I came this week I will. Anyway I will be coming the Sunday after Christmas, that is if all goes well.

My sister is not coming home at Christmas after all. You say it used to be the one day when all the family got together. It used to be like that here before the war. We always went to my auntie's at Birstall (that's the one that gives Betty and I lectures) and there used to be quite a gathering. This year it will be rather quiet.

About the bag, you need not post it, you may as well wait until I come, it would be safer knowing the post.

I better say cheeri'O as I have my skirt to press before I go to bed so just be what you told me to be, good

All my love

Darling
Jean

Replied 19.12

Aschersleben, 26.11.47

13.12

My Dear Hans,

I'm writing you a few lines again. I've been waiting for a

letter from you for the past 5 weeks and every day I am saddened not to hear from you. I hope that this week something will come. We were so happy to receive the parcel, you can imagine the joy on our faces. I am very happy with the combs, they are beautiful. The toothpaste too, it's so hard to come by here and when you do get it, it's rubbish. Dear Hans, Christmas is ever nearer and how wonderful it would be to have you with us. I still have hope that you may come. How is the weather where you are? It's lousy over here. Winter is setting in and we hope that it won't be too harsh, otherwise a lot of people will have to close their eyes. I got up a little earlier this morning and I've been writing since 7am. My boss was in the hospital for her second thyroid operation. She was in danger of suffocating if she caught a serious cold. Dear Hans, how are you? How is Miss Jean? Mum has been so busy with gleaning sugar beets. In a fortnight from tomorrow we will be making syrup. Mum wants to drive to the Harz with Mrs Lehmann to pick up some wood. It's 30km away. She always does her part and drudges just to keep us alive. It can't go on like this, there has to be some improvement on the horizon. Last night Mum and I were at Mrs Klingebeil's, who is from Stettin, and we had a little chat. They have a wireless, but nothing was on. Dear Hans, you wrapped your parcel so wonderfully, Mum was so happy with all the beautiful things, now she can repair things again. Now dear Hans, please write to me soon, or it would be even better if you came. We still haven't heard from Papa, hopefully we will receive a sign of life from him, we must not lose hope. I'll finish here.

Greetings to you, dear Hans and Miss Jean too, from your brother Horst and Mum. Looking forward to seeing you again soon. Maybe Christmas 1947.

Replied 14/12　　　　　Aschersleben 29.11.47
　　　　　　　　　　　　　　　　13.12

　　　My dear boy,
Thank you from the bottom of my heart for your lovely letters from the 17.11 and the 25.11,

which I received today. We were very pleased. In recent days 6 letters arrived, 4 for myself and 2 for Horstel. The latest only took 4 days. How is this possible? Was it transported by airmail? When I read it I cried my heart out as suddenly the great joy of our early reunion had been shattered. But I don't want to be selfish and only think about myself. You know that I always only want the best for you. You are old enough to make your own decisions. You are probably much better off. I can't offer you much, not even our homeland. If one thinks about it, it's probably the right thing to do. How much of what is written is accurate I can't tell. Many letters came back, including the one about the boy who stayed at the Brands, he used to be in your unit. It is probably a lot of propaganda. One cannot believe everything.

Where should you work and accommodation? You'll have to cater for yourself if you become independent. Will you be able to earn enough to make a living? You write that you might even be able to support us more. I wouldn't know what the lifestyle is there. In any case, be assured, I want the best for you and I don't want to stand in the way of your happiness. And we know how much you would like to stay with us.

Horstel was also very disappointed at first, I'm sure you will understand, because when one is so happy one longs to be with one's relatives. Maybe fate wants you to stay longer. May the dear God lead everything to the best. We must take everything as it comes. We are very happy that you have another parcel for us. It is the only joy we have left.

Oh, if only our dear Papa would get in touch soon, we wish it wholeheartedly. So my dear boy, we wish you and your future life the best. Hopefully one day we will be reunited. So often life turns out different to what we expect. Tomorrow on Sunday I will write again.

Be greeted and kissed from your Mum who always thinks about you and from your brother Horst.

To a healthy reunion.

Replied 15/12.47

92 Wharf St.
 December 14th 1947.

15/12

My dearest Hans

I received your lovely long letter Saturday morning. I was going to answer it last night in the hope you might have got it Monday morning, but I was so very tired and I hope darling you don't mind and me leaving it until today. I will post it at the main post office in the hope that there may be a chance of you receiving this on Monday.

I have changed my mind about having my holidays next week. I looked at the holiday notice, we can have them until January 31st not December 31st so I will probably have them in the middle of January.

My cousin next door is getting engaged today. You see his Mother does not approve of it, she thinks he is too young, but I don't think that is the reason. I think she doesn't want him to leave home and it would not make any difference what age he was. She would still object.

You asked what Lucy was like, did you mean in looks, disposition or what? In looks she has natural blonde hair, not quite as tall as I am but as hefty and a very pleasant smile. On disposition she's fairly even tempered. One of her faults is that she talks a lot and I mean talks. Sometimes I wonder where she gets all her energy from. If that description does not do, you had better wait till I see you, but I do hope she is not your type.

I am sorry to hear Fritz has not got his old job back, did you say he was a fireman and what is he doing now?

I did not call you the other afternoon whilst Mr Edwards was there. it must have been one of your other girlfriends. It wasn't me.

I am sorry darling but this is not going to be a very long letter and I'm going to Dora's for tea and I have to get ready and that will take me about 1 hour. Believe me I would much rather be coming to see you than going round there .Now I will have to wait till next week so be good till then

All my love

Always

Jean

----

4   Hans Klawitter A 572 859.

Saltby POW Camp.
Dec 15th 1947.

My dearest darling Jean,

I thank you so very much for your letter I received just half an hour ago. I couldn't wait till the mail was brought up here so I went down to the office myself and picked our letters out. It was a lonely Sunday. It would have been worse than that but I had your letters and read them four or five times at least. You see everything is alright and I've got your letter after all. I don't mind if you can't find time to answer at once for I know you've to do more work than only answering.

Have you had a nice Sunday? I was sitting here doing some jobs for me and was waiting for the meals as I told you on Saturday. Yesterday in the morning I received a letter from my mother. She got my airmail within 4 days I was astonished As she told me, she was weeping for the first hours because my news came unexpected. My mother was longing for seeing me again. You know how long I am away from her and I can feel it for her. She is wishing me the best for my future and after thinking it over she quite agrees with me in staying away from home."You are old enough to know what to do" my mother said. She's now worried about food, lodging and how much money I'll earn to do all the things on my own. I told her about everything. Do you suppose what she takes as a reason for my staying? I've written about you in nearly every letter and now she said I hope you'll find happiness in every way. I have to tell you her best wishes and greetings and all the best for the future.

It'll be better for you taking the holidays in January I think. I am glad for me that there are only 4 days left otherwise I would miss your calls very much. I don't know your cousin but my opinion is is that it is better to be young than old! Don't you agree? an old proverb says " married young is never to repent" and I think that's right.

I really didn't want an exact description of Lucy as you gave me one. If you like to hear it, I don't like natural blonde hair nor black. I prefer dark blonde. As you see there is no reason at all to worry about. I'll tell you more when you are coming next Sunday.

Fritz was the chief of a bank only volunteering for the fire service. There is somebody else now in the bank and they don't want him.

And now about that call the other afternoon. I am not going to say a bit about it. I'll leave it till Sunday. I hope you know why, don't you? You always start joking. Be good and remember always what I told you.

All my love

always yours

Hans.

92 Wharf St.
December 16th 1947.

166

My dearest Hans

I thank you so very much for another nice letter. It's so nice to be able to get up in the morning and find a letter from you waiting. I was surprised when you said you had got my letter Monday morning because other times it has taken two days. It must make a difference when I take them to the main post office.

It is better that we write to each other, not only to improve your knowledge of our language, but because there is not very much we can say over the telephone, with people listening in and everyone at my end listening to what I say.

I was so glad your mother understands about you staying here, it is better you stay here for a year then go to Russia for one, but I don't suppose your mother thinks that the reason you decided to stay do you? Have you heard anything about your father lately?

Iris is back in my office now, but at the moment she's not on speaking terms with anyone. Lucy upset her about a week ago and she wouldn't speak to any of us, not even me and I hadn't said a word. Now she is coming round, we are not speaking to her. It is the only way to cure people like that.

I do hope Hans that you don't mind me coming on Saturday instead of Sunday. But as I was telling you it is Susan's birthday on Saturday. Betty is giving her a bit of a party for the children on that day and she wants my aunt, uncle, mother and myself to go to the tea on the Sunday. If you could not have got away I would have come as arranged but it would have meant a lecture from my brother-in-law and I think if he did say anything I would tell him where to go.

You wanted to know if I had a nice Sunday. I will tell you what I did then you can judge for yourself. I got up about 9.00 and had my breakfast, I usually have the paper to look at, but much to my annoyance the paper does not come in till 9:45 on Sundays. Then I waited till lunch, had that. Then I wrote to you. About 3:30. I went to my friend's which is about 5 minutes away and went via Campbell Street post office. I had my tea there and just sat there till it was 10.0, then I came home. It wasn't very exciting was it.

I have not been out at all this week. I'm going to that party tomorrow night. I wish I wasn't.

I was very lucky this afternoon. I got some sweets, they are very hard to get this time. I went to my usual shop and got them from under the counter.

Susan is staying here tonight so I don't suppose I shall have a very good nights sleep. She usually wakes up at 7.0 and wants me to play shops with her. You ought to ask me then if I like children. I think you would know what my answer would be.

My dear be good and thank you for not minding about Sunday I do mess you about don't I. I'm very sorry that I have to.

All my love

Jean

P.S. <u>Six pages</u>

Wednesday

I called Saltby this morning. Alfred said you had gone to Stathern He said you had gone to do something to a lorry eh!!! would you please tell Alfred what I said he could not understand me. I asked him if he was any better and told him if he must die wait until after Christmas then I will make a collection

Love

Jean

16.12/47　　　　　Aschersleben 15.11.47

16.12

My dear Hans,

168

We are sending you lots of love and Sunday greetings. I'm sure you will have received my letter from 13.11 by now. Yesterday we went out the first time gleaning sugar beets. Frau Lehmann and I managed to do 1150 sq metres each by midday! A great haul, if we can collect as much a few more times I'll be very happy. It's a shame that it's such hard work. I felt awful last night, I had such a horrible headache I didn't know what to do with myself. Something must be wrong with my nerves. I can't wait for the gleaning to be over so that I can finally recover.

I still have a headache today. I constantly worry about you and Papa, if only the day will come when we are reunited. Yesterday a man was at Brandt, he arrived recently from England, he was from camp 19. He leaves tomorrow for Wittenberg. He was allowed to bring over 56 pounds of luggage, another in the group had 96 pounds! I'll take the day off tomorrow for my birthday, but I'll be back on the field on Tuesday. I have guests coming over so I shall bake a cake, if only you could be here too. Horst is very excited, he always looks forward to my birthday more than his own. Baking is a challenge these days as yeast and baking powder are hard to come by, and one cannot use as much sugar as one would like. The landlord has changed for the worse recently, I used to be able to wrap him around my finger (which was helpful) but I've had to have a strong word with him to be nicer to me.

Stay healthy my dear boy and write to us again soon.

lots of love from your Mum and brother Horst.

16.12   Aschersleben 19.11.47

16.12

My dear Hans,

I want to write a few lines to you again today, I had a lovely birthday with 10 guests. With your brother and I that made a full dozen!

We thought so much about you and Papa and how nice it would have been to have you here with us. I received a beautiful lamp, a hairbrush and skin cream from Horst; a wonderful bouquet from Mrs Ziemann from Stettin, an apron from Mrs Klingebiel, and a beautiful warm wooden blanket from the Höhls for which I was very grateful. I was disappointed not to receive a birthday letter from you, which I was expecting, maybe it will arrive tomorrow. We have had frost for a few days and have been unable to get a hoe into the ground to glean the sugar beets. I received a parcel from Aunt Grete containing a young rooster and some pork which made me very happy. I boiled down a pot of it for Christmas. Horst is insisting we go to the cinema to watch "die Fliedermaus", I don't really fancy going as I've already seen the film at home. It is so much warmer and cosier at ours, much nicer than in the cold cinema but I don't want to be a spoilsport. In 5 weeks it will be Christmas Eve, I guess we'll have to celebrate another Christmas without you? We were so looking forward to it.

Stay healthy and write to us soon.

Lots of love and greetings from your mum and brother Horst.

Replied 16/12   Aschersleben 27.11.47
                              16.12

      My dear Hans,

At last, after a long wait, we received 4 letters from you yesterday. Actually to me dated the 6.11 and the 13.11. and for Horst dated 13.11 and 17.11. We were so happy and thank you from the bottom of our hearts. Now that he received mail from you Horst is satisfied again, he felt very frustrated not receiving any letter from you for 5 weeks.

At present he is at the Höhls, when he comes back he surely will scold me as it is half nine and I'm not in bed yet. I'm up since 5 am this morning. Again I had tough days with gleaning sugar beets, it rained and it was so cold. I was covered in mud from top to bottom and then pulling the handcart for 11 Kilometers. Yesterday I had 125 kg and today 75 kg. Thank God I've made it now and we have 400 kg, just as I had intended. Also I nearly made it up to 400 kg potatoes.

The last couple of days I went out on my own, Mrs Lehmann did not fancy it. Inow we have to make it through to the cooking of the syrup, there is a lot of work ahead. Waiting 14 days for mail can drive one crazy. But we are excited that a new parcel is on its way to us. But it makes us both very sad that you now can't be with us at Christmas. I can't even send you a Christmas parcel, I would love to do it so much. We'll make a Christmas for you when you come home.

They will probably look after you with lots of entertainment? That makes me happy. Who is Ellen?

You wrote that you've sent the parcel on the 21.9.47, I guess you meant the 21.10.47? I assume you have lots of acquaintances there by now? I told Horst off for writing to you regarding a wig, I guess that is asking for too much. He knew straight away that it was impossible. He will get one from Halle, it will cost about 200 Reichsmark. It's a lot of money but he desperately needs it if he wants to progress in his profession. Now my dear Boy I want to end this letter for today. Stay healthy and be heartily greeted and kissed from your Mum and your brother Horst. Hearty greetings to Jean
See you soon.

Prenzlau, 22.11.47

My dear Hans

I am finally getting around to replying to your lovely, and long letter, today. But I do have a complaint to make: you have left a whole page free! Why? Are you that short of time? But I was still very happy. I am really and truly a troubled woman. I am working on the sugar beet fields from morning till late in the evenings. Perhaps you know what this means. I didn't know how it works but I have learnt a lot from it and also enjoyed consuming the sugar beet in abundance. The weather is very changeable at the moment, which does not help. Oh well, if we always had the right weather for our field work, it would be finished in no time.

Now dear Hans, my journey is behind me and it went quite well considering the circumstances. Travelling is horrendous and I stayed much longer than I had planned. I came home on my birthday and was quite angry with myself that I did not stay there for ever, although this would not be possible. What am I to do? Hans, I wanted to tell you so much but don't really know where to start. I have not found my way back into my old routine here. It is a fact that, when you have been somewhere different, it is even more difficult to pick up the pieces when you get back. What lovely dreams I used to have about a bright future, and now all these dreams have been shattered. I can only see rubble and ruins. How grateful I am that I still have my mum. She seems to always have the right words to help me on my way. I intend to go back to her. When my work is finished on the sugar beet fields I shall take up my tailoring again. Mum is extremely busy at the moment. She almost lost her second husband. He fell from a 15 metre height and is in hospital. We really have a lot of bad luck in our house. My dad's youngest brother has now also passed. I'd love to know if I will ever experience something nice in my life, something that will make me happy. It will be when I see you again. Although it will be a very sad reunion, I am waiting for it with anticipation and am looking forward to it. I can tell you everything. And I **have** to see you again. Am I right in saying that you too want to see me? I know it is wrong of me not to leave you in peace, but tell me, Hansi, if you do not want to hear anything else from me, let me know, seriously. You have not yet told me whether you received my photo and whether you were pleased with it. Please, please send me a photo of yourself very soon. I know it is allowed and I know it has already been taken. It would make me very happy. Words cannot describe how I long to see you. I cannot understand why I betrayed you! What can I do? I think I am driving myself mad, going around in circles. But the old idiom is right: you make your bed and lie on it. And I love you so very, very much. Hans, I am writing all this to you. The words just roll off my pen – it comes naturally to me. It must not influence you in any way.

Don't mind me, tell me honestly whether you feel my letter is annoying you.

I have no right to ask for anything anymore. I have to learn to resign myself to everything. I can bear everything. I have already experienced many shocks in my life.

Now Hans, I want to bring my letter to a close. Please fulfil my wish of a photo of yourself.

Write back soon. I am sending you my love and a kiss. Yours Vera.

Don't let me wait too long.

Dear Vera   18.12.47

Thank you very much indeed for your nice letter dated 22.11.47, which reached me today. I have some free time at the moment and want to write back to you immediately, as usual. Whether or not I left an empty page in my last letter is neither here nor there. I have sufficient writing paper and can buy more any day. Indeed, I have not much time on my hands. Most of my time is spent in my car, and in the evenings I have to do all the admin. My daily tasks are finished at 10 o'clock at night. This is how one day after another goes by and I think it will continue like that for a while longer. Please don't get upset when I tell you that I have to stay here until 31.12.48. There are a few reasons why I came to this decision. I have been offered a job which is rarely made available to PoWs. It is a position as an interpreter and they have offered me 80.00 RM (Reichsmark) per week. With it comes free accommodation (a flat) and meals. Of course I was offered this job as a civilian, not a PoW. There are some other personal reasons which encouraged me to stay. Time does not fly past without leaving its traces behind. All sorts of things happen over time. I know all about work on the fields, having gained a lot of experience myself. I have done the same type of work as you. One gets used to all sorts of things, especially when one is forced to. I am very pleased to hear that you had a good journey. I think perhaps that travelling is not much fun nowadays. Why are you angry with yourself because you came back from your holiday? One must never lose courage. There is always a way out – in every situation. We shall never exhaust our wisdom. You know only too well that you can write to me about everything that bothers you. I shall always be there for you to give you advice should you need it, and if I am able to. But you also have your mum who is much older than I am, and can talk to you about her own life experiences. There are many things in life which one had wished for. Although dreams have been shattered, one must not give up setting goals and plan one's life. There is always something worth living for. No matter how sad it is.

Obviously my home coming is now delayed a little longer. I too want to speak to you again. There is still a lot to talk about. I want to make it very clear: you must not think your letters annoy me. If it helps you to get over your worries, just write to me. I am pleased to receive your post. This is my honest reply. I received your photo and thanked you for it immediately. If the letter did not reach you, then it must have gone astray. I am sorry, but I do not have a photo of myself and I don't want a photo of myself either which was taken whilst I am in captivity because I do not wish to be remembered of this time later on in my life. It was a bleak and wasted time in which I have lost too much. However, I shall remember your wish. As soon as I have some photos done, I will send you one. Please don't mention the word 'betrayal' any more. Calm down and get rid of these thoughts. You should read my first letter to you again, it will remind you how and what I think about it. I believe you when you say that you don't find it hard to tell me that you love me in spite of everything. But is it any good to us, now that you are married? It does not influence me at all. I make my decisions without any influence whatsoever. One should give up 'demanding'. I had to learn that one can get much further in life with courtesy and polite requests. Please don't be quite so downhearted and desperate. Look Vera, chin up will help. To bite one's tongue also helps to overcome many obstacles. You might say "he can talk, he is alright and a long way away from here". Well you would not be completely wrong in saying this, but believe me I feel a lot more for you all than you might think. I can put myself into your position and feel for you. Life is brutal and inconsiderate. That's why you have to look ahead and you must not lose yourself. I know that you are waiting for this letter in particular. I am therefore sending it by airmail in the hope that it reaches you within a week at the latest, in other words by Christmas. Perhaps I should apologise for this letter, but it is exactly the way I feel and think. I have done a lot of thinking.

I am getting on well considering the circumstances and I hope you and your loved ones are too. Next week I shall be staying with some good friends to spend Christmas together. They have invited me to stay at their house for four days. I was able to secure four days uninterrupted leave. I am hoping that I shall feel a little like being at home. It would be the first time in a very long time. It is about 30 km from here.

I want to finish my letter now. It is already 12 o'clock midnight. I shall have to make do with five hours sleep.

I wish you all a very happy Christmas and a blessed New Year. I hope all your wishes will come true and I am sending you greetings (coming from the heart) from Hans.

Write again soon.

<u>5</u>

Hans Klawitter A 572 859.
POW Camp Saltby.
Dec 18<u>th</u> 1947.

My dearest darling Jean,

I thank you so much for your lovely long letter I received this morning. Do you know how it is always to be interrupted. The boss is still here. I hope he is leaving soon. You better hurry up with your calling back. He wanted Mr Nash.The air is clear now.

I have to make it quick now or otherwise you shan't get the letter tomorrow morning. Are you now used to receive letters in the morning? I hope so, anyway. It really must be a very good thing to be in bed and get the mail and paper. It is a long time ago as I did so.

I am glad there is a second way to get in touch with you. You are quite right. I can't say all what I want to say. There are mostly some people around, even if it is one of my fellows here.

My mother is quite satisfied now as she told me in her last letter I got yesterday. In any case it is better to stay here then to be taken away by the Russians. My mother knows, or at least supposed the real reason. In her last letter she wrote the following: "I know it is rather difficult for you to go away from Jean for you have missed everything for years. And therefore I don't mind you staying. I wish you happiness for all your life if god bless you and Jean". Do you know my opinion? A mother always feels what is true or not . And I hope you'll remember our last Sunday when I told you the real reason about my staying. I can't leave you behind when I leave. It is too far away. Don't think I won't trust you. You know I would miss you every minute. Do you understand me? Look, darling, I was away from home for such a long time and I'm so happy to have you, for ever as I hope. I think there is no more to say about it. Didn't I tell you all this already? But people never get fed up with talking about these things. We haven't heard about my father lately.

You know I don't mind you coming on Saturday instead of Sunday. I am so glad when you come. It was a long time to wait for me wasn't it? And now I am longing for Saturday. I hope the next 2 days will pass very quickly. Shall I tell you now about me as I spent last Sunday? I got up about 10:30. you are surprised aren't you? Yes; don't be too hard with me. I was really tired. Then I was waiting for the meals as usually. In the afternoon I did some work for me and as I looked at the clock it showed 10.00 hours, so I forgot my supper. Don't be afraid, I am still alright and didn't even fall unconscious for I was sitting all the time.

Have you enjoyed yourself last night? If it is too difficult to get sweets this time you better eat them yourself. Don't you agree?

I know your opinion about children. Didn't you tell me sometime? And I quite agree with you. A house without children is not a real home.

Do you mind when I close now? I have to go to Stratharn at once and this is the only possibility to bring this letter down. Otherwise it would be too late.

Let me say cheerio and God bless.

Be good till Saturday and

and all my love

always yours Hans.

29/12   Aschersleben 30.11.47
                            18/12

My dear Hans,

I want to send you greetings today, on the first Sunday of Advent. I answered your latest letters yesterday and Horst has written to you as well. I'm sure you are waiting for a reply to your letter from the 25.11. Hopefully it won't take too long to get to you. I asked at the post office if it would be possible to send the letter via 1st class registered post so it gets to you faster, but this is not possible yet. Once everything has calmed down, then it might well be the best for you to stay, if you find a good job. At first it was very painful when all hope was dashed. We hardly know each other anymore. But if it is for your own good, then it must be. You know my whole life is spent worrying about you.

Over the winter I wanted to look for a job, but Horst goes wild when he hears about it. He wants me to recover from all the strain. I just want to contribute so that we can move forward, we can't stay like this. We want to have our own life again. If we need to buy anything necessary, it's unavailable or unaffordable.

Horst imagines your return so often these days, that you will bring us cocoa, coffee and milk after your release. He is always up for a treat, none of these things are available here.

He just went to the cinema with a female friend, and asked me to join them - but I need to finish my mail and fix some of my old things, because on Tuesday and Thursday we want to get some wood. Hopefully the weather will be bearable. Then I have to clean the sugar beets because next Sunday we want to cook syrup and then again on 12/12. We need a lot of fuel, every two weeks we receive 50 kilogram coal which lasts hardly 8 days. That's why I'm forced to get wood, I don't mind doing it, hopefully I will stay healthy.

Horst is doing what he can, he has a lot to do in the business. Send our heartfelt greetings to Jean. Is she at home with her parents? We want to see what the negotiations bring for us. Maybe it will become part of the western zone, as that was taken by the Americans.

Now be greeted from the bottom of our hearts, sending you kisses your Mum and your brother Horst.

Aschersleben 30.11.47

My dear Hans,

With thanks I received both your letters from the 13.11.47 and the 17.11.47 in good health.

For quite some time the mail worked pretty badly and I did not receive any letters from you for 5 weeks. I am alive and well and I hope you are too.

Thank you that you made the effort for the wig, I should have thought about it more before I troubled you.

I ordered it now from Halle, it should be ready by the beginning of December. It costs 200 Reichsmarks, which is a hell of a lot of money, but I can't live without one. It is a light blonde wig, but one cannot get hold of any hair accessories or ornamental combs, which give the appearance of the wig beauty.

On Friday evening the specialist group "Hair stylist" had a

meeting at the police building which I also attended. Allocations of textiles and footwear were discussed. It looks pretty bad, mostly things for children are produced but nothing for adults. I was lucky that one of my customers, who works at the labor union, organised a pair of shoes for me. I got a pair of black loafers which look good, but how long they will last is a different story. Everything is very basic.

Amongst other things we will have specialist training in the beginning of next year for which I have registered. Firstly undulation, postiche, historic and competition hairstyling. I'm so much looking forward to this.

We were so happy about your lovely parcel, we could not open it up fast enough..

Who is Ellen who sent us a parcel. Is she older?

Now to what upsets me very much. It came so sudden that you are not coming home. But it is ok if one looks at it from the right angle. It would be different if you came to the E.z here, which still can happen. I'm sure you can't continue to send things over, your money is also scarce.

I recommend you to stay as long as you can with Jean, who might become your wife at a later stage. But I hope we will see each other again sometime. We got used to the waiting. It 's fate. If only our Papa would get in touch. Then it would be easier to bear.

We are looking very much forward to your future parcels. Lots of greetings to Miss Jean.

Be greeted from your brother Horst and Mum. Don't worry too much, one day you will come home. One hears a lot of rumours. We don't know what it is good for and one never should step in fates way. To a healthy reunion.

Today is already the first advent.

R 29/12   Aschersleben   3.12.47
                            20/12
I want to write your Christmas letter in good time, so that

179

it will reach you for Christmas, as there is no relying on the post. I am wishing you, dear Hans, all the best for Christmas and hope you will spend it in good health. Christmas here promises to be as gloomy as before, and one does not look forward to it. If only it had already passed. I think you are doing the right thing staying over there, as things are very miserable here all around. Who knows what it is good for. However do not let me spoil your festive mood, as our thoughts are always with you. I imagine that Christmas at the camp will be eventful as usual. I've already been in my new job for six months. How time flies! Mum and Mrs Lehmann went to the Harz to collect wood yesterday, and they are planning to go again the day after tomorrow. Mum struggles miserably, she often has migraine and she can hardly bear it. It's all too much. We are planning to make syrup on Saturday and Sunday – come back to lick the pots and pans!! Please write to mum and tell her to look after herself. She doesn't listen to me even if I stand on my head. This week we've had no mail from you, maybe something will arrive soon. What is the weather like where you are? Here it is cold and foggy. How is Jean and will she be coming to visit you for Christmas? At least that would distract you. Who knows if yours and Ellen's parcels will arrive before Christmas - We would be so thrilled. Every day I am awaiting news from Halle. My wig is supposed to be ready at the beginning of December, at least that will help me to move on with my training. Mum is so tired, she's already going to bed – one really feels sorry for her. Hans, you were going to have your picture taken in town – has that not yet happened? Tomorrow mum is going to get us a Christmas tree, otherwise we wouldn't have a single bit of Christmas joy. Now my dear Hans we are sending you all the best. Please write again soon. If only we would have news from our dear papa I will close now. Much love from your brother Horst and mum. Many Christmas greetings to Miss Jean and Ellen. Stay both healthy and cheerful. Auf Wiedersehen!

Hans Klawitter A 572 859.
Saltby POW Camp.
Dec 21st 1947.

My dearest, darling Jean,

First of all I want to tell you "I am so happy". As I came back here last night there was nobody here. I had my lunch and after that, still on my own I opened your little parcel. It is my first Christmas present for 5 years. It is a wonderful feeling to know there is somebody thinking of me. I thank you very much for your present. I can't do it only with words, therefore, I better do it next Sunday. Don't you think time is running faster when we meet. I was so sorry last night when we had to go for the bus. It was so nice going around talking about everything. I was lazy this morning getting up by 10:15, wasn't I? It was so nice to stay in bed. After doing some work and having lunch I pressed my suit for Wednesday. I am going to destroy now the sweets you gave me the other day. There is such a nice music at the moment. It is a German station with a program called "music for everybody". Yesterday I've got a lovely Christmas card from my brother. He and my mother send a Merry Christmas to you. Last night I went to bed quarter past eleven, the same time you arrived home I hope. Did your sister say anything about the parcel? Don't give it away before Christmas. and now, darling I would like to close. Don't be annoyed. I still have a lot of work to do for Mr Edwards is going to Leicester on Tuesday instead of Thursday. Therefore I have to make everything ready till tomorrow night. You'll get your Christmas letter besides this one. Be good and think of me

All my love to you

Hans.

Answered 22/12

92 Wharf St.
21st dec 1947.

22/12

My dearest Hans.

181

I arrived home about 11:50. Thanks darling for a very enjoyable afternoon and I hope it was for you to.

By the time I had put my curlers in and had something to eat
it was 11:40 when I got into bed, but I did not get up till 9:30.
I hope you are able to get something to eat. I wasn't really
hungry but thought I had better have something.

About that Christmas present. I don't want you to give me
anything. I will wait until next year, by that time you will be
in a different position and you may be able to give me something so I will wait till then.

My auntie just called me to the phone, I thought for a minute
it might be you but it was my sister asking me to take a game
up with me this afternoon.

Well darling, I do hope the letter you write to me will be
longer than this. I am very sorry it is so short but I will try to
write a longer one next time

be good all my love
Jean xxx

7

Hans Klawitter A 572 859.
Saltby POW Camp.
22nd Dec 1947.

My dearest Jean,
I thank you very much for your letter and Christmas card I
received this morning. As I told you already I got two more
letters. One from Edna, Leamington Spa, and the second one
from Joan Stratford on Avon. My fellow brought the mail
down to the dining hall as I had my breakfast. I opened the
other two letters at first and found the cards. Yours was the
last to be opened for I know so there was a letter in. And
reading your letter I like to be on my own. I was surprised as

I found that lovely card. It was the best one. Yours is always the best. Oh darling I thank you very very much for everything you are doing for me. If only I would know what I can do for you. You give me presents, your kindness and love. And I? I'll give you the same except presents. I am so awfully sorry that I can't make you a real Christmas present this year. I am so glad your birthday is coming soon. Hoping to make it right then. I told you in my letter already how much I enjoyed that Saturday afternoon. I can't thank you with words. Don't you think I better thank you next Sunday? By the way, it'll be my last Sunday here in Saltby definitely. I'll tell you later about it. Later on in the morning Alfred got a parcel from Ivan. It is to be divided between us two. There is some chocolate, nuts, cigarettes for Alfred a pair of gloves and for me a necktie. Isn't it nice there is somebody thinking of us? But I better would like you to come with bare hands. Your presence alone makes me very happy. Don't think I only do this lot of talking to fill the letter with. You know I really mean it when saying it. Believe me I could cry out to everybody how happy I am and how much I love you. My mother would be happier when she would know how happy I am. We'll write to her sometime both of us and tell her how happy we are.

Wasn't it a funny thing about you writing such a short letter. And I did just the same. Sorry darling I didn't have more time. I was working all day long for the timesheets and account sheets for us and the three hostels had to be checked. We must finish all these things till tonight for Mr Edwards is going to Leicester tomorrow already instead of Thursday. Alfred is doing my work now while I write this letter for you. I want you to have it tomorrow morning and the boss must post it tonight. You'll get then two letters from me tomorrow morning. How lucky you are darling. And now something about my last Sunday in Saltby. I know now why Mr Sanders has been here this morning. He wanted to see the boss about me. I have to leave for Stathern next Monday Dec

29th. It is the second time but I hope it'll be alright now. But please darling don't tell anybody about it. Mr Edwards begged me for but I can't let you wait till next Sunday. I like to tell you the news straight away when I get it.

I hope you don't mind writing with pencil but it is the one you put in your or parcel. I will always take it in future. It is half past 2 now. You've started your work already. After all I am glad to see you here next Sunday. I wouldn't miss Variety Show.

Well darling I'll close now. Do you answer this letter so I will get it on Wednesday morning before we leave for Great Dalby. Do you know I better would like to see you on Christmas? But don't worry. I'll have to wait till Sunday.

Be good, all my love and many kisses,

always yours

Hans.

92 Wharf St.
Dec 23rd 1947.

24.12

My dearest Hans

Thanks for keeping your promise and writing. I received it this lunchtime.The postman had not arrived when I came out this morning so I had to wait until then.

I suppose you can tell by the paper I am writing this at work. You should hear me swear when someone calls on the switchboard and I feel like gagging Lucy, she will keep asking questions. this is the fourth time I have started this letter.

I rang you about 2:30 Alfred said you had gone to Melton I will try and ring again if possible. It does not matter now you have rung me.

I told you I was going to a dance tomorrow night. There are four of us going don't worry all girls. A girl that works with Dora and Alice, I believe I told you about Alice (she's the one that was engaged) Alice and I can talk for hours when we get together so I shall not mind going now. I don't really like dancing. I would much rather stay at home.

I am sorry I have to finish this in pencil but my pen has run out of ink. Well darling it is nearly time for me to go and I want to post this on the way home so you will get it in the morning.

I will write to you either Christmas or Boxing Day.

I hope you have a very very Happy Christmas. I will be thinking of you all the time. I will try and ring on Saturday if possible. Anyway I will be seeing you on Sunday so until then

          All my love

   Jean xxx

P.S.

I have not given my mother the bag yet, also if you write to your mother give her my love

    92 Wharf Street.

    Dec 25th 1947.

My dearest Hans

I do hope you had a very Happy Christmas. I don't suppose you feel much like work this morning.

At the moment I am on my own apart from the dog he's here. My mother has gone to have a rest on the bed. I could have stayed in my auntie's but I thought I would come home and write to you. I wish you were here with me then everything would be perfect. I am thinking of you all the time.

My mother thought the bag was beautiful and thanks you very much for it. You said in your letter that you never gave me a present. You have. You gave me two lovely bracelets and a scarf. They mean more to me than anything else.

Alice never went with us last night. I don't know what happened to her, I was hoping she would come. It wasn't too bad. I would rather have gone to the pictures but I could not get out of going to the dance. I did not stay to the end. I came home at half past 11. Someone brought a bottle of milk. So I made myself some coffee (bottle coffee) . I got your letter and took the milk to bed and read your letter. I was really happy then. My sister left a present for me but I could not wait till this morning to open it so I did before I got into bed. In it there were some pale blue house slippers, they are very sweet, and she bought me a purse. I have always wanted one like it. I will show it to you on Sunday. I had some makeup from Gwenn and Alice. My mother gave me two pairs of nylon stockings and I gave her coupons.

I got up about 9:15 this morning. Scrubbed the floor and dusted and believe me it is no easy job to try and tidy this place especially when Susan has been. I finished that about 12:30. Then my mother and I went next door to have dinner. Now I have come home. I have the radio on and a nice big fire. All I want now is you to be here (the fire wants some coal on). We shall be going next door in a little while to have a cup of tea and I suppose we should stay there till about 10. I will then write some more to this letter.

Well darling it is now 12 o'clock. We came home later than I expected to. I will have to be up early in the morning. Betty, Susan, Cyril, my aunt and uncle from next door and my auntie Miriam are coming tomorrow for dinner. I have to go and fetch the baking tins to cook the turkey in. My mother lent it to someone that had not got a tin big enough. Tomorrow afternoon we are all going to the Palace Theatre. I don't know what I shall be doing Friday night but if Dora wants to go to a dance she will have to go on her own. Saturday I still don't know what I'm doing, I shall ring that is certain.

I hope you can understand this. By the way, could you understand the last one I wrote to you. I'm surprised if you could. It took me all afternoon to write that letter but I started it about four times then my pen ran out of ink. If I had not told you Wednesday afternoon I was writing I would have given it up as a bad job.

I shall have to wait until Sunday to hear more about Stathern. So till then darling be good.
All my love and
    Kisses
                    Jean.

8

> Hans Klawitter A 572 859.
> Saltby POW Camp.
> 26th Dec 1947.

My dearest darling Jean,

There is no letter no calls from you during these days. Do you know how that is? I am used to find your letters in the morning. Anyway. I hope you'll get this letter on Saturday morning. As you know I keep promises. Shall I tell you about myself? We started our journey by about 1:15 Wednesday afternoon. Mr Edwards pick us up at 2. The first meal was waiting already. We spend the afternoon with talking. I was thinking of you all the time. In the evening we played games. I felt tired when my usual bedtime came and slept till I was woken up at 10:15. do you know the difference between planks and a soft bed. I know now. It is wonderful to sleep in a soft bed. I really had forgotten all about it. but it is a good thing to be remembered after such a long time! Yesterday in the morning we went out for a little walk and had a meal afterwards. There was a lovely smell all over the house when we arrived, and I really got a shock as I saw the piece of meat on my plate. But I got it after all. In the afternoon I read a nice book and at night we played roulette. Clive came as Father Christmas after tea and everybody got presents. Suppose what I got? You can't darling. A packet of cigarettes, sweets, chocolate and a calendar for the desk. You know, one to change everyday. Clive made a real good job of it. He emptied his long bag asking "who is Hans" I answered "here". Here is something for you merry christmas he said and so it went around. He'd do it a few times for he'd made only small parcels. It was a very enjoyable evening. During all this time we drank some Port wine and so on. Don't be afraid darling. I didn't get drunk. This morning I slept again till 10:30. We now came back from a morning walk. I expect your call now during the course of the day. Do you think you'll be able to? I hope so anyway, darling. It really was a nice week. We're together on Saturday, a nice picture on Tuesday, holidays from Wednesday to Friday, picture tomorrow might be at the camp and with you to the variety on Sunday. Oh darling, I am longing for this Sunday. I'll see you again and it might be the last time in Saltby. I asked Mr Edwards last night what happens when my repatriation becomes due before they open our hostels. He told me I will become a civilian then straight away. That's good isn't it? I hope to find your letter tomorrow morning. Now darling let's close. Meal is ready. Be good and all my love Hans.

PS Many greetings to your dear mother and a kiss for you you

Hans and Jean at

Saltby

PEACEFUL TIMES

May your days be
GARDEN SHELTERED
Where
PEACE & GLADNESS
bide,
Where flowers of JOY
and
FRIENDSHIP
And LOVE grow
side by side

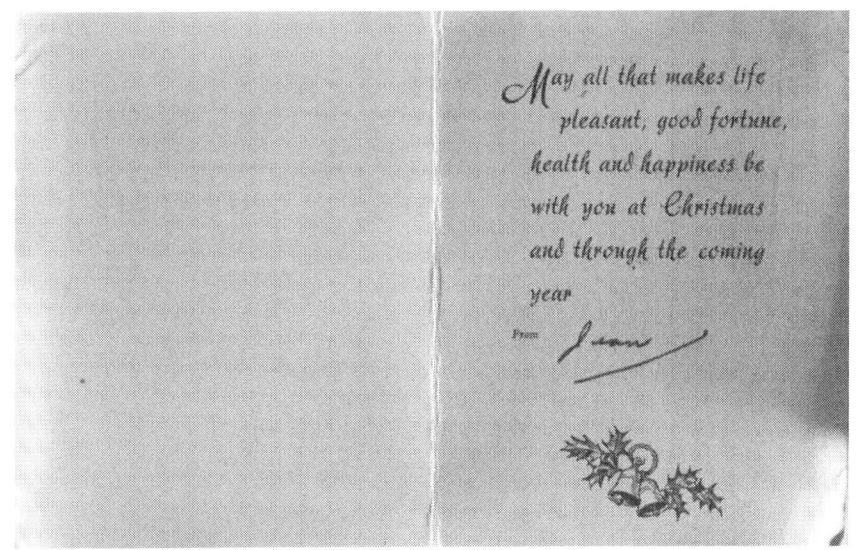

May all that makes life
pleasant, good fortune,
health and happiness be
with you at Christmas
and through the coming
year

From *Jean*

Hans Klawitter A 572 859.
Saltby POW Camp.
27th Dec 1947 8.00 p.m.

My dearest, darling Jean,

I must write to you in spite of your coming tomorrow. You don't mind do you? There is still a lot of work to do till Monday but I can't do anything now I am just going to write to you. You'll get this tomorrow. It seems safer than sending by post anyway.

Do you know how it is to be lonely. Mr Edwards all the time tried to make time as nice as possible. But I was always thinking of you. You don't suppose how much I waited for your calling. I looked at the phone but it only rung once and then it was Alfred. I was glad to get back here this morning for I knew you promised your call for Saturday. Mr Edwards was asking me about you and I was impolite. I don't like people being so curious. I didn't answer his question. It is alright for us to know about our own affairs. I don't bother about other people, don't you think so?

I don't know yet when I leave here on Monday. Anyway I'll ring you before. I'll put the new address at the end. I beg you to answer to that place for it'll make a nice start finding your letter the next morning. I don't know what's the matter with the mail. You should have got my letter this morning and also about your one. As I arrived here today my first look was at the table but it was empty. Nothing at all. At last got your call then and I'll tell you I really was going for it. It is not a long time till tomorrow afternoon because I'm going to bed early. I was working very hard this afternoon and therefore I am tired. It will be a long time to work tomorrow night making a nice long accident report for one of my fellows. Will it be my last work here? I hope so. I haven't heard anymore about our hostels. But I think they will be opened shortly. You know darling as close to Leicester as possible. I hope you also enjoyed Christmas. Just tell all about it tomorrow I hope. It would have been nice opening Christmas together but it is over now and will have to wait another year. You are quite right. "good thing need good awhile" I'll always remember it. I am rather interested what your mother said about that present. Did she mind me sending it? I hope not. I won't forget Clive as he came as Father Christmas. He made a very nice job with it. We couldn't help laughing as he made his comic gestures. Clive is a nice little boy he always kept me busy doing things for him.

Well darling I'll have to do some work at least and it is getting late

I like to say goodnight. a good night kiss for you and be good.

all my love always yours

        Hans.

PS
Give my best wishes and greetings to your dear mother
Hans.

The new address
H.K
L.W.A.E.C Hostel. Old Rectory
Stathern nr Melton Mowbray/Leics

Hans Klawitter A 572 859.
Saltby POW Camp.
Dec 29th 1947.

My dearest darling Jean

I've had my supper and feel alright after it. You asked a funny question tonight. Do you know what I mean. If not, I'll tell you. I mean your question: Is it worth waiting! If there is a chance for me to go to Leicester I take it even if I do not get food for a whole day. Please darling, always remember this. You should know how I wait for your call to hear your voice. I think I caught a cold while waiting in the cold lorry but don't worry it doesn't matter to me. Have you had a nice time tonight at your uncle's? A nice cup of tea is really a wonderful thing as I found out. But people wish company.

Well darling I thank you very very much for your lovely long letter. I got it early this morning and it was my first work to read it. You are right Christmas with you and everything could have been perfect. I'll tell you now the truth. it was my secret wish to spend Christmas with you, that's why I told you in my last letter I was lonely on the holidays I knew you're thinking of me all the time. I felt it. Anyway it makes me happy to hear your mother found the bag beautiful. Listen darling, You got two bracelets and a scarf but all that doesn't mean a real present to me. It must be something special. I won't say anymore better wait and see. I'll be your birthday next year and also another Christmas. When you come next time I'll give you a tin of ground coffee. I myself don't like that bottle coffee. You couldn't wait till Christmas day with your sister's parcel? Jean, Jean!! You didn't show me the purse last Sunday. Better do it next time. I think you better to have help to scrub the floor. I am used to it for instance. So you're very busy all day long cleaning writing and eating. Did you really only want me to be at your place to put some coal on the fire? Darling, don't be so hard with me. There is something else I rather do. Did you do the cooking yourself? How did you get on with that job?

I read your last letter easily. I am used to reading other people's handwriting. I also had to do it at home. I can go mad if there is somebody always asking questions whilst writing. Do you know that I am not allowed to give civilians a lift in one of our lorries? In spite of all this I did it because I know how it is to miss a bus. I don't mind taking somebody along when the lorry is empty. He was glad to get home a bit earlier.

When do you answer my letter? Tonight or tomorrow? Oh, I just remembered you're going next door tonight. I'll have to wait then till day after tomorrow. If there is any news about Stathern I'll let you know at once.

Well, darling it's getting late now. 10 o'clock. Please give my compliments to your dear mother. By the way, I didn't receive letters from home during the last week. Now darling be good and think of me.

All my love and a good night kiss

always yours

Hans.

11

Hans Klawitter.
L.W.A.E.C Hostel.
Old Rectory.
Stathern.
31st Dec 1947.

My dearest darling Jean,

I'm going to write as promised. I think I have settled already. The first meal is over. Breakfast prepared and now I'll take the rest I badly need. It will really be a very bad thing to miss your calls now, anyway I hope to get your letter tomorrow morning. I have got the same room I had last time I'm here. The only thing to tell you about the start I am alright and I hope you are to. And now darling, I have a wish. Please come on Sunday 4.1.48. Please darling. I am only here a few hours but so lonely. Please, darling, please. Be good. Come if there isn't anything very important for you to do at home. Look, that fellow here in the kitchen has his girl coming round from Leicester every Sunday. Don't worry about the meal you'll get it here. I would like you to come earlier than usual because you'll have to leave here earlier. I just heard the best time is 7.20 you'll arrive then in Leicester 9.45. Please darling don't be so hard with me. Don't let me wait another week, maybe I am dead at that time!! Look, as we arranged I'll have this Saturday and Sunday off and the fellow the following. So it'll be the best for you to come this Sunday.

The people here are alright. They're glad to see me again. The first question was, "are you here for good now". I'll have to get up a bit earlier now 5 o'clock is just the right time. Isn't it. What do you think about your working with me (the fire wants some coal on) getting up by 5.00 and to bed at 11 o 'clock. That's what I really like. I don't know yet when this fellow is leaving. He would like now to stay with me. But I think his time is nearly over. He'll be here this weekend at least. I don't know then about the next one. I'll have to work then on my own, and this is the second reason why I asked you to come this Sunday.

The warden came a few times and asked if my room is alright, if it is warm enough, if I'm comfortable upstairs and so on. I made the room as nice as possible. You should know what I like or not. Did I tell you I am not here as a civilian I am still attached to Saltby camp. It may only be for a short time for the civilian hostels are to be opened very soon and I'll get my job that I applied for. If you like to come with that other girl, go to 5 to Kensington Street, Belgrave Road and ask for Miss Dora Hill. She'll tell you which bus to take best I hope you'll ring me some times. You shouldn't be afraid because the telephone is here in the passage and the same one as in a call box.

Well darling I'll close now. Be good and fulfil my only wish. I hope you have enjoyed the film tonight.

All my love and many kisses
always yours
Hans.

92 Wharf Street.
December 31st.

My dearest Hans

A Happy New Year darling. I hope you have settled at Stathern alright and that you have had a good bed to sleep on. I shall have to wait until in the morning to know about that.

Thanks darling for your letters. I'll have to write about three letters to you now.

I heard from my friend in London yesterday. She has invited me down to see her. She likes me to go down so she has someone to go round the shops with. I think she finds London very lonely. She married a London fellow that was stationed in Leicester in Pay Corp. She used to say I had got to marry someone from London but it does not look as if I will. Anyway I think I will go and see her in the spring, it is too cold to go now. Talking of being cold it was terribly cold here yesterday. I have bought myself some lined gloves. I have to keep warm somehow.

There is not much I can say about Monday only thanks for coming. Has Mr Edwards said anything to you about me. I have an idea he knew I was the reason for you wanting a hostel near Leicester don't you?

Thanks for offering to send a tin of coffee, but you need not bother, we have some, but the bottle coffee is not so much trouble to make.

The little dog that comes in the morning has gone, we gave it some tea and cakes but it would not stay. I think Lucy must have frightened it away.

I know I am not going to a dance tonight. I have just rung Dora, she is ill in bed with cold. So I think I will go to the pictures on my own. I have not been to the pictures since I went with you.

Well darling I will say cheeri'O. Lucy is on her own this week and I am doing some typing for her. she keeps getting in such a mess. So happy new year

All my love
and kisses
Jean

Wednesday 11:30 a.m.

My dearest Hans

Thanks for your letter. I wrote to you last night and luckily I had not stuck the envelope down so I can write a few lines about Sunday. I do not know for certain yet whether I am coming on Sunday or not, anyway I will let you know. It is very nice of you to suggest that I went to see Miss Dora Hill but I would much rather come to Stathern on my own. I have made enquiries about the bus and there is a bus at 1:30, arrives at Melton 2.15. If the bus gets to Melton early there is a bus leaves to Stathern at 2:10, The next is 2.45

Darling I think you had better ask permission from the warden for me to come. You need only ask him if you can have visitors. I think he would like it better if you asked him

I think that is all I have to say for the time being the rest will wait until I see you

    All my love

92 Wharf St.
Jan 1st 1948.

My dearest Hans

Another new year has started. I wonder what is in store for us! Time will tell that. I meant to start the new year by being early at work, but I did not make it in time. I was 3 minutes late. I would have been later than that if the clock had not been fast.

Darling I missed not hearing your voice today. I thought I should miss not hearing from you but not so much as I have, it seemed a terribly long day. How do you like Stathern? Have you got a nice room and a comfortable bed?

Did you see the new year in? I went to the pictures. I got home about 9.30. I had some supper and went to bed. I could not be bothered to wait up till 12.0. I went to the pictures tonight. I was going to stay in but felt as if I could not stay in, so I went to the pictures on my own. I am glad you are not staying at Stathern for good. It is such an awkward place to get to.

By the way what made you think something was wrong the other day. What could be wrong.

I hope you get this before the weekend and be good

All my love
Darling
Jean

___.
Xxxx

R 3/1.48   Aschersleben 8.12.47

1.1.48

My dear Hans,

We wish you a happy and healthy Christmas. Enjoy it as much as you can, our thoughts will be with you. Yesterday I could not write to you, because in the evening I was cooking syrup. Half eleven I finished, from starting Saturday morning. I was up for 40 hours without sleep.This evening I will continue with the final 200 kilos, if I only had this behind me, it was a tough week, adding in picking up the wood from the Harz. Part of the trip we had to go up a steep forest path with the heavy, fully loaded handcart, we were terribly worn out and could only move the handcart forward inch by inch. We were more on our knees than on our feet. But this is over now. Excuse my bad handwriting, my hand is asleep, I can hardly hold the pen. Otherwise we are reasonably healthy, we hope you are too. Today I have to clean the last 100 kilos of the beets. We are now happy that we have so much syrup although it was secured with inhumane effort. Now we have something to put on our bread.

Now my dear boy we wish you again all the best, stay healthy and feel always assured that all our thoughts and our love belongs to you. Next time I will write more, I don't have much time today. Be greeted from the bottom of our hearts, we're sending kisses from your Mum and your brother Horst. To a healthy reunion. Heartfelt greetings to Jean

Dear Hans
Very best wishes
And all the best
For a healthy time
From your brother Horst and mum

Replied 4/1　　　　　Aschersleben – 14/12/47

2/1

My dear Hans

As today is Sunday I wanted to write you a few lines. It has
now been 14 days since I last heard from you. I am waiting every day. The post must be going very badly. We are
reasonably well and cheerful and we hope the same applies
to you. The weather is not great, foggy and damp. Christmas
is approaching. One can't really get excited about it as it all
makes one feel sick. There are some days when you'd rather
not hear or see anything. One lives from one day to the next.
What will father Christmas bring you? Mum is making a big
effort. I have already got a number of things for her. I will

write to you about it at Christmas. I received my wig this week. It looks good, but I want to get some changes made to the parting. It has cost a bomb. Now my dear Hans. I wish you from all my heart a good and healthy New Year, may it bring you lots of good things, and above all a healthy and imminent reunion. Neither your nor Ellen's parcels have arrived and I guess that yours won't arrive before Christmas. How is Miss Jean?

So, In the meantime I have had lunch, pea soup with pork, and pumpkin dessert for afters. It was delicious. We have also finished making the syrup. Mum was totally exhausted and slept only 5 hours in three days.

However it was well worth it, a hundredweight of sugar beet produced 22 kilos of syrup! Many women can take an example from that. Today mum has a very bad toothache again. Within the last weeks she has had two extractions.

Now my dear Hans, please do write again soon. Much love from Horst and mum. Good health and auf Wiedersehen

Jan 3. 48,
6.00pm.

My dearest, darling Jean,

I am ashamed because I didn't answer your first at once. I really didn't have a minute to spare yesterday. Do you know what it means working 15 hours per day? As I went up to my room last night the only thing I could really do was to have a wash and going to bed right away. I think I fell asleep in the very moment. At 6 o'clock this morning somebody knocked at my door and told me to get up. I would've been glad to get another few hours sleep. This morning I received your second letter. I thank you very, very much for both. Well, darling I was so glad to hear you on the telephone yesterday. I was waiting for your call all the days long. Now about your letters about marrying a Londoner. I'll have a word with you tomorrow afternoon. The warden told me this afternoon to make that room next to mine ready for your coming. I shall take everything from the office I want to keep that room as a second one for me. My day off starts tomorrow morning till Monday morning. As he told me, I always get my day off on Sundays for I have no place to go to during the week. So I hope to see you every Sunday?!!

I am quite sure Mr Edwards knew why I wanted a hostel near Leicester. That's the reason he was always laughing when I told him so.

I asked the warder as the postman came this morning what about a letter for me. He only said, sorry! Then I told him I can't work without getting a letter in the morning. I went off making my room and came down again half an hour later. He'd placed your letter then on the breakfast plate, stood by and was laughing at me as I came in and found your letter. He is a wonderful fellow to work with. He's been prisoner in Germany for about 5 years and was warden in Gaddesby before he came here. You might know him, Mr Pickering is his name. His lady came this afternoon. She is from Leicester. He gave me some things and made a nice cake. For him for today and for us tomorrow. Everything is prepared and I hope you'll enjoy yourself tomorrow. My only hope is you'll get the earliest bus as before. Don't worry, darling you're not the only one starting the work later on New Years morning. I got up at 9.30. You've been working then already. I like this place very much and I am getting used to the work. At any rate the meals are getting a lot better as I was told by the men. I am really glad to hear that. I didn't eat a tiny bit from breakfast to dinner.

Do you know when I went to bed on New Years eve? I think just the same time as you did. About 10 o'clock. I was tired and wouldn't wait till 12.00 hours.

Well, darling, I couldn't help laughing as I read in your last letter about asking permission for visitors. I've done it already days ago. You know I won't like any trouble for you, so I asked. The warden told me it is quite alright. He gave me the keys to get things from the store. I told you already about it. Don't be afraid about being thrown out. It makes a big difference between a POW and an English civilian hostel anyway.

I am on my own. The other cook and the porter went away before midday as it really was a hard working day to get my day off tomorrow, even if I should have to work like it tomorrow morning it is worth it. You know darling how I am longing for you. I truly hope the time tomorrow afternoon won't pass so quick. Better wait and see. Mr Edwards sent me a bicycle down this afternoon for there is no lorry to go around with. Well darling say cheerio till I see you tomorrow. Be good. My thoughts are always with you.

> All my love and kisses
> Always yours
> Hans.

> 92 Wharf Street.
> January 5th.

My dearest Hans

Darling I'm sorry I did not keep my promise and write last night. I suppose you can tell I am writing this at the office by the classy paper: it's about time the Min of Ag issued better note paper don't you think. Anyway I was too tired to start to write. I don't know if it's travelling on buses or it's you that tires me out. So I am writing this morning so you will get it tomorrow,

I think yesterday was one of the nicest Sundays we have spent together. You made everything so nice and comfortable, thank you darling for everything. I know darling you think me hard because I came on the 8.8 bus, but don't you think it is best that I catch that one, another thing it was good of you to come to Melton with me you have no idea how miserable I feel when I get on the bus. Was that the cook who was on the bus you went and sat with? I think his girl was on the same bus as I, at least she looked like the description you gave of his girl, she had to stand nearly all the way. As you know I got a seat. I think they must think I had better sit down or else I shall drop. The bus had not got out of Melton when the bus I was on was over taking the first bus, that bus overturned, the next thing there was clatter of glass, fortunately there was not anyone hurt.

Cheerio darling be good till I see you again

       All my love and kisses

           Jean

13

                  L.W.A.E.C Hostel.

                  Stathern.

                  Jan 6th 1948.

My dearest darling Jean

Thanks so much for your letter I received this morning. I slept till 9.30 today so I need not to wait for the postman. I found the letter already waiting for me. Don't worry, darling, I knew you're very tired as you left me as I really didn't expect your letter before Tuesday. I think it's travelling on buses that tires you out. Don't you think I was a bit annoyed because you didn't ring me early yesterday as I told you I heard in the morning that there was an accident on the second bus. So I was waiting and waiting for your call. My only hope was nothing has happened to you. I knew you're sitting on the right window side and if the bus had collided with another vehicle it only could be the right side then I don't know what I would have done if anything happened to you. Anyway I'm so glad nothing happened to you. I rang you I was so afraid somebody else answers the phone.

You need not to thank me for the nice Sunday. I have to thank you for coming so it was possible to spent the afternoon together. You know I like everything nice and comfortable it makes life easier. I don't think you hard because you wanted to take the 8.8 bus. It is only that moment when you start looking at the watch.

I just came back from the Warden's room. There was somebody from Leicester office. He told me I am a civilian already since I came here on the 1st Jan 48. So I'll get my first normal pay now on next Friday. The pay is £4-4-0 for the first time so soon as they open our hostels I'll get my job I applied for. So, darling, everything will be alright shortly.

As Mr Pickering told me as I came back on Sunday night he knew who you are. He remembered your voice. As soon as he is able to he'll pull your leg, in spite of that be clever and give him the right answer.

Well darling let me finish now otherwise you won't get this letter tomorrow.

Be good till I see you again

All my love and kisses

Yours Hans

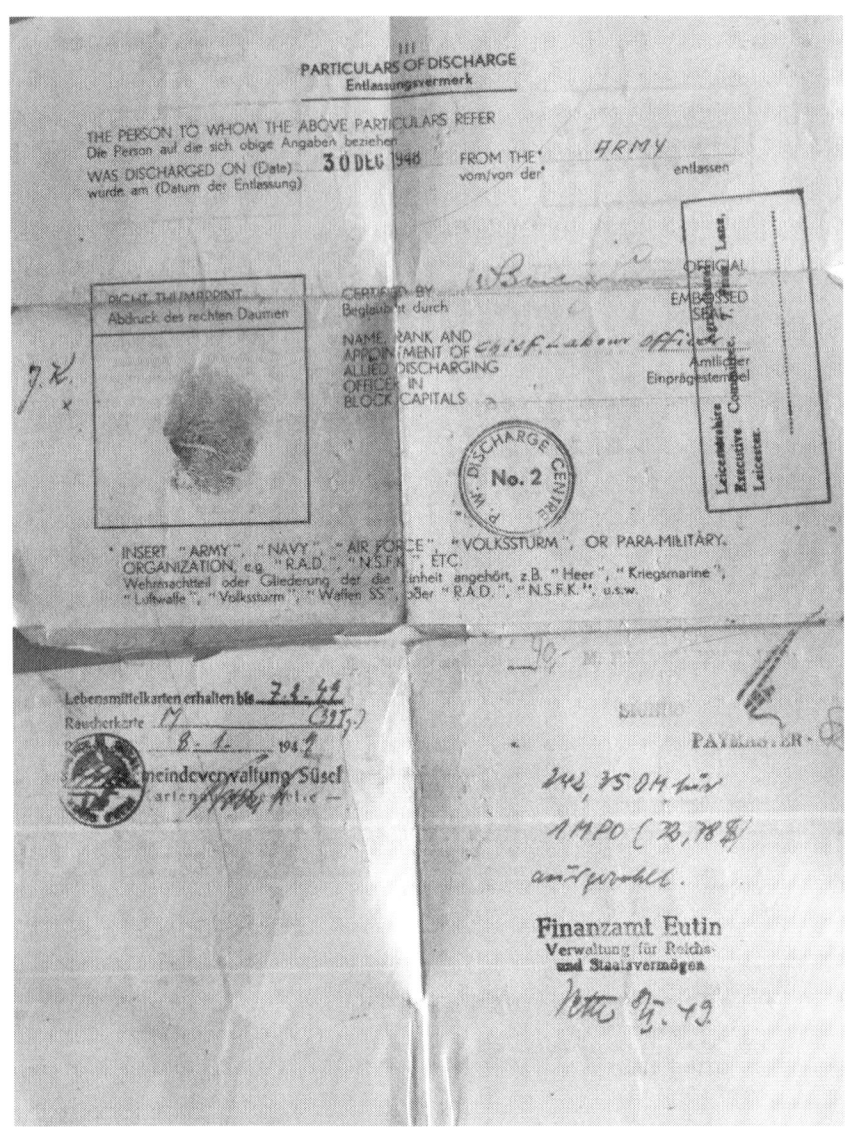

92 Wharf Street.

January 7th.

My dearest Hans

Thanks very much for your letter who posted it in Leicester for you?

I did not ring you Monday about the accident the buses had because I did not think anything more about it, and I did not think you would know until you received my letter. Darling never worry about me I have nine lives.

You said Mr Pickering knows who I am. I found that out Tuesday afternoon. I had to ring Mr Bodymore at Gaddesby (Mr Pickering used to be there) Mr Bodymore said 'I just missed you at Stathern' I pretended I did not know what he meant. Then he said 'here I've gone and fallen for you, and then I see you walking along with someone else at Stathern'. He is always joking and saying it is about time I went to Gaddesby. I tell him I should get lost if I went there. He said Mr Pickering had not told him as Mr Pickering did not know me, I don't think he recognised my voice. I think he knew you came from the Labour office Saltby. How else could you meet a girl from Leicester or maybe the cook told him, I couldn't lead a double life if I wanted to could I.

I have rung Saltby twice this week. On Monday Herman answered, and this afternoon Alfred answered. I said good afternoon asked him how he was, nothing more I can assure you.

I went to the pictures Monday with Dora and Alice, it was called "Dearest Fanny". It wasn't bad, it was in technicolour. I think you would have liked it. Tuesday night I stayed in, did some darning and I have stayed in tonight. I am in on my own, my mother has gone out with my Auntie and Uncle.

I ought to answer Bernhard letters and Muriel's (my friend in London) but I am not in the mood. I shall do it sometime before next year, it won't be this week. Thursday I am going to Alice's for tea and a good talk. Friday I am going to wash my hair and that takes me all night. Saturday I shall probably go to the pictures with Dora. That brings me to Sunday. Darling I won't be coming on Sunday, please don't mind darling, I know it is worse for you being out in the wilds, but darling I hope you will find some where to go. I had better see Dora. It is hard to explain, I know you think it funny because I see her and not you. But you see I don't want her to think I see her when it suits me. I hope you can understand, believe me darling, I would much rather be with you, even if it means being out in the cold and rain.

Anyway I will ring you sometime, I have to put my hair in curlers and it is getting late so I will say goodnight my darling be good.

All my love and kisses

Jean.

Xxxx

14

L.W.A.E.C Hostel.

Stathern,

7th Jan 1948.

My dearest, darling Jean,

I have a new idea, don't be surprised. I'll write a few lines every day and when I get your letter I'll post it. I got up at 5.00am so the other fellow has to do the dinner. Shouldn't I really have a few hours sleep now? No I rather write to you, as I got up this morning I thought of you, having another 3 hours to sleep. How nice it must be to lay in bed till 8.00 every morning. But don't worry darling I would like to do as you do. The other cook is leaving on Friday definitely so I'll be on my own than still having my day off on Sunday, I am sitting here in the room thinking of the nice hours we spent here together. I wish it could be the next Sunday again. As I think I'll be very lonely next Sunday. I wouldn't dare asking you about coming for you've said so already. Oh how hard you are. May I beg you again??

Night before last I went to the picture in the village (not W.L.A. Hostel). It was a real nice picture and I enjoyed it very much. You should have been with me, but I think you see better films in Leicester. As I heard yesterday there is a nice show, "Pantomime" in Nottingham. If I get my money on Friday I might be able to go one night next week but I'm not sure yet. I rather would go to Leicester to get the 9.50 bus from Melton to Stathern, can you make inquiries for me? Do you mind me coming to Leicester one night and see a picture! Maybe you'll have some time to spare that evening and we're able to go together. I am a very bad boy, aint I?

But if you would like to hear the truth darling I can't live without you. I have told you a few times already but I am not getting tired of telling you again and again. I hope you'll always remember what I said last Sunday. After I have bought the things I told you about I'll save my money and we may be able to do what we are longing for. Life will be worth than for me and I am quite sure we'll be happy. (I promise not to argue).

How lucky you are receiving a letter nearly every day. I hope I'll get your answer tomorrow. I was able to send my letter straight to Leicester with one of the men from the store yesterday afternoon.

Be good till I see you again.

All my love and kisses.

Hans.

92 Wharf Street.

January 9th 1948.

My dearest Hans

Aren't you lucky having a letter every day (almost). When I got a letter on Thursday morning, I wondered what was wrong. I thought you were moving or something had happened. It was a nice surprise to hear from you and know that nothing was wrong.

Did Mr Pickering tell you I spoke to him yesterday. He said Mr Bodbymore was a Stathern last Sunday but it was you that told him who I was.

I have made inquiries about the last bus to Melton. The last bus is 8.30, gets to Melton 9.15. That would give you enough time to go to the pictures. I leave at 5.15 and we would have to be at the bus stations for 8.15, that would give us 3 hours so maybe we would have time. Perhaps we could go to Nottingham one Saturday when you get settled.

I went to my friends' (Alice) for tea last night. I did not get home until 11.30. The time flies when I go there. Alice's mother is a very nice person, she always makes me eat such a lot. She never takes 'no' for an answer.

I am going to the pictures tonight with Dora to see "Duel in the Sun". It is supposed to be very good. I am not going out Saturday night, so I will stay in and go to bed early. Have a good week and darling I will think of you all the time.

All my love

Jean

P.S. I have just been speaking to Mr Bodymore. You would laugh if you could hear me speaking to him. He asked me if I still loved him, I said yes more than ever, he knows I'm only joking.

16

L.W.A.E.C Hostel.
Stathern
9th Jan 1948.

My dearest, darling Jean,

Thanks very much for your letter. I knew it had to come this morning: One of the men working for Mr Lawson (store) was here and took my letter to Leicester. I told him all the time he's been here not to forget that letter so he went off he was laughing at me for I told him than again. About the accident on Sunday night I told you all about in my last letter. That's what I usually say, don't worry about me. Look darling I hope you'll understand I don't want anything happen to you. Always be careful.

Mr Pickering didn't say any more about you. He only asked me yesterday if you are coming. I quite agree with you in going somewhere else. I know you have some more things to

do on Sundays than only coming to see me. Anyway I am not going away on Sunday. I don't know yet what to do, I'll certainly write to you, telling you again how lonely I feel without you being here,
You shouldn't be impolite to Bernhard, leave my letter for a day and answer his. You never fulfilled his secret wish to see him in Saltby so you should answer his letter at least.
Saltby must be a quiet place now when you only ring up twice last week. I called last night to have a word with Mr Edwards about my ration book. I told Alfred to tell him about it. I am still waiting for my civilianisation, but it must come now very soon. I want to be free doing whatever I like. Freedom is a splendid thing.
I believe you would much rather see me even if it means being out in the cold and rain. You've proved it already a few times without grumbling and I am very thankful for it. It always makes me feel happy. I am very glad there is the spring and summer ahead and it means a very nice time for us.
Mr Pickering told me yesterday afternoon you're on the phone but he didn't call me. I've given him instructions for the next time. I really wonder whether I get any money tonight. If not I am without any the following week. That does not mean I want some from you, not in any case. Anyway I've enough left to post your letter.
Now my darling I would like to close. I am waiting for your call. Cheerio then and be good, think of me on Sunday afternoon.

All my love and kisses
Yours
Hans.

176
L.W.A.E.C Hostel.
Stathern.

My dearest darling Jean

I am going to write as I promised last night. I didn't feel well as I got off the bus and had a nice headache as I arrived here. The 9.10 bus to Stathern was gone already so I had to wait till 10.10 and arrived here 10.50. I should have taken my overcoat for it was really cold whilst waiting in Melton. I really felt miserable. I think it was the shock I got when you told me you are not coming on Sunday. Don't worry darling I only was annoyed for the few minutes as you told me. I wouldn't say I was annoyed just a bit disappointed. I quite understand. As I told you I was so glad the last time passed so quick and I had only to wait another 3 days. I feel very very sorry you aren't coming. I was so longing for the Sunday if there is a chance for coming, please come. I'll be very lonely if you don't. I am better this morning darling. Do you post a letter for me today!

Look darling, I really got a shock as you said maybe I would say 'go off' to you. You made me very unhappy, darling. Don't you know how much I love you? Please darling, don't say such a thing again. You should know I never want to leave you. Have you forgotten why I stay here? I can't go leaving you here.. Look you are the only girl I know and love very much.

Now something funny. As I told you the warden cooked the dinner last night and something went wrong. The custard burned, the steamed pudding and the vegetable weren't cooked well. I was laughing as he told me. The men told me this morning about it. Please don't mention it to the warden. He can't be blamed. By the way I hope to be civilianised tomorrow. Mr Coy rung up yesterday afternoon and told him so. Anyway I hope it is true this time. So you'll see me a civilian the next time you come. Isn't it nice darling, now I'll have to close. It is nearly time for lunch so I have to do some work to get it ready.

Well darling never forget what I told you and be good till I see you again. Do think of me?

All my love and kisses

Always yours

Hans.

92 Wharf Street.

January 11th.

My dearest Hans

I haven't received your letter yet. I suppose the person forgot to post it. I was disappointed when there wasn't a letter for me Saturday morning. But still I have something to look forward to on Monday. If you post your letter today there should be two letters for me tomorrow. My mother has gone to Rothley with my aunt and uncle, so I am all alone except for the dog. I think Dora will be coming about 8.30. It has been pouring with rain all day. I have not been out and will not be going out if I can help it.

I have been numbering your letters you have sent me 14 between Dec 4 and Jan 1st. When I have finished this I am going to sit by the fire and read them all (the fire does not want any coal on).

What bus on Wednesday will you be coming on? There is a good picture on at the Odeon it is a musical and it is in technicolour. I think you would like it, the programme begins at 5.15 I will see if I can leave about 10 minutes early, then we would see all the programme, the second one begins at 8.20. If you want to see anything else I don't mind. I will try and draw a map and tell you where you can meet me at Kemps (jewellers) in Gallowtrees Gate facing Woolworths. You will get off the bus in Southgate St, if you go back up towards the traffic lights then turn right go down High St to the clock tower turn right again (Deans & Dawsons travel agents are on the corner) that is Gallowtree Gate and Kemps is not far up there.

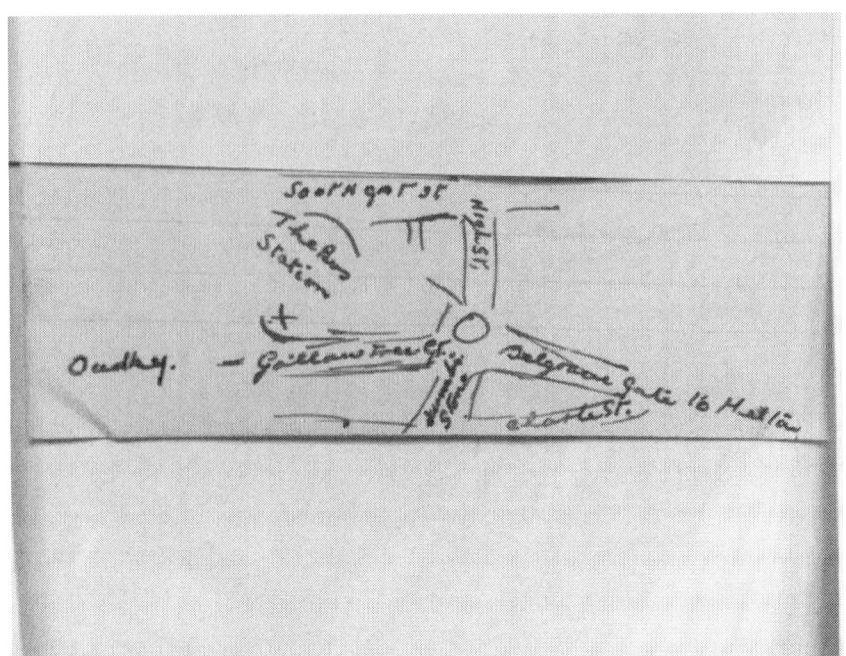

What do you think to my little map? I think it's good though it will be a miracle if you understand it. I almost forgot to say what time. I think it will be alright if I say 5.5.

I have to get the tea ready myself this week darling, there isn't anyone to wait on me. I better finish or else you won't get this tomorrow. I will be waiting under the clock at Kemps 5.5 Wednesday.

All my love and
kisses
Jean

____.

17

L.W.A.E.C Hostel.
Stathern.
Jan 12th 1948.

My dearest darling Jean

It looks strange to me you didn't get my letter on Saturday. The man I gave the letter to went off early Friday afternoon to Leicester. He promised to post the letter as soon as he gets there. He isn't back yet.

I thank you very very much for your two letters. One arrived on Saturday about 10 minutes after your call and the other one this morning. It was such a long day for me yesterday. Time did not go quick enough. Wednesday afternoon will change the situation anyway. I haven't got my money yet but I hope to get some till Wednesday. Mr Pickering offered me some money but I refused for I don't like to borrow. I'll take one of the buses on Wednesday afternoon and meet you there at the arranged place at 5.5 Your map looks very nice,

Now something about yesterday. I got up at 8.00 (lazy boy) for the breakfast is to be served at 9.00 on Sundays. Then I worked till 1.00 changed and after that I looked out of the window and found out it was raining so I rung up Saltby and asked the boys whether they are coming.

The answer was no, So I changed again and worked all afternoon, made the tea, supper and sandwiches for today. The time went quick and as I looked at the clock it showed 10.00 I went to bed early. The night was over at 5.15 this morning. I was so tired but had to get up. Isn't it a nice number of letters during a months time? That means nearly every second day one. Don't be surprised darling I also have 14 of your letters lying besides me. I really hoped there might be a bus leaving later than 8.30. The main thing for me is to get to Melton. I like to walk 8 miles to Stathern but I am thinking of you. You better take your supper along on Wednesday. It'll make an awful long time for you without any food. I would like to meet you at your office but I think you don't like it.

I'm so sorry there is nobody to wait on you this week. What do you think about me coming over for a week, getting the tea ready for you? Wouldn't it be nice darling? If you don't like me coming over I want to see you here next Sunday to give me a chance for making the tea.

Four of the boys here came after dinner yesterday into the kitchen thanking me for the nicest dinner they've had since long. That's what I like seeing other people satisfied.

It is late and I have to look at the dinners, I don't think I'll get your letter before Wednesday so I'll say cheerio till I see you. Be good my darling.

Loads of love as always

Yours forever

Hans. Xxx

92 Wharf St.

Jan 12th 1948.

My dearest Hans

Thanks very much for your letter, it was waiting when I got up this morning. Whoever you gave it to did not post it till Saturday morning according to the post mark.

I have not answered Bernard's letter yet and I do not think it impolite to keep him waiting a little while. After all, his wife might get the wrong idea about my writing to him. I know I would in any case. Anyway I am not going out tomorrow night so I will answer it then, heavens knows what I will put, I don't.

I rang Saltby today and spoke to Alfred I probably will not ring until next Monday I bet the girls at Grantham exchange miss us, do you remember that time someone was crossed on the line (it was the first time you asked me to go to Saltby) when we had finish a man said to me I have just been listening to a conversation between a German POW and an English girl. I had to laugh, the poor bloke would die of shock if he could see us now.

Please try and find Kemps when you meet me out on Wednesday because if Lucy saw you I would never hear the last of it. She is bound to ask where I am going. I'll just say I am going out.

Another thing is please go and have a rest when you can 5

o'clock till 11.00 at night is a long day. I love to receive your letters but darling I would rather go without than you miss your sleep. So please in future darling have your rest first then write if you have time. I have to go and catch up with my sleep now. So good night and God bless.

All my love
Jean

PS I received your letter this morning. Will you ring me when you get to Leicester? That is if you have got two pence. Don't worry about me not having anything to eat but what about you, I will bring something you can eat it on the bus, really common isn't it.

Same address.
Jan 14th 1948.

"Darling"

I am very sorry about tonight. I never realised you would be so disappointed when I said I would not be coming on Sunday. I was coming until my sister asked me to go to tea on Sunday, if I had told her I was going to Stathern she would start asking questions. I couldn't stand that. I get so fed up when people start telling me what I should do and what I shouldn't do. So I thought it would be easier to go on Sunday. Another thing, my sister is not at all well, besides not very happy living with her in-laws. I wish you did not love me so much then maybe you would do the same thing to me and I would know how much it hurt to be disappointed. I think it would do me good if you did. I will try in future not to hurt or disappoint you.

I hope darling you got back to Stathern safe and that you had something nice to eat, my mother had left the table set and a nice fire, when I had eaten I sat down and wrote to you so that you will get it Friday. At the moment I feel so mixed up and miserable, still darling by tomorrow I will have got over it. I will write tomorrow night too so that you will get a letter Saturday. Till then I will say cheeri'O and please try to understand me and what I do.

All my love and kisses

Jean

——.

Replied 24/1.48

Correspondence of a Prisoner of War

To	Johannes Klawitter.	14/1
No.	A572858.	

Destination	Prisoner of War Camp.
Road	No. 51 Allington.
District	Grantham/Lincolnshire.
Country	Great Britain.

From:

Name	Heinz Bieck.
Prisoner's No.	886160-1687.
Camp No.	14.
Squad No.:	10.
	Douai (North).

The print on top says 'don't write on this part of the paper'.

France, 7.1.48

Dear Hans

Thank you very much for your letter dated 13.10. It sounds like you have gone through a lot already as a PoW. Did they sentence you when you were captured? I experienced much the same. On 7 May 1945 * when I was captured, I had to raise my hands. It was in the room and they transported me immediately to the front, to Boston. On 23.5.43. we reached the 'Promised Land'. From there, we went on a four-day-

Pullman-journey to south Texas. I was down here until May 44. It was very warm there and I stayed in a 'non-labour--camp'. It was a training camp only. I learnt quite a lot there which I was able to put to good use later on. Our next camp was in the picturesque Maryland area, in the port town of Baltimore. I was employed as an auxiliary in a laboratory of a hospital together with an Italian lady, until August, when the hospital was closed down. In the following year I was allowed to work as an interpreter in a huge army laundrette directly in Baltimore. I can only describe my time in captivity as having been wonderful. Then, one day, I was asked if I would like to stay there or go home. Well, you can imagine what my answer was. I was very clear in my mind that I wanted to go back home. I left the USA in November 45. It was an excellent journey with 'Victoria Class' and took 21 days until we reached Le Havre. Then, suddenly, my dream of 'homeland' was shattered. We were put into a very large transit camp and we were told of our destiny. It was a stroke of fate – coal mines! We were supposed to be there 3 months, but it turned out to be 2 years. Conditions have improved somewhat nowadays, but when I first got there, I thought it would be the end, but a Prisoner of War can endure an awful lot! – I would be very happy if I could be where you are. There is no sign of release yet. All they do is dishing out loads of instructions. I suspect I shall be here for 5 years and more. Where you are one can put up nicely with the PoW life. How much do they pay you? Now, my dear Hans, I am also intending to go back home into the Russian Zone. I think it will be the right decision. I hope that this letter will be forwarded to your home address. I am sending you my best wishes and also to Auntie Hedwig, your cousin Heinz. Write back soon whenever the mood takes you, in English. I am sure it will be fun for you!?

*a mistake, must be '42

Aschersleben – 14.12.47

My dear Hans

Today I am sending you many best Sunday greetings as well as thanking you for your dear letter dated 23.11.47 and for your Christmas and your New Years greetings. As far as health is concerned, we are not doing too badly, apart from terrible toothache. On Thursday I have had two root extractions, as for several weeks I have had unbearable headaches, could not sleep at all. The dentist said that they should have been removed 6 months ago, as it could have ended badly. I thought that I'd have some peace after that, but immediately the next tooth began to give me trouble so there was no fuss to be made, it also had to come out. Thank god we have finished making our syrup, I am so glad, and we were so surprised with the result. One hundredweight produced 22 pounds, and the same x eight. That way we'll never have to eat dry bread. I have been busy 3 days and 4 nights, as when you have to borrow a press as well as a kettle, you have to be really on the ball, as everything costs 2 litres of juice per day. I re-cooked all the Schnitzels, with great success. I haven't had mail from you for two weeks. Not sure what's up with Horst, since you told him that you might not return for some time he has become really depressed. He is always so home-sick, and we cannot change anything when he is so homesick. He was so looking forward to your return. If you have to rely on yourself all the time, life is very difficult. But we do not want to complain, as it may be best for you, and we do of course want only the best for you. Please do be careful when driving. Have you found work for your future ? You are right of course, it is not like home anymore, but despite it we have managed to make it quite cosy for ourselves. I have become quite slim, although no comparison to before, but that's not the worst. As soon as I have some quiet I shall recover. Well, if you now speak English you can communicate with Jean. How will you spend Christmas? We have just had a conversation as to how we shall spend Christmas Eve. We are afraid of loneliness. Maybe we shall invite the Simmands, acquaintances from Stettin. Loneliness is particularly hard to bear on Christmas Eve and New Years Eve. But these days will pass as well. I am delighted that you have had two shirts sewn, but isn't white a bit delicate? Perhaps coloured ones would be more suitable? This is not something we can even begin to consider – I have mended Horstel's shirt 99 times over, by now everything falls off us in shreds. I do imagine that your salary does not allow you to be extravagant. For the last few weeks our landlord has changed a lot, he is as polite as never before. He obviously realised that his moaning gets him nowhere with me. I am much tougher than he is. Dear Hans, can you get powdered egg where you are? An acquaintance's husband sends this stuff, and it is wonderful. However he spends a lot of time in a teacher's family, so maybe he has better connections because of that. He recently sent baking powder, pudding powder as well as soap. Please do not be cross as I am writing this, as, if you can't get hold of this stuff, it doesn't really matter. I do not want to rob your pockets. We wish you a happy and healthy New Year. May it fulfil your secret dreams and all the best for your future. We also send our New Year's greetings to Jean. Be hugged and kissed from your ever worrying mum and your brother Horst.

In the margin – Maybe the next year will bring us a Wiedersehen

16/1   ## Aschersleben 21.12.47 (4th day of advent)

14/1

     My dear Hans
We thank you very much for your dear letter, unfortunately

you did not date it. I am very reassured that you have a good post lined up, and we wish you good luck and all the best for the future. This kind of salary you would not receive here, but maybe things will change in a year or so. It clearly is the best for you, even if it means that we have to put up with not seeing you. At least where you are you can spend your money on something, whereas the only thing Horst has is his Sunday suit, and he certainly can't wear that every day. He's been wearing his weekday trousers for ages, and they are practically falling off him, there is nothing here to buy. I have been many times to the protestant aid office as well as to the support bank, but always with the same result. On Wednesday it will be Christmas Eve, and it is good to know how you will be spending it – that really is very kind of your boss. At least I know you will have a good time over the holidays. But of course does that means Jean will not be able to visit? However she is surely pleased that you are staying there? Who knows where you are going to be sent to? Maybe you will already be released when this letter reaches you. Dear Hans, might it be possible to get us some soap? I feel embarrassed to keep asking you for things, you must think we always want something. Please do not be cross with us. The Christmas Stollen is all done. Miss Ellen's parcel has been en route for over 6 weeks now, we'd be so happy if it arrived in time for Christmas. Horst has to work today, but is free on the day after Boxing Day. Now my dear boy, keep well, and we wish you a happy and successful New Year. Our thoughts are always with you. Much love and kisses from your mum and your brother Horst. Regards to Jean

16/1   Aschersleben 22.12.47

14/1

My dear Hans
We thank you very much for your letter dated 12.12.47 which gave us great pleasure. The fact that you posted two

parcels for us on 22.11 makes us enormously happy – who knows if they will get here in time for Christmas? The day after tomorrow is Christmas Eve, so it would be just wonderful as we would have a real treat. Miss Ellen's parcel has been en route since 5.11 and has not yet arrived. Probably this is to do with all the extra postal traffic at Christmas. If you've bought everything for the two parcels you probably sacrificed all your money? But you're not allowed to do that – we do not want to be a burden to you. We shall make ourselves a delicious pudding with milk, it will be delicious. Currently about three transports per day arrive in Frankfurt/Oder, if only our Papa were amongst them. Some of the ones who arrive have been missing for 4-5 years, and they all say you must not give up hope. Winter seems to be finished here, it is raining lots and it has not been that cold. On Thursday we received half a hundredweight of briquettes, they will last us a long time. We shall receive more coal in the new year. Today we got some fat, we had hoped to get some butter for Christmas, but unfortunately only margarine. Tomorrow I shall bake us a white loaf as well as some Streusselkuchen*. How much I had wanted to send you a parcel, but we are only allowed to send two pounds per parcel to civilians. I am delighted that the gleaning has ended and I have some peace and quiet. In your letter you are saying that Edith is too lazy to write, but there is another reason: She has a sweetheart – well, she is certainly old enough. Let us hope she is luckier than the first time round. Our Horstel has lots of work, and he has some heart problems, I am really worried about him. He has grown too much, and what with the lousy food, I often feel so sorry for him, he is so pale. Please give Jean our best wishes for Christmas – we wish all the best to you both. Now my dear boy, we are sending you our love and kisses from mum and your brother Horst.

Here's to a healthy Wiedersehen

- a kind of crumble cake

16/1   Aschersleben Christmas 1947

14/1

     My dear Hans

Today we were delighted to receive your dear parcel, for which we thank you with all our hearts. We have been so happy about every single thing. Tonight we shall have hot chocolate made with milk, how wonderful, it will be so tasty. You should have seen how both of our faces were radiating with joy. It arrived yesterday at the post office and I was able to collect it the next day. Now we can wash ourselves properly! We so enjoyed every single thing! It seems that this time you did not shut the tin, but just tied it up with string, and sewn in. The weight was correct, minus 10 gram, 10 lbs. I guess the other one will arrive after the holidays. Ellen's parcel has not yet arrived. Let's hope it will arrive eventually. It is always so wonderful to be unpacking such a parcel, but Hans, it worries me to think that you are paying for all of it out of your meagre salary, leaving you with nothing. Mrs Klingenstein from Soldin and her mother were here for a few hours. Just now Horst and I have had supper, white bread with margarine, and hot chocolate. It was delicious. Horst was so delighted. Now I am all alone and about to deal with my mail. Horst has gone dancing, I had to encourage him, he always worries about leaving me alone, but it means that I can be alone with my thoughts, thinking about you and Papa. On Christmas Eve we went to church, but all the time I was thinking of you both. Father Christmas has been very busy – Horst gave me a bread-slicer, a very large baking tray, a toiletry box, and four bottles of eau de cologne, Russian leather and Old Lavender. Horst received his wig, a silver signet ring, cigarettes, and from his boss an open razor, a hair cutting comb and a pair of scissors, plus 20 Marks. The Hohls gave him a bottle of oil, a piece of bacon, and a large jar of cherries, apples and cookies. From Mrs Bode came a jar of currents, apples and also cookies. Bearing in mind all of this, plus all the wonderful things you sent, you can imagine how beautiful our Christmas table is looking. If only you and Papa had been able to be with us, we would have been so happy. What will the next Christmas be like? Christmas Eve Mr and Mrs Ziemann from Stettin were with us, so we were not too lonely. Tomorrow afternoon we are invited to theirs. I have to get more Kaffeeschrot, a quarter pound a month is not enough, we are such coffee addicts. At least I am looking a bit more healthy, and I shall continue to recover. For Christmas I really wanted to give you a signet ring too, but I did not know the size. Silver has to be handed in, but I know the lady well, so they have made an exception. Yesterday I received post from Aunt Lina and Uncle Erich, they send you their very best wishes. There is no news from Bruno either. Christel cannot go to work in winter, as she has nothing to put on her feet and nothing on her body, its' a real pity, there's always someone worse off, we have all become beggars. My shoes have disintegrated in the rain. I would never have gone out like this at home, but here nobody cares. When you see how the locals go around – a while ago a woman said she still had ten pairs of shoes, well I guess it's better than for those of us who do not have any. On Sundays I really do not like to go out – I feel most comfortable in my own four walls. If only things would improve – three years of misery are now behind us. Currently many transports arrive with prisoners, if only our Papa were amongst them. We hope you have had a really good Christmas, you so richly deserve it. Uncle Erich is intending to visit, but the rail connections are so bad. Ursel goes to a winter school in Grimmen. Now my dear Hans, I shall finish today's letter, please stay well and we wish you and Jean a happy and healthy New Year. Much love and many kisses from your mum and your brother Horst. Here's to a healthy Wiedersehen

24/1   Aschersleben 27.12.47
14/1

My dear Hans

Today being the third day of the holiday I would like to send you a few lines. Christmas has passed – But it was all worthwhile. I have a blond lady's wig, a signet ring and sweets, which for the present time feels plenty. And mum has a bread machine, an oven shelf, a toiletries shelf and a box with three bottles, including old lavender, eau de cologne and a folder for letters. All our thoughts were with you during the festive days. What did you do over the holidays? Your lovely parcel arrived on Christmas day, well the joy was enormous. The package could not have been opened fast enough. Mum made us all a cup of hot chocolate and we have not seen or drunk anything as nice for years. Plus all the other beautiful things. Ellen's parcel has not yet arrived –let's hope it gets here. I have been offered a new job in a large hairdressers salon, but I am sorry to leave my little boss. I don't really know, but professionally it is the way forward. I will have to discuss it with my boss. What are your thoughts about it? Now I shall describe to you how I spent the holidays. On Christmas eve we went to church and at eight o'clock the Ziemanns came. They are people from Stettin, and they did not want to be alone, and one can't really cope with it. On Christmas day I worked from 8 in the morning until 4 in the afternoon. On boxing day I worked until midday and to a dance in the afternoon. In the evening we went to the Rueckbrechts who are from Gross-Moellen. Dearest Hans, how did you spend Christmas? What happened at your boss's house?

I bet there was plenty to eat. Today we do not work, but we did work last Sunday. I was off for four days. Dear Hans, can you maybe get hold of decorative combs and hair ornaments? It is not easy for me to send these requests, as I do not want to trouble you. Tonight we are planning to go to the cinema, they are showing 'Marriage in the shadow" which is of course a propaganda film. I shall go there at 4.30 to buy tickets, let's hope we will still get some, as we have to queue. Oh if only our dear Papa would be on the list, there are now daily transports arriving. I always feel as though he may arrive any moment. I will be finishing this letter now. Many greetings to Miss Jean, we very much enjoyed her message. Lots of love from Horst and mum.

92 Wharf St.

January 16ᵗʰ.

"Darling"

I did not go to my sister for tea today. When I got home Saturday lunchtime my sister had come home ill, the doctor has been today and said she has got to stay in bed for a week. I was really fed up yesterday. I have got over it now. I went to Dora for tea Saturday, then we went to the pictures, My cousin comes on Saturday for lunch. She asked me to go to tea (Sunday). I had not seen my Auntie for about a month. I used to go every week at one time, so had Betty, she left off going before I did, I like to go to see her but she always finds something to lecture us on, My Auntie used to tell Betty off about using lipstick, when I bleached my hair I dare not see her, but when I did, much to my surprise she liked it. Anyway I went to tea today and I really enjoyed it. I got there about 3.30 then my cousin and I went for a walk, it has been a beautiful afternoon, at least the weather was, and that reminds me, when I come to Stathern make me do some walking, I don't get enough exercise or fresh air, at least that is what everyone says.

<u>Monday</u>
I received your letter this morning. Thank you very much I was very pleased until I read you had put the receiver down on Hermann then I was very annoyed. You should learn to control your temper more. You may be sure Hermann would have a very good reason for not going to Stathern. I am not going to say anything to Alfred or Hermann. You can do that yourself. I don't want them falling out with me. I spoke to Alfred this morning. Anyway he told me they had not been. Alfred said Hermann was going home on Wednesday and had rather a lot to do, aren't you sorry now, beside that it was a very cold day and windy, it is a long cycle from Saltby to Stathern especially for Hermann. I think you ought to ring Saltby to apologise for putting the phone down.
I will ring you tomorrow as I think I may be going to Melton to visit my Uncle. I will ring you from Melton. I have told Kath at Melton office I will call into see her if I go. Anyway darling I will call you tomorrow so be good.

All my love
Jean

PS You can please yourself if you ring Hermann but I think you ought to.

92 Wharf St.
Jan 16th 1948.
Darling
I was so glad to receive your letter this morning and know you arrived back safely. I hope by now you have recovered from your shock and that you are feeling much better. I was going to write to you last night but Alice came, we sat talking it was 10.30 before she went home. I took her a little way, came back and put my hair in curlers (it is my own) it was late to start to write so I thought I would write this morning

and post it at lunch time. So far I have not been getting on so well. I have been terribly busy on the switchboard, with all the interruptions I have had I feel like being impolite to everyone that comes in now.

You asked if I minded you going into Melton office? Of course I didn't I was only joking, you should know that by now. I think I do it all the more because I know you don't like me to joke about it. You can go wherever you want. To Melton office, Stathern WLA* Hostel, or even to Thorpe Arnold. I promise I won't mind a bit.

Poor Mr Pickering I bet he was in a mess Wednesday night. I thought you said he used to be a cook, I don't think that would make any difference, the English never do make very good cooks (that is just to let you know what to expect).

I have not seen my sister yet so I don't know any more about Sunday. I will ring you on Saturday.

It is now 12.35 and I want to post this letter. I will say cheeri'O, be good.

All my love
and kisses
Jean

* Womens Land Army

L.W.A.E.C Hostel.
Stathern.
Jan 18$\underline{th}$ 1948.

My dearest ,darling Jean,
I thank you very much for your letters I received on Friday and later today. Now it is Sunday. I am in a bad temper Hermann rung up and told me they're not coming. I didn't ask for the reason but put the receiver down instead. They shouldn't think making a fool of me. As Hermann rung me yesterday he told me they are coming down if the weather is alright. Now it is the best weather and they aren't coming.

I had heaps of work to do this morning, made a nice cake yesterday and carried everything up in my room. I just had finished as he rang up. Please darling when you ring Saltby during the next days tell them I am not their fool and I won't ask anybody from Saltby in future. I hope you're coming on one of your holidays next week. As I told you I am going to Allington on Wednesday. Mr Dam from Waltham office came paying out the men on Friday. I asked him if he's got money for me, the answer was 'no'. So I did some talking on Saturday morning. Mr Pickering rung up Mr Shilton for me. Mr Edwards is coming down here on Wednesday morning taking me to Allington for release and is bringing me back after it. So I'll be a civilian already when you come next time. Saltby Camp is to be closed very shortly and will be the first hostel for civilians. I am so glad I went here otherwise my application to Mr Barker-Swaine would be cancelled. Mr Coy turned up here on Saturday noon. I told him at once that I want to stay here as long as possible. When the Leicestershire hostels are to be opened I'll be able to go to one of them. He'll do for me what he can, he told me, "if they want you back, there are lots more to be sent without you". So I hope that case will be settled.

Now to your letters. You know darling I don't want you to get into trouble because of me. I also don't like when people start asking questions. You wish I did not love you so much! Darling I don't believe that. I never will disappoint or hurt you. I thank you very much for promising the same. I'll try to understand whatever you do. You felt like being impolite to everyone that came in? What about me. If I'd come I am sure you'd have thrown me out right away, wouldn't you? The English never make a good cook. Darling I'll tell you the cake you brought to Grantham the other Sunday was wonderful. If you think you are not a good cook I hope I am. It is 3.45 now. In half an hour I'll start preparing the tea and after that I'll do the sandwiches for tomorrow morning. It isn't bad at all today for there are only 3 men in for tea and supper. Mr

Pickering told me that I'll get another half a day off during the next week besides Wednesday. My going to Allington doesn't count. If Thursday suits you I would like you coming. Please come as early as possible (arrive here at midday). Don't worry about lunch and tea. There'll be everything ready for you. The warden doesn't mind. He was telling me you should come every day during your holidays. His lady is here this afternoon and taking this letter along for posting in Leicester. She comes from Humberstone

I'll close now darling. Be good and think of me. My compliments to your mother. By the way, I've got 4 letters from my mother last week. I would like to translate them to you when you come.

Now darling,

all my love and kisses always yours

Hans.

24/1   Aschersleben New Years Eve 1947

19/1

My dear Hans

Today is the end of the year and we are sending you many many greetings. Wouldn't it have been beautiful if we had been allowed to spend it together? May the dear God make it possible for the four of us to be reunited next year. Our thoughts are with you, dear-ones. Who knows what the new year will bring us, let us hope that our dear Papa will also return and that we will see our homeland again. Especially during the festive season our hearts are doubly heavy. May we all stay healthy!

Since yesterday we have winter weather again, frost and snow and seriously slippery. Tonight we'll be going to the Ziemanns. Horst does not want to go out dancing, he doesn't want me to be alone, and we do not feel like going to the theatre or the movies. We really do not have any reason to wel-

come the New Year in with a great fanfare – the times are too serious and too difficult. I wonder how you and your dear Papa will be spending this evening? How different it would all be if we could be together at home? I will finish this letter for today. Please stay healthy
Much love and many kisses from your 'always thinking of you' mum and your brother Horst

My dear Hans
We have just received your letter postmarked 17.12.47, which made us very happy. Well, finally you've received mail from us. You have a lot of trouble with us, bearing in mind that you are already saving up for the next parcel for us. We really shouldn't demand this! Please do not be sad that you weren't able to send me a birthday present. Haven't you already given me so many things, which have given me more pleasure than anything else. Bearing in mind how little you earn, this is a big sacrifice for you. Once you have been released you will have to think of yourself first, as it will be difficult to become a civilian again. The gleaning has finished a few weeks ago, but in a few months time it will start all over again. Horrendous! It starts with collecting wood in spring, once it gets colder, we have to heat more. Horst has just combed an acquaintance of Frau Brandt and in return was given 9 large briquettes, which means I can cook for a few days. Every little helps. We had a letter from the Ribortfs from Pyritz. They are now in the West and are well. They are staying with their son, and have raised a pig which they have now slaughtered. They receive 2 litres of full fat milk and also some low fat milk. Whereas we!!!! Do you remember Buchholz from the Savings Bank? The one with the crippled hand? They lived in the Selbsthilfe* they thought they had lost their only son 4 years ago, and when we had to leave three years ago they both committed suicide. Now the son has returned from Russia and has found neither parents nor a homeland. Isn't that awful? Tailor Papendorf now lives in Cologne and has opened a large tailor's workshop and a beautiful apartment, for which he pays 230 Mark rent. He's been so lucky throughout the whole war and didn't have to

leave. If you really do not need the linen you have sent we gladly accept it. Don't worry about the wig, Horst already has one. This cannot be expected of you! It's ok for you to write very 'small', I can read it very well. Horst is also writing to you. Lots of love again, mum

*a self help provision for children of the war

Aschersleben New Years Day 1948

My dear Hans

We have now taken the first step into the New Year, may it bring us only good things and above all, a Wiedersehen. We have spent the last night of the year quietly. Frau Ziemann made the coffee we had brought along, and I had baked doughnuts. Just like at home! There was herring salad on rolls. Do not laugh, but Frau Ziemann had bought a herring for 10 marks on the black market, isn't this pure madness? A normal mortal cannot compete with this – Horst would have to give up his weekly salary for not even three of those herrings! We also played Ludo and went home under the sound of the bells. Your and Miss Ellen's parcels have not as yet arrived, let's hope they'll arrive in the new year. Packages from this area often take 7-8 weeks. Yesterday we received a parcel from Uncle Gustav, with carrots, wheatgerm and a few pounds of peas. We are pleased, as everything helps. Now my dear boy, sending you everything good you can possibly imagine for the new year. Greetings to Jean and much love to you – kisses from your mum and Horst.

Here's to a healthy Wiedersehen

24/1   Aschersleben 1.1.1948

19/1

My dear Hans

It being New Years Day I am sending you a few lines – who knows what the New Year is going to bring us. How nice it would be if we heard something from our dear Papa. We now have daily transports arriving from Frankfurt/Oder. Today is a fine day, there's a bit of snow on the ground and some frost. Last night we spent with the Ziemanns, we came home at 12.30am It was ok, but not exactly what one imagines as a young person. Mum feels now very much better, her skirt keeps popping open, but for a while she hadn't looked well. Yesterday after work I combed Mrs Rueckbrecht. They are from Gross Moellen and were already rather drunk. They had given the father so much to drink – he was lying on the bed with his head wrapped in bandages – everyone was drunk. Then it was going to be my turn, but she didn't manage it. In the same house there lives several black marketeers, and I was asked to shave one of them, which I did, and was given 16 Reichsmark – well worth it. I shall save the money to buy tools, my first item will be some curling tongs. Tonight we have visitors again, the Rueckbrechts and the Klingelheils are coming. Dear Hans, believe me that some days I feel so depressed that I no longer hear or see anything. Count yourself lucky that you are still over there, as here you make yourself ill with frustration and anger. I'm not sure if this year things will get better. On 1st of February I shall start a new job in a ladies salon, it will be very hard for me to leave my old boss, but I have to think about my future and move on. And in such a salon one learns new tasks, which is the main thing. Please give my best wishes for the New Year to Miss Jean, did she spend the evening with you? This afternoon I shall check out if there is somewhere to go dancing, my regular haunt, the Baeckermuehle will be closed until Easter because of lack of coal. A real shame, it was the nicest place. Hans, do you remember when on Christmas Eve we used to eat white bread with sausage, and on New Years Eve we ate Bockwurst and rolls, and doughnuts? Alas, best to wipe it from one's memory.. My very best wishes again to you and Miss Jean

Your brother Hans and mum

Please write soon. Here's to a healthy Wiedersehen, hopefully soon

19

Darling Jean

I am going to write a few lines as promised it'll only be a short letter for I have lots of work to do till tomorrow morning. It was very nice of you calling me from Melton. Isn't it a shame I couldn't see you only 8 miles away? Don't worry, only two more days till Thursday. As I told you Mr Edwards is coming here at 9.30 tomorrow morning. I hope to be back early in the afternoon. Tonight I've to get my kit ready to take to Allington. I hope I get everything changed. That's my work for tonight after 9.00. It is 2.45 and I still have to get the leeks ready for tonight. Do you know what a lot of work with them? Alfred rung me about half an hour later. He didn't understand what you meant. He was telling me I should ring you in Melton office. I explained than to him and he was satisfied. I said goodbye to Hermann and think I'll miss him tomorrow in the main camp.

Thanks very much for your letter. I was waiting yesterday but I'd had it. Nothing for me. When you come on Thursday we'll have a walk around. You'll get plenty of fresh air and exercises. If you really want exercise I can give you an advice. Start Wednesday afternoon from Leicester and 'walk' to Melton, then you may take a bus to Stathern. Not bad is it? I was surprised as I read the lecture you gave. I quite agree with you. I am glad there is somebody who shows me how to make it better. I don't mind, darling just tell me and I'll try to do it better. And your letter was so business like that I really believe you're very annoyed. I hope you have got over it now.

Now darling let me close. It is getting later and the leeks are waiting for me. So be good till I see you Thursday. Think of me tomorrow.

All my love and kisses
Yours for ever

Hans.

January 21st.

My dearest Hans.
This is going to be a very short letter. I want you to get it tomorrow otherwise it won't be any good. I am coming tomorrow. I hope to get the 12.30 from Leicester. I hope my mother does not mind getting the dinner early. The next bus is not until 2.30. I will do my best to get the 12.00. I should get to Stathern about 2.30 then.
I rang Alfred from the call box. Mr Edwards answered so I could not say very much. He seemed rather embarrassed. I did not think he knew what I said.
I have been into the town this morning. I took Susan with me and I walked her off her feet. I bought a pair of shoes Betty gave me the coupons.
I better close now I'm rushed to death looking after the shop and Susan. My mother has gone to have a rest.
                    All my love
                Jean
            Aschersleben 4.1.48
    24/1   22/1
        My dear Hans
Today I am sending you my heartfelt Sunday greetings. I already replied to your last letter on New Year's Day. Horst was very pleased to have received a letter from you dated 19.12.47 and he will reply soon. Last night he went to the theatre, they showed the Magic Violin, he was utterly enthralled. He insisted I came along, but I didn't go. Everyone looks smart and me with my wooden clogs – better to stay at home. Today for lunch I made a dessert from the powder,

it tastes so wonderful. On New Years Eve we had the Rueckbrechts from Gross Moelle and Frau Timms from Stargard
with her husband, who recently also returned from Russia.
As soon as he walked through the door he went over to
the Christmas tree, where we had placed Papa's picture, and
said: I was together with this man as a prisoner of war, he
could not actually name him, but recognised papa by sight.
I showed him papa's last picture as a soldier, and he said
that there was no doubt at all that it was papa he was with.
Oh Hans, if only he were to return to us, we would be the
happiest of people. Herr Timm has lost 20 pounds since he's
been here, which he does not like at all. His wife has not
provided at all, not even added a spoonful of flour to the
sauces, she doesn't even have potatoes in the cellar. That is
pure negligence! Every week he buys a four pound loaf of
bread, costing 40 Mark, which is less than he earns the whole
week, so when the savings are finished it means being brave
and confronting hunger. Dearest Hans, when will you finally
be released? Please can you then send me your new address
in an air mail letter? That way you won't have to wait so
long for a letter. Your parcel has not arrived yet, and nor has
Miss Ellen's. Just recently, people have only received their
packages sent in October and November, so we were lucky
to have received ours on Christmas Day. Now my dear boy,
please remain healthy, lots of love. From your mum and your
brother Horst

24/1   Aschersleben 8.1.48

22/1

My dear Hans
Today we received Ellen's parcel. We are so pleased! Unfortunately we could not tell if it was complete, as the packaging
was damaged and had been repackaged on the journey. In any
case, including the packaging it weighed 1 ½ kg and contained the following: a sleeveless jumper for Horst, a knitted cardigan for me, as well as a pair of shoes which I will
take to be finished – then I'll be able to wear them for a long
time. Elastic, some thread, sewing needles and some darning

wool. We were delighted! Please give our deepest thanks to Ellen. Unfortunately I cannot write myself, as there was no sender's address, and also I don't know any English. Dear Hans, if you are sending anything in the future please continue to wrap it extremely well, as it would be really annoying if something was lost. You are spending your hard earned money, so it would be a real shame if it ended up in the wrong hands. Currently many parcels arrive from England. I hope that your second one sent 24.19 will arrive soon.
Sending you much love and kisses from your mum and your brother Horst. For a healthy Wiedersehen
Regards to Jean

<u>20</u>

L.W.A.E.C Hostel.
Stathern.
Jan 23<u>rd</u> 1948.

My darling

I thank you very, very much for your coming yesterday afternoon. I really was the happiest man of the world. Well I have to wait till I see you again next week. Probably I am coming on Wednesday afternoon. It was such a nice surprise as I came down and found you waiting already. I didn't expect you coming on that bus but I was so glad you did come as early as that. Anyway it was a most enjoyable afternoon. I arrived back here at 9.30 for I took the same bus back. The conductor was surprised to find me on the bus again – on my own. I could see it on his face. I hope you arrived home safely. The week is mainly over now and I'll have a quiet weekend. I've told Mr Pickering this morning that I want my half a day off on Wednesday or Thursday. So I'll work on Sunday. I am sorry I couldn't spare any time this morning to write to you so this is going to be a short letter. Otherwise it would be too late to post it. Do you remember the woman you met on the road? She came at the usual time this morning and her first question was, did you enjoy the afternoon? I said I won't tell you. She was joking all day long. The warden is going away tomorrow afternoon so I'll be on my own for the porter is going to Nottingham. Wouldn't it be nice you being here giving me a hand? There is a lot of work to do. You could easily do the cooking couldn't you? I would tell you what to do! Tonight I am going to the picture as I told you. Listen darling I think I better come on Wednesday for I've got to go to Melton for my passport photo as soon as possible. I think I can fix all these things then on Wednesday at the same time in the same place. I hope you'll write on Sunday and tell me all about it.

Now darling let me close. I'll have to hurry to the post office to post the letter. Think of me on Sunday afternoon. I'll write to you.

All my love and kisses
Yours
Hans.

PS What did Lucy tell you about the call?

92 Wharf Street.
January 25th
My darling
Thank you very much for your letter. I am really very sorry I did not write on Friday but I was very busy. I arrived home on Thursday about 9.10 and I did not sit down. I got Cyril some supper and I went up and down stairs about a dozen times. Then on Friday I cleaned through, that took me all morning. I was going to write after dinner but had to go into town to fetch some wool. I was unsuccessful. I went to the pictures at night and I knew it wasn't any use writing then as you still would not have got till Monday morning.

My mother has gone upstairs to have a rest. She does not seem too well, it's rather a lot for her to do, to look after my sister and Susan. Enough to wear you out, and she sits here watching me write this, asking questions. I feel like gagging her.

I have been very busy this morning. I have been doing the washing and started 10.15 and did not finish until 12.30.

Lucy did not say anything about you calling me last Wednesday, it was Iris you spoke to. She said to me you missed 2 calls whilst you were away. The first was from a girl I used to work with. Then Iris started to tell me about your call. She said she looked for my Uncle's number, then when she found it you said you knew it. She was annoyed. Then she said it was either a German or Pole. All I said was it would be a German, I don't know any Pole's. I have started her thinking.

Here I go again darling but please don't be annoyed. Do you mind if I don't see you on Wednesday as my mother is going out and it is a rush for her get Susan to bed and get the tea as well. Cyril usually comes but he's as helpless as I don't know what. I get very annoyed with him. I hope you don't mind. I know you will be disappointed but I will come on Sunday. I hope by that time my sister will have gone home and everything will be back to normal.

Please don't be too mad darling and just be good.

All my love and kisses

Jean

21

L.W.A.E.C Hostel.
Stathern.
Jan 25th 1948.

My darling,

As promised I am going to write your Sunday afternoon letter. Isn't it a lovely day? I wish you would be here and walk around Stathern with me. If all goes well I'll see you on Wednesday afternoon. Only 3 days till then. Would you be so kind and tell me why you're in such a hurry as you rung me on Saturday? I wished you a very good weekend but noticed that you had gone already. Had somebody come into your room? Don't worry darling. I hope you've had a nice week-end.

The dinner is over, the warden back and his young lady with him. Do you believe me when I tell you I was very busy yesterday afternoon? I wrote 5 letters. One to my mother, one to my brother, one to my cousin in France, one to Ellen thanking for the parcel and one to my grandma. Therefore I've all the afternoon today to write to you.

Just after dinner I had a little row with the porter. Don't be afraid it wasn't my fault and I didn't start it. So you need not give me a lecture this time. I only told him to go and have a rest and did the work myself. He's grumbling about everything and I know the reason. He is too old for a job like this and because I know, I controlled myself and kept my temper!! I am going to follow your advice. Well darling I wonder what you are doing at the moment. It is 3.45 and I bet you went to a tea party. Isn't it lovely such a nice cup of tea? And because I know I am going to mash a cup now for myself. Do you want one? Hurry up and come. I am a bad boy and can't stop joking. Do you remember what I told you on Thursday? Darling I love you so much and I hope our time is coming soon. I know we'll be happy all our lives. Mr Pickering's young lady has been here just now and fixed me up with stamps. She is a very nice person. She is going to take this letter along for me so you'll get it first post tomorrow.

It is 7.30 now so darling I've to start with the tea and do the sandwiches afterwards. I will close now. Be good, darling till I see you on Wednesday afternoon.

All my love and kisses

Yours forever

Hans.

22

L.W.A.E.C Hostel.

Stathern.
Jan 26th 1948.

Mr darling
I am very sorry I shan't see you on Wednesday but I don't
mind. I don't know if you could arrange for Thursday if not
I'll go to Melton on Wednesday afternoon to have the photographs taken and may go to the pictures later in the evening. I didn't expect you to cancel our arrangement but please
don't worry. I am glad I need not to wait for a fortnight. Did
you understand what I told you on Saturday as you rung me?
I mean about the pictures on Friday night. Mr P asked me
'who is keeping the seat for you' because it was late as I went
from here. I answered, it is of course one of the girls. So he
was going to tell you as soon as you rung me. He is always
trying to pull me a leg, but he's unsuccessful. I always have
the right answer.
Do you think it is a long time washing for two hours? That's
the time I need for my few things every week. I should be
used to doing it already for a few years. I'll do it another few
years and I hope to do it then in the quick and proper way.
I am really sorry I annoyed Iris last Wednesday. I thought it
was Lucy and I had given her another riddle. I hope Iris won't
start asking questions. I feel so sorry.........

Next page missing

92 Wharf Street.
January 27th.

My darling Hans
Thank you very much for both your letters. I really intended
to write to you yesterday afternoon but I had so many interruptions. I was speaking to Kathleen at Melton nearly all
afternoon. She speaks to me because she is very interested
in a boy that works in this office. Iris and I have been playing cupid but so far it has been going very slow, we can't get

them to meet. I think he had better get in touch with Saltby camp. It doesn't take them long to get to know anyone. I have to laugh when Kathleen starts to talk about you and Alfred. She was telling me yesterday about Allen but somehow she had got another story than me, it took me all my time not to tell her she was wrong. Another thing she said was that you are getting fat. So I am not the only one that needs exercise!!

I hope you don't mind not coming to Leicester this week. I told Alice I would see her on Thursday, I had forgotten that. I could have told her I was going out, she wouldn't have minded. I know you would not have minded but it wasn't worth coming when I will be seeing you Sunday.

I have just been speaking to Alfred, he says that Saltby is being closed down within the next few days.

I did not tell you where I went on Sunday. I was not going anywhere but Alice came Sunday lunchtime and asked me to go to tea. I went about 3.30 and came back home about 10.00. Alice's mother is very nice and she always makes me feel at home. I have just run out of ink. This is Lucy's best, can't you tell?

Lucy has been asking who I am writing to and she gets very annoyed because I won't say.

I am not going out tonight. I think I will wash my hair.

I will be seeing you on Sunday so just be good and don't see too many land girls.

All my love and kisses

Jean

L.W.A.E.C Hostel.
23   Stathern.

My darling, Jean

It is not long to wait now, only a night and a few hours to-morrow. So I am happy to see you soon. Saturday is nearly gone. After finishing this letter I am going to have a bath and I think I am going to bed early tonight. So you know how it is to be really tired. I am glad being able to sleep till 7.30 tomorrow morning. There was something wrong with the phone this morning. I rung about 5 times but as soon as I lifted the receiver there was no answer. I expected your call and thought it might have been you. That's the reason I rung you. As you talked to Mr Pickering afterwards Mrs Brown (the lady you met on the road as you came the last time) asked me 'who's girl is it really.' Because he was speaking longer than I was. Didn't you hear me laughing.

I thank you very much for your letter I received yesterday morning. I checked up for you just now about the picture. 'The upturned glass' It was on in Leicester this week and it is on Monday as well. I just forgot which picture house it was. I'll see again and tell you tomorrow. As I heard 'Golden Earrings' should be very good. It was just what I wanted to see. I rather go to Leicester and see you than to Melton. What do you think about me coming one day next week? But I would be glad if you don't cancel our arrangement again.

I was laughing as I read in the letter about the haircut. Of course I had it before the photographs were taken. My mother wouldn't have known me otherwise. I stopped fasting on Wednesday so you need not being afraid of me looking like Ghandi. Or do you want me to look as he is looking now. Anyway I am trying to get to Melton in time for your bus. I hope the driver will stop till your bus is coming in. Alfred told me Mr Edwards is going to take the job as Camp Labour Officer in Saltby after closing and changing into a civilian hostel. He was not quite sure. Really it won't matter for me.

Now darling I would like to close and get my bath ready. I am waiting for tomorrow afternoon. We'll have a very nice time. So be good till tomorrow.

All my love and kisses

yours
Hans.

92 Wharf Street.
January 29th 1947.

My darling Hans

I expected a letter today, I thought you said I would get one on Thursday and one on Saturday. But when I got up this morning there wasn't any letter, maybe I will have one in the morning.

I have just been speaking to Gwenn (don't worry not the one at Thorpe Arnold). We've been on the phone for 1 ½ hours. She was cooking dinner for tonight and had a steamed pudding on the stove, we had been talking so long that all the water in the saucepan had boiled out, and that was the end of Gwenn's pudding.

I was informed by the girl at Melton office that you are coming in to see me. I had to laugh. Kathleen rang last night just after you and Alfred had left. She knows I've seen you so she was telling me what Alfred was like. She wanted me to ask Alfred what you said about the concert at Stathern. I said I would find out for her. So you had better tell me. By the way have you spent your sweet coupons if not you had better do it before Saturday that is the last day for this months rations. I washed my hair Tuesday night and painted my nails a deep red. I think your face would go blue if you could see them. Anyway I would hate you to miss anything so I will do them again for Sunday.

Look, darling this is a very short letter but I have been talking such a lot that I have not had much time left to write, so be good till I see you on Sunday.

All my love
Jean
___.

L.W.A.E.C Hostel

Stathern.
29<u>th</u> Jan. 1948.

My darling,

I am so sorry I couldn't write to you yesterday. Perhaps you know that Mr Sanders and 3 gentlemen from the Min of Ag went around the hostels. I finished at 12.00 as somebody rung me and told us that those men are coming here. So I had to stay and wait. After they'd gone I went for the bus. It was 2.15 I arrived in Melton 3.00 went to the barber and afterwards to the photographer. As I finished all this it was 5.30 and too late to ring you. The photograph kept me waiting for 1 hour. When I left the barber I met Alfred. He didn't expect me in Melton. He wanted to see Kath but didn't know where it was. So I showed him. We stayed for about 10 minutes and I really was surprised how curious people can be. She asked me about Stathern, about WLA (how many) and so on. I don't know where I learned joking. I think from you darling. I told her there are about 30 girls that makes one for every during one month time. Do you know what she said: "Hans, I really didn't expect you to be as bad as that!" Oh darling I couldn't help laughing. Then she asked me if I know Jean from Leicester. I said no, but I am going to invite her sometimes to Stathern, You know her always saying 'really'! Half past five I went to the picture. James Mason in "The Upturned Glass". I enjoyed it but it isn't the kind of picture I like. In all his picture he is cruel. So in this one he's killing a woman. Maybe you've seen it in Leicester.

So Kathleen said I'm getting fat. Am I really? I didn't notice it till now. I don't eat a lot. The warden had a word with me on Tuesday because I didn't eat a bit for nearly two days. He told me if I wouldn't eat he's going to ring you and tell you about it. So I'd to start again. I was just trying to stop eating. Ghandi can do it why can't I?

At this time I would've been on the bus to Leicester but I am looking forward for Sunday. Alfred told me he doesn't know what date Saltby will be closed? I really got a shock as I went to the photograph and ordered 6 passport photos. He charged 9/6. I expected about 5sh and was lucky taking all my money with me. Otherwise I couldn't have paid. Listen darling can you make your coming on Sunday as early as the last time? If you've any trouble at home come on the usual bus. I'll come then to Melton and see you ¾ of an hour earlier. Are you going to ring me on Saturday? I'll be good and won't see many land girls. So you just be the same till I see you on Sunday.

All my love and kisses
Always yours
Hans.

92 Wharf Street.

30th January.

My darling Hans

I'm glad you saw a good film. I have not seen "The Upturned Glass" I heard it was very good. If it ever comes to Leicester I will have to see it. I went to see a good picture, it was called "The Golden Earring", it was very funny. I know I told you there weren't any good pictures, but if we see that picture it is in Germany just before the war and the SS are after an Englishman that dresses up as a gipsy. It was very funny. I did not think it would be.

I won't know you now you've have had your hair cut. I hope you had your hair cut before you had your photograph taken. Another lecture. don't I natter? Are you eating more now. I don't want you looking like Ghandi, so you had better start eating more.

I will be coming to Stathern on the 1.30 bus from Leicester. It is too much of a rush to get the 12.30, with luck I may be able to get that 2.10 bus to Stathern. If you can't get to Melton don't worry. I will find my way.

I have been speaking to Alfred nearly every day. I think they are going to make Saltby a hostel very soon and from what Mr Barker (he is warden at Sutton Cheney) says Mr Goodman is going as warden to Saltby.

Anyway darling, I will be seeing you on Sunday, so till then I will say goodbye.

>   All my love
>   Jean

.

3/2.48 ## Aschersleben 11.1.48

>   30/1

My dear Hans

I have received your dear letter dated 19.12.47 with great pleasure and thanks. The post is very bad, as your dear parcel has not yet arrived. Let us hope it won't get lost, as it contains the scarves and socks. Ellen's parcel seems to have been too loosely wrapped. I have just returned home, it is 16.30 and I had to look after my customers. On Thursday my boss sent me to Halle to buy goods, but don't ask, it was a real hassle on the train, people are like wild ones. I had bought goods worth 600 Mark and you have to be so careful as the perfume bottles are so fragile and in no time at all you can lose 100 M. I shall start my new job in Darmstadt on February 1st, and it pains me to leave my current boss, but I am young and still have a lot to learn, as one day I would like to start my own business. The weather seems to be getting colder but hopefully the winter won't be too cold, as this month there has not as yet been any coal made available, and unless I can get something through the back, as it were, we shall be freezing. This evening I shall go dancing, and so as not to leave mum alone, the Rueckbrechts are coming over. Tonight we shall have hot chocolate, which is such a pleasure, but unfortunately it finishes so quickly – but there's enough for one more lot. No doubt you will soon be released and start your work, and you will have to leave your car behind. I shall send my letter in the same envelope as mums, as we are running out of envelopes and you have to be thrifty. Yes Germany, how far have you sunk! I hope Miss Jean is well, please send her my best regards. Soon the masked ball season is going to start here, when it's carte blanche for the craziest time and everybody goes mad. Last week I went to the theatre – they showed The Magic Violin. I can't get mum to go out, she says she will not go to the theatre in her wooden shoes, but it was truly wonderful. This week we shall go to the cinema to see 'Spaete Liebe' a rare occasion as normally they only show R films, which I'd rather not see. I hope to have a letter from you this week, and above all the parcel. Please write again soon and be receiving my best greetings from your brother Horst!

If only our dear Papa could be with us. I have a feeling though that he might soon return for a healthy Wiedersehen!

3/2.48   Aschersleben 11.1.48
                        30/1

    My dear Hans

Although I have not heard from you for a fortnight I am writing you my usual Sunday letter with much love. This evening the Rueckbrechts and the Timms are coming to visit, at least I won't be alone. Horst wants to go dancing, it's only two minutes away from us, he so loves dancing. Well, he doesn't have much else I guess. How is the weather where you are? Real winter hasn't set in here yet, which is just as well, as this month there will be no coal available, meaning we will have no heating and we'll have to eat everything uncooked. Dearest Hans, could you please buy us a washing line? It's so unpleasant to have to borrow even the smallest thing. We had to leave our beautiful big lines at home and

how urgently we need them! It really is time that important items start to get manufactured here, such as coffee
grinders, meat grinders, hammers, pliers, etc, as surely nobody likes borrowing. At the fair in Leipzig there were small
meat grinders, but where should this money come from,
they cost 120 marks. Have you been released yet? When
will the big day arrive? Let us hope that your second parcel,
sent on 24.12, will soon arrive – we are awaiting it every
day. I shall now end my letter for today, my dear Hans, as I
am about to make supper. Lots of love and kisses from your
mum and your brother Horst, he is also just writing. He can
get on one's nerves, and then he laughs his head off.
 To a healthy Wiedersehen

> 92 Wharf St.
> Feb 2nd 1948.

My darling Hans
I arrived home safely about 9.30, you know I had a seat all
the way. It was a German POW that stood up to let me sit
down. I rang Mr Pickering this morning, he wanted to know
what I had been doing on Sunday. He said you were not well
and that you had gone to bed. Now I'm going to ask you what
you ask me. 'What's the matter?' Mr Pickering asked me if I
saw his girlfriend when I got off the bus. I told him I got off
the bus at Abbey Park Rd. She hoped I would be able to walk
with her through the town. I think she is scared of the little
man that is going about Leicester.
Kathleen has been told off for talking to the girls in Leicester. Mr Scott reported her to Mr MacHardy so now she is
going to the Land drainage Department.
2 Germans have been here today, one of them came in to ask
what time it was. I told him he meant (I can't spell the German for 'what is the time') then he wanted to know where
I learnt Duchland I told him that was all I knew, I could not
tell him the rest of the half dozen could I?
I still have not got a name for my pup (little dog). Betty calls

him Joe but my mother does not like it.

It is nearly time to go so darling I will have to say cheeri'O and please take care of yourself. I hope you feel better this morning.

All my love

Jean

<u>25</u>

L.W.A.E.C Hostel.
Stathern.
Jan. 30<u>th</u> 1948.

My darling Jean

If you speak to Gwenn the next time tell her to put more water into the saucepan to avoid the water boiling out whilst being talking. You should have told her your old saying: 'it only happens once in lifetime.' I always remember it when anything is going wrong. So she needs not to worry about that.

Just what I expected Kath to do. I was dead sure she would ring you as soon as we left the office. Isn't it funny? That was the only reason I went with Alfred. What about a concert in Stathern. I didn't say a word about it for there is no concert in Stathern. A village like this isn't able to give a concert. The people from here have to go to the next villages for a dance, She hears more than anyone of us said. Do you think I wouldn't tell you first? If there would be a concert I would go with you and nobody else.

I gave my sweet coupons away because I have not enough money this week to buy them myself. I think I'll get my first money tonight. It's payday anyway.

I just came back from Melton Mr Coy told me last night to go to the Labour Exchange for my National Health and Unemployment cards. He picked me up this morning and brought me back again. So this letter will be short for I still have the fish to do and it is 3.00

Friday is our fish day. It doesn't mean much work but it is to be done in time. It is only two more days till Sunday darling. I'll rush down now to the post office and post it. I don't know yet whether I go to the pictures tonight or not. I've to get tomorrow's breakfast ready tonight.

So be good darling till Sunday

All my love and kisses

Always yours

Hans.

26

L.W.A.E.C Hostel.
Stathern.

Feb 2<u>nd</u> 1948.

My darling Jean,

I am very sorry you rung this morning and I wasn't here. I got up at the usual time and felt dead tired. So I finished the potatoes after breakfast and went upstairs again for a few more hours sleep. As I came down at 12.00 Mr Pickering told me he was speaking to you. I wonder what nonsense he asked you. He told me he was pulling you a leg. I hope you arrived home safe last night. I did. We arrived here at 10 o'clock. After doing the sandwiches I went to bed just after 11.00.

Did you notice Kath getting off the Leicester bus last night? She was on the second one.

Well darling I thank you very much for the most enjoyable afternoon. I only wish you could come every Sunday. I nearly fell asleep on the way back. And so did Mr Pickering. He kept asking me how far is it to Stathern? Anyway I am looking forward now for Thursday. I am sorry you forgot to take the eggs along but don't worry I'll bring them on Thursday. Did you check up about the pictures? I hope there'll be a nice one. If not it doesn't matter. The main reason of my coming is always to see you. I didn't know what you meant about that man going around in Leicester. I remember now. I read something in the paper. Darling of course I don't want you to meet him, I only said so because I didn't know what you're talking about. Please be careful when you go out at night. See that somebody is going with you. If there would be a later bus or train back to Melton I certainly would've brought you back.

Do I get your letter tomorrow morning? Please darling. I hope you have posted yours already at this time. I've to hurry now to the post office to post this one. I want you to get it tomorrow. You'll get another one on Wednesday.

So be good darling and remember what I told you yesterday. God bless you.

All my love and kisses
Always yours
Hans.

27

L.W.A.E.C Hostel.
Stathern.

Feb 3rd 1948.

My darling Jean

I thank you very much for your letter I got half an hour ago. Don't be surprised darling. I am going to answer at once for Mr Pickering shall take the letter to Melton when he goes out at dinner time. I am glad you arrived home safely. A POW gave his seat for you? It was very nice of him, of course every man would've done it.

No wonder Kathleen was told off for talking too much. Her conversations most times ended after a two hours talk. So you had two visitors yesterday. I also wonder where you leaned your German!! Did you buy a dictionary? By the way a little correction. Don't say you leaned Deutschland (that's spelt right). Deutschland means the country. The language is called Deutsch – German. You hardly could tell him the rest of the words you know, except yes and no.

You haven't got a name for your pup yet. So I'll help you then. If you like it, call him Johnny. Nice, isn't it?!!! That's the name of my cat in Saltby. Maybe it is alright for a dog as well. If you're interested I'll write the translation for 'what time is it?' down. It is 'wie spät ist es.'

I was lucky this morning getting two more letters besides yours. One from my mother and one from my brother. He is always joking. I noticed something stiff inside like a big photograph. I opened it and found one. But not from him. It was a picture showing a girl and a man talking. He told me in the letter he saw it in a shop window and bought it because he found it very nice and just right for me. I couldn't help laughing. You should see the addresses on the letters. I wonder how the post found this place, but it is the first time they wrote this address.

I hope I'll get your letter tomorrow morning to know about the pictures. My photographs didn't arrive this morning. So the warden is going to have a look when he goes to Melton today. My mother and brother send many, many greetings to you.

So darling be good till I see you on Thursday. Do you finish a bit earlier or shall I have to wait til 5.15?

I'll say cheerio now and beg you to think of me.

All my love and kisses

Always yours

Hans.

R 24/2   **Aschersleben 17.1.48**

3/2

My dear Hans

I would like to thank you very much for your letter dated 29.12.47 which gave me great pleasure. I'm always so happy when I receive post from you, just a shame that the mail is so slow. The weather is spring-like, it looks as though everything will be green soon. I have just returned home, I have had a client who needed a water wave, you see my work never ends. On Thursday begins our special training, water wave and undulation, there will be around 25 participants. The course is 11 weeks long and I'm really looking forward to it. Today we received your letter about your new job, especially as 'chef', I can imagine it must be good to cook if all you have to do is help yourself to ingredients. If you were to get a job as a cook here, you would first have to go to evening classes to retrain in preparing post-war recipes allowing for lack of ingredients. I was really delighted to hear that you have two rooms, at least like that you and Jean can be together in peace and quiet having coffee and talking. However your working hours seem to be pretty long, so please do not work too hard and look after yourself a little. Was the concert at the camp organised and performed by the German prisoners? Dear Hans please do not be surprised if mum and I are coming to England to visit you. We have become globetrotters, and nobody is safe from us. Tomorrow evening I shall go out dancing again, as far as I'm concerned I would go every night, but mum makes sure I don't go too often. Life here is monotonous, every day the same. If only our dear Papa would make himself heard, but hopefully he will arrive soon. Dear Hans it does not sound as though you are employed as an interpreter, or maybe that will be later on? Anyway, being a chef is also very nice. In a fortnight I shall start my job in the ladies' department, I'm just really keen to learn as much as possible, because once you've learnt something nobody can take it away from you. Have you been discharged yet? Tomorrow I shall wash and set mum's hair. Dear Hans, I am enclosing a postcard I really like. We are both well and cheerful. Many good wishes for Miss Jean, and now, my dear Hans, I shall close this letter. Our best wishes from your brother Horst and mum, here's to a healthy and imminent Wiedersehen. Please write soon.

R 3/2.48   Aschersleben 18.1.48

cribe.

My dear Hans

Thank you for your letter dated 3.1.48. Well, you are now a chef? How did you get this job? It is definitely not a bad job, at least I know you won't be starving, but a fifteen hour day is pretty long! Does that mean you will not be getting the post as interpreter which was promised to you? At least you won't be far away from Jean? You also have a nice abode, which is great. If it wasn't so far away, there would be room for all three of us. If it was in the Western zone, it would be not bad at all. Jean will be pleased that you are still near her. Have you actually been released yet? Now it is Sunday again, and we are having a nice supper. Horst was given half a pound of butter by the Hohls, isn't that nice? I have baked us some poppyseed rolls, and we shall have the last of the hot chocolate. I've been looking forward to supper all day. They are all such rare treats, Winter still hasn't set in, just as well considering the heating. It sounds as though you were very restrained on New Years Eve. We thank Jean very much for her greetings and respond with the same, with all our hearts. On Friday I spent another few hours queuing at the Provisions Office, there were applications for underwear and aprons, but as I got to the staircase everything was gone already. We have now been here for two years and have received nothing apart from a few pairs of underpants and a few socks. If only there would be a dress or a summer coat, so one didn't have to walk around in the same cardigan weekdays as well as Sundays. I have had Ellen's shoes adjusted, just a pity that one of the heal leathers is so worn. It really is too sad that we have to live like beggars. Your parcel has not arrived yet, let's hope it comes soon. Dear Hans, maybe soon you'll send us a lovely picture of yourself? And of Jean? You can imagine how curious we are. Can you perhaps get some shaving soap for Horst? His beard is growing, and his skin is so sensitive. Please stay well. Lots of love and kisses from your mum and your brother Horst.

92 Wharf St.
Feb 4th 1948.

My darling Hans

I thank you very much for your letter and for the lesson in German, learning what to say will be hard enough. I think spelling German will be beyond me.

I am glad you have heard from your mother and brother, you will have to show me the card your brother sent you. You will have to write your address more clearly. When you answer the letters, give my love to them.

About tomorrow. I will not be able to leave early. We can go to see. 'It always rains on Sunday' it begins at 5.20 so if you meet me outside the Odeon (that is the place we went to last time). I had better give you a map just in case you have forgotten where to go.

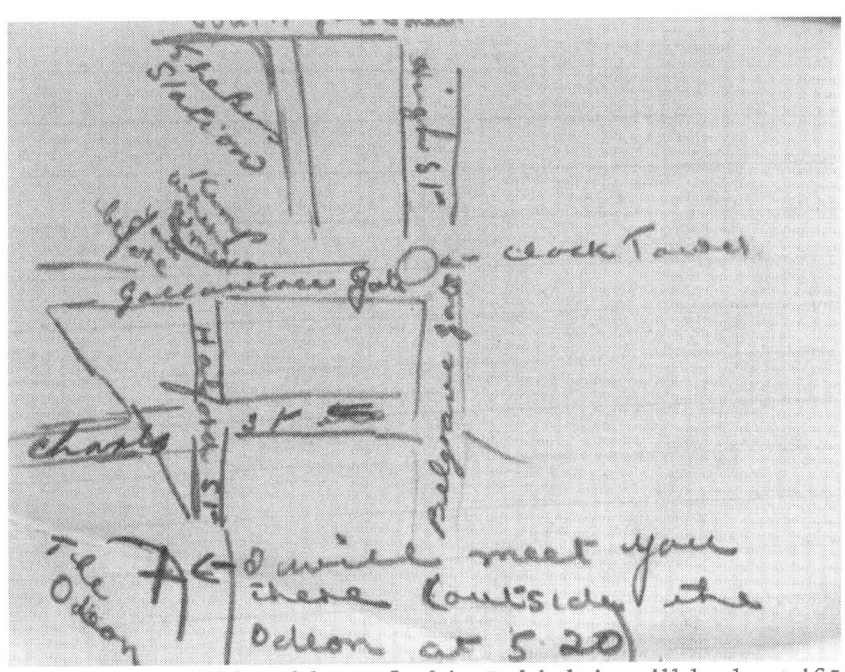

I hope you will be able to find it. I think it will be best if I meet you there because I can get down there in 5 minutes. Then we will be able to see all the picture. You see I have not cancelled our date. Are you surprised? So darling I will see you tomorrow. I will see you outside the pictures, The Odeon. I have put that again so there's no mistake.

All my love

Jean

.

28   LWAEC Hostel,
Stathern.
Feb. 6th 1948.

My darling Jean,

Another morning's gone. I arrived back safely at 10.30 and you don't suppose how tired I was. Mr Pickering was waiting for me. I had something to eat and went to bed at once. I felt rotten. It didn't take me longer than a few seconds till I fell asleep. Anyway I feel a lot better this morning.

Wasn't it a terrible afternoon yesterday? I think the title of picture was wrong. It should have been It keeps raining every day! You know I don't mind rain. I walked around the town from 4.00 till 5.00, the streets deserted and the rain running down my face. That maybe the reason I had a headache from as I went on to the bus.

I haven't rung Alfred yet and I am not sure if I invite him for Sunday. I think I better take the afternoon off and have a rest. I really need it. I don't know what you are going to do on Sunday. Perhaps a little tea party? Drink a cup for me will you? I hope you'll enjoy yourself. Anyway I'm not going out.

Nearly everything is going wrong today. I just remembered that we are going to have peas for dinner. I hope they'll be ready till 6.00. There is fish in the oven and the oven is still stone cold. Heaven may help me with the dinner. But I don't worry if it is not ready. Everything happens once in lifetime. Now darling let me finish. I'll write a long letter on Sunday. Have a good weekend and think of me.

Be good and all my love and kisses. Always yours
Hans.

PS Were the eggs alright?
HK.

92 Wharf St.
Feb 6th 1948.
My dear Hans
I hope you arrived home safe last night, it was about 8.50 when I arrived home. I had my supper and I was in bed by 10.0. I have to get up early now to put the dog out but so far I have been too late.

I have been speaking to Alfred this morning, he asked me if you had been to Leicester. I told him you were going to ring him sometime today so he said he would call you. I did not ring him. I had to get him for the Labour Dept so I did not have an excuse.

I spoke to Mr Bodymore today. He asked me if I was going to Stathern. when I said I wasn't, he wanted to know what was the matter and why wasn't I going. He said "I suppose you will be becoming a Frau soon." I said "what do you think?" He wanted to know how much German I know, I joked and told him I spoke German very well. Then I heard the cook 'man' speaking in German so I told him not to tell to him I didn't know a word.

I am staying in tonight. I may wash my hair and nurse the pup. He's just like a baby, every time I sit down he wants to come on my knee, he will be very spoilt, my mother is just as daft with him, she makes hot milk for him in the morning.

I will say cheerio. I want to go upstairs to see Connie. I think she has got tomorrow off. My pen has run out of ink again and it still leaks. I will have to take it in to have it repaired sometime.

Have a good weekend darling and don't do anything I wouldn't.

All my love and kisses

Jean

..

92 Wharf St.

Saturday 9.45pm 7.2.48.

My dearest Hans

I have just finished cleaning out. I have had a bath and now I am writing to you. My mother has gone out and my sister has gone home so I am all on my own, well not quite, the pup is with me, he's sitting on my knee, he's getting a little devil now. He has been chasing the cat around (the cat belongs next, door my auntie has shut it out). I rang Dora this morning to see if she was going to the pictures, but she was going out. I was glad really because I did not feel like going to the pictures and I have got rather a lot done tonight. Alice and Dora are coming to tea tomorrow. I could have gone round to Alice's tonight, she usually stays in Saturday night (I have the cat and dog on my knee now).

I don't think I will be going to Gaddesby. I may meet a strange German POW in Grantham or London, but I would not go to a strange men's hostel. When I met the POW I knew it was safe. Gaddesby is not the only place I have had an invitation to go to. I have had one from Ashby, Shelbrook hostel. Mr Marshall says I hold the world record for holding a man off with a poll 19 miles long (that is the distance from Leicester to Ashby de la Zouch). Then there is Mr Barker, he's at Sutton Cheney hostel. He is always asking me to go out there. He has three sons, one is 26. I go in for older men. I won 2/6 this morning. A gentleman that rings up quite often from the Air Ministry at Grantham bet me 2/6 that Mr Hodgson was not in. He was, and I won 2/6. He wanted to make the bet that we should go out to dinner one night. I told him there was no bet in that case. You know I would not go anywhere like that or to any other hostel except Stathern.

I was going to ring you this morning but you beat me to it. You ought to save your money. I would have rung you sometime in the morning. I hope Alfred comes tomorrow and that you have a very nice weekend. My sister has asked me to go to tea next Sunday. I will try and get out of it if I can. I told my mother who I had been to the pictures with on Thursday, all she said was "what time does the last bus go back to Stathern" but she must have told my sister because she wanted to know all the ins and outs.

I have to say cheeri'O now darling and good night and God bless.

All my love
Jean

R. 7/2.48   Aschersleben 20/1/48

7/2

My dear Hans

Today I am writing you a few lines and tell you some news. We have been reckless and bought ourselves a radio. What do you say to that? Mrs Klingebeil from Soldin got it for us, her brother in law works for the company in Berlin, otherwise it would have been impossible to get one. In any event we love it and it means we are no longer so lonely. We have been without a radio for three years. Just now beautiful music is being played. It is a small 3 valve Lorenz, but the sound is wonderful. Can you imagine how much it cost? Please sit down, it was 700 Mark, practically all we've got, we have thought about it a lot, as here there is lots of talk about a new currency, so, in case we were to lose our few saved pennies we thought it better to invest them in a valuable object. And it does give us real pleasure. We shall now save really carefully and buy ourselves and electric iron. It is supposed to cost 250 Mark. They are all crazy prices. Today we had another surprise. We received a parcel from Uncle Gustav containing stuff from the slaughtering of his pig. It contained a liver sausage, a three and a half pound piece of pork for roasting, and a lung, plus one pound of semolina. Isn't that wonderful? I had sent them four cups which I had in Thuringia, because Aunt Erna wrote that they do not even have a cup for each of them and they could not find any. They were so pleased with them. That way we all help each other. If we refugees don't help each other, nobody else will. Horst has gone to see the doctor; he often has heart problems. Let us hope it is nothing serious, I so worry about him.

The doctor did a very thorough examination, there is nothing wrong with his heart, he just seems to have grown too

263

rapidly, and because of this his internal organs have remained a little bit behind. He will have to have an x-ray
of his lung. The main issue is that of health. My dear Hans,
love and kisses from your mum and your brother Horst. To a
healthy Wiedersehen

<u>29</u>

L.W.A.E.C Hostel.
Stathern.

Feb 7<u>th</u> 1948.

My darling Jean

Thank you very much for your letter I received this morning. It is now 6.00pm. The Saturday is nearly over. I am quite
comfortable in the kitchen tonight. I took the wardens wireless down here, have a German sender on with nice waltz
music. I know something better, you being with me, for instance. Then everything would be perfect. But I'll be on my
own tomorrow. I was speaking to Alfred for the last half an
hour. He accepted an invitation to Melton yesterday. And so
I've had it. So I'll be able to have my badly needed rest. The
warden is gone to Leicester this afternoon and the porter has
the day off. It is very quiet because there are only two men
in. Nice isn't it? I wonder what you are doing now. Look darling you need no excuse for ringing Alfred. Do you think I'm
jealous? I know I can always trust you and you told me so
didn't you?

Mr Bodymore seems as if he likes fun. Don't worry darling
one day you'll find that our language isn't as difficult as you
think. You should've heard me as I started to learn English.
I was afraid of myself talking to anybody, however I noticed
that it turned better from time to time. You know yourself
how it is at present. Still bad I think. Everybody is noticing
I'm a German except my own fellows. As I came back on
Thursday night there were two fellows sitting besides me.

One of them asked me what time it was and I promptly answered in English. At the Melton station I met somebody from Saltby he was talking with. Then he was indeed very astonished. You know I'd that raincoat on. So he couldn't make me out.

I would like to see your little pup. You may bring the next Sunday if you like. I don't mind. If the weather is nice we may have a little walk around and take him along.

It is now nearly time to prepare the supper. And there with, the Saturday ends for me. Did I tell you Friday was an unlucky day for me? I told you already about not getting the oven hot. After dinner I was boxing with Mr P, slip in front of the stove and fell with the right arm on the hot plate. The success was I burned my arm badly. I hope it'll be alright till I see you next week.

After finishing this letter I'll do the sandwiches, then the tea and have a rest afterwards. Now darling let me tell you how I feel today. I am very lonely, longing for you, but I'll have to wait another three days at least. I hope those days will pass very quick. It is only a week till I see you here again.

Well, my little sweetheart, I'll like to close now. Be good and all my love and kisses always yours.

> Hans.

30

L.W.A.E.C Hostel.
Stathern.
8.2.48.

My darling Jean

Thanks so much for your long letter I received this morning I hope you have got my letter this morning too. I took your advice and had an hour's walk last night. I went out at 5.30 and came back 6.30. That means half the way to Saltby and back. On my own, of course. As I came back I met one of my fellows from Redmile and talked to him for half an hour. I hope I'll be able to do it now every night.

So you're on your own Saturday afternoon too. Mr Shilton and somebody from London have been here and left half an hour ago. There're a lot of visitors coming lately.

I am glad to hear you're not going to Gaddesby. It really surprised me how many invitations you've got. No wonder you refused to come to Saltby as I asked you first!! I am also glad to hear that you feel safe when you meet POWs.

You are always lucky in winning something! I tried for the last few week on the football pool but without success. For this season (4 weeks) I've got Leicester City but I am sorry to say there is not any much chance for me. They've lost the first match yesterday already.

Please darling fulfil my wish and come next Sunday. Try to get out of that tea party of your sisters. You know yourself how much I am waiting for those days. It's very nice of you telling your mother who you went to the pictures with. She seems to become interested and that's what we want, isn't it darling? Don't worry if your sister asked you about, tell them the truth. The sooner the better, but I'll leave everything to you. You know how much I trust you.

I hope you'll tell me in your next letter what day suits you best this week. Find out where there is a nice picture. I think the film Maryland should be good. Anyway I'll leave it to you.

It is 3.30 so I'll have to post your letter. Be good my darling and think of me.

All my love and kisses yours
Hans.

Replied 9.2.48.   Prenzlau. 11.1.48
Dear Hans   9/2.

Today is Sunday. A silence surrounds me, which puts me in the mood of writing to you. I have already answered your previous letter. Unfortunately, I was not in a very rational state of mind and I should not really have written to you at that time.

This is the first real Sunday I have since I have been back. My relatives are at a meeting. I have to look after the house and the animals. When I look out of my window I can enjoy this lovely view of a dung heap. From time to time a goose looks into the window. It would climb on to the kennel below the window. I am sure you can get the picture of what it looks like around me. As dawn comes, I have to feed the animals: 3 cows and 4 young cattle. They all need good portions of fodder. A few days ago I plucked up the courage to milk a cow. My hands are still hurting but I am sure it will get better soon. You can see that I have all the best intentions to come to terms with my situation. If only I could be satisfied. You wanted to set a limit in your last letter. Hans, I felt it. I assume my letter was too open for you which prompted you to restrict me somewhat. Why don't you come home? What keeps you there? I do not know this country in which you live, nor do I know the people and cannot judge you. You prefer to live there in peace, relative security and have a satisfactory income instead of coming home. This is not meant to be a reproach. You will know what is good for you and why you are doing this. We can only describe our fatherland as a poor country. I can understand that you are not longing to get back. I would have gone from here too if I were not bound to stay. I would love to live in the Harz Mountains. I particularly loved being where Marga lives. Also all my friends have moved over to the West. Well, I have to be patient for one more year and not to give up hope, and my belief in you until you come back to me. Yes, I want to tell you everything that happened and then, maybe afterwards I can bear everything better. But one year is a long time. Your letter sounds very discouraging. It is harsh, when one has dreamt of a happy future and it turns into the rough and meaningless reality one has to bear. Nothing would matter to me, I could accept the hard work I have never been used to, if my marriage were based on a good foundation. But I am suffering again and again due to these disappointments. Nevertheless, it is my fate. Little by little, when I stop fighting against it, I will be completely and utterly dull. I am still young and try to fight back.

Manfred got engaged at Christmas. Mum did not want to

know anything about it but I told her that everyone should be allowed to make their own decisions. He is 19 years old. When you are young, the whole wide world is before you. Otherwise nothing has changed here. I don't know yet when I will have my operation.

Wishing you all the best and sending my greetings Vera.

92 Wharf St.
February 10th.

My darling Hans

Thank you very much for both your letters. It was a nice surprise. I also had a letter from Bernhard this morning, he said when I see you I was to give you his greetings and best wishes for your staying in the UK. Bernhard said he had been to see his mother who lives in Berlin, he said he felt like a repatriated POW again (I do not know what that feeling is) when he was going through the Russian zone to Berlin. It is very strict on passports and luggage. He has seen for himself now.

I think I shall be coming on Sunday but if I do I don't think I will not bring the pup. I will bring him in the spring when the weather is nicer. Do you mind if I do not see you in the week because I have promised Alice I would go to tea Wednesday night. I will be seeing you on Sunday, that is only 4 days off, so darling, it is not very long.

I am using Iris's notepaper and writing this at work. I was going to write last night but was too fed up and tired.

I did not tell you what I did on Sunday, well I'll tell you. I got up at 7.40, I had to, the pup was barking. I dusted round and then went for a walk in the morning. After lunch I stayed in and waited for Dora and Alice to come, that is all I did.

I have brought my knitting to do at work in the hope that I may get my jumper done, so I will say cheerio darling and get on with it. So be good, and don't be too annoyed about coming to Leicester in the week.

All my love
Jean

.

92 Wharf St.
Feb 12th 1948.

My dearest Hans

It was a very nice surprise to hear you yesterday afternoon, almost like old times. I thought you were pulling my leg when you said Saltby Camp Labour office. At first I thought maybe you had gone back to work in the Labour Office. Did you enjoy your afternoon out and have got over your long cycle ride? Hasn't it been a lovely day today when it's like this I get so fed up of sitting here. I would like to be at Croxton. I don't know what Stathern is like, I have only seen it from the bus but I don't think it is as pretty as Croxton is. Do you think we might go to Belvoir Gardens this spring or summer, it would be a nice walk?

I went out to eat last night at Alice's, her brother who is in the peace time RAF came home on leave with his wife. She was saying they are back learning German. He is stationed at Weybridge near Ipswich, they have a little cottage 12 miles from the sea (just what we want). Anyway to get back to what I was telling you, they entertain a POW every Sunday, so his wife and I had a lot to talk about, and from what she said about learning German I don't think I will get past the first ½ dozen words I know. I think they had better make a new order in Germany that everyone learns English. don't you?

You would have laughed this afternoon. Iris goes with a boy from Radcliffe on Trent, Nottingham. She is going to see him tonight and she was to have rung him this afternoon at 2.0 to say she was going but she forgot all about it till a few minutes ago. She nearly went to Nottingham without telling him she was going.

This was going to be a long letter but the German from Staughton has been in to see us (I didn't learn any German). I will write again on Friday so till then be good.

All my love

Jean

.

<u>31</u>

L.W.A.E.C Hostel.

Stathern.

12<u>th</u> Febr 1948.

My darling Jean,

I thank you so much for your letter. As I got in on Wednesday morning I told the warden that I wanted the afternoon off. I wasn't annoyed because you couldn't see me. The Sunday is not far off and I at least spoke to you on the phone. Taking your advice I'd some exercise. It was such a nice day (except the evening) to have a ride on the bicycle. I made the 12 miles in one hour and 5 minutes. Not bad, is it? Mr Edwards came in the afternoon and I sat on my old place as I saw him coming. He opened the door and went to his table before noticing me. Then he was surprised seeing me in Saltby. Not long after that Mr Shilton, Mr Wrightmann and another gentleman came and Mr Edwards went around the camp with them. So I'd a chance to ring you. Later in the afternoon I went with Mr E. down to Melton and drove a lorry from the garage back to the camp. About half past five I took another lorry back to Stathern. And I was lucky for it was raining hard. I just came in time for my dinner and found everybody working (eating). One of my fellows came with me and drove the lorry back to Saltby.

I am coming to Melton then on Sunday and I hope the bus driver will wait again. It is better and gives us another ¾ of an hour. What was it as I rung you yesterday? Was Lucy

270

standing by and listening? I'll be a mysterious person to her. When she is listening again next tell her it's Santa Claus. Maybe she's satisfied then. Your little pup is just right getting you out of bed at 7.40. That's early to get up on Sunday isn't it?

That's the right way to do your knitting. Can you manage the switchboard and the knitting at the same time. If not I'll come over and give you a hand. Listen darling isn't there a possibility once to come early on Sunday and have dinner with me? Tell your mother why I would like you to come earlier and I am sure she wouldn't mind. Please darling, try to come earlier and let me know on Saturday morning.

Now darling let me finish. Time is getting on and I still have to do my dinner. My mother sends the best greetings. So cheerio now and be good.

All my love and kisses
Yours
Hans.

R. 17/2   Aschersleben 25.1.48

12.2

My dear Hans

We are sending you many Sunday greetings. Unfortunately, we did not receive any mail from you during the past week. Also, your parcel has not yet arrived – it has now been en route for two months, but then that from Miss Ellen took nine weeks to arrive. Have you thanked her from us – I asked you to do that a fortnight ago! Today the weather is horrid and foggy. In the morning I went to church and in the afternoon we both went to Mrs Klingebeil for a birthday coffee. There was even coffee made from real beans. Fantastic! She brought it back from Berlin – it cost 530 Mark. That is not something us mere mortals can afford, we do not have that kind of cash. Horst would have to work for about five months in order to earn that kind of money. She also brought back some cocoa, half a pound cost 250 Mark – clearly phenomenal prices. Horst has just gone dancing, he has been looking forward to it all week. Well, he is of course welcome to it, but he is only allowed to go on Sunday nights, and I make sure that he looks after his health, bearing in mind the kind of food served there. He does listen and he knows I only want the best for him. On Thursday he started his course – you can imagine how excited he is – he completely lives for his work. He is part of the A team on his course, meaning he is one of the six best participants. He really makes a big effort to move on. Our radio provides a lot of beautiful entertainment, it is something so wonderful which we have had to do without for so long. Do you have the opportunity to listen to the radio? And how is your new job? Do you not have an assistant? And have you met Jean's mother? And does she have siblings? I always want to know lots of things, don't I? As we cannot discuss things in person, one has to ask about this and that in letters. Let us hope that next week we receive mail from you, and also finally your parcel. Now my dear boy stay well, best wishes to Jean and special love and kisses from your mum and your brother Horst

Here's to a healthy Wiedersehen

r. 24/2   Aschersleben 31.1.48

12/2

My dear Hans

As I have not heard from you for a long time, I am sending you some greetings today. Your dear letter dated 15.1.48 arrived today – thank you very much. Today was my last day with my current boss – on Monday I will start my new job. It was difficult for me to leave there, as the work was good, And I miss the ladies' department. Our evening courses have now started and I am really enjoying myself – one learns so much and the man who manages it is the most famous hairdresser, Herr Hoermann, a ladies hairdresser. I should have started in their salon, but I had already agreed to take on the job, so could not cancel. How are you anyway, and as far as I understand you you are not too far away from Jean ? Is the temperature as mild as it is here where you are? Today it was 10 degrees Celsius, but we can put up with it because there is no coal. Please forgive the bad handwriting, today we had so much work that my hand is shaking. Your dear parcel has not arrived yet, we wait for it every day. The post is very slow. Hans, how about a four-week holiday, currently some people are here on holiday from France, but I do not know if the same applies to England. It would be so nice to see each other again. Dear Hans did you remember the decorative hair ornaments and the combs? Or maybe you did not receive my letter? In March there will be a great hairdressing competition in Halle, and four submissions have been requested from Aschersleben. I would so much like to participate, and it may be possible, but ornaments are missing. I shall make a big effort and practise. What do you say about us having bought a radio? Tonight they are broadcasting some brisk dance tunes, that's what I like. You cannot imagine how much I love dancing, but clearly this is not of the most importance. Dear Hans, do they sell strong hair pins, grips and styling brushes, these are things we really cannot find here. I do not want to trouble you with these things, but you really cannot find them here. Please do not be cross. I will now close this letter and please give my best wishes to Jean, with love from your brother Horst and mum. Here's to a healthy Wiedersehen

R 17/2   Aschersleben, 1.2.48

12.2

  My dear Hans
After two weeks, we finally received your letter dated

15.1.48. We were very pleased to hear from you again. This constant waiting is very painful for me! Whenever the post does come and I know you are well, I am always happy again! My! – you received a lot of post from us all in one go. It would be much nicer, if the pleasure of receiving mail is spread evenly over a period. I wonder if you have been discharged in the meantime? This means that you are entering into an entirely new phase in your life, and we are sending you, my dear boy, all our love and best wishes for the future. I'll be thinking of you. Will you be staying there and carry on with your Chef's duties, or do you want to work as an interpreter? I am sure you know what you want to do next! I can well believe that you are enjoying the cooking. The main thing is you have all the ingredients you need. I can't say that I always feel like cooking, because I have to rack my brain as to 'what can I do' as we get very little fat here! For this decade we were allocated syrup instead of fat. Horst is suffering from terrible bouts of heartburn. He mustn't eat so much syrup and I am already toasting the bread for him. Well, it does not help to bend over the clients all day long. I am so grateful that Horst does not have any problems with his lungs! He had a chest X-Ray on Wednesday! I am always quite worried about this, he really shot up too fast and his organs were unable to keep up with it! Lots of people now have TB. Dear Hans, we heard from Frida recently and she is sending her love to you. Would you send us some tea too, and can I give her some? As you know she lives in East Frisia where they cannot live without tea. They part with their last bit of fat in exchange for some tea! If I send some tea to her, she will give us fat! It would be such a help to us, but I don't know if you can easily buy it and whether it is very expensive. It is lovely to know that your written English is very good now. I am sure it is of a great advantage to you. Yes, you should buy yourself a suit because you can't wear the same clothes all the time. You want to feel 'human' again. Just buy whatever you can get, which is something we cannot do here. Would you be able to send us some cocoa and stock cubes? We would love to have some more. Mrs. Schulz also received another parcel from her husband. He sent a blue suit to himself, 1 pound coffee and cocoa, sewing thread, and for her a most beautiful pair of shoes. He often sees a family, where one of them is a teacher, and they help him a lot. I can get the ring for you but I have to take some silver to the jeweller, which I don't have, so I shall give them syrup and - Bob's your uncle! I finally managed to obtain a hammer! Do you have any of those small mats for the table which shine and can be wiped clean? We use newspaper sheets instead of a mat.

Please keep well and we are sending you our love and kisses, your mum and brother Horst.

Please give our warmest wishes to Jean. Here's to a healthy reunion.

Exactly three years ago today was the dreadful day when our homeland was taken from us!

32

L.W.A.E.C Hostel.
Stathern.
Feb 13th 1948.

My darling Jean

Thank you very much for the nice letter I got today. I really slept very well after the cycle ride. I can't complain about the other nights. People could carry me away and I wouldn't notice. That is a very sound sleep indeed.

Isn't the weather getting nice this afternoon I also don't feel like work on such a nice day, but as you know I've to. Otherwise the men would kill me when they come home and there is no dinner.

Croxton is very nice but I think it's much nicer round Belvoir Castle. There are lovely places for picknick. We'll certainly go there as soon as the weather condition allows it. Didn't I tell you not to be afraid of learning German. Many people have done it successful. It just wants a bit of understanding and practice and I think you can have both. I'll help you with it. So you'd a lot to talk about entertaining POWs. Don't forget darling there's a civilian who wants some entertainment!! I'll like your idea about everyone learning English. It really would be nice if all people speak the same language.

I see for men from Stoughton it seems to be allowed to come to the showroom but not for a poor man from Stathern. He's to walk around Leicester for one hour till he gets wet through. Don't worry darling he doesn't mind.

It'll be a busy afternoon today, fish and that takes some work. Besides that I've got to get the leeks ready for tomorrow. It is now half past two so darling I hope you don't mind when I close now. I'll write a letter tomorrow afternoon for you when you come on Sunday. Don't forget to try what I begged you for.

So be good my sweetheart till Sunday. I'll think of you all the time.

All my love and kisses
Yours
Hans.

Belvoir Castle

P.S. I hope I have not
missed any words out
JP.
     92 Wharf St.
     Feb 14th 1948.

My darling

I am writing this letter in a hurry again, as you can tell by my writing. It is getting late, at least it is late to me 10.30. I wasn't going out tonight as Dora was going to the dentists again and I was going to stay in and do my odd jobs, but when I got home this evening my mother said she was going to see my cousin so I went with her. You see my cousin is going to Germany next Thursday she is joining her husband. She doesn't want to go very much. Her husband has 7 years more to do in the army. They have been married 6 years, and they do not have a home, so she really has to go otherwise her husband will be an old man before they have a home. She has a daughter 1 years old, she is going too. You would think she would want to stay here with the baby.

As you know I had to stand up, there wasn't any POW to stand for me, I did not mind. It does not bother me having to stand. Anyway I got a seat after a while. I arrived home at 9.30, took the dog a walk then I went to bed at 10.30.

About Wednesday I think you had better meet me outside the Gaumont better known as the City picture house. I had better draw a plan, it is in the market place. The picture begins at 5.15, so if you meet me, I will see if I can leave 5 minutes early. I hope you can understand the map. I will say goodnight and God bless and not forgetting the kisses.

All my love
Jean

33   Same address.

Saturday 14th Feb 1948.

Darling

I'm sitting in the kitchen and counting the hours till tomorrow. Exactly 19 hrs 10 minutes, 25 sec not too long is it? I expected your call this morning and I was very glad as you told me you were leaving on the 12.30 bus, but I was sorry to hear then that it was a mistake. I don't mind darling and I told you only to try it.

By the way I think I'll be able to buy my suit next weekend. I only want next weeks pay and that makes £11. Don't you think that's enough? I think I better go to Leicester one day next week and have a look around. Melton seems not to be the right place.

I wonder what was the matter as you rung me up. You're speaking so low. Was somebody else there to learn you a few more words? My first thought was you'd a cold.

I was busy this afternoon making some tarts for us and the warden but he just got a call that his girlfriend is not coming. I've told him how sorry I feel for him. I am so glad I'll be luckier tomorrow. Now darling I'd like to say cheerio I have to get the brussels ready for tomorrow dinner. Be good darling and all my love and kisses.

Yours for ever

Hans

<u>34</u>

L.W.A.E.C Hostel.
Stathern.
Feb 16<u>th</u> 1948.

My darling

I am so sorry the Sunday is over. I thank you very, very much for your coming. My only wish is the time shouldn't pass so quick. I always feel like being home when you're with me. So you know what I am always thinking about? You're coming one day and stay for good, but I am afraid I've to wait some time. How did you get home darling? I watched you as you're standing on the bus and you looked so tired. I felt very sorry for you. Did you have to stand all the way? The boys on the bus should be ashamed of themselves keeping their seats. I hope you don't get fed up with coming out here. It is not very pleasant really standing all that way. If there only would be a later bus back I would bring you right home. Well darling I hope to get your letter tomorrow morning to know you arrived home safely. Find out about Wednesday and let me know in time. If possible I'll buy a suit already on that day. That means you may see me wearing it when we meet at 5.00 I arrived here at the usual time 10.00. Mr Pickering had done the sandwiches so there was nothing to do for me. I was glad because I felt really tired. Don't think me too bad when I tell you I am just finishing the last sweet. But I didn't touch a cigarette yet. I am going to stop smoking if possible. There is a bit of work for me to do today. Fish tomorrow for breakfast. I don't like it but I've to do it.

I haven't got any mail this morning. A letter from my mother was due but I was unlucky. Anyway I hope to get two tomorrow. I would like to ring you now to hear how you got home but you told me to save my money. I hardly can wait till tomorrow. If there is a possibility I'll try to buy some eggs for you. We'll have a word about it on Wednesday.

All my love and kisses

Yours forever

Hans.

Aschersleben 13.1.48

17/2

My dear Hans

Thank you very much for your two letters, dated 14.12 and 30.12.47, which reached us yesterday and today, and found us in good health. The letter you wrote to Horstel on 29/12 has not arrived. Today it has been raining all day. We are pleased to hear that you have spent a good Christmas, and have even received a present, although sadly nothing from us, which makes me feel sad. I am assuming that by now you have been released. All the best for your future life. We think of you all the time. How come you didn't want to go dancing, bearing in mind you are such a handsome lad and so far have not really been able to enjoy life. Clearly dancing is not the most important thing, but it sounds as though the people over there are more cheerful and inclined to celebrate. Of course we have lost the war and that creates an altogether different atmosphere. Oh yes, my dear boy, who knows when you will ever sleep in your own bed again? We only have one top eiderdown and two pillows from our dear grandma. Horst sleeps in a bed which belongs to Frau Lehmann. How far have we come, having to sleep in borrowed beds. It seems that fate has decided for you to remain where you are for the time being and that does not trouble me too much. We are struggling because we are so lonely, and away from home. If you really do not want me to take on any work, and if this is your Christmas wish I guess I'll have to fulfil it. You see I wanted to support Horst a little, and we have to move forward, and people who are in work find it easier to get the coupons for reduced-price groceries. So many times I have come away empty-handed. Horst absolutely does not want me to work. The peace and quiet suit me well, and whilst at summer I weighed only 108 Pounds, fortunately I have now gone up to 124 Pounds. Isn't that good? Of course the wonderful things you have sent have very much contributed to this. You cannot imagine what a pleasure it is to drink the chocolate with milk, as well as the broth, and on Sundays the most wonderful pudding! This has given us so much pleasure, and not just once! I so often think of grandma, if only I could have spoiled her a bit with something so nice. She had done so much for us all throughout her life, yet had to waste away so slowly, dying of hunger. It makes one's heart bleed.

R 17/2   Aschersleben, 3.2.48

My dear Hans

We were so happy to receive your lovely letter dated 24.1.48. It took longer (9 days) to get here this time, the first airmail letter only took 4 days. Horstel had not left for work when the letter arrived, so he opened it and it made him very happy. We sat down, close together, on our splendid chaise longue and I had to read the letter out loud. Honestly, one should have taken a photo of us to show how carefully I read your letter. Well, now you are free. Our heartiest wishes and all the best to you. I have to say that you were very frugal. You know now, my boy, how important it is to start saving in one's youth because when you get older you can reap the benefit. Carry on the way you are and never forget that you still have a mother who is always worried about you and only wants what's best for you!! I have to confess that I still worry about the parcel. It was posted 10 weeks ago. One of Horst's clients received a parcel last week, which was posted on 5.11.47. We are so looking forward to receiving the leather soles and the other lovely things like the stockings and scarfs. Every item in the parcel is so valuable to us. Dear Hans, don't you get the cash from the bank for the cheque of £28? It would be much to your advantage if you could get the cash and then buy yourself some clothes there. Because you can't get anything here, not for money and not for good words either. Look after your cheque for 72 Dollars, because – who knows how long our currency will be valid. Buy yourself a good suit, even if you have to pay more for it, you will get more pleasure out of it. I am sure when our Papa comes back, he will have nothing. Looking at the poor fellows here, my heart bleeds. I wish you could see it one day. But even if Papa comes home without anything, the main thing is he comes home. Werner's opinion differs from ours. He says that some people don't bother about their relatives much, otherwise they would not stay away voluntarily. I wrote back that everybody has their own opinion, because there are people who think such a lot of their relatives that they decide to stay away voluntarily – however difficult it might be - and make the sacrifice in order to help their relatives. Maybe he will think about what I said. It looks like you have some really palatial furniture! We wouldn't say no to this either! I am so glad to hear that you are corresponding with Heinz. I wonder if he will be allowed to return home soon? We are looking forward to your photo. Don't you want to send one of Jean too? Tell Jean we are thanking her very much for her greetings and also for the fact that she takes such an interest in us. We are very sad that you cannot get to us during your leave. I wrote to the Repatriation Camp in Pirna and asked about Papa. Today I received a card from them saying that he has not arrived there yet. I got the most beautiful signet ring for you today, which will be engraved with your initials and it is ready for collection in 10 days-time. We hope you will be pleased with it. I am sure you will like it. If the lady in the jeweller's shop did not know me so well, I would not have managed to get this ring without providing the silver. Instead of the silver I gave her a few pounds of syrup. This way we both got what we wanted. If I knew for sure it would not get lost, I would post the ring to you. I don't know how best to do it because I would not want it to get lost, it is far too precious. Let me know what you think about it. Dear Hans, whatever sewing thread you can get, please buy it. I have had a jacket made out of the rest of a blanket and the thread is almost all gone. Did you not receive Horstel's letter, in which he asked if you can get some small ornamental combs? Please can you see if you can get them for him? He would like some for his wig. I don't think they are very expensive.

Now, my dear boy, I am sending you best wishes and lots of love and kisses, your mum and your brother Horst. Here's to a healthy reunion.

Please give our very best wishes to Jean!

L.W.A.E.C Hostel.
Stathern.
Feb 19th 1948.

My darling Jean

I am sorry my day off is gone and I have to work now for a few days till the next one is due. I arrived back safely at 10.00. Don't be surprised for I was home so early. Mr Pickering didn't expect me so early so I had to make the tea myself. He also told me the suit is very nice but the main thing is that you like best. How did you get home darling? Was the pup alright? I hope you didn't forget to give my greetings to your mother. If you did, I would like to remind you. I always enjoy the pictures very much whilst being with you. Everything is more interesting and you feed me well (with sweets). I am glad it is a bit quiet this afternoon for I did the sweet (tarts) in the morning. This morning the breakfast nearly went wrong, I woke up, it was still dark and so I didn't know what time it was. What else would I do as to sleep again? As I woke up the second time it was nearly light and the porter still sleeping. I knocked at his door and asked for the time. It was 6.20 (breakfast 6.30). You can tell how I rushed down to get everything ready. After all breakfast was only 5 minutes later and nobody noticed. The warden was on to me again today because I didn't eat any dinner. He asked me what you're doing to me for I never eat anything the day after I was with you. He is going to tell you. Give him the right answer. I really didn't feel like eating and think the sweets are the reason. We emptied your pocket to the very bottom didn't we?

I am so glad I have got the suit now. It is only the first thing. When I go shopping the next time it'll be a shirt and a pair of shoes and socks. I can do that with a fortnight's earnings.

Now I'll say cheerio my sweetheart. Now be good.
All my love and kisses
Always yours
Hans.

92 Wharf St.
February 20th.

My darling Hans

I arrived home safe and sound about the usual time. My mother had gone out, the pup was quite alright, my mother had left the light on for him. I think she thinks he is afraid of the dark. He has something wrong with his ears at the moment but they seem a lot better today. The eggs were packed well, they were not even cracked. Thank you very much for them and especially for the tea, we never manage to make our tea ration last all the month. One of the Germans came into Leicester yesterday afternoon to say goodbye. He is going home next Wednesday to the British zone.

What is the weather like at Stathern? At this moment it is snowing quite fast. I think there is a lot on the way and it's very cold with it. Alfred rang here on Thursday morning for Mr Edwards, I don't know what was the matter, but he wasn't very chatty. He pleases himself, I couldn't care less one way or the other. I went to the pictures last night to see "I walk alone". That is the picture you thought would be good, but if we had gone to see it we would not have seen it all because that picture began at 5.0, and the next time it came on was 8.30. Anyway it wasn't all that good. I am going to Alice's tonight. It is her turn to come to see me, but her father is working late and she would rather I go when he is not in. Alice and her father do not get on well together.

I will have to say cheeri'O have a good weekend.

All my love and kisses
Jean

.

LWAEC Hostel,
                                        Stathern.
                                        Feb. 20th 1948.

My darling Jean

This seems to be the first week I only got 2 letters, that means if I get the second one tomorrow. Anyway I hope so, well, darling how are you? I've seen that man today and told him to bring the dozen eggs Wednesday next week. I think it is the best when I bring them along. You might smash them on the crowded bus on Sunday. Isn't it lovely weather? I've told you how much I like snow, it always reminds me how it was as I was at home. We'd snow every winter. A real one. Let me know what day it suits you best next week. Do you ring me tomorrow? I'll wait for your call. It is rather early today 2.00 o'clock. We'd our dinner a bit early, because it is Saturday tomorrow and my favourite fruit, leeks, for dinner. Some of the men are in and one came down and got the leeks for me. So that makes one job less for me. It isn't very pleasant to go to the garden now. The warden is going home this weekend so I'll be on my own. A quiet weekend again. I received a letter from my mother today. I'll tell you something about it when I see you again. Is the pup better now? My mother told me not to forget to give you her greetings. I am well darling, and I hope so from you and your dear mother. Please ring me. I would like to wish you a good weekend. Another tea party on Sunday? Well darling I'll close now. Be good and think of me over the weekend.

                        All my love and kisses
                                Yours
              Hans.

Replied 21/2.48

To: Mr Hans Klawitter.
              LWAEC Hostel.

Old Rectory.
Stathern nr Melton/Leics.
Great Britain.

20/2.48

France Feb 4 th 1948

Dear Hans I was delighted to get your kind letter telling me that you became a civillian. Thank you very much. So I lose no time in replying to this letter. My mother told me about your intention. That's the best you can do, for things look different after a year and you are able to get profession again at home. It's a pity though that I can't be over there but those are little wishes. Now I'm going to tell you about our life in France. It's awfully boring inside the camp and the job doesn't agree with me at all. I'm longing for home and a job on the air. Time hangs heavy upon me but that must change. For two and a half years I'm occupied under the earth, it's really enough indeed. I could tell a tale of this pretty time, but later. Let me hope for the best that the prisoners time will go over pretty soon. It's no earthly use to become a civillian in France, because that's a matter of itself. I better like to go home. O yes, I meant to come over there to take a job like you. With girls we don't have any contact. And we also are not allowed to go out. The only thing we can do is a deal of work every day, one gets used to it. After work one feels a bit run down, that will go over. It's a long time since I had a better time. In the States. Sometimes I had a jolly time especially in the nice town Baltimore. I'll tell you later of it. I didn't know you were engaged at home, I hope you are not sad about this girl. Much luck to your love affair with the little charmer over there. My repatriation should be this year. What do you mean about going to the R-zone? I'm intending to do it, as I have no relatives in another zone. If I had the change to be in England I would do the same like you. I wonder is that really so, that the Russians being so barberous? Time will show! My only object is to help my parents. I have a feeling that all come right to the end and one day we will meet us again at home! The main thing, we are all o.k. Are you engaged as an interpreter or cook in the hostel? It seems to be a very nice place. Well, Hans now I will close and hope you will let me hear from you soon. All the best to you, your cousin Heinz. Give the best respects to your mother and Horst. Are you allowed to take leave for home? In France the civillians get a month leave. They get a card like a Punch worker, we have the same too. We just need to be free. So Hans my only object is to receive many letters of yours because practise makes perfection and that wouldn't be wrong

R   21/2   Aschersleben, 8.2.48

20/2

My dear Hans

Today is Sunday and I am sending you all my love. The weeks are flying passed us, nearly half of the month of February is gone, and it will not be long till Easter! Horstel's letter dated 25.1. arrived here the day before yesterday. He will reply to you tonight. This afternoon he has gone out dancing. He does not go there in the evenings any more. He was so angry when, a fortnight ago, a married woman approached him and asked if he would come back to her house! You should have seen him how disgusted he was and I could not stop laughing! Mind you, I agree that there are so many women out there without any conscience whatsoever. I am glad he finds it abhorrent, at least he will not stray from the straight and narrow. I told you before, that I had a jacket made out of an old blanket. I had also a blouse made with short sleeves from some material which I managed to obtain some time ago in Prenzlau on Horstel's clothing allowance card. Guess what the tailor charged. I was so surprised I nearly fell through the roof. The bill came to only 31 Marks. Soon it will be impossible to make an earnest living from an honest job. Dear Hans, can you still get some sweetener? I am sure you will think to yourself: "These two need a lot of sweet stuff". We eat soup every evening and then we need some for baking. It does not last very long. We are getting a lot of pleasure out of our radio. With your new job, do you have an opportunity now to listen to the radio some times? This week, I bought some seeds for Uncle Erich's garden. They are very hard to get this year. Did you not receive Uncle Erich's letter? He wrote to me saying that you could not have received his letter because he has not heard from you since. It's all very depressing! Syrup instead of fat, fat free cheese instead of meats, and the meat feels like rubber in your mouth. You have to chew and chew. I do wish the food situation would improve. It cannot go on like this for much longer! What will the future bring us? I am so glad that things are much better for you. I am sure you will keep your job. At least you get good food there! I expect Jean will be with you again today. Do give her our love. We are still waiting for the second parcel which you posted on 24.11. – in vain I am sure. I think it is better if you don't send two parcels off at the same time! My dear Hans, I will close my letter for today. I want to write to Uncle Gustav. Please stay well. I am sending you all my love and kisses, your mum and brother Horst. Hoping to see you in best shape!

37   LWAEC Hostel,
                                 Stathern.
                                 Feb 21st 1948

My darling Jean,
I thank you so much for your letter and the call this morning. I've told the warden that the call was for me but he didn't believe it and answered the phone. I was standing beside him. My only hope is that you are able to spare me an evening next week? Please tell me why you sent that empty fourth page. Did you think me to answer on it? No, I am not going to for this letter shall be a bit longer than one page. Mr Pickering left about 12.00 and my special friend the porter has his day off. So I am on my own (there's no pup). Mrs Betts has just been and brought me a few apples and oranges to fill my spare time with eating them. I was busy all afternoon, pressing my suit and there is still my washing left. I'll do it

when I finished this letter. It is rather quiet because there are only 2 men in tonight. I've had a talk with Alfred this afternoon. Only for half an hour. He told me that Saltby will be closed definitely on the 6th March, that's a fortnight today. Mr E is trying to keep Alfred and the other fellows for 14 more days to hand everything over. Anyway he's not coming tomorrow but promised to see me before he goes home. He hopes to go next month. The war-ag don't know yet whether to take Saltby as a hostel or not. They can't make up their minds. Why didn't you tell me darling, that you can't manage with the tea ration? I've told you on the phone what the weather is like. It was snowing very fast last night, but the roads are alright. If there are no buses on Wednesday I'll walk to Leicester. I don't mind. You know I want exercise. I am so glad you're coming next Sunday. Let me know till Wednesday what you think about my coming over. I would like to say cheerio and be good my sweetheart. God bless you.

      All my love and kisses
      Yours forever
         Hans.

      92 Wharf St.
      February 22nd.

My dear Hans

I hope you have had a lovely weekend? I don't suppose Alfred came to see you. I could have gone to my sister's for tea, but when I looked at the weather I didn't feel like turning out. It is even too cold to have a wash and get ready.

I have been busy. I went out nearly every night last week. Look darling I don't think we had better arrange to meet this week, because the weather is so unsettled at the moment and I have promised to go to see my auntie at Birstall. I was going last week but did not have time and Alice is coming on the Thursday for tea. I told you I was going to Alice's last Friday. It snowed quite a lot going back home and someone landed a snowball at the back of my neck. I did not do anything special yesterday. Dora came to tea and then we went to the pictures, that is all I did.

I have got to write to Bernhard sometime when I can get in the mood. I usually have to make an effort to write any letter, except to you. Well darling I had better say cheeri'O this is the last sheet of paper on the pad. If it isn't ink I run out of it's paper. I do hope you have had a good weekend. Be good.

All my love
& kisses
Jean

.

92 Wharf St.
Feb 24th 1948.

My dearest Hans

I thank you very much for both the letters you have sent. I am one behind already this week. About that plain sheet of paper you asked about. I put it in by mistake I think I never really finished that letter. I was writing that when one of your fellows from Stathern came in to say goodbye. By the time he had gone it was too late to finish and catch the last post. By the way, he came in again yesterday, but that will be the last time. He goes home today. You should have heard him calling the English, he did it to annoy Iris and I but he couldn't. He is going to write when he gets home. I have just been ringing Saltby, Alfred has gone out. I have been speaking to the other fellow, he speaks very good English, it is the first time I have spoken to him. Lucy has gone to London today. A girl she was with in the ATS is getting married today so Lucy has gone to the wedding. The fellow the girl is marrying is one of Lucy's old boy friends but he got away.

I went to the pictures last night, it was quite good. It was called 'The Assassin'. I thought it would be another war picture but it wasn't, it was a cowboy. I am going to stay in to-night, we have had the sweep (chimney) and there is rather a lot to do. I am going to see my auntie tomorrow night and I did not see any of my relatives last week. If I want to visit all my relations it would take me years.

Just be good till I see you
All my love
Jean

.

<table>
<tr><td>39</td><td>LWAEC Hostel,
Stathern.
Febr 25.th 1948.</td></tr>
</table>

I thank you very much for the letter I received this morning. Don't be surprised darling. I am writing at my old place in Saltby. As I couldn't see you today I went with one of the lorries to Saltby and paid a visit to Alfred. It might be the last one in Saltby. I would have liked to go on a bike, but I think you'll agree that is a bit too cold today. I went up to Saltby Village with the lorry and walked the little way to the camp. Alfred was surprised to see me for I'd rung one hour before I arrived and told him there was no possibility for me to go. I'll ring you this afternoon. I hope you aren't busy. I thank you for your explanation about that plain sheet of paper. I thought the letter wasn't finished. Look darling, don't care what that fellow said about the English. You know what I think about the English people and always remember that. Now darling, let me close. I've to see the QM this afternoon. He is going home next week and I like to have a look around before he leaves.

Be good, till Sunday, all my love and kisses
Yours Hans.

92 Wharf St.
Feb 25th 1948.
My darling

Just a few lines to let know that I am OK. When you rang this afternoon I was just going to wash up for Miss Scarlett and fill the kettle for Iris. That is what I meant by doing my good deed for the day. I told you it was my turn to do the tea next week. For heaven's sake don't come in to see me because the German from Stoughton has been in twice today (don't worry he has a girl) he came in this morning to bring the time sheets and then he came into the town this afternoon and he called in again. What with Willi coming in three times last week then two this morning and one this afternoon. They will be asking me if I would like an extra room to entertain the POWs in. I was surprised to hear you this afternoon especially when you said you had walked to Saltby. When I said you needed more exercise I did not mean you to walk 12 miles. Anyway have you got over it? I could not talk to you very much because Iris was there, it's not that I mind, but when anyone is listening to what I am speaking about I can never think what to say. So I thought it best to say cheerio.

I went to my Auntie's tonight, that is one that objects to me seeing Germans, also the one I am probably going to Eastbourne with. So goodnight and God bless until tomorrow.

Thursday

You had better cancel what I said on the other page about walking to Saltby. I believed you.

Don't worry I don't care what other people think about the English, everyone is entitled to their own opinion.

Anyway darling I will try and write tomorrow to let you know about Sunday so till then.

All my love

Jean

<u>40</u>   J.E.G Klawitter,
          L.A.E.C Hostel, Old Rectory,
          Stathern nr Melton Mow-
          bray.

Febr 27.th 1948.

My darling

I thank you so much for your nice letter. Did you really believe that I walked from here to Saltby? I think I would never have arrived in Saltby. You could have come then to pick up the bits. You must be very busy, darling, entertaining all those men from Stoughton. Look, I think I'm a bit more polite because I ring you at first and ask if you like me coming in and if not I stay away. But they know how to do it, they go and see you without asking. I don't know any Willi's. Karl's or Fritz's from that camp.

Alfred rung me this morning. He's going to Nottingham tomorrow and on his way there he would like to see me for a few minutes. So he is coming once at least.

When are you going to your Auntie's? Do you stay at home over Easter? I don't know yet whether the hostel will be closed over Easter or not. If so I'll be the only one here then.

Isn't it a lovely afternoon again? It is so hot in here today. I don't know what is the matter with the stove. It never burned as nice as today as long as I've been here. I've to look at the fish every five minutes to avoid them getting burned. All the doors and windows are open and I can't get it cool. It is hotter than it was last summer.

I've just got the eggs for you and put them in the dairy to keep fresh. Laid within the last two days. I'll pack them well and you can take them on Sunday, if you like.

As I came down this morning I noticed that there was no electricity in the small stove and just the small stove is my only help in the morning. I was only 10 minutes later with the breakfast. Did you notice how long it took you to toast two slices of bread? And I'd to make sixteen today. I nearly went mad, holding the bread to the open fire and was surprised it only tasted a bit smoky. I bet you would've laughed.

There's a lot to talk about on Sunday, that means no sleep for you whilst being here!!

You know it is Saturday tomorrow and I've to get the leeks from the garden it's nice, dirty work.

I am looking forward for tomorrow morning, saying in your letter you're taking the 12.30 from Leicester!!! Or am I wrong?

Now darling I'd like to say cheerio. Be good and look after yourself well. Remember you are very dear to someone.

All my love and kisses

Yours forever

Hans.

92 Wharf St.
Feb 27th 1948.

I can't start to thank you for the letter because you did not send me one. I don't really mind darling, it's hard to think what to say when nothing ever happens especially when you don't get a letter to answer. Anyway, by the time you get this I will have spoken to you. I am going to ring you tonight. I can tell you better that I am not coming on Sunday. I could say I would come but if I feel like I feel today I wouldn't come so I think it is safe to say I won't be coming. I do hope you are not annoyed. I promise I will come next Sunday, even if I am half dead. You are not the only one with rheumatism. I have it in my hip. Don't worry I can walk.

I have been trying to write this all afternoon but this is all I have done.

Anyway darling I will write a long letter tomorrow till then

All my love

and kisses

Jean.

41

L.A.E.C Hostel,

Stathern.

Saturday 28.2.48.

My darling

Saturday night and not as usually a Sunday to follow, but another working day. Thanks for your letter (without address). It doesn't matter really. It is only a minor matter. I also have to thank you for your call this morning. As I told you on the phone I felt rotten after your call last night. I never before noticed how just one word can change me. It started last Monday as you told me in your letter not to come on Wednesday. Since that Monday I had nothing else to eat during the week than my porridge every morning and a few cups of tea during the day. I don't feel like eating. I nearly dropped one morning as I did the breakfast. Look darling I know you can't understand how it is to be in a strange country, with strange people about. There is no place to go to and you are the only one I know. Didn't I tell you how much I love you and how I am longing to see you and talk to you? There is quite a lot I wanted to talk to you about tomorrow and I made everything so nice and comfortable for you. And then just this little word, 'No!' I would like to ring you now straight away and beg you to come, but I know even that call would be unsuccessful. So I better leave it. I know when you say 'no' you mean it. Be sure that I would come if you'd called me, if I even could hardly walk. I can't tell you how much I hate a weekend like this one. And now my next chance is Wednesday if I may say so. I am not sure yet. I better wait for the mail on Monday morning. A Wednesday doesn't give me time to talk to you because it is just a rush to the pictures and then back to the bus. But in spite of all this I am glad and thankful for every minute I am able to be with you.

The warden is in his room and I am sitting in the kitchen. I couldn't stand any company tonight. I took the bike and went for a ride to Harby and back.

It is now 7.30 I'll do the supper and leave it on the table, have a bath and go to bed.

Are you better by now darling? I hope so in any way. I'll try to write a few more lines tomorrow. So good night for now and God bless you, my darling. Be good.

<u>Sunday</u>!

Here we are again darling. I've had a nice rest last night and feel better. I went to bed at 8.15 and got up at 8.30 this morning. Just 12 hours. There is some work left for this afternoon, the sandwiches for tomorrow. After that it is time for supper and there with this lonely Sunday gone. I am really glad. The warden is also on his own for his girl friend didn't come. I may go to bed early tonight. All last week I went to bed at 9.15. Pretty early isn't it.

Now darling, I'll say cheerio and start my work again. I hope you've written today that I may get your letter tomorrow.

Be good, till I see you Wednesday

All my love and kisses

Yours Hans

92 Wharf St.

February 29th.

My dearest Hans,

Thank you very much for your nice long letter. I am wondering if I shall get such a nice letter tomorrow after the short and not so nice letter I sent you on Friday but I hope by now you have got over that and you are not feeling so sorry for yourself.

Anyway darling it isn't such a nice day and I could not have been bothered to get myself ready to go out. So it is a good job I told you I was not coming today.

You say I in the past 6 weeks that I have cancelled six meetings. I can only think of 3. Sorry. You must have read some of my letters twice.

Did you see Alfred yesterday? Alfred said he may be coming into Leicester before he goes home. He hopes that will be within the next three weeks. When you rang from Saltby last Wednesday Iris wasn't listening on the line, but there was someone on the line because when I said cheerio to you the line cleared straight away I had not put the receiver down so it would be the girls on the Grantham exchange. I have just had to make the fire up, no one to do it for me, and I have been trying to get the American Forces Networth on the wireless. They usually have some good music on about this time (2.30) but it is hopeless. We never can seem to get any overseas programme on until 7.30. It does annoy me because all the programmes on the BBC on Sunday afternoons have been heard in the week. I will have to send a complaint in about it. I believe I told you Iris went to Paris for a holiday last year. Well she met a fellow whilst she was there and has been writing to him since, she had a letter on Friday asking her to marry him. Iris says she is thinking it over, but believe me she is almost on her way to Paris. Are you coming into Leicester on Wednesday or Thursday? Whichever day suits you but if you can make it Wednesday I could wash my hair Thursday, I will have a look and see what is on the pictures. You have the "Mercury" but I may as well tell you what is on. At the Gaumont (that is the one in the market place) 'Personal Coleman' and another with Laurel and Hardy in it. I have seen what is on at the Picture House and the Princess in the Odeon. 'Build my gallons high' sounds like a gangster film. Then there is the Savoy (that is near Charles St) 'An Ideal Husband' that is an old fashioned film about 1900 in London. I hope you can let me know which you would prefer to see. I don't know what time any of them begin until tomorrow.

I do hope Sunday wasn't so bad for you, so till then (Wednesday)

All my love and kisses

Jean

PS Don't you think
this is a long letter?

JP

42

L.A.E.C. Hostel,

Stathern.

March 1ˢᵗ 1948.

My darling

Thank you very much, darling for the letter I received this
morning. And such a nice and long one.

I think it was lovely yesterday. All the way to Melton there
were people walking about. I am sorry, darling I made a mistake as I said you cancelled our arrangement 6 times in the
past 6 weeks. I meant to say 8 weeks.

Yes, Alfred came down on Saturday and was sitting here for
about one hour. He looked so hungry so I gave him a bit of
our dinner. He seemed to be satisfied. I met him again last
night as I arrived in Melton.

I meant to hear somebody talking as I rung you from Saltby.
Don't you think they've recognised our voices. We always
have the American Forces Network on our wireless because
they bring a lot of German music. Don't you think I better come and try to get that station for you? That would
be a nice Sunday. You ought to write to the BBC to change
the programme for you, but be careful. Maybe they put 'The
hour for housewives' on instead.

You didn't tell me Iris has a boyfriend in Paris, but she's
alright marrying him. Tell her my congratulations. That's
a very good decision indeed. Yes, darling I am coming on
Wednesday afternoon, but please don't tell me again not to
come.

I leave it to you what picture we're going to see. Choose that one you haven't seen yet. If you rather see that gangster film it'll be alright for me.

The Sunday really didn't turn out so bad as I thought at first. I took the 3.45 bus to Melton and met one of my fellows I was together with in Wartnaby Hostel. Then in Melton we met another one. After a cup of tea at the bus station we went to the pictures and afterwards again for a cup of tea to one of the coffee houses. I took the 9.15 and was back here by 10.00 when the porter told me there was a visitor for me at 9.30 and he is coming again. I was just going to bed as somebody knocked at my door. It was that second fellow from the Labour Office Saltby you'd spoken to the other day. He come from Langar and couldn't get back to Saltby because it was very foggy. So I've put him up for the night and he went back on the lorry this morning. The first of my visitors who stayed over night!!

Well darling I'll say cheerio. Be good and God bless. Let me know till Wednesday where and what time to meet you.

All my love and kisses darling

Yours forever

Hans.

92 Wharf St.

March 2nd.

My dearest Hans

I thank you very much for both your letters. It was a nice surprise to find two letters this morning, long ones at that.

I am very annoyed because you don't eat when I do not come to see you. You also make me feel very ashamed. I know it isn't fair to you, but I can not help it. I still like to feel free to please myself what I do, maybe in time I will change.

About Wednesday (don't worry I am not going to cancel it) I think the best place would be the Gaumont in the Market Place, the picture house we went to last time. I will meet you outside because it begins about 5.5. I was speaking to Alfred this morning, he was saying that he is coming to

Leicester Saturday afternoon with Mr Hill of Melton to the De Montfort Hall to a concert. A German conductor is coming 'Furt wanglet' (I think that is how you spell it). Since last Monday we have had to sign a new kind of time sheet. It is a book now you sign what time you arrive in the morning, if it is after 9.5 you get a red mark against your name. So far I have not got one because 9.5 is my usual time. Then you have to sign at night.

I think I had better say cheeri'O. Iris wants me to cut her hair. I don't know how she dare take the risk. So till Wednesday be good

All my love

Jean

.

92 Wharf St.

March 3rd.

My dearest Hans

I have just finished my supper and cleared the things away. My mother has gone out. I think she was going to someone's birthday party but she won't be late home. I have the dog on my knee. I have to pick him up because he keeps scratching at my stocking and I am afraid he might ladder them, so it is a case of having to pick him up.

Well darling thanks for a lovely evening. I enjoyed it and thank you very much for the flowers, they are lovely. I have put them in water and they seem to have livened up.

I was going to tell you tonight about the letter Iris had. For a bit of fun Iris sent to a lonely heart club for particulars, this morning she got the replies, it has been very funny to read what they want and about some of the men, it has been quite a joke.

Well darling I had better say goodnight and God bless you. I will post it in the morning. I hope you receive one Friday.

All my love

Jean.

.

Aschersleben, 15.2.48
                                        2/3.48

My dear Hans

I thank you, from the bottom of my heart, for your letter
dated 3.2.48. There is a lovely programme on the radio at
the moment, which makes a welcome change and provides
entertainment! What do you mean by 'the black Heinrich'?
Maybe when the food gets burnt? This must not happen to
me because our food is very scarce! It looks like you are not
earning as much now as you would have got, had you taken
on the interpreter's job. But you do get good food in your
current job, do you? Buy as much as you can afford in terms
of clothing. If we have asked you for things and you do not
have that much money, then please do not buy it for us. I do
not want you to go without for our sake! Of course, it would
also be much better for us if we were given a clothing card allowance so that we can buy the most essential things. We are
looking forward very much to your photo and hope it will
get here soon. Erna Schünemann is now in West Germany
visiting Frida and Christel. She also intends to come and see
us. We are looking forward to seeing her again. If your ship
had departed on 5.2., then you would be here already now!
I collected your ring on Thursday. It looks very nice but is
quite a lot bigger than Horstel's ring. Horstel is writing to
you at the moment and we shall put both letters into one envelope, because they are very hard to come by! Now, my dear
boy, stay fit and well. I am sending you all my love and kisses.
Your mum and your brother Horst. Give our love to Jean.

Aschersleben, 15.2.48

2.3.48

My dear Hans

Finally, I am writing to you today to thank you for your lovely letter dated 24.1.48. I was, as ever, very pleased to hear from you. This morning I was working again. I combed the hair of twelve ladies. I think maybe I am silly because I should try and relax a bit instead of working on my day off. Now, I want to tell you all about my new job. I like it very much. I am now working in a Ladies' salon and I am getting an awful lot of pleasure out of it, as you can imagine. The most important thing is that I am learning such a lot and gaining more experience. Whatever I learn cannot be taken away from me! This afternoon, I went dancing again. It is always the same. The masked ball period is coming to an end. However, I never saw any! On Shrove Tuesday I went dancing in the Bestehornhaus. Usually, only the 'upper class' frequents there. It is still one of the best places on the Square with a well-behaved audience.

We are expecting another visitor soon. Erna wants to come and see us and we are looking forward to spending some time with a relative again. Otherwise, we are always meeting up with strangers. Although we are quite well-known here now and don't feel like strangers anymore. I can quite believe that it is such a lovely feeling to be free again. If only our beloved Papa could contact us, mum would be so relieved. We are hoping to get some news from him soon.

I would be very happy if you could get me some ornamental combs and other hair decorations, but only if it does not cost too much money. If it is too expensive, then please do not buy it. Mum has bought you a signet ring. Now you have a reason to come here on holiday to get the ring, but it is so far away. It is always easier to write about something than it is do actually do it. Dear Hans, give my love to Jean. Who knows what the future holds for us. There is a lot talk about a new currency. Well, we can't lose much more. Come what may, we can't change anything. I am going to close my letter for today. I am sending you my love, your brother Horst. Here's to a soon and healthy reunion. Write back soon!

43   L.A.E.C. Hostel,
Stathern.

March 4 <u>th</u>. 1948.

My darling

Thanks very much for the very enjoyable evening we've spent together. I arrived back here safe and sound at 10.00. The 9.10 bus to Plungar was still waiting as we arrived in Melton. Did you get back well? Can you suggest what I am eating just now? I am finishing the dates. I had a few on the bus last night and the last few have to be 'destroyed' before they get bad. How were the eggs? I hope alright for I packed them well.

Look darling about Sunday. As I told you the warden is going home over the weekend and doesn't know yet if he is coming back Sunday afternoon or Monday. As you know I have to do the sandwiches for Monday, Saturday night is too early so I'll have them to do the Sunday afternoon. I hope you'll get the 2.10 from Melton and I am coming to our bus stop here at least. If the 2.10 is gone take the 2.45 (Redmile or Bottesford on the bus). If the weather is nice we may have a little walk around.

Mr Shilton is to come this afternoon. He's been already in Gaddesby. Something like an inspection. We don't know what he really wants. You should see my kitchen today. Everything clean and shiny (I also cleaned the windows) I was scrubbing, sweeping, dusting and the women stood at the door and were laughing about me. They told me I looked just like a housewife. They kept joking till they went.

Did you enjoy the picture? I think it was very good. By the way I am coming again to Leicester next week. I want to see that film 'Two girls and a sailor' and also want to buy a shirt. I'll have a look at the Mercury tonight on what days that picture is on. There's a lot of nice music in. If you can't see me I'll have to go on my own, but maybe you could spare an evening for me!!

Well my darling I'll say cheerio till I see you on Sunday. Don't be surprised if I am in Melton.

Be good sweetheart and God bless.

All my love the kisses

Always yours

Hans.

92 Wharf St.
March 4th.

My dearest Hans

This is your weekend letter. I have to write tonight or at work where I never seem to have much time. I haven't much to tell you. Tony Woods (he's the fellow that you saw with Kath Williams last Sunday) he came down to our office this morning (he usually comes down to bring his morning paper). I thought he was serious with Kath so did Iris, but this morning he was quite worried saying Kath was getting too serious, he was going to tell her tonight that he wouldn't be seeing her again. We (Iris and I) were pulling his leg saying that he had had it, he would be married before he knew where he was. I was speaking to Kath this morning. I thought she was going to tell me she had seen you because she started asking me if I had spoken to Alfred lately (I think she rather likes Alfred she is always asking me about him) then she gets round to you. Anyway she did not say she had seen you because I put her call through before she could.

About Sunday, don't worry if you are not able to get to Melton I will be able to find my way. I ought to know where to get off the bus now. With a bit of luck I might catch the 2.10 bus to Stathern, if I don't I will ring you from Melton. So till then be good. Goodnight and God bless

All my love
Jean

44   L.A.E.C. Hostel,
                             Stathern.

                             March 5.th. 1948.

My darling

I was surprised reading your letter that you wrote straight away on Wednesday night. I thank you very very much. Please don't bring your pup along when you come. I am afraid of dogs which bite!! Have you a nice supper on Wednesday night? Half a dozen fried eggs and bacon? I didn't eat anything except some jam tarts, that is because I nearly finished the dates on the bus.

I was looking for flowers all the time I came to see you but there's only pots at the market and I think we hardly could take a few pots to the pictures. So I at least was lucky this week. I know you like flowers and so do I.

Everything alright for Sunday, darling? I've had a busy morning. Can't you guess? I'd to clean my two rooms upstairs. Finishing at 12.30 I was just right for dinner.

I've never heard about heart clubs and don't know what it means so you'll have to tell me on Sunday.

So be good, my sweetheart, till I see you on Sunday. It is only 2 days off.

All my love and kisses
Yours forever
Hans

P.S, I'd a letter from my mother today. She sends many greetings to you. HK

Dear Hans   5/3

My mum gave me your letter dated 18.12. on 1 January. I was very pleased but the first lines were sufficient to make me very sad. It is the first letter from you in which you have knowingly hurt me very much. You did not misunderstand me when I mentioned an empty page. I did not want to remind you to save paper. But enough, it is completely irrelevant. I do understand that you don't want to write to me anymore. I have nothing more to ask of you. I mean that being polite and thankful is more my style. But I don't know if I will be able to, Hans. Of course, one has to try, but at the moment I have other, completely different worries. I am not well Hans, but I want to tell you that my physical pains are much easier to bear than my psychological pains. I am expecting to lose my gall bladder. I have been getting treatment for many weeks now. At first I thought I would go to the Greifswald Clinic but now I have decided against it. I will stay here. The trains are not reliable and the journey would be too much for people who want to come and visit me. In case anything happens I am sure my mum would inform you whether I want her to or not. I am quite composed but am awaiting the operation with some trepidation. I am sure everything will be alright in the end, either one way or the other. Your letter was written in a very strange way, Hans. You do not have to be more precise. I understand what's behind it. You don't really need to write more, maybe it will hurt me.

Yes, one can get used to working in the fields. You will find it easier next year. One cannot write very well in bed, at least I cannot write any better in bed. I am happy when you write to me.

On the side: All the best. Heartfelt greetings from Vera

45

Same address.

March, 6.th. 1948.

My darling,

As I read your letter this morning I thought you'd cancelled again because you started " This is your weekend letter" I was glad it doesn't continue. Anyway darling, I thank you very much for it. No wonder Kath takes it serious. Maybe she thinks she must hurry to find somebody who is willing to marry her. As I told you I nearly got a shock as I saw her the other day. She seems to enjoy life. I'd like to see her in say five years. I think Kath will be very disappointed. It might be possible that she is interested in Alfred, but I mean as it's the second time then she's had it. I have pressed my suit for tomorrow. But there is still some work left. Cutting some wood for the fire and bringing a bucket of coal upstairs. There is something else, but I won't tell you. You better see and taste yourself tomorrow.

So you mean you ought to know where to get off the bus? Don't fall asleep for the last stop is Redmile right in front of a POW Hostel!! I hope you'll be able to get the 2.10 and arrived here just when I finish work.

I was waiting for your call all morning, but Miss Philips must have been busy on her way to meet Alfred. Did you see him. You ought to for he's going home soon.

It is 4:30 now. I'll get the tea ready and start my secret work afterwards.So I'll say cheerio, my darling and be good.

All my love and kisses
always yours
Hans

92 Wharf St.
March 8th.

My dearest Hans

I suppose I should really write a long letter and try to explain but I'm not in the mood. I will do that some other time because I should explain it is not enough that I just say I am not sure that I love you enough. There is another thing, you say I looked happier when I had told you. You seemed very pleased with yourself. why? I was glad you were.

About Wednesday I had better meet you in the same place same time as last time, that is outside the Gaumont at 5:15. I have been to the pictures tonight. I went to see " A man about the house", it was very good. I was going to stay in but this dinner time I saw Dora. She said she felt fed up, so did I. So we decided to go to the pictures.

I was speaking to Kath this morning. I felt really stuck for words. she asked me if T Woods had said anything. I did not know what to say. So I said "No". I thought she would have been hurt if I had told her we (Iris and I) knew about it before she did. I did not like Tony Woods for that, at least he could have told Kath first. Kath said she was probably coming into Leicester one day this week to buy some shoes. I hope it is not on Wednesday. She said she had seen you on Sunday.

When you rang this afternoon I had got Mr Simpkins baby on my knee, he was talking to Mr Scott. Mr Scott had come in for a cup of tea. Mr Simpkin often brings his little boy in. He has 11 children, his daughter has a baby older than his. Mr Simpkin is the National Farmers Workers Union leader. A real communist. He is very nice though.

> Well darling I will have to say goodnight and
> God bless.
>   All my love
> Jean
>
>   ..

46   L.A.E.C.Hostel,
                                           Stathern.
                                           March. 8 th. 1948

My darling.

I thank you very very much for that wonderful Sunday after-noon and I think it was the best one we spent together. Did you arrive home well? I got back here 10.00. After doing a few little jobs for the breakfast I went to bed and dreamed of you. At 4.30 this morning however, the bell rang and I'd to get up. After my morning work I went to bed again and told Mrs Betts to call me at 12.00, but I was surprised as the porter came upstairs and told me it is 2.00. I asked Mrs B why she didn't call me at the time I told her. Her answer was " You slept so nice so I couldn't wake you up". She is like a mother to me.

Well, my darling, how are you today? I was very glad you got a seat last night. I always feel sorry for you standing there in the bus and a long way to go.

Wasn't it alright darling having a little talk yesterday? You really looked strange to me and I was very much surprised as you told me you're not sure if you love me. Do you know what I think and my only wish is? You'll come one day and tell me yourself that you're sure. And I'll wait.

I really was astonished yesterday as I started talking about my holidays, but if your mother objects it's quite alright then darling. It would be a difference if I knew her and could have a word with her myself. So we may go to Skegness for one day and that will be enough for me.

Well, my sweetheart, time is getting on and I'll have to say cheerio. Think of me and God bless you.

Remember always that you mean everything to me

All my love and kisses

only yours forever

Hans.

92 Wharf St.

March 10th.

My dearest Hans

The bus went out on time last night because it was 8.45 when I arrived home. I had my supper and was in bed at 10.0. Thank you for the flowers they are lovely. I was speaking to Alfred this morning, I told him I was going out to Saltby this afternoon if the weather kept like this. He said he would meet me with a bicycle. It is just the place to be, at Croxton, and of course Stathern. Alfred was saying he will be on his way home in 5 weeks time. He's hoping to go to Scraptoft camp before he goes. That is about 3 miles from Leicester so it looks as though I shall see Alfred before he goes.

I am not going out tonight as far as I know. I may take the dog for a walk. In fact I shall have to take him out, he hasn't been since last Tuesday. He has been in the yard but not out for a good walk. I don't think he cares much for walking, it is a good job he doesn't, because he won't do much walking if he waits to go with me.

I will say cheeri'O. Iris wants me to talk to her. I will write tonight, heaven only knows what I will put because I don't do much.

Anyway be good

all my love
Jean

.

47   L.A.E.C Hostel,
            Stathern.
            March 11th. 1948.

My darling Jean,

Isn't it a lovely afternoon!! Be sure I don't feel like working inside today. I am writing this on my knee and I think you can tell. It is too hot in the kitchen so I took my easy chair and went outside and I am sitting in the yard under the kitchen window. Thank you very much for the most enjoyable evening.

I would like you being here now. We'd have a nice walk, take something out with us for a picnic and have a very nice time. That's what we'll surely do in the summertime. We'll have a very nice time.

Sorry darling, I troubled you again with a question last night, but it was my fault because I understood your letter wrong. You see I still have a lot to learn and I'll spend some time with reading your letters. Don't you think that's the best way? You'll learn a foreign language much better when there's somebody you can talk to. But there is one difficulty, that is, when this somebody comes only once a fortnight.

You always tell me don't feel fed up. If I'd been able to see a picture every time being fed up,the men wouldn't get a thing to eat. So stick to it. That seems to be the best way to be cured. I'll ring Alfred this afternoon and ask him if it's coming on Sunday. He promised to do so for it is the last chance for him. Saturday would also suit me. Or better, when you ring Saltby tomorrow tell him please to give me a call.

You didn't expect me on the market place yesterday did you? It was a nice surprise for me anyway. I hurried down from the bus station for you told me once you start about 2.05.

I caught a nice little rat this morning. Don't be afraid, not upstairs. Outside the house!

Well darling I'll have to say Cheerio now. Be good (I know you're always good) and think of me.

All my love and kisses
Always yours darling

Hans.

92 Wharf St.

My dearest Hans

This is going to be a very short letter, but I thought I had better send one even if it is only a few lines. I was going to write to you last night but I took the dog for a walk. I took him with me to see Alice and did not get back until 11.00. You ought to have seen me walking down Swain Street Hill with a bottle of milk in one arm and the dog in the other at 10.45. About Sunday. Alice asked me to go to tea but I do not want to go very much. I ought to see Dora this weekend. I have not seen her on Sunday for ages so I don't think I will come. I hope you don't mind. Anyway darling I will have to say Cheeri'O if I want you to get this tomorrow morning. I will write you a long one at the weekend so til then

All my love

Jean

.

P.S.

Please don't count the mistakes

48

L.A.E.C Hostel,
Stathern.
March, 12 th. 1948.

My dearest darling Jean,

Thank you very much for your letter. I rang Alfred this after-noon and he told me he may go to Mr Edward's. He men-tioned it to him last week. I hope you'll tell me tomorrow you're coming on Sunday. It'll be lovely weather. Will be like today and we'll have a nice walk around Belvoir Castle. It is wonderful up there. I've been awfully busy this morning. You don't suppose what I did. Some gardening. That's just what I want, working in the open air. So I cleaned all the yard and started on the front side of our hostel. It should look nice when the flowers grow there. I think I better do a bit every morning. That'll be a better exercise than walking. I hardly can stand on my feet now, it started last night. Pains in the old wound. That's the real reason I went out but it was worse afterwards.

As Alfred told me his ship is leaving on 14th April. His last working day is 20th March. So he knows his date at last.

I feel sorry for the pup. Can't you take him to the pictures once? It'll be a nice change for him, wouldn't it? Only running about the yard and I bet the yard is only small.

Don't you really know, darling, what to write to me? You'd better tell me a nice tale then or enclose a book. I know it is hard for you to say anything. It would be different if you would be sure! Then there'd be a lot to talk about.

Now, my sweetheart, be good. I hope to see you in Melton on Sunday.

> Till tomorrow
>
> All my love and kisses
>
> > Hans.

<u>49</u>   L.A.E.C Hostel,
                       Stathern.
                       March, 13.th. 1948.

My sweetheart

Thank you so much for the letter I received this morning and I was waiting for your call. I don't know what's the matter with my leg. Honestly I am very glad you're not coming tomorrow. Everything was alright on Friday afternoon as I asked you to come. It started Friday night and I hardly could walk then. The warden told me to stay in bed Saturday morning, but you know me. I don't like other people doing my work. So I got up at the usual time and as you rung me I was just fit to walk to the phone. After dinner I sat down and went to bed afterwards. Upstairs on my hands and feet. I've had it last year in Saltby but it is worse this time. I think I've a fever for my head is rather hot. Anyway I hope it'll be alright til Wednesday. Do you think you can spare me an evening? As I told you on the telephone I only slept half an hour last night. I was reading until 4.30 this morning, fell asleep then at 5.00 my bell rung. It really was a good job I hadn't any cigarrettes left for I'd have smoked some!!

It is 9.30 now and I'll be glad when I get upstairs safely. A quick bath and then to bed. I've got a good book just in case.

Did you think of that white scarf for me? If you're able to get one without coupons, please get it. I think to spend about 15s for it.

Now, darling I am going to say good night and God bless. Be good til I see you next week. As usually a good night kiss from your Hans. I'll try and write a few lines tomorrow afternoon.

Sunday is nearly over. I rung Alfred this morning and he told me he's not going away. So I asked him to come down and here he is. I got him down once at least. My leg is a bit better today and it'll certainly be alright on Wednesday.

Let's say cheerio now, darling and be good

All my love and kisses

 Yours forever

   Hans.

  92 Wharf St.

  March 13th.

My dearest Hans

Thank you very much for your letter and for ringing me Friday afternoon. It was a very nice surprise but unfortunately Iris was there and she was there again this morning. I always find it hard to talk when she is there.

I am regretting already that I told you I wasn't coming tomorrow. I am very sorry I hurt you but I told you on Wednesday I wasn't coming. I did not say maybe. I can go to Alice's tomorrow if I want but I am not going, Dora is coming to tea. I will take the dog a walk in the morning and do some washing, that all depends on the weather.

I went to the pictures last night (Friday) and have been again tonight, I went on my own Friday night I was fed up. I don't go to the pictures every time I'm fed up.

I met Dora this afternoon and we went into the town. I took the pup with me. One of the girls in the shop my cousin manages wanted to see him. She had never seen a Dachshund pup. I did not get anything (I will try for your scarf in the week) from the town. I went back to Dora's for tea and from there to the pictures.

Darling I hope your leg is better now. I have never heard you complain about it before, does it hurt you very often? If it does I should go to see a doctor, he may be able to give you something to relieve the pain, or do something.

Well ,darling, as you may have guessed by the writing I am in bed and tonight we put the clocks on one hour that means one hour less sleep in the morning so I will say good night god bless you and keep you safe

So till I see you again be good

All my love

Jean

50   L.A.E.C Hostel.
                            Stathern.
                            March 15th 1948.

My darling Jean,

May I thank you very much for your lovely long letter I received this morning. It was quite alright, darling you didn't come yesterday. Look, you told me Sunday last week you're not coming and I only rung and asked you on Friday because the weather was changing so nicely.

I feel a lot better today and can walk almost naturally. I know I've never told you about the leg before because there was no reason for. I'd it the last time as I came here in the first days of January, but it was worse this time. It hurts very much but I can stand it. I'll get over it in a few days. There's no need in seeing a doctor because they couldn't help me. There're still two bullets inside and they couldn't take them out as I was operated in the hospital without cutting the muscles. So I'll have them as a souvenir for lifetime, There're a few more pieces of metal inside the body but they don't hurt me yet.

I think I've told you already in my last letter that I've been in a nice mess yesterday morning. I read in the paper about putting the clock on one hour and forgot all about it later on. Three of the fellows here were going to work on Sunday morning taking the 9.10 bus for Plungar. They were waiting for me to ring the bell at 8.45 but nothing happened. So they waited a few more minutes and then one of them came upstairs to call me. Still half asleep I'd a look at the clock and told him it is 8.00. Afterwards I remembered. They got the breakfast then at 9.45.

 Can you spare me Wednesday evening? I would like to come.

Two of my fellows from Redmile are working here in the garden for a few days. Be sure it'll be a change for them. They're going home in a fortnights time.

Now, darling let's say cheerio and God bless. Take care of yourself well, and remember what I told you Wednesday on our way to the bus station.

> All my love and kisses
>> Always yours
>>> Hans.

92 Wharf St.
> March 15th.

My dearest Hans

You were right I did go out yesterday afternoon. Dora came early(3.00) so we went to Anstey and walked over the fields to Bradgate Park then through the park to Cropston. We couldn't get on the bus at Cropston so we had to go back to Woodhouse Eaves and get the bus from there. There were a lot of people on the buses yesterday I think when I come to Stathern I had better catch the bus before the 8.8 (that is if the weather is good) then I will be sure I'm getting on the Leicester bus

You did not say anything about coming to Leicester next Wednesday when you were here last week. I did not think you were coming. I am going out for tea on Wednesday. My cousin asked me last Saturday to go. I am staying in tonight and have promised to go to the pictures with Dora Tuesday. That is all I am doing

I'm glad Alfred was able to come yesterday. I didn't think you would get him there.

You remember me telling you about Kath going with a fellow at this office (Tony Wood) and he thought it was getting too serious well one day last week, he had an awful letter from Kath's mother calling him black. The night before he finished with Kath her mother bought him some cigarettes. She wrote asking him to send the money. He read the letter to Iris and I, but we couldn't help but laugh at it. So you have been warned. Keep away from Kath's house.

So till then
All my love
Jean.

R 15/3.48   Aschersleben, 23.2.48

                                    15/3.48

     My dear Hans
Thank you very much for your letter dated 2.2.48 and also for the photo. We can recognise you very well. When you get your new suit, you will have some nice photos done. Once

318

you have a radio in the kitchen, cooking will be more fun because you can listen to music whilst you cook. Winter is upon us now after all. We have minus 18°C. Our bedroom is very cold, almost unbearable. And we still don't get any coal, we are lost for words. And who suffers? Well, to a large part it is the refugees. We are without clothes and heat. The others get deliveries right into their cellars and who fills our cellars? We get nothing because we cannot give them anything in return. Many people steal the briquettes from the train station but I just cannot do it. I never refuse to work hard if there is something to be had in an honest way, but if it is dishonest, then I can't and will not do it. It is also very dangerous to climb up those carriages and take the coal, not to mention being caught! When it gets warmer I shall go into the woods again. What else can we do? Dear Hans, Horst laughed out loud when you told him to stop smoking. I know you mean well, but he hardly smokes one cigarette on a Sunday. He does not get any pleasure out of it. He will give it up, because we are saving up for an electric iron. Do you never get a Sunday off work? Auntie Erna and Uncle Erich and family are sending their love to you, and also Uncle Gustav and family. Tell us what you are eating these days. Do they write the menu out for you or can you choose what you want to cook? Now, my dear Hans, I would like to conclude my letter to you. I shall have to get something ready for our meal. We are having a vegetable soup with peas – everything in it was gleaned.

We are sending you all our love and kisses, your mum and your brother Horst. Give our love to Jean. Can you get baking powder there? We can get neither yeast nor baking powder.

Aschersleben, 23.2.48

My dear Hans

Today I am sending you my usual Sunday greetings. I didn't receive any post last week. It looks like the post is getting here very slowly. The parcel still has not arrived. I said to mum 'those who interfere with parcels should be punished in a way that they will always remember'. It was posted three months ago and I don't think that there is now any hope of it ever getting here. I went dancing again this afternoon. It was quite nice. Where else can one go and what else can one do? Winter arrived two days ago. It is very cold and today it is snowing a lot. We had given up on winter this year and were already looking forward to spring time. Alas, it was not to be. Dear Hans, how are you doing? How are you getting on with your cooking? How would you feel about doing a typical English Sunday Roast? I am very busy combing ladies hair every Sunday morning. Dear Hans, do you also listen to Radio Leipzig? This evening, I listened to Radio Leipzig again. They played film music. It is so lovely to have a radio again. It used to be very quiet in our home without it. Dear Hans, how is Miss Jean? I hope she is well. What is the atmosphere in general in England? Still PEACE!!! Or WHAT?? Our guests have still not arrived. We are looking forward very much to seeing Erna again. I am sure using the train in this weather is no fun. It was lovely to receive your photo. It looks very nice – pity about the dark shadow on it. You can't imagine how cold our bedroom is – it feels like an ice cellar! Mum has already prepared a jug with hot water. I shall finish my letter for today. I am sending you, dear Hans, and also Miss Jean, our love, from Horst and mum!

Here's to a healthy reunion in the not too distant future.

Write back soon.

Replied 15/3.48   Aschersleben, 26.2.48
                                                    15/3.48
        My dear Hans
We thank you very much, from the bottom of our hearts, for your lovely letter dated 17.2.48. You don't know who Auntie Frida is in connection with the tea? It is Frida Simon,

Papa's sister. I am sure you know her. She lives near Bremen. Frida Simon sent a message through someone, that, should you get some leave -- then we must go to her and you should come too, if you can't come as far as Aschersleben. You can't do much in 12 days and I don't know how long your journey would take and, of course, I don't know how much it would cost you either!! Two days ago Erna Schünemann came to stay with us. It was lovely to see her again and she had no problems coming over! She is staying with us until 2.3. and is sending her best wishes. We are so happy to think you have got something else for us! Can you not put Jean's address as the sender on the parcel? Mrs. Schulz' husband did something like this and the parcel arrived within three weeks. You know what, dear Hans, we have now given up hope of ever receiving the parcel which you posted on 24.11.47, it is really sad. What a pity it had to happen to us. We were so looking forward to it and we really could have done with everything. My black yarn is now all gone. I had a skirt made for every-day use from an old blanket. It won't last very long, I know, but we cannot get much here. Good luck with your new suit. Get yourself to look nice and smart. We can't wait to receive a photo of you and Jean, but please show a nice and pleasant face, not a sad one! Ask Jean to write to us. You will translate it and enclose the translation and – Bob's your Uncle! I shall try and send the ring to Gertrud. I hope it will be alright! Yesterday, we went to the cinema with Erna. The film was called 'Dog Days' and it was very good. Yes, I also hope that your apprenticeship was not done in vain.
I want to finish my letter for today. Please take care and stay well. Lots of love and kisses from your mum and from your brother Horst. We are hoping for a healthy reunion and are sending our best wishes to Jean!

Replied 15/3.48   Aschersleben 1.3.4

15/3

My dear Hans

I did not manage to write to you yesterday and send you my usual Sunday greetings. Erna left us this morning and we are feeling quite lonely again. She liked it here. She is starting a new job on 1 April in a hotel on the island of Juist. This is where Christa lives as well. It is about time she got out of Altenpleen, an awful wasteland area. Horstel is sick, he had to lie down yesterday. He had difficulties in breathing and also has a bad cough. He had to do a 'sweat cure' and is now feeling a little better already. He just can't stay in bed for long. But sometimes you cannot just shrug it off your shoulder that easily.

Auntie Erna is sending you her love. We had a letter from her today. She would love us to go and stay with her. I don't really know when we can go there. Horst told me that the hair dressing salon where he works may undergo some renovations in May and the employees will have to use their annual holiday if the shop closes. If this happens, then it would be possible for us to go and see her. The fare alone is quite expensive. We need at least 200 Marks. But it is so lovely to see our relatives again. Dear Hans, I think it would be best if I gave Erna the ring to take with her and she can post it to you from there. She will come past our house again on the way back. We are not allowed to send any silver by post. We shall find a way of getting this ring to you so that you can start enjoying it. We are so glad that the harsh winter weather is easing off. We were very worried about the lack of firewood. I am anxiously waiting for the weather to get better, so that I can go to the forest again and stock up on the firewood. I am sure it will get better soon. Please forgive me for my bad writing. I am listening to the radio and making lots of mistakes. Now my dear Hans, stay fit and healthy. I am sending you all my love and kisses, your mum and Horst. Give our love to Jean. Erna is sending you her best wishes. She will be home again by tomorrow afternoon.

<u>51</u> L.A.E.C. Hostel,
Stathern.
March, 16th. 1948.

I would like to thank you personally for your nice long letter I received today and I'll tell you it was a real surprise. After having spoken to you now I am sure I've to see the picture on my own. It is not so nice but can't be helped. I don't want you to cancel your arrangements with Dora because I know how it is to be told off. Anyway it was very nice of you writing in the afternoon. So you at least thought of me.

Did you have a nice walk then on Sunday afternoon? Only a few miles to Cropston isn't it And then the way back. Is that the exercise you want? I think it only will be the first nice Sunday such a lot of people being on the bus, because everybody is going for a walk.

Nobody could tell me yet what that picture "Saigon" at the picture house is like. Even Mr Pickering hasn't seen it yet.

I didn't know what to think about Kath. I couldn't help but laughing about that cigarette bill. That's the way to do it. Be sure you'll never see me there. I wouldn't like to get a letter like that from your mother.

Aren't you lucky this week, darling getting letters Monday, Tuesday, another one tomorrow. One on Friday and one on Saturday!! And I'll see you then on Sunday and that's certainly the best day of the week. We"ll have a nice walk around if the weather keeps fine. Otherwise, a nice and warm room is waiting for you.

My leg is better today. Anyway it had to be because I am going to Leicester tomorrow. What if I would call in tomorrow? You could only do one thing. And that is to call all the men from the office and have me thrown out. Poor people to be disturbed whilst having an afternoon rest. I better smash that clock tower so I'd have a reason to come in and ask for the time

Now, darling, I'll say cheerio. Be good til I see you tomorrow 2.05.

All my love and <u>kisses</u>
　　always yours
　　　　Hans.

P.S. I'll hurry up from the bus station!

　　　　　　　　92 Wharf St.
　　　　　　March 18th.
My dearest Hans

How did you like the picture. I think I will be going to see that on Saturday. I received your letter this morning. Thank you very much. Why didn't you save it until you saw me, by the way you did not put the beginning in.

I had a letter from Bernhard this morning. I have not answered his last letter yet. I am going to answer this one straight away. Bernhard has not got his family with him yet. Apart from that he hasn't anything to complain of.

I will be coming on Sunday on the 1.30 bus from Leicester. If the weather is nice and your leg is alright we shall be able to go for a walk. I did not see Dora on Wednesday night. I went to an aunt's for tea. I came home about 9.30.

I haven't been out tonight. My mother has started my dress, even though I don't do anything she likes me to stay in and thread the needle.

I will see you on Sunday so till then

All my love
Jean

　　　　　52　　　　　　　　　　　L.A.E.C. Hostel,
　　　　　　　　　　　　　　　　　Stathern.
　　　　　　　　　　　　　　　　　March. 18<u>th</u>1948.

My darling Jean,

324

After all the miseries I am back safe and sound. I arrived in Stathern 11.30!! Aren't you surprised? You can't suppose what I was doing. After I left you at the Gaumont I went in and saw the picture. It finishes at 7.55 so I'd plenty of time to go to the station. Wasn't the weather nice at that time. Just enough rain to get wet through after half an hours walk. The bus was not waiting for me so I'd to wait for it. There was a fellow from the R.A.F sitting with me upstairs and started talking about courting. He never fancied I was a German. Now, darling, let's have some explanation about my late arriving. The Plungar bus had gone but fortunately the Redmile one was waiting already. It was still empty so I went right to the long backseat and lay down for a sleep. It was 9.20 then. I didn't even hear the bus moving and as I woke up I found myself in Bottesford (the last stop), but it was a good thing the bus had to go back to Melton on the same route via Stathern and so I arrived a bit later. I looked at my clock this morning and found out it was 5.45. As you know the breakfast for the first few men should be ready by 6.00. I never before in my life dressed as quick as this morning. I was so tired that I hardly could open my eyes. You'll be surprised to hear that I even, on my way to Leicester in the afternoon, fell asleep. Sometimes one gets tired. What I need is a weeks rest. I really enjoyed the picture. It was funny and about people who won money on the football-pool. I hope you also enjoyed the tea at your cousins.

I read in the Leicester paper last night they're going to increase the bus-service on the Leicester-Melton route commencing Saturday 20th. There may be a later bus back to Melton than I hope. We would then be able to see the pictures through.

Isn't it really funny, darling your office out of bounds for me? Don't worry I don't mind. I didn't know what to do in the afternoon so I walked round to the Odeon and saw "Saigon". It was not bad at all. I posted the letter on my way there. As I looked at the watch it was 4.55 and I thought there might be a chance to see you at 5.15. But it was too late to get the letter back.

As you started running down that street yesterday I thought you'd seen me and were running away. So I had to start running as well. I checked up my weight yesterday and found it was 12.2 stones instead of 13.7 st last time. Done well with my exercise haven't I? I'll continue a bit longer and my weight will be -/- in a years time.

Isn't it lovely again this afternoon. I'll go to the garden after finishing this letter and put some potatoes in. I like to be outside in the sun,

Well, darling, I'll do my outside job now. I'll be in Melton Sunday 2.00. Be good til then

All my love and kisses
Yours forever, sweetheart
        Hans.

                                          L.A.E.C. Hostel,
              <u>53</u>   Stathern.
                                          March, 19 <u>th</u>. 1948.

My sweetheart Jean,

This'll be a very short letter, darling, for I've lots of work to do this afternoon. I don't want you to miss a letter on Saturday morning. I was hoping to get one today, but I have to feel sorry for myself. I'd one from my mother instead. Is everything alright for Sunday? I expect you then in Melton on the 2.15 bus. Mr Pickering is going home this weekend so I'll have to hurry with my work Sunday morning. I think I'll do a lot on Saturday afternoon for instance potatoes, greens. I am well and I hope so for you and your dear mother. As I learned today we (hostel staff) are to be paid by the hostel officer commencing next week. The slips are to be signed with a fountain pen with a golden nib. I hope we'll get it also every Friday. It is Alfred's last day today so I think I better ring him this afternoon for he'll certainly forget it being busy with packing his things.

Now, darling I'll say cheerio.

Be good and take care of yourself well. Till Sunday

All my love and kisses

Yours

Hans.

92 Wharf St.   March 22nd.

My dearest Hans

I arrived home safely at the usual time, 9.30. I gave my seat up to let an elderly lady sit down. I thought she needed the seat more than I, but I did not have to stand long. Did Mr Pickering tell you I rang this morning. I could not ask for you because Mr Shilton wanted him and when I went on the line to see if we were still connected, it was too late they cut off.

  I have to take the dog to the vet. He has a few bare patches on his back. I am taking him before he loses all his hair.

I will write a longer letter later on, so be good

All my love

Jean

P.S.

Should I have put

love Jean

54

L.A.E.C. Hostel,
Stathern.
March, 22 <u>nd</u> 1948.

My dearest darling,

I am very sorry I talked so cruel to you yesterday and I wish you'd forgive me. I am really sorry darling. I thought about it and I didn't even notice I might frighten you away, but you know how I am longing to see you. I've told you I love you and I always will do so. I am sure we'll have a very nice time together- just the best time of our life-. Anyway I promised you not to talk about it anymore and I certainly will keep my promise.

Now something else, darling. Did you remember it was 21st March yesterday? Beginning of the spring and just two months til your birthday. Please think about it if there is anything you'd like to have. You know quite well I'd like to give you something very nice. The best is just good enough. Don't worry about the money. I know best how to spend it because I know it isn't easy to earn. I always like to see you happy and gay, and always keep smiling, darling.

Please, let me know about coming to Leicester this week. If you can't spare Thursday evening, I've had it, but remember I'd like it very much to come and go to the pictures with you. .

I'd like you to come earlier Easter. Shall I ask that fellow again for some eggs for you? Your mother may need some if she's going to make a cake for the Easter holidays. I forgot to ask you yesterday.

I got my money this morning for that win on the race . £3-4-6. Nice isn't it. That is 16 times as much as we put on.

Do I get a letter tomorrow morning? I hope you wrote last night after you got home. I just learned you rang Mr Pickering this morning and didn't even ask for me? Oh oh!! So busy!!

Now, darling I'd like to say cheerio. Be good and God bless. Look after yourself well and remember how much you mean to me.

So till I see you on Thursday
(As I hope crossing my fingers)
All my love and kisses
    Yours forever
        Hans.

<u>55</u>   L.A.E.C. Hostel,
        Stathern.

March, 23rd 1948.

My darling Jean

Your letter was rather short but I don't mind for I know it is a job to write at work. I don't like to be disturbed whilst writing to you. I hope that fellow is coming this afternoon so that I could ask him about the eggs and I want you to get them before Easter. That means there must be a possibility to see you before or otherwise I've to bring them straight to 92 Wharf St. Your mother would be a bit surprised then, I bet.

I went out for a walk last night about 8.30 and went nearly up to Harby and back. You know that corner where the bus stops, a few land army girls were standing there asking where I was going to. I said I was only out for a walk and they offered me company. You should've seen how annoyed they were as I told them better to get going. There'll always be the right answer from me. I suppose the girls talk about everything at night and so they'll know me shortly and what I think about the whole lot. So I hope they won't even talk to me any more.

Now, about the ending of your letter. Listen, darling, you know what best to put there. Please yourself and do it as you really feel. If you put the same as you always did I'll know it is true.

Please, darling don't forget to let me know about Thursday till tomorrow 10 o'clock for I've to tell the warden that Mrs Betts need not come tomorrow afternoon.

I'll say cheerio, my sweetheart and God bless. Be good til I see you again. Don't forget to arrange to come early Easter!!!

All my love and kisses

    Always yours darling

      Hans.

Replied 28/3.48   **Aschersleben 7.3.48**

                          23/3.48

My dear Hans

Thank you very much indeed for your lovely letter dated 21.2.48. Your letters always reach us quicker than our letters reach you. Today, the sun is shining again and the whole world looks different already. We had such horrible fog for five days, it was so thick that we could hardly see anything from one side of the street to the other. It was very difficult to breathe. Horstel was sick for eight days. He was in bed for quite a few of them. He is very restless and would rather go to work. On Monday he is going for another chest X-Ray. I am always worrying about him because he has grown so much and so quickly. Health is the most important thing. I am very happy to read that you have bought yourself a new suit. I am sure it will make you feel a lot better. You will look very smart at Easter. Will you get some time off from work? How kind of you to send us some more sweetener! The parcel has still not arrived here, I think it is becoming more and more hopeless but it is very sad for us. I am finding it hard to understand because Mrs. Schulz gets all her parcels, and very quickly, even the one from Canada which contained 12 pounds of food. We are just very unlucky in this respect! The thing is, if you have not got very much then it is even more painful. Dear Hans, please can I ask you something? Would you be able to get a shirt for Horst? His shirts are becoming impossible to repair, and I would love to give him one for his birthday in May. He needs a size 36. You would make me very happy if it were possible to get me one. He managed to just about get through the winter with his old shirts, but he can't carry on with them. I am trying so hard to get things here, but it is just impossible. If you could also get some more white, dark brown and dark blue yarn, because we have to do such a lot of repairs to our clothes, we can't get any cloth patches either. I hope Erna can take the ring with her when she comes by next and then post it to you from there. Give Jean our love. Please take care of yourself and stay healthy! I am sending you lots of love and kisses, your mum (who is always thinking about you) and your brother Horst. Here's to a healthy reunion!

> 92 Wharf St.
> March 25th.

My dearest Hans

I am going to try to write a long letter but I am going to write to Iris as well this afternoon.

I arrived home safe at 1.40 in the morning and I did not feel a bit tired. I didn't feel like getting up this morning.

Do you know what Mr Pickering was telling Mr Sanders yesterday, because Mr S said to me "has he come" I wondered what he was talking about, then he said "I brought him into Melton and he was going to catch the bus to Leicester". I knew ~~what~~ who he meant then. He wanted to know if he had to start saving for a wedding present.

56

> L.A.E.C. Hostel.
> Stathern.
> March 25th 1948.

My darling Jean

Don't you think I'd better start a letter in case you don't come tomorrow? There're only eight men for dinner tonight and two tomorrow morning. So it'll be easy enough for me. I think there isn't much hope for me to see you tomorrow. Now, everything depends on your sister, but of course I cross my fingers.

I am on my own at the moment. The warden is in Melton with some visitors from Leicester. Mr Shilton and I think the other fellow is Mr Hazelding. Never heard of him. They left a few minutes ago. After all I stopped in Melton yesterday afternoon. Rung Mr Pickering after I'd spoken to you and told him our emergency slips were posted already. So he told me to stay away for the afternoon. I saw a very nice picture called "The yearling" and was back in the hostel at 9.00. Then I made my list out about meals till Monday and went to bed.

Now I think I better get going with my dinner. The boys are coming in earlier tonight to get home in time for supper. I'll write a few more lines tonight. Be good my darling and fulfill my wish.

Thanks very much for your call darling. It'll be a nice day. I just wonder what bus you're coming on. Anyway I'm glad you're coming after all.

I overslept this morning. We were playing darts last night till 11.00. As I woke up this morning, the sun shone through the window. It was 10.00 and both the men were sitting in the lounge, waiting for the breakfast. One of them came upstairs at 9.00 and as he found me still sleeping, he didn't want to disturb me. The warden was up earlier than I. it is now 2.30. Maybe you'll be on the next bus. Everything is ready for us to go.

Cheerio now, my sweetheart and be good. I'm sure we'll enjoy the afternoon.

All my love and kisses
Yours forever

Hans

L.A.E.C. Hostel,
Stathern.
March 28th 1948.

57

My darling,
Well, darling. The last holiday is half over. I thank you very much for your coming on Friday and yesterday. I really enjoyed these days and I think there wasn't a better Easter time for me for years. As I told you I always feel like being at home when you're with me. Everything is so nice then and I like to wait on you and make everything comfortable. I like to see you pleased.

Mrs Betts came this morning and brought the cigarettes she's got for me and the money as well. Afterwards she told us it's her birthday today and she likes to give <u>us</u> a present. I couldn't help laughing.

Did you get home well last night? I went to bed at 11.30. Maybe you noticed me leaving the bus again after I left you. Three of my fellows, also civilians, were standing outside. So I went to have a word with them. All three had one over the eight. I think I was glad they kept quiet whilst being on the bus. One said " that's the last time I drink beer". All the people were smiling. He was about my age. See, that's why I don't drink anything. I am quite sure when I meet my fellows and go for a drink I won't know when to stop and I don't like to be ashamed of myself and other people seeing me drunk. So I think it is better to keep away from alcohol.

You're quite the same yesterday as you've been a long time ago or better as I know you. I thank you very much my sweetheart. You made the days pleasant for me.

Well, darling, I'll say cheerio. Be good and God bless. Take care of yourself when you go out.

> All my love and kisses
> > Yours forever darling
> > > Hans.

Replied 1.4.48   Prenzlau, 29.2.48

Dear Hans

Thank you very much for your letter 29.2. which I received a few days ago. I had intended to reply much sooner but did not find the time to write down all my thoughts. Today is Sunday, it's quiet and it feels lonely like so many Sundays.

First of all I would like to thank you for the lovely photo. I noticed that the house in the background, which used to be very small, has become a very much larger house. I would have noticed it anyway, even if you had not told me.

You did know before you posted the letter to me, that it would not make me happy. Is it really necessary that we both hurt each other with our letters? I did not know, however, that my previous letter was unfair towards you. In the meantime, I have listened to a lot of Prisoners of War who returned home telling their stories and talking of their experiences. Mum's husband's son has just come home from England. And I am very sorry. Hänschen, you will be lenient with me, won't you? I have to hurry. Otto has taken the horses for an inspection and he will be back soon.

Yes, Hänschen, I want to become free of prejudices and spend my energy and concentration on my husband and the farm. I don't know if I can succeed. One has to be healthy for this life. I was saying today that sometimes it feels like I am just wasting away. I avoid going to the doctor's and I don't like undergoing treatment, not even for serious health problems. Today I got out of bed at lunchtime. I was unwell for several days. My gall bladder gives me a lot of trouble.

16.3.48
I am hoping to post this letter today, otherwise you have to wait too long for my reply. I received your letter of 3 March yesterday and want to reply to it immediately after this one. What has happened in the meantime? It would take a lot of time to tell you and I don't want to keep moaning and groaning about my aches and pains. I can go to the hospital but my fear is my business and I have to put up with it. I have other reasons than fear for not wanting to go into hospital. If I do go, I will not be able to work 100%. The motto here is 'work' Sundays and on Bank Holidays, all day long working in mud and dirt. I am forced to work with some very odd people. My family have already stopped coming. If you could watch me for just one day, quietly and invisible to anybody, you would say "poor Vera". Never mind, I do not deserve anything better. One day I shall tell you everything because you are the only one I can trust. Your last letter has reconciled me. Yes, we want to remain friends and always want us to be honest and open to each other. Hans, to be sincere is not as easily done as it is said. I have to think of you in order not to be unfair to Otto. Life could have been so lovely if I had not betrayed you. My remorse started very soon after the deed and this is what plagues my heart. Now I am here, all alone, and think about how different things could be.

Now to your previous letter. It made me very happy. I understand your letter and am sorry that I upset you with my letter. It seems I really do have a special gift to hurt people. It comes from being bitter and unhappy. Please forgive me but it came as a bit of a shock to me. I had hoped to see you soon. It would be absolutely unbearable for me – the thought alone is – if I had to leave this world without having seen you just one more time. And this is why I want to get well again. I am happy to read that you are thinking of me and you want to keep all your fingers crossed for me. You have written a lovely letter Hansi and I thank you for it. I can read the same passages again and again. When we meet again you must tell me everything that happened to you. My heart is heavy when I think of our reunion. I cannot stop the tears in my eyes. I have not played around with you Hansi, and I don't think that you were having these thoughts in your mind really. Yes. I know I have hurt you enormously. Unfortunately, it is not a dream but the naked truth. I hope this letter gets to you quite quickly. I would prefer to give it to you personally. When are you coming home? And you are not coming alone? Will you have just one day to spend with me? Or do I have to wait a long time? Please write to me about your plans.

Mum is sending her regards. She tells me that she has written to you on your birthday but has not had a reply yet. Mum finds it very hard to accept that things are not the way what they should be with me. I am confiding in her quite often. But everybody gets what they deserve. Manfred is very sick and we are extremely worried about him. The wedding is supposed to take place soon as he has already started his own family. We have a lovely little orphan girl now. She is so much like my little sister who passed away. We spoil her a lot of course, she is mum's only happiness.

I have to go back to work now.

I hope to go back again soon but I shall not be able to get home quite so often.

Otherwise I am alright and I hope you are too. Write back again soon.

I am sending you my best wishes (coming from the heart) yours Vera

92 Wharf St.

March 31st.

My dearest Hans

Thank you very much for your letter, did you forget to post it, it was written on Monday (dated for Sunday 28th) and I did not get it until today. I have run out of ink so I will have to write the rest in pencil. I hope you don't mind. I arrived home safe on Sunday about 11.15, but it was cold waiting for the bus, there were a lot of people left behind. I don't know whether there is another bus that comes from Waltham, there used to be one.

I think there is something wrong with your telephone. I rang twice yesterday, the first time there wasn't a reply the second time engaged, then I did not get a chance to call again. I was going to get up early on Monday morning, but it was almost 9.00 before I woke. Dora came round at 10.30. Of course I wasn't ready, but Dora is used to that, she always had to wait for me. I always used to make her late for school. Anyway we started out about 11.15 to go to Bradgate Park, but there was a terrible long queue, so we got on the Lough-boro bus and went to Rothley. We walked to Woodhouse Eaves, it started to rain so in a pub we went. After we had had our dinner there, when we came out and it was pouring, so we got on the bus and came home. At night we went to see a good picture called "The Unfaithful". That is all I did on Easter Monday. I went to the pictures again last night to see "Easy Money", it was very funny in parts. I think this is a long letter don't you? I know there's only three pages, but the paper is wide.

The showroom door keeps opening, I look up to see who is coming in and it is only the wind. It has been terribly windy this afternoon in Leicester. I expect it is worse at Stathern.

I will have to say cheeri'O. Lucy is on her own today so I will

have to offer to do the washing up. So be good
All my love
Jean

<u>58</u>

L.A.E.C. Hostel,
Stathern.
March 31<u>st</u>1948.

My darling Jean,

I'm sorry I can't see you this week. I still remember Sunday afternoon and you saying " you've had it chum!" I don't even mind if you're busy at home. There must be something wrong with our phone. I really was waiting for the call till 5.15. Then I knew it was too late.

Now about me, Easter Monday. I went down to Melton on the 4.10 with that young fellow who stayed in. We were going to see the picture "Fear in the night". Just in time I remembered there was a fair on and we went there till the picture started. Walking around I decided to do some shooting and try my luck. After the first two shots I had two prices. I thought it would be best to make it half a dozen for the one useful. Five more shots and I had what I wanted. Half a dozen....... Sorry darling I am not going to tell you what it is. I've told you on the phone better to come and see yourself. It shall be a surprise for you. Maybe you'll like it maybe not, but I just wanted them for <u>you</u>

There was rather a crowd about and one of them asked me if I'd been a sharpshooter in the army. I said yes but in the German army. He started to shake hands afterwards and told me I was a good show. Anyway I am glad I have got something for you, darling. Did I tell you about the queue on Monday night? I took the 8.10 bus to Plungar and there's about 100 people waiting for the 8.55 to Leicester. I've never seen a lot like that, and then only two single buses.

My fellow from Goadby Marwood hostel was here last night and told me there is a boxing match on tonight. I couldn't tell him a thing because I wasn't sure if you could spare me

Thursday evening. I'll ring him up now and tell him I am coming to see him. If the boxing match is too late I prefer to go to the pictures.

I'd a letter from my mother this morning. The first one since about a fortnight. She and my brother are alright and she sends many Easter greetings to you. I told you she asked me why you don't write once. If you write a few lines and I'll put them in my letter the next time. Of course you may please yourself.

Well, my sweetheart, I'll say cheerio. I'd like to answer my mothers letter and ring you afterwards from Melton. Please let me have a letter at least in the morning. So long and be good.

>All my love and kisses
>Yours forever
>Hans.

R 13/4   **Aschersleben 15.3.48**
31/3

   My dear Hans

Thank you so much for your letter dated 2.3.48. We went to Güsten to visit the Schmetzgens, who also used to live in Pyritz. We had not been there since July, even though they only live about one hour by train from here. I felt so ill and did not really want to go, but they wrote to us again asking if we can come. It always makes a nice change when meeting up with friends. They are sending their love to you. I might go to Berlin with them on 7 May. There is going to be a big meeting on 8 May with lots of people from Pyritz. I would love to go because I shall be able to meet a lot of friends from 'the good old times'. On Friday, weather permitting, I shall go to the forest to get some more wood. I am very pleased that you are enjoying your cooking, and – most of all – baking. I can well imagine that you like that. I suppose if you want to gain more experience, you will be changing jobs again? Who would not go for it!! I went to the post office yesterday and wanted to report the missing parcel, but I could not do it from this end. Apparently the sender of the parcel has to lodge a complaint. They may be able to look into it at their end. I am so dreadfully angry about it. I was so looking forward to receiving the stockings because we can't get any here. Horst is writing to you today as well. Now, my dear Hans, we are wishing you a happy and healthy Easter holiday. Will you get some time off work? I hope you will have a nice time. I suppose Jean will come to see you during the Easter holidays. How is the photo coming along you promised us? I hope it'll turn out really nice. The ones from your work were very nice! We are receiving some lovely music on the radio again today. Are you still listening to Radio Dresden? We get Radio Dresden quite often too, they always have a good programme. We also tune into Radio London. Give our love to Jean and wish her a happy Easter from us. We are sending you all our love and kisses, your mum and your brother Horst. Here's to a healthy reunion.

R 13/4   Aschersleben, 15.3.48
        31/3.

        My dear Hans!

I want to thank you from the bottom of my heart for your lovely letter dated 24.3.48*, which reached me again in good health. I am well again now after having been in bed for four days. There is no bigger punishment for me than to have to stay in bed and not being able to go to work. I had a very bad bronchial catarrh. One cannot take anything to do with the lungs lightly, aone has to be really careful. Eight days ago I had another chest X-Ray and everything seemed to be alright then. Yesterday we went to Güsten and met up with friends from Pyritz. Our training course finishes at the end of April, then we have our final hairdressing exam and a 'cosy' get-together. I am going to produce a wonderful hairdo. I would have loved to have had the bits to decorate the hair and I don't know whether you managed to get any. We are in Class A, six of us, not many because lots of them are not interested in this profession. I, for my part, enjoy ladies hairdressing very much. Wow! I can see you already as a head chef – we will not be able to keep up with you. I am also trying very hard to progress and achieve a high standard of hairdressing. Sadly, your parcel has still not arrived. Every time we think we have something to look forward to, it seems to go wrong. I do have another wish but hardly dare to write it down. Mum must not, under any circumstances, get to know about it, otherwise there will be one hullaballoo. If at all possible, would you be able to buy a pair of pretty shoes for mum, in size 39? Maybe I can make up for it when next you are here again. That's my wish. You have no idea what mum's clothes look like, sadly. We have still not heard anything from our beloved Papa. But, we are sure that he is coming home one day. I want to close my letter for today. Give my best wishes to Miss Jean and to you, dear Hans, we are sending also our very best wishes, from your brother Horst and mum. Write again soon. Here's to a healthy reunion. We are wishing you a happy Easter with lots of Easter eggs and are sending our love to you and Miss Jean. Yours Horst and mum

* clearly a date error

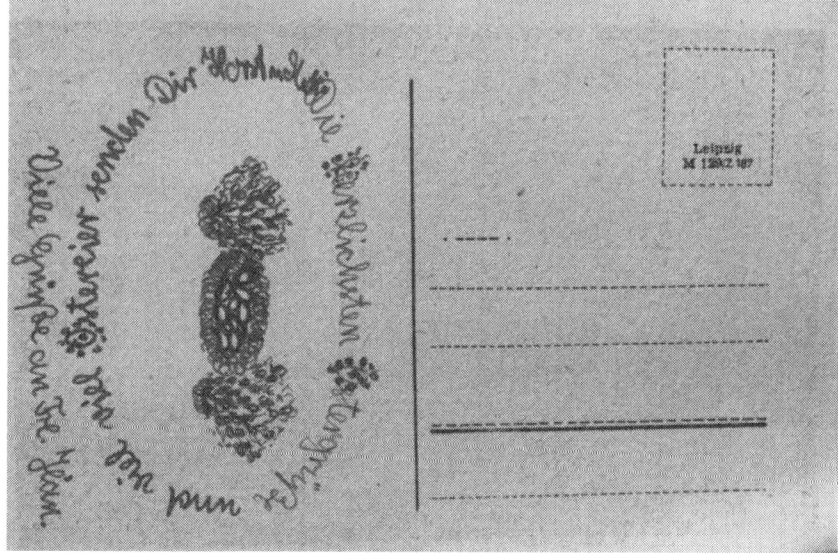

In the circle it says:

We are sending you our love for Easter and hope you will get many, many Easter eggs.

Yours

Horst and mum

Give our best wishes to Miss Jean

92 Wharf St.
April 1st.

My dearest Hans

Thank you for your letter and I did like getting a letter this morning.

I am glad you had someone to go into Melton with Easter Monday, even if it was only that fellow - though this may be hard to believe, I do hate you being on your own. I'm glad you were able to get a <u>prize</u> (that is how you spell it). I always thought those shooting ranges were crooked, but I was wrong. I am glad you told me what you had won. I couldn't have waited, but you hadn't ought to give in to me so easily. I am spoilt at home without you spoiling me too.

When I rang on Wednesday afternoon I had forgotten you were going into Melton. I spoke to Mr Pickering, he was telling me that he was going to London for the holiday and how everything got messed up.

If I do not stop speaking to POW's I will get myself in a mess. There is a fellow from Stoughton coming into see me tomorrow, and Alfred said he was coming in whilst he was at Scraptoft. Charlie's been in today and I think I will have to tell the other fellow not to come in yet. I think three is too many to have in, in a week. I don't mind Alfred coming but I should not like them to come together. I think Alfred would take a poor view of me.

I will write to you mother sometime if you will tell me what to put. If you will lend me your dictionary I will write in German, then you can have a laugh.

I can say you are lucky now. You will get a letter in the morning and I won't. I don't really mind. I have had three letters this week and I have only sent you 2. I will write a long letter on Sunday, but I won't promise.

Have a good weekend. I think you will enjoy "The Golden Earing". I am not going anywhere. I promise to be good and you be good too.

All my love

Jean

59

L.A.E.C. Hostel.
Stathern.
April 1ˢᵗ 1948.

My darling Jean,
Thank you very much for your lovely long letter. I received it this morning. It was the first one this week. I am sorry I really forgot to post the letter I wrote on Monday. I wrote it before I went to Melton and forgot all about it as I went to the fair. We'd to hurry to get to the pictures on time. I noticed the letter in my pocket as the bus left Melton, and the main reason for my going was to post the letter. I wanted you to get it on Tuesday.

There was something wrong with our phone. I was here til 2 o'clock yesterday and all day Tuesday waiting for your call. The warden rung up the post office yesterday and there came a man this morning to have a look. It should be alright now.

I left here yesterday at 2.00 and stopped in Goadby Marwood til 5.00. The warden there rung Mr Shilton whilst I was there. I asked her who was answering the switchboard. She said it was always the same, kind girl there. I didn't say anything else. In the evening my fellow and I went to the pictures. It was called "The Locket" and I enjoyed it very much.

The warden told me you asked for me yesterday in the afternoon. What was the matter, darling? Anything important? Did you forget I told you I was going away?

Well I'll say cheerio, and be good.

All my love and kisses

Always yours

Hans.

92 Wharf St.

April 3rd.

My dearest Hans

I do hope you have had a good weekend. I can't say yet whether I have had a good one or not as it is only Saturday (I will call you on Monday)

Last night (Friday) I went with Betty to look at a house one of my auntie's has to let, but she isn't taking it because she doesn't like the district and the house was rather dark inside. I thought she would put up with anything to get a home on her own. At the moment she is living with her mother-in-law, they get on fairly well together, but sometimes they don't hit it off together. In case you are wondering who Betty is, it is my sister. Susan is staying the night. She stayed last night too. I don't know why but I think she must have taken a liking to me. As a rule we have an awful job to get her to stay. I have been to Lucy's for tea today. You won't know me next time you see me. I have been to have my hair permed this afternoon, I am wishing now that I hadn't. I feel as if I am bald, they have cut it short (you know how I like short hair). I went to a place in Birstall that is near to Lucy and she asked me to call in to see her when I had finished. I wasn't going for tea, but when I got there she had the tea all ready so I had to stay. I had a very good tea and I did not come away until 9.15. Dora had been waiting for me from 7.0. She did not mind. I am not seeing her tomorrow, but I have to take Susan, home otherwise I may have gone to Stathern.

So you think I am trying to make you jealous do you? Well it is the last time I tell you when anyone comes in. I did not think anything could make you jealous or so you told me.

You ought to see my pup now, he is getting lovely now. I will bring him one Sunday to Stathern, but I think I will wait until his back is better. I have to take him to the vet again next Thursday.

I had better get going to bed otherwise mother will wonder what has happened. It is 11.30 and I was on my way at 10.30. Then I thought I would write a few lines to you.

Be good, goodnight and God bless

All my love
Jean

<u>60</u>

L.A.E.C. Hostel.
Stathern.
April, 4<u>th</u>.1948.

My dearest darling Jean

Thanks so much for your nice letter. I am on my own today, but there's nothing to worry about. As I told you on the phone this morning Mr Pickering went to Leicester and the porter to Nottingham. I told the warden about my going out and then he told me that there's a rule that one of the staff has to be in the hostel all the time. I couldn't expect the afternoon off so I've to stay.

So. you like to get a letter every morning. Be sure so do I. However, you seem to be very busy and then there's no reason to mind. Mostly, the shooting ranges are crooked. The first two times I shot, I missed but by then one should now how the gun is. I've always had luck in shooting and I brought good a lot of prizes home. I never had trouble of that kind whilst being in the army.

You mean I shouldn't have given in so easily in telling you what I'd won. Look, darling, I would have liked to keep it a secret but I just couldn't let you ask without giving an answer. That doesn't mean spoiling you.

You seem to have quite a lot of acquaintances at Stoughton. How does this other fellow happen to know you? Is he working with Walter? And I'll remember there's something out of bounds for me. I am dead sure Alfred'll come in to say goodbye. I think he's going to Scraptoft at the end of this week.

We'll write a letter to my mother when you come next time. That is if there's time to spare. I'll certainly lend you my dictionary and we'll have a lesson. I wouldn't laugh because I know how I was starting to speak English.

I was surprised as Mr Sanders brought our money yesterday afternoon.

By the way I don't know yet if you've got my Easter card. You never mentioned it. There's nobody in for tea and supper today so it's an easy Saturday. It smells nice at the moment for I am cooking the ham. Did you give that bit to your mother? Or did you put it on your sandwiches?.

You should have seen the boys here yesterday as they came in at night and smelled fish, chips and green peas. They're standing at the door before I rung the bell and that seldom happens. One said " I just want yorkshire pudding now to be happy". He was lucky for I'd made some. Chips for all the men means lots of work for I've to do them in an ordinary saucepan. Starting at 2.00 I finished at 5.30. No wonder I went to bed 9.00. And all that in front of a red hot stove.

I heard you talking to the warden yesterday. The kitchen door was open and I rushed to the phone as he just said "cheerio". Listen darling, I'll tell you again there's always time to spare for you. Please remember.

I'd a letter from my mother today. She wrote there's something wrong with the Russians. After all she's very glad to know I am safe here. She also sends many Easter greeting to you.

Will you kindly remember my coming to Leicester on Wednesday? Please, spare me that evening. I enjoy a picture much more when you're with me. I leave it to you to choose a picture. I am sure I'll like it then.

Well, my sweetheart I'll say cheerio for today.

Well, darling, Sunday work is done and I am going to Melton now. The warden and his girlfriend are here so I'll ask her to take the letter along. You'll sure have it tomorrow morning. Wasn't it an awful day? Raining and snowing all the time. Now the sun is shining again. Mr P told me there is "Gone with the wind" in Leicester all next week. Can you find out which picture house it is on? I'd like to see it because people talk a lot about it.

Well, my sweetheart, I needn't tell you to be good for you promised to be. Cheerio till I see you Wednesday and look after yourself well.

All my love and kisses

Yours forever

Hans.

92 Wharf St.

April 5th.

My dearest Hans

How are you? It seems ages since I heard from you. What happened Sunday? Were you too busy at the W.L.A Hostel!!! Or was it Mrs Betts daughter? You know I am only joking I know you wrote I expect I will get it in the morning. I wrote Saturday night, but I did not post it till late Sunday night. I forgot to post it in the afternoon. I took Susan home and it was not until I got to Betty's I found I hadn't posted it, so I made a special journey to the General Post Office at 10.00. I have been to the pictures tonight. I went to the Gaumont to see" Mask of the Cain", it wasn't too bad. The supporting picture was the best, it was an old one made about 10 years ago called "Topper" it was very funny. It is time for me to go to bed again. I am going to ring in the morning. Good night and God bless. I looked in the paper to see what was on the pictures. At the Princes's is "Sundown" it is an old film but very good so I hear. I will meet you outside Kemps at Gallowtree Gate at 5.15.

You know where that is don't you. Where I met you the first time. So till Wednesday be good
All my love
Jean

	61	L.A.E.C. Hostel.

L.A.E.C. Hostel.
Stathern.
April 5th.1948.

61

My darling,
It was a very nice surprise for me to get your letter this afternoon. I went to Melton yesterday and saw a real nice musical picture "Carolina Blues" it was called. An American one. The second picture was of course a cowboy picture.
I think you like to have Susan with you. What about your sleep? Does she wake you up in time on Saturday?
I would like to see your new hairstyle. I remember my mother when she came from the hairdresser. She wouldn't go away for the next two days. I know you like short hair, but I hope it is not too short.
I don't think you're trying to make me jealous. You know quite well I was only joking. If you don't want to tell me anymore who is coming to see you, alright, I don't mind.
Are you going to bring your pup along when you come on Sunday? I'll save a nice bone for him to be busy. Mrs Betts has a pup too. She's always coming for a bone. I think dogs like me.
Well, my sweetheart, I'll say good night now. The men got

the supper and for me it is time to go to bed. You know my time is 9.00. So just be good and a good-night kiss from your Hans.

<u>6th April</u>

Thanks very much for your call this morning. I love to see you tomorrow. You know quite well how dear you're to me. Does it matter what you look like? Not to me, anyway. I'll leave it to you about the picture.

I'll take the 1.10 bus tomorrow and go to have a hair cut at Melton. It'll look better when my hair is also short. Don't you think so? Has Alfred been yet to see you? It should be the time now he's going to Scraptoft. Will you ring me when he's there to let me have a last word with him?

I got a letter from Gertrud this morning. You know that's the one who was living next door to us. She's sent a nice picture. I'll show it to you tomorrow. Now, darling, I'll say cheerio. Be good till tomorrow.

All my love and kisses

> Yours forever
>> Hans.

R 13/4   Aschersleben, 21.3.48

5/4

My dear Hans

Unfortunately, we did not receive any mail from you during the week, but I want to send you our loving Sunday greetings anyway today, on the first day of spring. We are not too bad health wise and Horst is better now, only he is very pale. He is also very busy at the moment. As Easter is upon us in eight days, you can imagine how busy it is in a hairdressing salon! The day before yesterday I went to the Harz forest with Mrs. Lehmann, in order to get some wood. The first trip was quite horrendous. On Tuesday got one load for Mrs. Lehmann. By the time we have brought home ten loads, we shall be quite pleased and not worry about the next winter any more. Yesterday afternoon, I spent five and a half hours chopping the wood up and this afternoon I put it all in a big pile. Horstel cannot give me a hand because he is too busy at work, and he is not very strong. I do feel sorry for him because he tries very hard and wants to contribute towards achieving a better life for us! If the salon gets renovated and Horst gets two weeks holiday, we want to go to Vorpommern. We would love to see our relatives again. But now the situation is getting more intense again, I don't know whether we should go. I am so happy to know that all is well with you. I wish I could say the same about Horst! I just hope it is going to be alright. Well, you are listening every day too. I wonder if you have a visit from Jean today. You are quite alone most of the time! I am listening to some lovely music on the radio again. It takes my mind off other things. I think we might get our electric iron after Easter. We had hoped to get an extra ration of sugar and flour for Easter, but we hoped in vain. Oh well, we have to be satisfied with what we've got! The main thing is we stay fit and well. Erna moved to Christa's on 17.3. Werner wanted to take her there and pop in to see us on his return journey which means that he would come this week. I had intended to give Erna the ring but I shall have to send it to her now and she can post it by registered mail to you. I hope it all works out alright. We are sending you and Jean our best wishes for Easter and our love and kisses, your mum and Horst. Here's to a healthy reunion.

> 92 Wharf St.
> April 7th.

My dearest Hans.

I was surprised when you rang this evening. I can tell you now why I asked where you were. I heard the operator say 'Press button A". I thought maybe you were in Melton. Mr Smith was sitting with me when you rang (he was the other side of the table) he usually comes in at 5.0 and at lunch and tea times. Mr Whiteman never said anything, I did not give him a chance. I don't really care what anybody thinks. It's just I like to keep my private life away from L.A.E.C. Funny I am not.

Iris is still away. She sent another certificate in so she will be away another week. I went to see her last Tuesday night but she had gone to her sisters. I suppose I ought to write to her but you know what an effort it is for me.

I told you yesterday that I was taking the dog to the vet. I got ready to take the dog. It started to rain and was very windy so I did not bother. I will have to take him on Saturday. You should see him now, he looks so sweet, he is asleep on my knee. I am going to a dance tomorrow night, it is an R.A. dance. I am going with Betty. I have been trying to do something with my hair. I ought to have said I like short hair on men but not on women! I am going to let mine grow long from now on. Have you started smoking yet? I have got used to people saying they are giving smoking up. Every time cigarettes go up they stop smoking. After a week they are smoking more. That is why I laughed.

I will say good night. I will write a few lines tomorrow.

Good morning, nice day if it wasn't so windy. It is really 'good afternoon' for it's 3.15.

Thank you very much for your letter, I am sorry you did not get one.

You ought to be nicer to the land girls they are only being friendly. What is the matter, do they frighten you or something.

Don't come down to Melton on Sunday I am not sure what bus I will come on. It all depends on what time we have lunch. I won't come tomorrow, although I would rather come when there isn't anyone in the hostel. I will be seeing you on Sunday. I will be as early as I can so til then I will say cheerio.

      All my love

Jean

62

L.A.E.C. Hostel.
Stathern.
April 8th 1948.

My darling Jean

I thank you very much for the evening, I enjoyed everything. Did Mr Wightman say anything to you? I know it was a shock to you as he suddenly turned up. But believe me it was a shock to me as you tried to get your hand free. Does it make such big a difference to you? Look, my darling, my opinion is not to care about other people. Let them talk whatever they want. We know ourselves quite well what to do. It is only natural with two people being very fond of each other. "Nationality makes no difference"! So I use your own words. That's what I can't understand you making it a big secret. Don't worry sweetheart everything will be alright in time.

I arrived safe and sound at 10.30. 5 or 6 land girls from here were also waiting for the 10.10 bus and asked me to take that one. I said yes and as the 9.45 passed by, I jumped in and off we went. You should have heard them swearing. That means I better stay in at nights. The lot may wait for me outside.

Are you going to see "Gone with the wind"? I better wait now until it comes to Nottingham. I may be able to see it there.

Isn't the weather wonderful today? Rain, sunshine, warm and cold. They're playing "April showers" on the wireless just now and it really is in time. I only hope we have a nice summertime and know we'll spend some very nice days together. Darling, that's the time I'm waiting for. Outside somewhere, nice weather and with you. Let me tell you there's nothing else more wonderful.

Don't hear other people talking about your hair. I like it very much, and I'll tell you, honestly, you looked lovely and I certainly mean it.

Well now, about our football match. Everything was arranged last night and we'll play one night next week. They've put me in as centre forward, but I've told them I am not a non-stop train to run about the field with 60mph. Anyway I think we'll manage. Let me know in time about the weekend.

Well, my darling, I'll say cheerio. Be good and look after yourself well

       All my love and kisses
        Yours forever
           Hans.

    92 Wharf St.

    Sunday 8.30.

My dearest Hans

To begin with I have not been out today. I came home from work at 11.00. I went to bed straight the way. I got up this tea time. My head is a lot better but my throat is still painful. I may go to work tomorrow, it all depends what I feel like in the morning. I hope you believe me, if you don't I can't help it. I am writing with a pencil that is only 1 ½ inch long, it was the only thing I could find. I don't know where my pen is. I couldn't find it and I left my pencil with Lucy. I wish you the best of luck on Wednesday. Is the Stathern team a good one?

I will say goodnight and God bless. I will write a few lines in the morning when I get your letter, if there is one.

Thank you very much for your lovely long letter. Did you ring up today? If so you will know that I am not at work. If I am no better tomorrow I will have to go to the doctor. As you know we are only allowed to have two days off without a doctors certificate. If Iris was at work I would go, then I could have the week off. What do you mean you don't mind talking to the land girls but most of the time that's not the finish. You flatter yourself don't you?

That is about all I can think of at the moment to tell you. I will try to write a long letter tomorrow.

All my love

    Jean

<u>63</u>   L.A.E.C. Hostel.

                 Stathern.

                 April 9 th .1948 Saturday aftern.

My dearest love,

Thanks a lot for your nice letter I received this morning. And many thanks for your call. How are you darling? I hope you're better when you get this letter. You'll have noticed that I was upset, as you told me, but not because you're not coming. It was your asking 'don't you believe me?" you should know by now that I do believe you. There is nothing to joke about. It just came a bit unexpected, that's all. I'm very sorry I can't come on Wednesday but I hope you can arrange for Thursday instead. As I told you we are playing Wednesday night. Come and look at me. Please don't laugh. I can see you smiling. Anyway, Didn't you know our phone is the same as a call-box? That means we also have to press button A.

You're quite right right keeping your private affairs away from the LAEC. Curious people should always get the right answer. I feel very sorry for your little pup. I mean you can't take him to the vet today. Don't you think it'll be the best to stay in bed for a few days. A lot of people have got a cold. I've got mine a fortnight ago and can't get rid of it. But I don't like to go to bed.

So you went to a dance. You didn't mention it last Wednesday, but a fortnight ago you said something about going on the 9th. What are you doing with your hair? Please, darling, leave it as it is. It really looks very nice.You'll be surprised, my dear but I didn't smoke today for I haven't got any. I've had a very nice afternoon again yesterday. Only five hours in front of that little stove, starting at 1.30 and I finished at 6.30. After doing the supper and went straight to bed. I also felt rotten.

I ought to be nice to the land girls? You've had it chum! Everybody else, but not me. There was a dance at the W.L.A Hostel last night. Of course not for me. Instead I made a very nice supper and told one of our own men to go over and tell the others. Not 10 minutes later all the men were here for supper. So they'd to stop the dance til the men came back. We'd a good laugh. The girls can't frighten me, but there's some difference as soon as they take the uniform. Most of them forget how to behave. They don't know the limit. That's the only reason. Besides that I am not a flirt. I like to talk, but most times that's not the finish.

Well, darling, I'll finish now for today and write a few more lines tomorrow. Good night my sweetheart, and God bless. A good night kiss from your Hans.

Sunday afternoon

How are you, my darling. Such a lovely day and you in bed. I hope you feel better by now. I really don't know what to do this afternoon. Maybe I am going to see a picture, but I really don't care when I have to go on my own. Did you write to me yesterday, I don't think I'll get a letter tomorrow morning for there's hardly anybody to post it for you when you're in bed. Shall I come and keep you company? "Out of bounds" would be your answer, I know.

Well, my sweetheart, I think I'd better close for know. I'll go for a little walk as long as the weather is nice. Don't you think I'll have plenty of exercise on Wednesday night? Don't forget to keep Thursday free for me, that is if all goes well.

Cheerio, darling and look after yourself well. You know how much I miss you today.

All my love and kisses

Yours forever
Hans.

Aschersleben 28.3.48
9.4

My dear Hans,
Today is Easter, but I'm very sad because we did not have any news from you for 2 weeks now.
No Easter greetings arrived, that takes away my joy of Easter. In the morning I went to church, Horst could not come with me as he had to look after some private clients, there were several… 20 ladies. He puts a lot of effort into fulfilling everybody's wishes. He is doing very well at his new workplace, his boss is very pleased with him. As an Easter present he received a bottle of lavender worth 20 Reichsmark and 2 curling hair irons worth 25 Reichsmark each. That made him very happy. He received plenty of tips this week: 13 Reichsmark, 15 eggs, 10 cigarettes, 1 litre of milk, 6 sandwiches and cake. Through his work he develops many relationships that are of benefit to us. Through one of his clients we got hold of a dinner set for 6 people and 5 mason jars. It makes me really happy that we can have our own things again. Also the Easter bunny did have something for me. I received a beautiful real silver chain with a silver rose, a kitchen broom and a scrubbing brush. These are things that I am really happy about. But our Easter joy would be better. if we would not have to be so alone. We wonder how you will spend your Easter celebrations? And where is our dear Papa!! Many others are returning, but we still are waiting in vain. This week I went three times to pick up wood from the Harz, it was very tiring, but one doesn't want to be worrying over stocks again. It is so beautiful in the forest, such a wonderful silence. We received mail from Auntie Lina, she sends her regards. They are waiting and yearning for Bruno, or a message from him. I wonder if you have visitors today? So you have

some Easter joy. Now my dear Hans I want to finish my letter for today. Stay healthy, be kissed and greeted from the bottom of our hearts from your Mum and your brother Horst. Send our love to Jean. To a healthy reunion.

L.A.E.C. Hostel.
Stathern.
April 12th.1948.

My darling,

I was waiting for your call this morning. I told you I was going to ring up at 12.00 to make sure for I thought you may have been very busy during the morning. Believe me, darling, I am really anxious. How do you feel today? My only wish is that you will be better in a day or two. If I only had had a word from you. Did you send for the doctor? It is awful to stay here without knowledge how you are. I hope to get a letter tomorrow morning.

I went to Melton yesterday afternoon and saw the picture "The bell comes down". It was not good at all. Mr Coy and his wife and son came yesterday so I nearly missed the last bus to Melton. He's had a look at the new houses opposite the hostel.

I am rather busy today doing the sandwiches in the afternoon. We're going to play football tonight before we see the other team on Wednesday

I would like to come round myself and see what's the matter with you. Please, darling be very careful and look after yourself well. I would like to wait on you now. I thought about ringing up your number, but I don't know if you're in bed. If you happen to go to the office tomorrow ring me as soon as possible. You know how much I am waiting for news. Very well, my sweetheart, I'll say cheerio and God bless. My thoughts are always with you.

> All my love and kisses
> > Yours forever
> > > Hans.

<u>64</u>   L.A.E.C. Hostel.
                              Stathern
                              April 13 <u>th</u>. 1948.
My dearest love,
I've to tell you something at first. Perhaps you've noticed it's
Tuesday today. You really are cruel to me. Don't you understand how I am longing to hear from you? I know you're
ill for you told me yourself on Saturday. It must be serious, otherwise you wouldn't have left the office during the
morning. I was waiting for mail twice yesterday and just the
same today, but not a sign from you.   Are you afraid of asking your mother to post the letter for me? I am sitting here
and waiting for news. Please let me know what's the matter.
I hope you feel better today. I am alright except one thing I
told you about.
We're playing football last night, however, the real match is
tomorrow. It won't be too bad for us.
This letter will be a very short one for Mr Coy just came in
and it is nearly 4.00. So I better hurry to post the letter.
Well, my sweetheart, cheerio and God bless. All the best to
you.
All my love and kisses
     Yours forever
                    Hans.

Replied 6/5.48

Aschersleben 29.3.48
                    13/4.48

          My dear Hans,

Today, on the second Easter day, I want to send you a few
lines. Mum and myself are very sad that we have not received
any mail from you for two weeks, especially now with the

celebrations. Maybe the mail is not working properly? Your lovely parcel has still not arrived, It is such a shame, all the beautiful, precious things. Now dear Hans, Easter has passed. How did you spend the Easter time? I went dancing yesterday and today, after all I can't leave my little crush Gisela on her own. I planned to go again this evening but my feet hurt very much and need to recover after so much work. I have a very nice circle of customers. We also had a very nice Easter present from the business. I received a big bottle of lavender worth 20 Reichsmark and a pair of curling hair irons worth 50 Reichsmark. It is really nice considering I have only been there a few weeks, actually already 8 weeks now. Where does the time go? I received 93 Reichsmark and 16 eggs in the Easter week. That amazes you, doesn't it? From Mum I received sweets, cream, passport cover, and money. To Mum I gave a silver chain with a rose pendant, a scrubbing brush and a broom. Dear Hans, how are you and Jean? Did you celebrate Easter well? Are you already in your other job as a head chef? We assume so as we haven't received any mail. On the 6.4.48 is our final Hairdressing exam. Please wish me luck. On the 12.4.48 is a big hairdressing competition in Leipzig, which I would like to attend, to watch. The boss has requested it. There one can learn a lot. Dear Hans, did you get the hair accessories? It would make me very happy. I'm so tired, I hardly can write any more! Now I want to close. Dear Hans, and also Jean , be greeted from the bottom of our hearts from Horst and Mum.

What about the picture?

To a soon and healthy reunion!

R 13/4.48   Aschersleben 31.3.48
                                                    13/4

        My dear Hans,
Thank you so much for your lovely letter from the 15.3.48.

We already thought you did not want to have to do anything with us anymore, because we did not receive any mail from you for nearly 3 weeks. You seem not to write every week now because the letter before the last was dated 2.3.48, a 13 days difference. Maybe you don't have much time. It is always such a joy to receive a message. So you've sent another parcel. We are so happy about it and hopefully we are more lucky this time.

Yesterday Mrs Schulz was with me. She received a parcel from her husband on Easter Saturday with coffee, tea, cocoa, sweetener, sewing thread, yarn and lots of other things. The parcels only took 3 weeks and all arrived here intact. She says he always shops in London and already has sent her 5 pairs of shoes and also different pairs for the children. He made friends with two families, who also send lots of things. Not everyone has such luck. Dear Hans, Erna could not come to us again. Now I have sent her a "signed for" parcel as she had forgotten some of her things when she stayed with us. I enclosed your ring. Fingers crossed it will arrive in your hands and wear it in remembrance of us. We hope it will give you some joy and you will like it. We are very sorry that there is no photograph, we've already waited so long for it. You must know what you can afford. At least you've sorted yourself out with the shoes. Take care with your leg, surely you will suffer from pain for a long time when the weather is changing. Stay healthy and write again soon. I have to prepare supper now, Horst just arrived from the shop. He is off again soon to the course. Now my dear Hans, be greeted from the bottom of our hearts and be kissed from Mum, who always thinks about you and your brother Horst. Lots of greetings to Jean.

To a healthy reunion.

    92 Wharf St.
    April 14th.
My dearest Hans

I was surprised to hear you had not heard from me. I sent a letter on Monday. I have not very much to tell you I am still alive and very much better, but I have to stay in bed until Friday. The doctor came last night and said I had tonsillitis. I am getting used to that. I have had it three times. I suppose the best thing I could do would be to have my tonsil out but I would have to wait until I get enough courage. Alfred is on his way home now and as far as I know he never came in. I wish I had made a bet with you. I heard from WIlli today (he used to be at Stoughton) he said things were worse than he expected. I have not very much more to say. Nothing happens. I am in bed all day and night. I have a beautiful view of Raven's factory.

I will write again and I will ring as soon as I go out. I will have to close now, my mother is going to post it. So cheeri'O
All my love
Jean

.

65

L.A.E.C. Hostel.
Stathern.
April 15 $\underline{th}$ 1948.

My dearest love,
Thank you very much for both your letters. I got the first one yesterday and the second one today. So I at least know how you are. Will you be able to come this Sunday? I hope so. Our match last night was not too bad, however we lost. We don't need an excuse for we played for the first time together. The result 3-1. I've scored the goal at least. I am really surprised at myself because I am not at all stiff today. I told you I was going to have this afternoon off. There's nothing special on the pictures in Melton and no reason to go to Leicester for I can't see you. So I may go to Nottingham for the first time.

You want to know what I mean saying talking to the land girls is not the finish. Well, you know yourself I don't flatter. But they come again and again and one can't get rid of them easily. That is what I would like to avoid. If anybody asks me a question I certainly answer it for I don't like people thinking I am impolite.

No, darling I didn't get your letter until Wednesday morning. I think you can imagine how I was waiting. When do you think you'll have enough courage to undergo the operation? Shall I go with you and hold your hand or have mine taken out as well? You'll be surprised to hear you would have lost your bet because Alfred was in Leicester. One of our drivers from Saltby went to Leicester on Monday and as he came back he told me that he's met Alfred in the Market Place. What about your bet now? Give her the money!! Well, darling, I'll say cheerio now. You should have enough time now to write a letter as long as a book. My only wish is you being well by now. I'll post the letter where ever I go so you can see where I spend my afternoon.

Take care of yourself, my sweetheart and be good
All my love and kisses
    Yours forever
        Hans.

66

L.A.E.C. Hostel.
Stathern.
April 16 th 1948.

My dearest love,
The week is nearly over. I hope you got my letter this morning for it was 6.00 as I posted it last night. I don't like you being without one for two days. How do you feel today, darling? Are you able to get up tomorrow? I wish you would come this weekend for the next week is the fourth week since you've been last.

As I did the greens yesterday, one of the land girls came to see me about something. I went up to the lounge and asked her what the matter was. It took her a long while to get to the point. After all she asked if there's a possibility for me to come to the W.L.A Hostel as cook. I told her politely that there's no possibility at all and if somebody would ask me I certainly would refuse. After a while she asked if I was going to Nottingham in the afternoon. Then she told me she was also going to see a picture and if I would wait for her at the bus. I was going to get on the 1.50 but it just left when I came round the corner and there she was, waiting for me because I was not on the bus. So we took the 2.10 to Melton and on the way she tried to tell me wits. The people were looking at us so that I really was ashamed. I told her to behave herself and keep quiet or I would change my seat. I left her at the market and went to see "Crossfire". The picture just started and who came in? She!! Seeing me and shouting was one thing. I had enough then for the second time. I left the picture house at 8.20 to get the 8.45 back to Stathern. It was a nice surprise to find her waiting outside again. Believe me how glad was I when I arrived here at 9.45. We left the bus and as I turned round to the hostel she asked if I would mind her coming round this afternoon. That was the last thing I wanted to hear. I told her straight what I thought and just then a soldier turned up and asked her where she'd been so long. He was waiting for her since 8.00. I was so glad there was somebody else so I got rid of her. And then you try to tell me the girls are just friendly. Anyway I've told her if I see her coming to our hostel I'll lock all the doors. See, that's what I meant with a talk not being the finish. You can't get rid of them when you start talking.

We've started something nice with playing football. The next match will be against Machinery-Dept. Waltham War-Ag on Tuesday next week. I asked what about a rest at night after a days work. The answer was, "catch up with the sleep at night". So let's have another go. I hope we'll be a bit luckier next time.

Isn't it lovely again this afternoon. I don't know how you can stop in bed. But I forgot "Uncle Doctors" order. Will you let me know about the weekend, darling. You know how much I am longing to see you. I think I've found something suitable as a birthday present for you, but I won't tell you.

Well, darling, I'll say cheerio and get going with my dinner. I hope the letter isn't too long. Be good sweetheart.

> All my love and kisses
> > Only yours forever
> Hans.

92 Wharf St.

April 17th.

My dearest Hans

I am well on the way to recovery now. The Doctor came this morning, he said I could get up, but that I wasn't to go out until about Sunday. I see him again next Tuesday. I had a letter from Alfred on Wednesday, he wrote it last Saturday. He said he was sorry he never had a chance to ring to say goodbye when he left Saltby. He said he would ring me at the office last Monday morning, of course I have had that, being at home. I am still waiting to know how you got on Wednesday night. How many goals did Mr Pickering stop or has one stopped him? Susan and Betty are coming down this afternoon so I will get her to post it. The pup has been in bed with me most of the time he is up and down stairs all day long. I have to put him on the bed to keep him quiet otherwise he barks so, and he doesn't take up much room in bed.

I will say cheeri'O. I hope you have a very good weekend and don't treat the land girls too bad

All my love

Jean

67

L.A.E.C. Hostel.
Stathern.
April 17th 1948.

My dearest love,

I thank you so much for your letter. I hope you got mine this morning and had some fun in reading it. So I've to start the fourth week without seeing you. Isn't it an awful long time, darling? I always hoped secretly that you may ask me to come and see you. So you are able to leave the bed tomorrow. May I come to Leicester on Wednesday? Please, let me know, darling. I told you in my last letter about our football match. I am still in my old position (centre forward) for next week. I didn't feel a bit stiff on Thursday but you should have seen me yesterday. Walking like a baby.

Mr Pickering was a good goalkeeper except the balls he couldn't get. He gave us a lecture before we went to the playing field. "Don't smoke before the match, during half time and just after the match'. I nearly got a shock as I saw him catching the ball with a cigarette in his mouth. There was something to joke about afterwards. The spectators had the most fun.

You really took the pup into your bed? Is that the only way to keep him quiet. Poor little fellow. I quite agree there should be enough room left when he's with you, but wait a few more months till he gets bigger.

Well, my darling, I think I better have a nice rest this afternoon for there's no one in, except myself and I don't bother about tea and supper for me.

Well, my sweetheart, I'll say cheerio. Be good and have a nice weekend. Take care of yourself

       All my love and kisses forever

         Yours Hans.

92 Wharf St.
April 18th. 1948.
My dearest Hans.
Thank you very much for your letters, I hope you have had a good weekend. This will be the 3rd weekend I have not been to Stathern, not the 4th as you said, I am probably going to take the dog in the park in a little while. Dora is coming to tea. I stayed in yesterday and that is all I have done and doing this weekend. My- the land army girls do take some getting rid of. I think you had better learn how to run fast not how to play football. When I see you remind me to ask what she was telling you on the bus I can't make out what you mean by wits! I still say she may have only been trying to be friendly or did she try to make love to you. I don't know and will probably never know whether Alfred went into the office or rang. Lucy has rung up two or three times to see how I am. She says she misses not having anyone to argue with, we are always arguing about each other's country, but we have some fun doing it. The weather is changing again, it looks like rain. Just my luck, beautiful weather whilst I was in bed, now I am able to go out it has started to rain. I will ring you one day next week. I have to see the doctor on Tuesday to get another certificate. I will probably have another week off, it will make a nice long holiday.
Dora has just come. I had better get ready so I will say cheeri'O.

All my love
Jean

.

<table>
<tr><td></td><td>L.A.E.C. Hostel.</td></tr>
<tr><td><u>68</u>.</td><td>Stathern.</td></tr>
<tr><td></td><td>April 19th 1948.</td></tr>
</table>

My dearest darling,
Thanks very much for your letter. There's nothing much to

tell about the weekend for nothing exciting's happened. I went to Melton to the pictures (Hey, Rookey) an American one. It wasn't too bad at all. You're quite right this was the 3rd weekend you haven't been, but I meant I am starting the 4th week today and I think that's also right. I am glad that you at least agree with me that the land girls take some getting rid of. I also think I'd better learn how to run fast. You don't know what I mean by wits? Do you know what "wit" is? WIT. What I wrote should've been the plural form. Maybe I was wrong. I don't mean to give you lessons in your own language.

I'd to go to the post office this morning to get some cornflakes. As I went round the corner she came out of the p.o. dressed in shorts and asked me how I liked her in shorts. The first moment I didn't know what to answer. Then I told her to get going and dress before she goes to the village and she promptly asked if I could wait til she comes back. I went to the post office and on my way back I'd the first lesson in how to run fast.

Anyway, my darling, I hope you are coming next Sunday. May I come on Wednesday? You may be able to meet me somewhere when I come on the 4 o'clock bus. Please!

As I told you in one of my last letters there'll be another football match this week. It is tomorrow night at 6.30. Didn't you say you wanted to have a look? You'll be able to now. Come in the afternoon and have your tea here.

Well, my sweetheart, I'll say cheerio. Please let me know about Wednesday. Look after yourself well.

All my love and kisses

    Forever yours

        Hans.

R 20/4.48   **Aschersleben 4.4.48**

                                  19/4

    My dear Hans,

Today on Sunday, you should again receive the most loving

Sunday greetings from us. Hopefully we will receive mail from you soon. I am alone at home, Horst went out for a bit and I have to sort out my letters. I want to write six today, which will take me probably until the evening. Aunt Else and her family are sending their greetings. We were planning to drive to them in April or May. We are not quite sure if we should do it. It is quite risky at the moment and we don't want to put ourselves into harms way. Maybe everything will calm down soon. We had mail from the Stresses. They regret that they are not together with us. It is very lonely where they live, there are only 6 houses. It would have been so nice if we could have stayed together, we always got on so well with each other. If another war should start, what will happen to the poor prisoners of war? I must not think about this!! Yesterday and the day before I was sawing and chopping wood. The sawing alone is a torment. Tomorrow I will take the hard wood to the carpenter to be sawn with the circular saw, I am not able to do it myself. Thursday we went to the Harz and on Tuesday we will pick up another load. We are now allowed to go there only once a week, we can't push for more. I've got heart problems again, it does not work as I would like it to. I have also lost a lot of weight, I can't eat enough to regain weight. At the moment only syrup and sugar are available instead of fat. Since autumn we have not have any good butter, where should one get the strength from? Now my dear Hans, we hope that you will receive the ring pretty soon. I hopefully it is already at Erna's and from her, it is not so far to you. Stay healthy and be greeted from the bottom of our hearts from your Mum and your brother Horst.

92 Wharf St.
April 20th 1948.

My dearest Hans

I have had a letter every day this week but it is only Tuesday and I shall be very surprised if there is one for me tomorrow. I have been into town this morning but it has made me tired. I have been to bed this afternoon for a rest. I am going round to see the doctor tonight. I am sorry but you will have to wait a bit longer before you see me, because I am not supposed to be out after 7.00. I will let you know about Sunday later on. I will have to see what my mother says. Lucy rang yesterday afternoon and I had a chat with her, I also spoke to Mr Scott, he had just called into the showroom. Mr Coy had also been and he told Lucy he had got a house at Stathern, you probably know that. Have you heard from Mr Edwards yet? I do know what WIT means but (if you don't mind me telling you) you don't use it in that way. I will explain when I see you. Have you seen anything of her. What is her name or haven't you found out yet? Susan and Betty have just come. I will say cheeri'O

All my love

Jean

69   L.A.E.C. Hostel Stathern.
April 21$\underline{st}$. 1948.

My dearest love,

I thank you very much for the letter I received this morning. I hoped you'd ask me to come but I agree with you better not to go out after 7.00. So I better wait a few more days. We played our match at 6.30 and lost again but everybody gave his best. You should see me today. I really could say, 'What, in my state of health?' As I told you I always was afraid of getting kicked on my leg and exactly that's what has happened last night. I fell and unfortunately the other fellow kicked in my side instead of the ball. It just took me about 5 minutes till I could get up again. This happened ten minutes after I've started, but I played till the end. Two of my fellows helped me back to the hostel for I could hardly walk.

So, you've been into town yesterday, but you didn't even ring me. I didn't know you've to ask your mother about Sunday. But you always say your mother doesn't ask where you're going to?

Isn't it funny you're writing if you don't mind me telling you? I take an advice wherever I can, you know I still have to learn lots to speak your language properly. I'd better wait then for your explanation.

Well my sweetheart I'll say cheerio.

All my love and kisses

Yours forever

Hans.

92 Wharf St.
April 21st 1948.

My dearest Hans

Thank you so very much for your letter. How's your leg? When is the next match going to be played?

I went to see the doctor Tuesday and I have another week off. Aren't I lucky the weather being so nice. I took the dog in the park yesterday afternoon but today I have not been out, my throat is sore again so I thought I had better stay in until it goes. Did you go into Melton yesterday and did you get your raincoat? I'm sorry I did not ring you on Tuesday, but I forgot. I walked all over town trying to find some navy and white material and some ribbon for my mother. I went in about every shop and I was so fed up and tired that I forgot to phone you. Cyril (that is my brother in law) is going to decorate the living room and my mother and I have been getting it ready. Betty and I are going to have a go at the ceiling. I did not mean I would have asked my mother if I could go to Stathern. I thought it would be quicker to put it like that instead of saying – If I am going to Stathern my mother may say it is too cold to go there in those draughty buses. Then what could I do, my mother has to look after me when I'm ill. You will find my writing different today for I am using an ordinary pen and I can get on much better than with my fountain pen. I hope you can read it. I was speaking to Lucy yesterday, she said she had a message for me that she forgot to give to me the other day. This is the message - Albert rang and said he was going back to Germany and wished me all the best. Alfred would be pleased if he knew he had been called Albert.

I will say cheeri'O be good. Don't get chased by too many WLA girls eh!!!

> All my love
> Jean

.

70

L.A.E..C. Hostel.
Stathern.
April 22 <u>nd</u> 1948.

My dearest love

Unfortunately I didn't get a letter today as you did. I posted one for you last night anyway. The picture wasn't to bad. George Formby in 'South American George.' Perhaps you've seen it. Don't laugh, it only took me 15 minutes from the station to the picture house. But I really think that walking about Melton has done me good for my leg is a lot better today. I at least can walk normal even if it is a bit painful. That means I'll be fit for the next match in a few days.

How are you darling? Do you feel well again? Such a holiday (as you call it) isn't too bad, but I better like to work every day instead of spending holidays in bed. What did your doctor say on Tuesday? Are you allowed to go out? Please, my darling, let me see you this weekend. It'll be four weeks Sunday. I've to go to Melton again tomorrow, on the way I'll get my ring back. I left it yesterday to have it made a bit smaller. Did I tell you that I've got the ring my mother wrote about? I received the parcel day before yesterday. It's a rather nice looking ring. My mother sent it to my cousin (now living in the British zone) and she sent the registered parcel here. It only took 4 days. You really have to come now and have a look at our garden. After the last few rain showers everything is growing nicely. Anyway it looks like a garden now.

Well sweetheart I'll say cheerio. I am still waiting for your call. 'One day next week' you said.

By the way, I haven't heard from Mr Edwards yet. You know he forgets very soon.

All my love and kisses

Yours forever

Hans.

P.S. What do you think about receiving 5 letters during the week?

R 24/4.48   Aschersleben 11.4.48
                              22/4

My dear Hans,

We thank you for your latest letter dated 28.03.48, which we received yesterday. We had to wait nearly 14 days for this letter from you, it just takes such a long time to get to us. For the last 8 days I haven't felt well at all. I have a very bad cold. I shortened and stacked the wood and I sweated a lot doing it. I have so much pain in my back and in my ribs. On Tuesday we want to go again into the forest, but I have to see if I will feel better by then. It is not really women's work. On Tuesday evening I went with Horst to the graduation evening of his course. He came third. Everybody said he should have been first, his work was certainly wonderful, but they can't put a refugee above the locals. Ah, it does not really matter. Tomorrow morning at 4am Horst will travel with several of his colleagues to a big hair dresser competition in Leipzig.His boss wants him to attend as a spectator and he will learn a lot. At the moment he is out looking after his private clients, he is always busy. I dreamt last night that I was with Horst at yours, Jean was also there. You looked well fed. Jean was tall and slim with dark hair, right? We are looking forward to the pictures, then I will see her. Thank God, Horst is feeling better now. Please look after your leg, is there still a splinter inside? Don't you go to a doctor? I am sure it would be better to have it looked at. It is more effort for you to go to the cinema than for us. It only takes us 3 minutes to get to one of them and 6 minutes to others. Recently we went again, firstly I fell asleep, then Horst. We had to shake each other to stay awake. At the moment a lot are coming back out of the Russian prisoner of war camps, if only Papa would be one of them. Dear Hans, are you in need of a coat? Will you get one there? Auntie Erna asked me to send her greetings. They are all waiting for us to visit, but we don't know when we can make it. One is dreading the long journey, but it would be lovely to see them all again. It has been nearly one and a half years since we last saw them. Now my dear Hans, I want to close my letter for today. You certainly will have visitors again today. Stay healthy and be greeted from the bottom of our hearts from your Mum and your brother Horst. Please greet Jean heartily from us. Horst will write to you again in the week. To a healthy reunion.

    92 Wharf St
    April 23rd

My dearest Hans
I am writing a few lines tonight (Friday). I am very sorry I

wasn't able to write to you before so you would get it on Saturday morning. I have been really busy today and I mean busy. Betty came down and we started to clean the room out and believe me it is no easy job. It is a fairly big room but unfortunately we only have the one room and the shop. We had to put the furniture in the yard except the sideboards and table. It took all morning to get the place ready. Betty washed the ceiling and I stripped the old paper off the wall. You should have seen me working a minute and stopping for 2 minutes rest. There is still a lot of paper to get off. I will have to get up early (about 10) and make a start. Cyril is going to put one coat of paint on tomorrow night and another on Sunday. My mother will be going out and I couldn't very well go out on Sunday leaving them to do our room. Could I? So, you would wait half a year for me. Am I worth waiting half a year for? Still time will tell. What is or was the time limit? I will write a few lines either tomorrow or on Sunday or both.

Goodnight and God bless.

Saturday

Betty has finished the ceiling. She dropped the paint once and we could not do anything for laughing. Betty took Susan to the doctors this morning and he said she was sickening for the measles. I have been so busy I almost forgot to get the sweets for last month I had not spent yours or mine. It just shows how much I think about sweets. I have been to the pictures tonight to see 'Indian Summer', it was very good (it was not about India). I should not have gone really, but Dora came round and I could not ask her to stay in, in the mess we are in. You would laugh I have to send my doctors certificate to work first, then to the National Insurance. Every time I send it I write a little note to Lucy asking her to post it on to the National Insurance when Mr Bembridge has seen it, but every time Mr Bembridge sends it back to me and Lucy spends half the time trying to find out where it is. I hope you have a very good weekend and just be good.

All my love
Jean

71

L.A.E.C. Hostel.
Stathern.
April 23 rd 1948.

My dearest love

Thanks ever so much for your letter. Did I keep my promise every day a letter for you? You'll get the next one when you come on Sunday. I also thank you for your call. Did you say you wanted to go home early? Then you'd better come a bit earlier. Anyway I understand quite well that you better get home before it gets cold at night.

As I told you on the phone yesterday my leg is getting better. Fit to be kicked at the next match. There may be one next week but I don't know for sure yet. If you get kicked it can't be help. I didn't even leave the field and the success was I went down two more times (without having seen the ball). It's a hard job to stay on your feet when every step is painful. But why being worried about all that, it's almost over and we'll see what surprise the next match brings.

How lucky you are. Another week off and always sunshine, but do you know that's only because I only had one wish now 'Good holidays and the best weather for you!'

If you would've told me a few more times there was a WLA girl on the phone I certainly would have put the receiver down. And that means you would have had it. Lately I always get running when I see the land army girls and I've always been successful. I've got my raincoat alright and everybody says it's very cheap for £2-10-0. 'll see you day after tomorrow. These two days will be the longest days of the week. I wish I could go to bed tonight and wake up on Sunday morning. That would be very nice.

Did you get your living room done? I better come and see what it looks like, don't you think so? I bet you looked nice after doing the ceiling.

When you come on Sunday try to get a seat right on the back of the bus. It won't be too draughty there. And then keep your mouth shut. You're only allowed to speak when you arrive here in Stathern. Remember that please!

So you mean your mother is the only one to look after you when you're ill. And what about me? Everything out of bounds. Be sure I would look after you and wait on you. It would be the nicest thing I can think of.

You know then that Alfred called after all. What about your bet? 'Give her the money!'

I've got a nice letter from my mother yesterday and remind me to read it to you on Sunday. Some funny things happen.

Don't you think the WLA get's hold of me. I sooner leave my shoes on the way back and get going.

Well my sweetheart, be good and please don't change your mind about the weekend. Cheerio till Sunday.

All my love and kisses
Always yours
Hans.

<u>72</u>   L.A.E.C. Hostel.
                                   Stathern.
                                   April 24 th. 1948.

My darling

Thanks very much for your call on Friday evening. Anyway I told you I don't mind waiting another half a year till you find time to see me. It's just bad luck it has to be done on the Sunday we arranged to meet after 4 weeks. Well darling don't you worry about me. I certainly will be alright. Is there any possibility for you to come one day during next week. Say Monday or Tuesday. And then of course Sunday again. It is 3.30 now and fortunately I finished my work for today. Two men are in today, I've done the tea and supper for them. At the moment I am listening to the wireless. I wonder what you're doing this afternoon. Tea party somewhere or getting your rooms ready for tomorrow?

Mrs Betts offered me to go along with her to see one of her daughters in Beeston (Nottingham). They're two nice girls 18 year old she said she can't see me sitting here weekend after weekend lonely and alone and I should enjoy the week-ends at last after working hard for six days. I quite agree with her. But what should I do in the hostel to enjoy myself? Running up and down the stairs or playing darts with myself? The warden has gone home today and is coming back with his girlfriend tomorrow afternoon.

Well my sweetheart don't do to much work tomorrow, don't overwork yourself. Cheerio and a kiss from your Hans. Be good and

All my love and kisses

Yours forever

Hans.

73   L.A.E.C. Hostel.

Stathern.

Apri,l 26th 1948.

My darling Jean

I thank you so much for the nice letter I received this morning. I really was afraid there wouldn't be one for me but I was lucky. Anyway I posted one for you in Melton last night. I see you've been very busy over the weekend. If you only let me give you a hand. You know quite well I like to help. Rather than sitting here on my own. Nothing exciting happened. I went to the pictures last night and it was a real good one 'Lloyds of London' it was called. On my way back on the 8.10 a couple of the LA girls sat behind me. You should have heard the noise. I would've be ashamed of myself. As I left the bus here I said to one of them she ought to see a doctor. There's something wrong with her. Because people of her age should know how to behave. You should've seen her face, but that's the only way to cure them. So that's how you do it work one minute and rest two. I quite agree with you that you could hardly let Cyril do all the work and go out as well, but I also would like you to make sure there's nothing to do for you next Sunday except coming here.

Did I say anything about half a year being a time limit? You know how much you mean to me. I am sure a lot of boys in my place would have told you off but I won't because I love you so much. It is hard for me to wait 4 weeks to see you but can it be helped? It isn't my fault and your illness isn't your fault. Can't you spare me Wednesday afternoon? Please, don't make it such a very long time. Another 6 days to go till Sunday. There's no match to be played this week so I'll take Wednesday off as usual. Please ring me or let me know in time I don't like it very much to go to Melton. Just see a picture and go straight back. And there's not use to go to Leicester if I can't see you.

Mr Coy told me just now that he's got a letter saying for sure he's got one of these houses. I think it'll take another fortnight till the houses are ready.

Well my sweetheart I'll say cheerio. Just be good. I am always thinking of you.

All my love and kisses

Yours forever

Hans.

92 Wharf St.

April 28th.

My dearest Hans

I thank you very much for your letter. I am sorry I could not see you today but I have really an awful lot to do. Why it is taking such a long time is because we are having to have four coats of paint on, Cyril can only put one on a night.

Did Mr Pickering tell you I rang twice? He said on Tuesday night that I was driving you about silly. I told him that was your fault. He said I was very wicked and that I ought to have a better excuse than spring cleaning, I ought to say I wasn't very well. I told him I always tell you the truth. He did not believe me. I really am busy. I am going to wash and polish the chairs when I have finished this letter. The last coat goes on tonight, then tomorrow I will be really busy putting the things in order. Had the WLA girl on the bus been speaking to you, given that you told her to see doctor. I went to see the doctor Tuesday morning. I felt sure that I would have to go to work today but no I have got another week off. If I want to start work on Monday I will have to go to see him on Saturday, he told me to please myself. I rang Lucy yesterday to let her know she had to sit at the switchboard another week, she said she ought to have double pay and a week off when I go back. I will have to wash my hair tomorrow night. You should see it now, it really does look terrible. Friday night I will have to have a bath (I can't wash my hair and have a bath the same night). I thought I had sprained my wrist. On Monday I helped my mother do the washing. We did the door curtains and the tablecloth and a lot of other things, I rang them out. At night my wrist was painful. My mother could not help but laugh because I had sprained my wrist ringing the table cloth out, anyway I asked the doctor he said I had twisted it.

I will say cheeri'O I really hope you enjoyed this afternoon I will be coming on Sunday if everything goes well.

All my love

Jean

P.S. Mr Pickering wanted to know how many young men I had, I told him I would let him have a list if he was interested.

74   L.A.E.C. Hostel.

Stathern.

April 29th.1948.

My dearest, darling Jean,

Thanks very much for your letter. There was a lot of news in it for me. I knew you rung twice, but I never asked Mr Pickering what he said to you. I am really surprised. I was really sorry I couldn't see you yesterday and hoped you may come round to the pictures with me. As I went to the bus station I was always looking for you thinking you might spare half an hour to see me off. But no, nothing at all. I am very glad you've finished your cleaning now. It'll make the last days a bit easier for you I hope. It seems strange to me when the doctor tells you to please yourself. I never knew it was like that. Are you sure if you start work again on Monday? You thought you'd sprained your wrist ringing table cloth out? Do you know what I did on my last washing day? I washed my new bath towel, rung it out and found one pieces in each hand after doing it properly. I tore it right in the middle. Just a strong wrist that's all you want, but don't worry darling, I'll be pleased to do little jobs for you, later on you certainly won't have to sprain your wrist again. I enjoyed the afternoon seeing 'The Lady on the Beach' and 'The Way Ahead' at the Odeon. I think it's my favourite picture house. It would've been nicer being with you. Please, darling, make sure there's nothing else to do for you next Sunday. Don't you agree 5 weeks being an awful long time. Were you afraid to speak to me on the phone yesterday because your aunty was there? It took you a long while to get them few words out.

Well my sweetheart, I'll say cheerio. I am almost sure there'll be no letter for me tomorrow, just be good and think of me.

All my love and kisses

Yours forever

Hans.

92 Wharf St.

April 29th.

My dearest Hans

I am not going to thank you for the letter I had this morning. It is a good job Stathern is about 20 miles away, otherwise I would have been over with a frying pan. To finish the telephone conversation. I was not going to the pictures when I rang you. I was coming home to wash my hair. I believe I told you in my last letter, but I changed my plans. I had a bath this afternoon and was going to wash my hair tonight. When I got back I was so tired I could not be bothered. So I do not know when I will be able to do it. I am going to see Susan tomorrow, she has the measles and wants me to take the dog. I have not finished spring cleaning yet but we have some of the things back in place. The room looks quite nice. There would not be so much to do if my mother and I were tidy. About Sunday – I will see what bus I come on. Don't bother coming to Melton then you can have your lunch. Goodnight and God bless.

   All my love
   Jean

75   L.A.E.C. Hostel.
Stathern.
April 30th 1948.

My darling

Thanks ever so much for your call last night. I really was in a nice mood as I wrote that letter on Wednesday. Please forget it.

As you can imagine I am very busy this afternoon. Fish and chips, but lately only once a fortnight. It is really warm in the kitchen and reminds me on my time in Louisiana. And it'll be 5.30 before I am able to open the windows and get some fresh air.

There was a nice queue waiting for the dinners as you rung last night, but nobody said a word. What did your auntie say about the cake? I am sorry if I caused trouble for you. In that case I better don't ring you again at home.

Well darling how are you today? I hope everything is alright for Sunday. I'd better wait till tonight and see tomorrow morning's mail before I say anything. It is my wish for this weekend anyway. Do you want to stay in or go out on Sunday, that means if the weather keeps fine. Otherwise I would get the fireplace ready. Anyway I'll see that you're comfortable.

Did you go the pictures yesterday? What are your rooms look like now after a week's work? I think I better go and see for myself without asking, don't you think so?

Well my sweetheart I hope you'll not mind this short letter. I'll be seeing you Sunday.

Till then be good.

All my love and kisses

Yours

Hans.

76   L.A.E.C. Hostel,

Stathern.

May, 1st 1948.

My darling

Thanks very much for your short letter, but in spite of it – thank you. I'll tell you something, don't start threatening me. I mean frying pan and so on. Maybe that's just what I wanted you to do. But if you would have come, there's no need to bring a pan along because I've three here – different sizes. Or did you want to hear something about cooking. I should be obliged to give you my advice. So you managed to have your baths. Twice a week should be enough. It is rather early today, 1.00 o'clock. I am waiting for 3 more men to come for their dinners. You might be sure I'll go down to Melton and wait for you. After such a long time I am going to take care of every minute. I'll get the fire ready upstairs in case it is cold and raining for I don't want you to get another cold and that means I had to wait again 5 weeks. Don't worry about any lunch darling. You know I seldom take any at all. Well, I'll finish now and write a few more lines tonight. So long darling.

Sunday

After all, I went to the pictures last night. Finishing my washing at 4.00 the warden told me to go if I want to for there's only one man in. So I had to hurry and was just in time for the 4.45. The picture was called 'Brute Force!' Something about a prison. If I only would know what bus you are going to take from Leicester. I thought it over and decided to wait here otherwise I may miss you. Everything is ready darling. It is rather cold so I've set the fire ready to be lit. Now I am counting the hours till you arrive. Only a few more.

Well my sweetheart, I'll say cheerio. Just be good.

All my love and kisses
Yours forever
Hans.

92 Wharf St.

May 4th.

My dearest Hans

Thank you so very much for your nice long letter. I am sorry you did not get a letter today but I was very busy yesterday (you had better tell Mr Pickering). My mother and I did quite a lot of washing in the morning and I had to have a sleep in the afternoon to get over it. I washed my hair in the evening, it took me an hour to set it.

I arrived home on Sunday at the usual time on the bus. It was raining a little bit but nothing to bother about. I start work tomorrow and I am not very keen on the idea. I have got so used to being at home I don't feel much like going out at 8.45, but I suppose I will soon get used to doing it again. I seem to work much harder at home than at the office. I went in to see Lucy this morning to tell her I was going to come back and I promised to take the dog in for her to see.

When I have finished this letter I will see if I can get the shirt. I think they are hard to get, so Cyril says but you did not have any trouble getting yours.

You have got a cheek. You mean me to come on Sunday don't you. I told you on Sunday I would see. It looks as if I shall have to come now.

I was going to write a long letter but I am afraid I am not in the mood, so it will be a short one. I will ring you in the morning if I get the time so till then

   All my love
    Jean

<u>77</u>

L.A.E.C. Hostel.
Stathern.
May 4<u>th</u>.1948.

My darling Jean

Look darling it'll be too late buying the shirt next week. There's only 17 days left and a parcel takes about 12-14 days to get home. I am sorry I forgot to tell you about it on Sunday so I'd to trouble you today. I tried to ring you half an hour earlier but there was no reply. Maybe your auntie was out.

I am glad to hear you're alright and so am I. So you start work tomorrow. As I told you (and you know it best) there was no letter from you today but 2 from my mother and 1 from Ellen instead. She's got mail from Alfred. He arrived home safe and is very busy for the first few weeks. It doesn't seem to be too bad at his place. Ellen told me that her sister married an ex POW and is going back with him as soon as he leaves the UK. Nice isn't it. I think Ellen wouldn't mind getting married.

My mother sent me 2 lovely big photographs. One of herself and one of my brother. She told me to put the others away now because these two are the best ones. I'll show them to you when you come on Sunday. Don't forget to come because I am waiting for that shirt. Well, darling, that's all so far. It smells very nice at the moment (Irish stew tonight and rolled jam pudding). You'd better come and taste it.

Well sweetheart I'll say cheerio. I'll write again tomorrow. Just be good and let me have a nice long letter.

All my love and kisses
Yours forever
Hans.

Mutti

Horst

R 4/ 5.48   Aschersleben 18.4.48

My dear Hans,

Unfortunately, we have not had any mail from you for ten days, but anyway I want to send you a few lines and loving Sunday greetings. Enclosed are two pictures of us and I hope it makes you a little bit happy. Finally we have some good pictures and they captured us pretty well. Now you can put away the other pictures that you already have of us, because I really do not look very nice on them. For a few days now we are having beautiful spring weather. Hopefully the day after tomorrow is also beautiful as we are collecting wood again. I was ill for 8 days, I caught a cold. Now I feel quite good again. I went to the doctor on Tuesday, the lungs are healthy but I have bad rheumatism and a valvular heart disease. That's what one can get in these times and does not need at all, because the long break is over. Werner stayed with Erwin in the West, I'm sure he will try to get Grandma to join them. Agnes from Stettin is now also back with her sisters. She was quite a long time in the Rostock area and had to work pretty hard. Horstel really enjoyed attending the hairdresser competition in Leipzig, he was very excited about it. I recently knitted the jumper that I'm wearing in the picture. At least something new to wear again. Yesterday we went to the cinema. They showed a very beautiful film Via Mala. If you write, please add some lines for Horst. You know how much he is waiting for it. We don't know yet when our journey will happen, definitely not before Pentecost as there is so much to do in the salon. Hopefully we will soon receive the pictures of you and Jean, they surely must be done by now! Maybe you meanwhile have received the ring. I sent it to Erna 3 weeks ago. Now, dear Hans, I will end my letter. We hope it will reach you in best health. Stay healthy, be greeted from the bottom of our hearts and be kissed from Mum and your brother Horst. Lots of greetings to Jean.

Dear Hans,

I don't have a lot of time at the moment. I will write at the beginning of the week.
I have not received any mail from you.
Lots of greetings to you and Jean from your brother Horst

92 Wharf St.
A May 5th 1948.

My dearest Hans

I am very sorry I did not ring you this morning. I really intended to but was so busy I forgot and when I did remember Lucy was talking to me. She is going to make an underskirt and she is using my table to cut it out on. So she has been with me most of the day. It seemed ages since I had been to work and I wasn't very thrilled with going but it wasn't so bad. I soon got used to being there and I don't feel as if I had been away. Thank you very much for your letter, I did not expect one. I am glad to hear you have had 2 letters from your mother and 1 from Ellen. What makes you think she would like to get married? You ought to have played cupid to her and Alfred, you could have told Alfred it was about time he settled down and stop leading girls up the garden path. I was always curious to know how friendly Alfred and Ellen were. You would never say and I had not the nerve to ask Alfred, I got a shirt. It is a blue one, size 15 with the collar attached. I also bought myself a summer dress. I had to go to 2 or 3 shops to get the shirt but I finally got one in Belgrave Gate. I hope your brother will like it. I am not used to buying mens clothes and I have never taken any interest in them. So you would like me to give up my job at the end of the year. I wish I could too but you can't live on air. If I married you I wouldn't mind working if I thought we would get somewhere in life, I want a family whilst I am young but I want my children to have a good education and a good start in life, especially if we stay in England. It would not bother me if I had to struggle though life, I think I would be quite content to go from one day to the other, but I couldn't with a baby, that is why I have to think of the future. I hope you can understand what I mean, I have not put it down very well but I hope can you sort it out. By the way I will be coming on the 2.30 bus. It is such a rush for me on the 1.30. I have taken the dog to the park for a walk, because he had not been out all day. My mother won't let him go out in case he gets lost, I don't know what I should do if he did. I have grown quite fond of him. I have always liked dogs so where I go my dog goes too. I went to the pictures last night to see 'The best years of our lives' It wasn't bad but it was a very long picture it began at 7.10 and we did not come out until 10.0 (by the way I went with Dora). I am seeing her again on Saturday I suppose we shall go to the pictures again. There isn't anything else to do in Leicester only go to a dance and I hate going to Saturday night dances waiting for someone to ask you to dance. I always feel as if I am waiting to be picked up and I am not really keen on dancing. Only when you can go with a crowd and have some fun. I enjoy that. I have tried to make this letter as long as possible and I think it is long but a lot of nonsense. There is one thing if I married you I would not have to write any more letters to you, or at least I hope I wouldn't. I will ring you in the morning (Thursday).

Be good and be careful

All my love
Jean.

78   L.A.E.C. Hostel.
          Stathern.
          May 3rd 1948.

My darling Jean,

I thank you so very, very much for the lovely Sunday afternoon. After all I enjoyed the afternoon and really I felt lonely and rotten as you left. But I don't worry, my darling, looking forward for next Sunday. I could've called myself words as I noticed I didn't even thank you for the sweets and dates. Anyway I'll thank you now, even if it's a bit late. I really must say we'd a nice little talk yesterday. I quite agree with you there's a lot for you to think about but be sure I also spend hours to think things over and I am always coming to the conclusion that we'll master the situation. There's an old saying in Germany, 'difficulties are there to be dealt with not to surrender to'. And that's what I always think. You know I'd work for you not minding what kind of work it is and I think we would be very happy. Don't think I'll only tell you nice things now and don't keep what I say. I always stay to my word and you know that as well. Why didn't you ask questions before darling? I should've known then that you also are thinking about it. And please don't think I just love you because you are the first girl after this long time behind wire. I've asked myself this question lots of times and I'll be honest to you. There are lots of nice girls about but I didn't see one yet I could like more than you. I always said to myself nobody else can mean more to me than you. I think you should never let the thought come into your mind that it is just because you're the first girl I met here. Isn't it fate that we met? Hundreds of times it was up to me to change things for a better way. I could've been at home since 1946, but I didn't take any action and went to England. I could've gone from Saltby to Langan when we came from Wartnaby. I stayed in Saltby. It is just as if it was yesterday as I asked you the first time to come and you said 'no!' Then it was you who asked when the next concert was, and after the first few Sundays the best time of my life began and then it was when I became afraid of losing you. You knew nothing about me and I knew nothing about you. Another few months and it'll be the day when I met you first, one year ago. How time flies but I'll never forget the afternoons we spent together. A few of my fellows grew jealous when you came to Saltby and I was so proud of you and I still am and always will be. My mother wrote in one of her letters she thought I'd forgotten her and only think of you because I mention you in every letter. I really am always thinking about you. The first thing in the morning and the last one at night. I just remember us looking for nice houses last night. I was so happy and you also seemed to be and that's how it always will be.

Well my sweetheart my thoughts carried me far off whilst writing this. I hope you don't get tired reading it. Please don't let me down next Sunday, come and I'll be more than happy. You know it doesn't take much for please me. Don't you forget to let me know about the birthday present. Look around if there's anything you like to have and tell me. Only 18 more days to go. Well, my darling I'll say cheerio. Time is getting on and I've to do my work. So just be good and think of me.

Loads of love and kisses, only yours, my sweetheart

Hans.

Correspondance of Prisoners of war.   Postage Paid.
Replied 7.5.48

	Mr Hans Klawitter.
Sender Bieck.	LWAEC Hostel.
Heinz.	Old Rectory Stathern.
Grade ------	Nr Melton Mowbray/Leics.
Prisoner no. 886160-1687.	Great Britain.
Address -14 Kdo 10.	
Douai (Nord).	
March 27th 1948.	

My dear Hans. I thank you very much for your kind letter. You must excuse my not replying to your letter earlier. But I've not had any time to write. Tomorrow we have Easter, and you'll take a walk with your girlfriend. I would like to be in your place. I don't need to wait long to do as you do! in a few weeks I'll be a civillain. I'll say there are many ways that lead to Rome! Trusting to hear from you soon and all the best to you. Your cousin Heinz

<u>79</u> L.A.E.C. Hostel.
Stathern.
May 5 <u>th</u>. 1948.

My dearest, darling Jean,

I hope you've had a nice long rest on Monday afternoon. I'll have one today but 3 hours will do for me. Perhaps I'll take the 4.45 to Melton, see a picture and be back at 9.00. How is the work darling? You haven't rung yet and it's 12.30. I imagine how busy you are, saying hello to everybody after 5 weeks absence. Anyway you'll have settled down again by tomorrow. There'll be one day my darling when you're able to finish that job and stay at home and somebody else doing the hard jobs for you. Please don't blame me if you're to come next Sunday. Blame my brother for it is his birthday present. I am quite sure you would come without me asking you. There was nobody else at your Auntie's yesterday was there? It was as if you've got your voice back. The laundry girl hasn't been yet. I am waiting to get my coat back. Did I tell you I sent it a fortnight ago to have it dyed navy blue? It'll look a bit better than prisoner brown. By the way I think I told you it doesn't matter what colour the shirt is because I don't know what suits he's got. On that photograph I got yesterday he looks like a film star. I really can't believe it's him. Well, my sweetheart, I'll say cheerio. Mrs Betts just shouted for dinner. Be good and do as I do – think of me.

All my love and kisses
Yours forever
Hans.

Replied 6/5.48   Aschersleben 21.4.48
                                          5/5.48

         My dear Hans,

Finally I come to sending you a few lines. Unfortunately, I
have not heard from you for a long time. You will certainly
have a lot to do as well. How is your health?. Please take
care especially with your leg. We are still healthy and well,
which we also hope for you. Here all of a sudden spring has
arrived, everything turned green overnight and the wonderful air! I just finished my walk. I have to get out into the
fresh air, as I am in the shop all day. I'm very pale. I went to
the hairdresser competition in Leipzig on the 12.4.48. I left
here at 4.10 in the morning and left from Leipzig the next
morning at 4.35. It was great. Hairstyles were shown and the
sea of colours, just amazing. There was a dance event from
9pm to 3am. And then without sleeping straight to the shop.
I knew where I should have been, in bed. It was all very beautiful and the presentation was great. How is Miss Jean, is she
healthy again? One has to take care in this kind of weather.
How much we would like to see and talk with you again. Because one does not have any relatives to pour one's heart out
to. It would be really nice if Frau Streese would live closer to
us, then Mum would have support. And from a man of word-
how is the situation in England? Here at the moment it is
calm again. All sorts is going on in Italy. Now, dear Hans, I
will close. Please write again soon. Dear Hans and Miss Jean
be greeted from the bottom of our hearts from your brother
Horst and Mum. To a soon and healthy reunion! We have no
message yet from Papa. A lot are coming. He will too.

92 Wharf Street.
MAY 6th 1948.

My dearest Hans

I thank you for the letter. I am very lucky, one every morning. I wish I could do the same. So you would get one every morning but you know me, always very busy.

I waited until the middle of the morning to ring you, I was not very busy and I thought I should be able to talk to you, but just as you came to the phone Mr Smith came in and was sitting in my office picking the horses out. Could you tell that someone was near?

Did you know that there are only 6 districts now, quite a lot has happened whilst I have been away. It is now Melton and Belvoir Agriculture C. and there isn't any Leicester district, that has been split up between 5 districts. Mr Gowling and the rest of the Belvoir staff are moving to Melton office after Whit.

I think Mr Edwards is at Billesdon Camp now. I had to get a Mr Edwards at Billesdon and he was not there so I thought that sounded as if it might be the Edwards from Saltby.

I had a letter from Willi this morning and he did not call me his dearest. I am now broken hearted. It looks as if I will still have to be faithful to you.

You ought to know by now that once I have said what I will do, you may as well save your breath than try to change my mind. So I will be on the 2.30. It usually gets into Melton at 10 past.

So I will be seeing you on Sunday. I hope I don't forget the shirt.

All my love
Jean

——.

L.A.E.C. Hostel.

Stathern.

May. 6Th 1948.

My dearest darling Jean

What, no letter? No chum you've had it! Thanks very much for your call darling, So, you got the shirt. That's very nice of you and I thank you very much for it. I'll get everything ready for the parcel that I just have to put the shirt in. Do you also want to write a few lines to him for his birthday? We'll do it together on Sunday.

I hope you're coming Whit Sunday or Whit Monday. There's a funfair in Melton and as I heard in Leicester too. So if you want anything from the shooting range, tell me. I just thought of it. What about you coming here on Whit Sunday and I'll come on Whit Monday over to the fair in Leicester? But no, you certainly want to go with one of your friends or go to a tea party somewhere. Anyway we'll talk it over on Sunday. Please, darling, try and get the 1.30 from Leicester. It is better for you to get on the 8.55. Bring your coat along even if the weather is nice. It's always cold in the evening. Tell your mother not to be afraid, I'll look after you while you're here.

I didn't even hear you saying cheerio this morning. I asked if you had posted a letter for me and noticed that you'd gone already.

My fellow from Groadby–Harwood went to Gaddesby yesterday as second cook. He changed because he was booked as kitchen cleaner and didn't get cooks pay. I better like to stay here where I am my own master.

The warden asked for a new kettle the other day so they brought a few things yesterday. Don't laugh the kettle just holds 3 pints. So it must be enough for 15 men. I'd a good laugh when I came back last night and the warden told me.

Well sweetheart, there's nothing else. Just be good till I see you on Sunday and think of me.

All my love and kisses

Yours forever

Hans.

Monday night 8.30

Hello sweetheart, how are you today? Fine I hope. Did you get home well? It was so good you got a seat alright.

I never thought there could be a Tuesday morning after those two lovely Easter holidays and I bet you didn't feel much like work. I was thinking of you at 9.00. That was the time when we got up yesterday. Wasn't it nice? Just to hear you calling me, come down and find you there. Fact not only fiction. I have just fetched myself a drink of coffee and – broke the cup. It means good luck you know. What are you doing tonight? Having a nice little talk with your mother? I wish you would!!! Remember that I back you up whatever you say or do. I have had another letter today from the Swiss Caritas Union, South Africa saying that from April 1st parcels may be sent to the Russian zone too. So, everything is alright. The boss didn't say a word about the chicken. We've put a poisoned one down for the fox and hope for the best.

Well, my darling. I'll close now and go to bed. Are you thinking of me?

Please give my regards to your mother.

> All my love to you and a thousand kisses
> Forever yours, my sweety
> Hans.

R: 7/5. 48 Aschersleben 23.4. 48
6/5.48

My dear Hans,

We thank you very much for your dear letter of 13.5.48. in spite of airmail, it took 8 days to arrive, but we are very pleased to have news of you again and see from it that you are still well. It's not great for you to get so many letters in one go and then nothing for such a long time. Yesterday was a hard day. We were in the forest and on the go for 15 hours. Horst was so scared, but there was no other way. We cut down 48 dried-out fir trees and then chopped off all the branches and dragged them out. It all took time, because you have to search out somewhat thicker wood : it's not worth the long trip just to get thin wood. A woman was with us, she had already loaded up a lot, but there was such a strong wind coming from in front, right at us, that she had to unload her best pieces of timber after a short distance. So we loaded two of her full bags on to our cart. We had already loaded up more than 5 hundredweight for ourselves anyway and then we had to face the steep hills, she nearly collapsed. We pushed her cart a little way ahead and then went back for ours tortuously until we arrived back home. If it hadn't been for the sweets or sugar she gave us, we couldn't have carried on. I have finished the thin pieces of wood and I will have to get the thicker pieces sawn for me. On Sunday the Schmetzkes from Gusten are coming to visit us. Meantime, I hope you received the ring because, from what Erna wrote, it got safely to her and she forwarded it on to you on 13.4.48. I am sure it will be in your hands soon. I hope Jean isn't seriously ill! We don't yet know for certain about Horstel's leave, but it almost certainly won't be before Whitsun now. If at all possible, we want to go to Western Pomerania. When we get there, we will pass on your greetings to everyone. We get very little post from you any more. You don't have to be sad because you can't actually give us anything! When you send us parcels, is that worth nothing? You know it makes us very happy.

The man, Schulz, is very friendly with some families and they support him a lot. This week he sent a packet of soap. But you don't need to be cross about that, not everyone is able to do it, that's why I didn't write to you about it. Schulz will be discharged in July. Then he'll bring 15 Kilos of coffee with him. They'll be able to change this for a lot of food. Just be careful playing football, it's not good for your leg yet.

Now my dear Hans, stay in good health for me, with love and kisses from your mum and from your brother. Hoping to see you soon!

L.A.E.C. Hostel.
Stathern.
May, 7$\underline{th}$.1948.

My darling Jean,
Thanks so very much for your nice long letter. It doesn't take very much to please me. Just a letter every day and your presence here over the weekend. I've read your letter over a dozen times this morning and I must say you think about everything. And even that makes me feel happy. You mean I should've played Cupid? No, darling that's nothing for me. Everybody must know himself what to do. In my opinion nobody could even give an advice in a case like that. They are personal affairs and I didn't want to interfere. No wonder you grew curious to know how friendly they were. Don't you think you better should've bought your summer dress next week? You could have saved 4 coupons according to today's newspaper. Yes, I would like you to give up your job at the end of the year if all I thought about goes well. I know some people think one can live on air but I don't and I know so well you would not mind working after marrying me. It seems the main problem to me that in married life we should stick together in bad as in good times. Certainly I want to get somewhere in life and that's what I'll work for. My principle is that my children shall have a better life than I had and a good education. If you don't bother, if you have to struggle through life going from one day to the other, I don't like it. Look my sweetheart, it is nice when times are quiet and peaceful, but there might be a time something going wrong and then it is necessary to master the situation. I know it would be easy only for both of us but we want a family. We both agreed about children. You've put it down al-

right darling. I know now you misunderstood me when I was talking about not losing the best years of our life. A family whilst we are young and then enjoy seeing the children grow up in happiness. That should be the ideal of all the married couples and that's what I live for. Anyway we'll have a nice talk on Sunday. See, if we should happen to go to Germany, that means if times get better there would always be the possibility to get back to my old job and live a peaceful life. Life just has its good and bad times and I reckon the bad time must be over soon. Don't say again you put a lot of nonsense into your letter. I find it nice to talk about everything. Do you think it is a reason to get married just to spare the times you're writing letters to me?

Well, my darling, I'll say cheerio for today. Fish today, but no chips.

So just be good and think of me.

All my love and kisses

Yours forever

Hans.

Same address.
Friday night 7.5.48.

My dearest, darling Jean,

I finished early tonight because there is no pack lunch to-morrow. It is only 7.00 o'clock. You know my work I like best is writing to you. I'll write a few lines to my mother afterwards. How are you today, darling? Wasn't it a grand day today? It really is a shame to sit inside. Somewhere out-side, just the two of us. I'll always remember that lovely place near Croxton and you missing the bus. I was rather busy this afternoon. I saw a few of my little friends – the rats – in the yard and chased them successful. I never knew I could run that fast for I got 2 with my stick. I sat on a piece of wood one rat just underneath one on my leg. What else could I do than keep quiet. And Mr Pickering and the women were standing on the kitchen window laughing at me. I didn't want to frighten it away. You should have been here. Is the table high enough for you? There is nothing to be afraid of. Are you going away tonight? I hope you'll ring me tomorrow. A few more lines tomorrow and on Sunday. Good night my sweetheart and God bless. Many kisses.

Saturday 5.30

Well, darling, here I am again being all on my own. I've done my work and I am sitting in the lounge now listening to the wireless. It is quiet, not a soul about. Mr Pickering is gone home to see his doctor. He was pretty bad when he left here. I hope he got to Leicester alright. If it is like this tomorrow we'll have a nice walk. Thanks so much for your letter. I think you are lucky to get one every morning, but just tell me if you don't like it. There's always time to write to you darling. I wish I would get a letter every morning. I noticed there was somebody with you as you rung me. I told you in my last letter that you finished the conversation rather quick. How should I know Leicester district has finished. I certainly would've told you. What do they call Leicester office now? I knew Waltham office has to change quarters. You'll find out if it is Mr Edwards from Saltby and if you don't mind, remind him to send the recommendation. You poor little girl. So Willi didn't call you his dearest. Don't let that break your heart. I'll call you my darling and hope that'll make up for the loss. He's writing to you anyway but you better be faithful to me! I know quite well that I can't change your mind once you've said no. Alright, don't get excited, I'll come down for the 4 o'clock bus. I'll just have to wait one more hour, that's all. There's such a wonderful music, Vienna Waltz, just now. Well, sweetheart, I'll say cheerio for now and God bless. A kiss till I see you tomorrow.

Sunday

I am waiting for the warden now. Maybe he's missed the bus because he usually arrives here at this time. It doesn't mat-

ter for me. I'll take the 2.10 and meet you in Melton.
So long then darling. Just be good.
                    All my love and kisses
                        Yours forever
                            Hans.

        92 Wharf St.
        May 10th.
My dearest Hans.
Are you surprised to get a letter (you ought to be) if you're
not. I am writing this at work, so you may have guessed by
the paper, it is the best LAEC can do. It won't be a very long
one because we go at 5.45 and it is now 5.0 and I have to look
after the board as well. I get so annoyed with anyone that
messes about and does not know what they want.
I arrived home at 9.30 and I was very tired. I took the dog a
walk, and I was soon after that in bed. I have been tired all
afternoon as well, it must have been that long walk we went
on. Lucy said this afternoon she would love to see me marry
an Irishman and have to live in Ireland. She said she wouldn't
half laugh. I asked her what I had done to her, that she could
wish such a horrible thing to happen to me. Mr Scott came
in this afternoon. He is Labour officer for Melton and Belvoir
now, Mr Coy is Labour supervisor at Saltby Camp, he hasn't
started there yet. I should think that is why Mr E is at Billesdon. I will let you know whether I am going with you on
Wednesday to the pictures, tomorrow. I will ring my cousin
in the morning to see if she is going out, if she isn't I will go
tomorrow instead of Wednesday.
Thank you very much for the eggs and everything. I am always happy when I come to Stathern. I wonder if we would
always be as happy as that?
I will have to say cheeri'O I want to do my hair I am going to
the picture tonight (with Dora)
                            All my love
                                Jean

L.A.E.C. Hostel.
Stathern.
May, 10th 1948.

My darling Jean

Did you get home well? I hope you didn't have to stand up for long. Wasn't there a prisoner on the bus to give his place to you? I packed the parcel this morning and sent it away. It wasn't possible to send it by airmail anyway I'd it registered. It'll take about a fortnight and the weight was 4lbs.

And now about Whitsunday. Mrs Betts told me that the Belvoir Castle usually is opened on Whitmonday. Wouldn't it be nice to take the Knipton bus and walk up to the castle? We'll have a word about it on Wednesday. Please make it possible to come along to the pictures. It should be better now as you saw it 3 years ago because it is in colour this time. I haven't seen anything of my little friends in the yard this morning. My stick is ready behind the door. I thank you very much for the nice afternoon. If it only could be every day like that. Please, my sweetheart, don't forget to tell me about the birthday present. I'll be very much annoyed if you don't. There must be something you would like to have. Think it over till I see you Wednesday.

Very well darling I'll say cheerio. Just be good 'my little girl'

Loads of love and kisses
Yours forever
Hans.

Countryside around Belvoir Castle

My darling Jean,
I hope you've arranged everything by now for Sunday and Monday. Well, darling. I want to see you on Sunday. It is very important. Don't ring me tomorrow and please no other private calls or conversations from the switchboard. Somebody made a big mistake somewhere. I heard a lot half an hour ago and tell you about it on Sunday. I am in a very hurry now. It is almost 3.00 and I haven't done a thing yet. Mr Edwards brought our money just today and I couldn't get away from talking. So it made me a bit later than usually. How are you today, darling? Everything is alright as far as I am concerned. I hope you do post a letter for me today or you'll ring me up from somewhere in Leicester. Are you working tomorrow? I heard the office finished work today at mid-day. You lucky girl. Anyway it'll be easier for me tomorrow for some of the men are leaving tonight. The rest then

tomorrow after lunch. I had a letter from my mother this morning. She hopes you're alright again and sends all the best wishes to you I am sorry, darling, but I've to say cheerio now. I'll tell you all about it on Sunday. Just be good and don't be worried.

All my love and kisses

Your forever, sweetheart

Hans.

92 Wharf St.

May 14th 1948.

My dearest Hans

Thank you so much for your letter. All I can say is I am sorry you did not get one from me, but you know how busy I am. I will warn you now that this letter is not going to be very long because it is now 2.30 and in about ½ hour I am going to get a cup of tea. I am going to get my hair set this afternoon. I can't ask to speak to you very well when I ring Mr Pickering for Labour Dept (Never mix business with pleasure). I spoke to Mrs Betts when I rang on Thursday. Did she know who it was? I am coming on Monday. I will try and be as early as possible. The buses are running every ½ hour so if I catch a bus about 10.30 I will be at Stathern about 12.0. I may bring the dog with me. If my mother is going out I will bring him, but if not, I will leave him at home. I think it would be too far for him to walk to Belvoir.

I will say cheeri'O see you Monday.

All my love

Jean

LAEC Hostel.

Stathern.

My darling

Thank you ever so much for your nice letter. It is 1.10 now

403

and I really had a lot to do before I could finish at 12 o'clock. Our porter sent a doctor's certificate and so I've all his work to do as well. I told you I didn't feel like work yesterday morning, but does it help? The men want their dinners. There is only one thing, 'get cracking'. I wish I could have spent another day with you. Anyway I'll never forget what you said about me coming along to Leicester before you got on to the bus in Melton. It made me very happy. So Mr Barker Swaine didn't say anything about the calls. I only hope to meet him once. Don't let him be too nice!! Oh yes you are such a shy girl. And I feel sorry for you other people putting the blame on you.

You don't want me to bring any flowers? Alright, but only for today. After today I know what to do myself. Don't worry I save my money wherever I can, but on the other side I like to see you enjoying anything I bring.

Well, my sweetheart I'll say cheerio. Do you work on Friday. Ain't I lucky to have my birthday on a Sunday and be able to see you the very same day?

Short page

I'm sorry but I'd to cut that piece off. It was silly writing it today.
Very well darling just be good. See you at 5.15. Think of me.

All my love and kisses
Only yours forever
Hans.

<u>P.S.</u>
I think I made a mess of this letter. Please forgive me. There is one of the men with me in the lounge and he keeps asking questions.

L.A.E.C. Hostel.
Stathern,

May 11th 1948.

My darling Jean

Thanks very much for the nice surprise I'd this morning. One letter on Tuesday seldom happened. Are you trying to write to me every day? Don't get too annoyed if people disturb you whilst writing a letter. You ought to tell them not to ring between 5.00 and 5.45. So you're very tired when you got home on Sunday. Don't you think we better stop walking around?

I am not quite sure if you told me Lucy was Irish. Give her my compliments and tell her if she wishes you again such a horrible thing she'll make my acquaintance one day. I'll see that you come to the right one from across the Channel. Mr Coy told me last night that he's going to Saltby as soon as they open the camp and he asked me to come along and work with him. He said Mr Edwards has had a good staff there. I hope you know by now how things are going tomorrow. Anyway I'll get another letter in the morning telling me all about it. Don't thanks me for the eggs. That's quite alright. I am only trying to help you a bit and you know I like to do it. I am very glad to hear you're always happy when you come to Stathern. Why does it take such a long time than for you to decide whether to come or not. You need not to wonder if we always be as happy as that. As far as I am concerned we certainly will be. You know I like to see you always happy. There's no question about that. I've told Mr Pickering about my holidays (3rd week in August) and everything is up to you now. You know my plans don't you? Could you fulfil my wishes. I don't think I ask to much.

Well my sweetheart, I'll say cheerio. Just be a good girl till I see you tomorrow. Think of me.

All my love and kisses
Yours forever
Hans.

L.A.E.C. Hostel.

Stathern.
May 13ᵗʰ 1948.

My darling Jean,
I heard you rung Mr Pickering this morning but didn't even ask for me. You must have been busy. Perhaps you'll ring again. There was another call for me last night from Saltby, but that fellow wouldn't tell his name to the warden. Seems to be a mysterious man. He only said he'll ring again. So I'll wait and see. How are you darling? Did you get home well last night. Did you take the dog a walk or have you been too tired. I mean we walked rather a long way. Remember we left the picture at 8.20 and arrived at the station at 8.30. So we really made it in no time. Did you call Dora yet? I hope it'll be alright for you coming for the day. Make it as early as you can and have your dinner here. I'll get something nice done. Did you listen to the telephone conversation this morning? We'll get 6 more men after Whitsunday and have to feed 4 of my fellows who'll go to Redmile Hostel shortly. If we get a van or lorry for the hostel I'll have to go every night and bring the dinner over there. It is a good thing it isn't far away. That'll make me a total of 23 then. Not too bad isn't it? Only 24 hours a day. I don't mind work as long as everything is going well. I think Mr Pickering is going to ring you now, but no chance for me. Did you say yesterday there shan't be a letter for me on Friday? I didn't realise that moment there are two days to go till Saturday. Oh! How cruel women are!!
Well, darling I'll say cheerio. Isn't the weather lovely this afternoon. I would like to go swimming somewhere. Are you going along?

All my love and kisses
Yours, my sweetheart
Hans.

R: 16/5.48   Aschersleben 1 May 1948

15/5.48

406

My dear Hans,

Yesterday we received your dear letter of 20.4.1948, for which we thank you very much. So you received the registered parcel from Erna safely. We are very happy that this way we've been able to carry out your wish. The whole thing was really fast. Silver usually tarnishes, you have to rub it now and then with a woollen cloth. I do hope that you are pleased with it. Is 1st May a holiday over there too? Well I won't see much of it, the weather is a bit cooler than usual. Hopefully Jean is well again? Dear Hans, don't strain your leg too much playing football, don't play too hard. Do you often bake cakes? What types can you get over there? Do people come round for coffee sometimes? We expect our trip will be after 10th June. On the 6th of June, Horst is taking part in a hairdressing competition in Halle and after that we wanted to go on our trip from there. Yes, I often miss Frau Streese badly. I was sick again this week for a few days. How can I provide for us, when we have to get wood? What can I cook with? And supplies for the winter also have to be got. It horrifies me that I'll have to go foraging this summer. If only I can cope with it! I often don't feel well nowadays, but you have to pull yourself together. I daren't let Horstel notice it at all, because he'll be very unhappy. What will be, will be. You don't need to concern yourself about it. But if only Papa were with us, I wouldn't have these big worries! It wears you down. But some time the day must come when you are both back with us. Now my dear Hans, stay healthy. With warm greetings and kisses from your mum who is always thinking of you, and from your brother Horst, Warm regards to Jean. To a healthy reunion! At the same time, we wish you joyful and healthy Whitsun celebration days.

L.A.E.C. HOSTEL.
Stathern.

Sunday, May 16th 1948.

My darling Jean

Thanks very much for your letter as for your call yesterday morning. So you knew all about that complaint. I thought there must be somebody else you are talking to because it wasn't I. I didn't want you to get into trouble because of me and that's why I told you not to ring here. Anyway I hope it was very interesting and you enjoyed it. The last men left yesterday afternoon. At 5.00 I took a lorry and went over to Redmile Hostel to bring some food for the four fellows. I was at 6.30 and had a look around the fair. You know temptation. I just took a gun and did some shooting and I'll show you the success tomorrow. Don't you think it would be impolite to leave all the things at the range. Just to be polite I borrowed a basket and carried the things home. I just read in your letter 'never mix business with pleasure.' No, you don't, not at all!! Mrs Betts didn't recognise your voice on the phone. She thought it was Mr Pickering's young lady. I'll get our dinner ready for 12 o'clock tomorrow and hope you'll be here by that time.

Mrs Betts had her daughter coming yesterday and her 3 year old grandson. He's a nice little fellow. We were friends in no time. At 9.00 last night he came around on his own to say goodnight to the uncle. I was surprised as somebody knocked at the door and he came in. So you are bringing your pup along! Don't be surprised but I'll have one shortly. When I went to Redmile yesterday I saw two little pups but still too young to take them away. The fellows will look after him till he grows a bit bigger. Well, my sweetheart I'll get something ready for dinner. So long then darling and just be good. Many kisses. In a few minutes you will be here again. Everything is ready. So, come and get it.

So long, my sweetheart. Just be good.

All my love and kisses
Only yours darling
Hans.

92 Wharf Street.
May 18th.

My Dearest Hans

I thank you for such a lovely weekend. It was the best bank holiday I have spent. My I only wish is that I could be there this afternoon. There isn't much doing at LAEC today and I am very bored sitting here doing nothing, but I suppose things will be back to normal tomorrow. I had a postcard from Iris this morning and she won't be back for another fortnight. She has been away for over two months now, but she will be back for when I go away which is a good thing. Barker Swain came to see me this afternoon and he never said a word about me speaking for 20 minutes, in fact he was very nice. I can't understand it, he probably thinks it is them that keep me talking and not as it should be, me keeping them (I am such a shy girl!!!) I am using an office pen and I am in such a mess I have ink all over my hands and everywhere. I will meet you outside the Gaumont just after 5.15 and don't bring any flowers, save your money, it is such a shame to take them to the pictures, the tulips you brought me last week are still alive. I have just been debating with myself weather (wrong whether) or not to go to the pictures tonight or to clean out my bedroom which I ought to do, but I am not in the mood for cleaning today. I could not eat my sandwich on the bus and that woman was talking most of the way. So I saved it and had it for my lunch at 10.30 today. It was just what the doctor ordered. I will have to say cheeri'O see you tomorrow.

All my love

Jean

.

L.A.E.C. Hostel.
Stathern.
May 18th. 1948.

My dearest darling Jean

Thanks, my darling, thank you very much for the wonderful afternoon we spend together. I never before enjoyed anything as much as I enjoyed that afternoon. I think there can't be anything better than spending a day just the two of us somewhere outside. I only hope it isn't too far off when everything becomes true. So, to say I felt rotten as your bus left Melton last night and really I don't feel like work this morning. After a day like yesterday the following week seems endless to me. I am so glad it's Wednesday tomorrow and I shall see you again.

Did you have a nice conversation on your way back last night. That lady looked rather funny to me. I think she thought herself something better than anybody else. Well, my sweetheart, how do you feel this morning? Did you come home alright. I arrived at 11.00 and after doing a few odd jobs for today's breakfast I went to bed at 11.30. The result was that I overslept this morning. I remember the bell at 4.30 and turned round again. When I woke up again it was 6.00. You should have seen the running about, doing everything for the porter as well. He's coming back tonight. After finishing my breakfast here I went to Redmile and was back at 8.45. That makes me a bit late with everything but I don't worry. Dinner will be ready in time. I am still waiting for the warden to come. He must have missed his bus. Well, my sweetheart, I hope you didn't forget to post a letter for me today. If you don't ring me tonight, I'll ring you tomorrow morning.

Thanks again for everything and just be my best girl.
             All my love and kisses forever,
                  Yours ,Hans.

L.A.E.C. Hostel.
Stathern.
May, 20th.1948.

My darling Jean

Many happy returns of the day. May all your wishes be fulfilled and you all your life be happy and gay.

I am really sorry I can't spend this day with you, but hope to be able to do it next year. May my only wish also become true. Well, my darling I arrived back at 10.30. I took your advice and had my supper at the Melton bus station and honestly I felt a lot better after having a sandwich and fish and chips. Anyway I shouldn't have told you I didn't eat anything during the day. Well, I promise to eat here before I leave next time.

Did you stick to your promise not to open the little parcel before Friday? It wasn't so difficult at all, was it? Anyway you promised and I know you kept it. I saw you looking for me last night as the bus left, but you didn't see me did you? I was upstairs on our side and even at the window. I didn't really have a decent birthday for five years, not as it used to when I was at home. It'll be different this year, because it is a Sunday and you will be with me. That will be a nice day for me. I had a look about Saturday afternoon. There's a bus at 2.00, 3.00 and so on every hour. If I don't make other arrangements (I mean taking a bus from Stathern) I'll be in Nottingham either at 2.45 or 3.10. The Redmile one takes more than one hour.

I'll have to say cheerio now and ring you first thing in the morning. So long, my sweetheart and just be my good girl.

All my love and kisses

Only yours forever

Hans.

LAEC Hostel.
Stathern.
May, 21st 1948.

My darling Jean,

It is your big day today and I am really sorry it's only once a year. I was so glad to hear that you liked the manicure set. I didn't think it would be so difficult to get one. So, my call was the first one in the morning. That's what I want it to be. As far as I know you've been a good girl all the year so I hope you'll get many presents. Wasn't it funny saying you don't know what to do when taking half a day off? You know I like you to be here every day or better, all the time. I knew you would keep your promise not opening the parcel. What's that, telling me I am crazy? I think I should know it myself best, but, sorry, I didn't notice it yet. By the way I don't want a strange nursemaid. I can't help it but I don't like strange girls about. My lip is alright, it was better already when I arrived here on Wednesday night. I didn't feel as if someone has hit me, but I think it must have looked like it. So you count me as the second one who can't make out something about you. Don't you think yourself you're wrong? I think I know you better than anybody else. I know what you want and I know what I want and that's the principle thing for me. Isn't it lovely this afternoon. It is a shame to spend your birthday sitting at the switchboard. I always took the afternoon off when I was at home. Remember it is only one a year. Well, my sweetheart, I'll say cheerio. Be seeing you tomorrow. As near to 3.00 as possible. Just be good and think of me.

All my love and kisses

Yours forever

Hans.

92 Wharf St.

May 23rd 1948.

My dearest Hans

Did you have a good supper at Redmile and get back to Stathern safe? I got into Leicester about 10.45. I had to get some
supper to eat with the egg. I thought I had not better leave
it until this morning it might have gone bad. It was nearly
12.0 when I got into bed I was dead tired so I soon went
into another world. I looked for you on the bus but I could
not see you. Were there two buses going to Redmile? I wish
I could have gone with you. I felt lonely sitting on the bus
on my own. It would be nice if we could go for a walk in the
evening then go home together. I would like that now but I
have to make sure that I would like it for the rest of my life.
I am glad you did not buy a coat for my birthday. I am glad it
was the manicure set. I will be able to keep it all my life and
remember all the nice things we have done together. I went
to see my auntie this morning to see what train we are going
on. I think it will be the 8.45 to London. I have to get my bag
packed as I am going to send it in advance, then I won't have
to bother with carrying it. I put my costume on this morning and I am getting thin, my skirt could do with an inch taking in. My auntie wanted to know if I was in love. Dora has
a boyfriend now, he works at the same place as her. I won't
have to bother what she is going to do on Sunday now.
I will have to say cheeri'O I must get ready for the party, my
cousin has just come, so be good

All my love

Jean

L.A.E.C. Hostel.
Stathern.
May 23rd 1948.

My dearest darling Jean

Thanks very much for the nice afternoon. I enjoyed the
picture very much, even sitting in the first row for a few

minutes, very nice wasn't it? I went to bed at 11.30 after doing a few odd jobs and having my supper for there was nobody at Redmile when I arrived there, My fellow was sleeping already. It is 3.45 now, I slept till 8.15 this morning. My fellow got up at 7.30 and fetched the key out of my room but I must have been tired not hearing him. So when I came down the fire was made up and breakfast almost ready. Mr Pickering told me that Mr Whitemann was here on Saturday afternoon with two people (married couple) to take the warden's place. The woman is about 26-28 and shall take his job. He doesn't know where he's going to. You know I don't like a woman here and I am not taking orders from her. Anyway I hope she doesn't interfere with me, or lots of trouble are ahead. I want to avoid that. How did you get home, darling? Was the egg still alright? Don't forget to let me have your address. I can't wait till you write first from there. Please, come back on Saturday and let's spend Sunday together. Well, my sweetheart, I'll say cheerio. My fellow talked to me all the time asking to go to the picture. I don't want to spoil his first weekend here.

So long and be good, just my best girl.

All my love and kisses
Yours forever
Hans.

92 Wharf St.

May 24th.

My dearest Hans

Thank you very much for your letter. I had left the letter you sent me on Saturday at the office. I don't know whether Lucy saw it or not but it was on my table, and she had been in with a postcard for me from Mr Barker he has gone to Cleethorpes for a few days. What pictures do you go to see? I can tell you went to Melton by the postmark.

Has the new warden started yet? And where is Mr Pickering going? What is her husband going to do, work on the committee? Tomorrow is the night I go to the concert. I spoke to Conie and Aunty this morning. I meant to ask you what Heinz was like, but I don't expect much from what you said. "Wait till you see Heinz" (I don't know how you spell his name but that is how we spell the name of some sauce). I really had not ought to be going out tomorrow because the railway is collecting my luggage Wednesday morning and I have an awful lot to do. I shall never get packed in time I don't know how I do it, but I always have to rush about at the last minute. I suppose that is a part of my national character. My cousin's party went off very well. Susan stayed the night so that Betty did not have to go early but we were not late leaving it was about 11.30. I was very tired. My mother has gone out with my auntie tonight to see some friends. So I am all on my own. There is a new girl in the showroom, she has been there about a week now. She is only there temporarily, seeing to anyone that wants to go to the Harvest camp. It hasn't taken long to learn her life's history. Lucy asks her all the questions and I sit and take all in. This is what we know so far – she is married and going to have a baby. She had only known her husband three weeks before she married him then he went abroad. When he came home she found out what a temper he had, now they have a free fight about every night. That only goes to prove that the old saying is right 'marry in haste, repent in leisure.' I don't think I am becoming hasty do you? Maybe you had better think that over too. I will ring you sometime this week before I go. If I come back on Saturday let us go for a picnic at Belvoir or Stathern. I think it had better be the latter because it will take too long to get to Belvoir. I wonder if the new warden will mind me coming to the hostel? But still it won't matter much if she does, we managed last year at Saltby so one more year won't make any difference.

I will have to say goodnight my love, because I have to get something in my case, so good night God bless.

All my love and kisses
Jean

.

My dearest, darling Jean

Thanks so very much for your nice letter. Be sure it didn't take me long to get to sleep on Saturday night. I sleep rather well as I noticed this morning. Having a very nice dream, I dreamt I heard the alarm and you said it's a bit too early. I agreed and the bell stopped after a minute. When I woke up it was 5.45 instead of 4.45. You should have seen me running about to get everything ready in time. So you see I think of you day and night. I also was looking for you as our bus left, but unfortunately there was another one besides yours. Don't think you were the only one feeling lonely on the bus. You know I would like to be with you all the time. I understand you quite well, darling. Make sure you like to be with me for the rest of your life. It would be so nice and I am sure there's a wonderful time for us ahead. A nice walk at night, sometimes to the picture or theatre and then at our home. Darling, that's the time I am longing for. So you are leaving at 8.45 on Saturday morning. I bet you are busy already packing your bag. Look, darling, I don't want you to get thin. I hope you don't take me for an instance and stop eating. Otherwise I promise to have my regular meals again. What do the auntie's want to know! What did you tell her? I bet you said 'no!' So, after all you're free from seeing Dora on Sundays now. She'll be busy from now on. Are you going to spend time with me? After all we went to Melton yesterday and saw two very nice pictures. 'Dance Hall' and "Time to

Kill' On the way I posted your letter. I was back here at 9.00.
Well, my sweetheart I'll say cheerio. Just be good and be my
best girl. Do you think of me?

All my love and kisses
Yours forever
Hans.

L.A.E.C. Hostel.
Stathern.
May 25.th 1948.

My dearest, darling Jean

I am awful sorry I didn't write this afternoon, but I really
was very busy. The first time something burnt. What else
could I do? Something else instead. Then I had to make a
cake and couldn't get the ovens hot. Trouble, nothing else.
The warden is leaving on Friday. Anyway that woman is
coming the same day. I wonder how I'll get on with her. I
haven't even seen her yet. So I better wait till I say anything. It is very nice of you to spare me tomorrow's evening. I'll enjoy the picture at least. I am getting on nicely
with my fellow. We were busy cleaning the dining room and
lounge during the last two days. It looks better now. Well,
my sweetheart, I'll say goodnight and God bless always. It's 9
o'clock and I am going to have a bath before I go to bed. I will
write a few more lines tomorrow. A goodnight kiss, yours
Hans.

Wednesday. 26.th May 48

Thanks very much for your nice letter I got this morning. It
is 11.30 now and I just finished because I want to take the
1.10 and have a haircut in Melton before I come to see you.
Do you mind if Lucy saw my letter? Don't take any notice,
darling and I am sure you know yourself what to do. Mr
Pickering doesn't know yet where he's going to. Probably
back to Gaddesby Hostel. As far as I know the new warden's
husband is going to work on a farm, living here in the hos-

tel. So you went to the concert last night. I thought you said you're going on June 25th. That's what I understood. Anyway I hope you've enjoyed yourself very much. Do you think you are the only one who has to rush about at the last minute to get the train. It was always the same at my home when we went away for the weekend. I always told my mother to get ready in time but we always had to run for the last 100 yards. I usually ran ahead to get our tickets. That means I've had training at it. Don't worry we'll never miss a train. I think it hasn't much to do with the national character.

I quite agree with you about that old saying, but it isn't always the same. Don't you think we know each other fairly well by now? There is nothing to be thought over by me. I've told you many a time darling, I am quite sure and only waiting for your answer. Alight, we'll go for a picture somewhere the Sunday after your holidays. Listen, sweetheart, the new warden won't mind you coming to the hostel. Don't forget it isn't a POW camp. You're right, we managed last year and we will manage now as well (I didn't say anything about another year). We can always stop here in the hostel if the weather happens to be bad. There's a nice warm kitchen or even the lounge.

Isn't the weather awful today. It's raining here all morning, but nothing can stop me from going to see you, not even if it rains forks and dogs. Well, my love, I'll get washed and changed now. Cheerio till I see you this afternoon and just be my best girl. Think of me.

All my love and kisses

Forever yours

Hans.

Replied 3.6.48   Prenzlau, 14.4.48

25/5

418

Dear Hans

Your lovely letter dated 2.4. reached me two days ago and I thank you for it from the bottom of my heart. I will try and reply today. Mum is coming tomorrow and she will take it to the post office for me. Yes Hans, I am bedridden again. The pains are so awful and it was reading your letter that started the pains. I did not go straight to bed, but they became unbearable and I had to lie down again. I am trying very hard to cope but it is pointless. The complaint is called 'gall colic' and there is no medication for it.Nobody can help, you just have to endure the agony. I have changed my doctor and hope I can have the operation soon, it needs to be done. I want to be free of this awful suffering. Here I have to put up with a lot of humiliation already, so Mum wants to take me home when it's all over. My husband's sisters give me hell. Whilst I am in bed doubled up with pain, I overhear conversations like: "What does he want a woman like her for? A sick wife is no good to any farmer" and similar remarks. This does not make a sick person feel any better. Otto told me yesterday that my complaining and whinging is getting on his and others' nerves. I shall have to go somewhere where I am not getting on people's nerves. I know I shall only be a burden to my mum, but I am hoping to get better soon. My recent attack was caused by your letter. I Mum wanted to visit me and decided to give me the letter personally. She thought I was still bedridden. When she came my attack was behind me and I was doing some washing, which had been soaking for a few days already. I was so happy to see a letter from you and, of course, I in the end disappointed. In the evening, when I was in bed, I thought about your letter and then, suddenly, I suffered another attack. I can't take anymore, Hans. You have upset me a lot. Have you acquired a new view of life or are you doing something against your will? Now I want to get to the main part of your letter: it seems I was a bit too presumptuous I admit, so I want to be honest at least. Perhaps I really believed in a different outcome but it is right that you have opened my eyes. You must have forgotten everything that was dear to you and you have to do it. The knowledge that you are happy will help me. It will calm me down and humble me. As my start into happiness has misfired, I want to make myself believe that I will find my inner peace again once I am back home. Yes, I grieve the loss of my child so much. To nurture and love her would have been a worthwhile task for me. I have always aspired to being a good teacher and the knowledge that I will never be able to have my own child (I meant to tell you this as well) is dreadfully painful for me. We had to suffer so much deprivation and hardship when we fled, not to mention the collapse of our country and how pathetic the aid was in those days.

Well, I don't want to start on this subject again. I am sure you will hear quite a lot from your mum. When you get home, I assume Jean will be your wife. You want to bring her along when we meet again? The fact that you are taking Jean to your home will change everything. We must not meet again. You will not be able to come on your own because imagine how Jean feels while you are coming to meet me. She must love you very much if she is happy to go to Germany with you. I do not want to cause her even the slightest pain. I cannot share her interest that she wants to see me as well. Why should she want to meet me? Hans, I cannot see you both, this would be the worst thing that could happen to me. In fact I think it would be for the best if we could say our 'goodbyes' now. I hope I will find my peace then.

When I am better again, they will accept me back into my teaching profession. They have already enquired about me. If only I had all this behind me. And who knows, perhaps things will get better between Otto and me. I want to close my letter and hope you can read everything. I am sending you my (heartfelt) greetings, Vera Schulz.

PS: This is what happiness looks like. You will not appreciate it, just return it to me.

R: 26/5.48   Aschersleben 11.5.48
                                  25/5

My dear Hans,

Thank you very much for your dear letter of 24.4.1948 which I want to reply to now. Yesterday afternoon I came back from my Berlin trip. It was wonderful at the Pyritzer reunion, there were many old acquaintances there and, everyone was happy to see everyone else again. I was asked to pass on greetings to you, above all, from Herr Lange, and Herr Bahr from the District Office. You actually met Lange, on the crossing from America. He has been with his family since Christmas. He said, if he had known everything about conditions here, he would have carried on staying there. He is hardly recognisable, so skinny, but Bahr looks much worse. Everyone was saying it was the best thing for you that you stayed and that at least you could manage to get some clothes for yourself. Willi Rollenhagen is still in French captivity. Waltraud married Waldow's son, has a little boy and lives in the West. Liselotte will soon be 18 years old and Soehni is already a tall nine-year old boy. Rubi is also at home. Frau Rollenhagen was there too, she and her husband are divorcing: she is now much thinner than she was at home, her grandmother also looks awful, she is already 83 years old. Neises have settled in Templin, Uckermark. Mausi is still missing in R. Kurt got married in the west, Grete is also married and Johanna is about to be married. Frau Zietur was there too, with her daughters, it was hard to recognise her. Herr Zietur, who was seriously wounded at the time in Pyritz, died in Flensburg. Also, your schoolmate Franz, who lived in Seestrasse, sends you greetings. Mader, the butcher, and his wife, were hardly recognizable, same as Frau Seiler. Albinus, the road maintenance manager, was also there. Otto Michaelis, the Turkish man from the West, and his wife are also divorcing. The daughter of the pharmacist Strache, has married a R like Kirschnicks' daughter, (he worked for the public services). The faces all looked so familiar but you had to think hard for a long time to match names to faces. It's been a long time since we have seen each other. There were a lot of young Pyritzers present. There is another reunion on 10th July. Horst is very keen to go with me then. On June 9th we will probably begin our trip to West Pomerania. Hopefully everything will work out. Please congratulate Jean heartily on her birthday. Aunt Emilie also sends you fond greetings. She spent four months in hospital with a thigh fracture, but can't walk yet. At 81 years' old, it's incredibly hard for her to manage by herself. Dear Hans, please forget all about playing football, it could seriously hurt you, especially now that you have already settled in nicely.

Now stay in good health, with warm greetings and kisses from your mum and your brother Horst.

    92 Wharf St.

    MAY 27th.

My dearest Hans

I am sorry you will not get this letter Friday morning (but you know how it is, BUSY). What did you think when there was a letter? I spoke to Mr Pickering today and he said his leg was much worse today. Mr Edwards went to see the doctor this morning, he did say what was wrong but I was no better off when he had told me. I got on very well at the concert, it was very good, but I am afraid I have started something. Heinz said maybe we could go somewhere next week, fortunately I am away but what will happen the week after? I met Arnie's girl, she is very nice. She is Irish from Dublin and does not like Leicester. They have been engaged since a year last April. I asked Arnie when the ban for speaking to English girls was lifted, and he said last October or September, in that case you were right I did see you before the ban was lifted. Well, darling I hope you get on with warden OK, remember if you don't, they will move you to a camp hostel and I don't think that would be so nice for you. How's Horst getting on? Has Mary changed her affection to him yet?

Well darling I will say goodnight and God bless I will write next time from Eastbourne.

All my love

Jean

L.A.E.C. Hostel,

Stathern,

May, 27th 1948.

My dearest, darling Jean

I am back safe and sound and was lucky to get the 9.10 in Melton last night. So I arrived here at 10.00 had my supper and went to bed. I enjoyed the picture very much, I always do being with you. Did you enjoy it? It is bad we have to leave before the second one is finished. Don't you think I better move somewhere near Leicester to be able to get a later bus. When you come Sunday after next remind me to show you a letter and a photograph. I got one this morning, saying everything I wanted to hear. You didn't have time to finish our conversation about the concert last night. Are you going to tell me about it? My fingers are always crossed that the nice weather today continues for a week so you may be able to enjoy your holidays. Forgive me, sweetheart for this short letter, but there are lots to do for me. I am going to help the warden with that list of equipment. I say cheerio and just be good. Think of me.

All my love and kisses

Forever yours

Hans.

L.A.E.C. Hostel,

Stathern,

May, 28th 1948.

My dearest darling Jean

I am so awfully sorry I didn't post a letter for you today for I thought you wouldn't get it in time tomorrow morning. There's nothing exciting happened till now except the arrival of the new warden. She seems to be very cautious, looking about the place. I hope she never looks at the pots because there may be something inside jumping against her face. What do think about rats? She likes them almost as much as you do. I could hardly answer your questions on the phone for she was standing at the door, talking to one of the men.

Saturday 29th

Another day is gone. It is 2.15 and I am still waiting for 3 men to come. The best thing to tell you about is the new warden. Anyway you'll see for yourself week tomorrow. I've told her you're coming on Sunday and I hope she wouldn't mind. Her answer was "not in the least. You're not in my way". In the course of a conversation I said that I don't her interfering with me, otherwise I may loose my temper and I don't want to cause trouble. So she knows what I want her to know. Time will show how everything goes on. Thanks very much for your letter, darling. I was waiting for your call this morning but nothing happened. You certainly must have been in a rush. Anyway I hope to get your letter from Eastbourne on Monday. Mr Pickering wanted to go home this afternoon and went to the bus but came back after a few minutes because he couldn't stand the pain. He went straight to bed. Maybe I'll take him home tomorrow afternoon. Now about the concert. I am glad to hear you enjoyed it. I told you before how it would go on after the first time to the concert for I know my fellows better than you do. I am not afraid you've started something. Don't you worry darling. I am not afraid of being moved to another place, but before I go I'll certainly see Mr Barker-Swain. The only question is a hostel nearer to Leicester. Horst is going on alright. It is very nice to work with him, I know him for long while. I haven't seen Mary the last few days so I can't tell if she's changed affection to Horst I've told him already that I put all the WLA on him to get a rest myself. Don't you think this is going to be a long letter? I only hope you won't get tired of reading it. It's 5.00 now I'll get something to eat for myself. I will write more tomorrow afternoon, night and hope to get your letter on Monday. So long my darling and just be my best girl. Xxx

Sunday May 30th

Well, darling my work for today is done. I'll have a bath and change now, but I don't know yet what I am going to do. The warden left this morning for Leicester. Fred Dann took him in the van. That means from now on I've to deal with her highness, the new warden. After a few days I shall see how we get on together. She just came and asked me if I want her to do anything. I've told her about the packed lunch and she's going to have a go at it. Cheerio for today, my sweetheart, and again – be careful xxx

Monday May 31st

I really didn't expect you to write on Saturday soon after your arrival for I know there's a lot to do and to settle down. After all I went to the pictures last night and saw a very nice one 'Home but the lonely heart' it was called. I don't agree with a few things I saw there, but it wasn't bad at all. I think the warden changed her mind because she's getting on a bit better now. Perhaps she noticed she can't boss me. Anyway I've told her straight on Saturday. What are you doing now all day? Wouldn't it have been nice just for the two of us to spend such a holiday. I would love it very much and I think so would you. I shall see how long your letter takes to know when to send the last letter. I suppose you can't spare much time writing to me. I don't really mind, my love, as long as I know you enjoy yourself. I'll go and see Mr Pickering on Wednesday and take a few eggs for him. I got some yesterday. He was pretty bad when he left here yesterday. I'll write a few more lines when I've finished tonight. Don't get tired of reading.

All my love, my darling. It is just 3 o'clock and received your new address. Thanks so much darling. I'll post this one at once and answer your letter tonight. So just be good and thousand kisses.

All my love
Forever yours
Hans.

92 Wharf Street.
May 29th 1948.

My dearest Hans

Thank you very much for your letter I read whilst I had my supper. It took me all my time not to open the other one but I promised I wouldn't until Friday, so I have put it away. Thank you very much for the glasses. I have not unwrapped them. I thought they would be better left. I was not going to write tonight but I have just written a few lines to Iris and I thought I would do a few to you. So you are too busy to eat are you? I think you are crafty. You will make yourself ill then you will have to get yourself a nurse maid because in that case, I would not have any sympathy for you.

Thursday

How's your lip this morning? Do you feel as if someone has hit you? I spoke to Mr Edwards this morning. I told him he had warned the wrong one if they had thought it was you that would have told Mr Pickering. I have just been speaking to Mr Pickering, he says there is something about me he can't make out (that makes 2 at Stathern). I told him to let me know what it is he can't make out. The weather isn't so good today. I only hope it will change for the 29th to the good. I am not going out tonight, it is really a good job because I have such a lot to do. I will say cheeri-bye now because I am nearly at end of the paper and I could not write another page so

All my love
Jean

THE ANGELS
ROYAL PARADE
EASTBOURNE
MAY 29th 1948.
10.30

My dearest Hans

I am writing this letter in bed. I have the room on my own unfortunately, I hate sleeping on my own at home so I don't know what it will be like, being in a strange place. My auntie and cousin have a room on the floor below. I was writing a postcard to my mother to let her know I had arrived safe, when my auntie came in and asked me if I was writing to my German, so I said no, but I am when I have finished this. She is always fishing to find out what she can.

I am terribly sorry I did not ring you this morning darling, but I did not have time. I said I would meet my auntie at 8.00 but I did not arrive until 8.40 and the train left Leicester at 8.45. They were mad with me, they had been waiting since 8.25. Anyway we had a comfortable seat all the way to London. We had arranged to go to the West End for lunch but it was pouring with rain so we went straight on to Victoria station, had our lunch there and then continued the journey down here on the 1.45 from London. It is quite a nice hotel right on the seafront. The food is very good which is the main thing and the bed is very comfortable. Tomorrow I don't suppose I will be doing anything special, my auntie and cousin are the sort that do not believe in buying Sunday papers, listening to the radio and breathing so you may have no fear of me going off the straight and narrow path.

Look darling now that the new warden has started I will not ring you at all whilst I am at work. If she doesn't know who I am, don't tell her I work at the LAEC because it is nothing to do with the LAEC. It's a funny way of putting it but I hope you know I mean.

Well darling I will have to say goodnight. God Bless I will be thinking of you all night and I hope then I won't be afraid.

All my love

Jean

Mr J Klawitter
L.A.E.C. Hostel
Old Rectory
Stathern
Nr Melton Mowbray
Leicestershire

Dear Hans
Thank you very much for your letter I received
it this afternoon. The weather hasn't been too
good up to now but I am hoping it will improve.
Went to Beachy Head this afternoon and just
about got blown off the top. We are going to
see a show tonight and I am hoping it will be good.   Jean

> L.A.E.C. Hostel.
> Stathern.
> May 31st 1948.

My dearest, darling Jean,
I thank you ever so much for your lovely letter I received

this afternoon. I promised to write tonight and so I will. It doesn't matter what time I go to bed because 5.15 tomorrow morning I've to get up. I didn't know you hated sleeping on your own. Are you afraid of somebody carrying you away. Just tell him my address before he does. It's quite alright you didn't ring on Saturday. I thought you would be in a hurry. I am really glad you're comfortable on the way. Good food keeps you in a good mood and going. Isn't that right? Look darling I've no fear at all of you going off the straight path. I just want you to be safe wherever you go and whatsoever you do. I got a letter from Mr Pickering this afternoon. He sent the reference I asked for. I've never seen a better one. I'll show you next Sunday.

Tuesday June 1st 1948
How are you today, my darling? It is such a nice weather here today. Are you enjoying yourself and think of me working in the hot kitchen? I had to make a cake this morning and tarts this afternoon so you can guess the temperature. I've a walk around the garden from time to time. I had the wireless upstairs in my new room last night when I was writing to you. It looks nice. Bedroom and sitting room in one. You'll see on Sunday. I expect a letter tomorrow morning if I am lucky. Well, my sweetheart I'll have to say cheerio now. I've a bit more to do, cooking for 20 men. They have put a few more men into Redmile Hostel. So long and be my best girl.

> I am thinking of you as always
> With all my love
> Forever yours
> Hans.

R 1/6.1948   Aschersleben 16.5.1948, Whitsun
                                    31.5.

430

My dear Hans,

We thank you heartily for your dear letter of 4th May 1948. So, then you have received our photos already!! Today is Whit Sunday. This afternoon I went for a walk with Frau Ziemann. Today, also, we received post from Frau Streese. Gertrud has been ill again. Dear Hans, did you send the parcel off? Because in your letter of 13.4.48 you wrote that you wanted to send it that week, but it hasn't arrived here yet, that's already taken 4 weeks. Wouldn't it be better if you sent smaller parcels? Maybe they would be quicker? If you could get a shirt for Horst, we would be really happy, he is really very badly provided for with shirts. Aunt Erna, Uncle Erich and Uncle Gustav and family asked me to send you their very warm greetings. On 8th June Horst is going to Berni Höhl's wedding and on 9th June we want to leave for our trip to West Pomerania - hopefully everything will work out. Heinz Bieck is staying in France until January. How long do you actually have to stay? Surely you must have a contract? Here we've had several substantial thunderstorms, one day after another. It's already quite warm. Your photos are taking a lot longer than they would here, they're taking their time with them, aren't they? Horst has been insanely busy at work because of Whitsun and even today he was still 'on the go' until midday – all the ladies want to look their best for the festivities. Our journey to West Pomerania will cost an arm and a leg, but we are all so keen to see each other again. What more can you want from life? The day after tomorrow we intend to go back to the woods to get firewood, we stopped for a few weeks, we were too exhausted, but now we need to pick ourselves up and go back a few more times. Aunt Lina and Christel have gone to Uncle Gustav's and Uncle Erich's for Whitsun, they don't have to travel as far as we do! This evening I am going to read a little, while listening to some music. I suppose Jean will have been with you again today? Or did you have the day off? Now my dear

Hans I must finish this letter. Just stay in good health! With all good wishes and kisses from your mother and from your brother Horst. Best wishes to Jean as well.

~~92 Wharf St~~
The Angles Hotel,
Royal Parade,
Eastbourne.
June <u>1st</u> 1948.

My dearest Hans

I did hope you would receive my letter Monday morning so that I would have one today. I got up early especially to see if there would be a letter for me, but I know there will be one for me in the morning. That reminds me darling don't send a letter to this address after Thursday because it may take two days to get here. Well darling the weather hasn't been too good (have you uncrossed your fingers). It was fine on Sunday though it was windy. Sunday morning we walked to Beachy Head, had rest in the afternoon and went to listen to the brass band in the evening. On Monday ~~morning~~ it poured nearly all day. In the morning we went round most of the shops. I brought a tablecloth to work on and I stayed in the afternoon to do some, fortunately this hotel has a beautiful lounge and the windows are very big so you get a good view of what goes on. In the evening we went to see a play called 'Peace Comes to Peckham'. it was very funny. I have not been anywhere special today. I went for a paddle this afternoon, but I did not stay long, it was too cold.

Well darling I will say goodnight God bless.

2.6.48

Well darling half of my holiday has gone already. I think you had better be transferred down to Sussex AEC as near to East-bourne as possible, that would just suit me. I was going to post this today but I went out without it so I sent a postcard instead (the warden will be able to read that). How is Mr Pickering? Is he any better now? We went up Beachy Head this afternoon oh, it was windy it would certainly blow the cobwebs off you up there. We have been to a show tonight, it was very good called 'On with the show'. I took my Mother's scarf with me and I think I must have dropped it in the theatre. I went back to see if it was there but they told me to call in the morning. I am hoping it will be there. I am coming home on ~~Sunday~~ Saturday so I will ring you and let you know about Sunday morning. I will say goodnight, God bless

Love and kisses
Jean

P.S
Please darling don't take any notice of the mistakes I feel too tired to read it through.

Jean and cousin Gertie at Eastbourne

LAEC Hostel.
Stathern.
June 3rd 1948.

My dearest, darling Jean,
I bet you are enjoying yourself because I only had one letter

on Monday afternoon. I'll see you on Sunday anyway. I went to Leicester yesterday to visit Mr Pickering. It took me one hour to find his place but was successful after all. I read in the paper yesterday that there was a storm off the Sussex coast during the last days doing some damage to fruit trees. Was that somewhere near the place where you are? Well, my love, how often could I tell you how much I miss you. You know I would like you to have many more holidays, but better somewhere near me. I can't even ring you now. After I left Mr Pickering yesterday I went to the Gaumont and saw 'Rio Rita.' It was very funny, just what I wanted to cheer me up a bit.

Here's everything alright and the warden is much quieter by now. There was some trouble night before last and Mr Sanders came out yesterday. She said she's fed up already and doesn't know whether to stay or not. Anyway it doesn't matter to me if she goes. I am doing my job as good as I can. By the way I bought a new pair of shoes for my second suit yesterday. I told you I was looking for shoes with crepe sole. £1-5-0 isn't too bad I think. They look very nice and I hope you'll like them. Well, my sweetheart, I have to say cheerio now and get on with my work. Just be good and my best girl. I am always thinking of you.

All my love and kisses

Forever yours

Hans.

R 4/6.48　　　　Aschersleben 23.5.48

3/6.48

My dear Hans,

Thank you very much for your lovely letter of 7.5.48. The package with the shirt didn't actually arrive on Horstel's birthday, I felt very sorry, but what can one do? Also, the other package isn't here yet, when did you send it? Tomorrow we want to go to the woods again. Then next week one more time and we'll be done for the time being. Then on June 9th, if everything goes well, we can start on our trip. And if we are in good health when we come back, the blueberry season starts and afterwards, the foraging. It's already starting to get to me. Then it'll be nothing but foraging. That you or Jean could get hold of a shirt makes us very happy and we thank you very much, if it wasn't so necessary, I wouldn't have bothered you about it . Horstel's birthday is now over, he had a few guests. He wants to have a little bit of enjoyment and I let him have it gladly. Did you manage to see Jean on her birthday? How old is she now? Supplies are alarmingly low, so we will have to call a halt to the cake-baking soon. That was always a little Sunday pleasure. Hans, dear, when you go into town next can you see if you can get some braid about 8-10 meters long, dark brown or black, about 2-4 cm wide. I want to have a winter coat made for me out of the remains of two covers. I must have the braid as the material is too thick to turn under. Otherwise, I have no other news. Many greetings from the heart and kisses from your mum and your brother Horst. Many greetings to Jean. Herr Schulz is leaving England on 28th May '48.

(Postcard) 23.5.48
To: Frau Hedwig Schünemann,
Aschersleben / Harz,
Hinterbreite 24,
S. Brandt /

From: Erna Schünemann,
Isle of Juist,
Nordsee Hotel,
Ostfriesland /

Juist Island, 10.5.48.

Dear Hedwig and Horstel,

I have received your dear letter with many thanks. A card will have to do, as I have no other writing paper. I've had to spend a few days in bed – everything has come at once.

I haven't yet received my Permission to come to Aschersleben, today I went to the Military Government to see what can be done. The "To"* were very nice and asked why I hadn't come sooner. I received news from Hans that he has already received the ring. It only took five days – don't you think that was quick? If you ever want something else again, let me know and I will gladly get it for you. I paid 2.30, but don't send me the money, buy a little something with it, whatever you like.

I haven't had any post from Mum yet, but post came from Werner today. Your photo is very nice. Don't forget to send Hans his, to look at occasionally. There is no vinegar essence here either, only plenty of vinegar. Do you want that? With warm greetings to you both,

Your Erna.

Happy Whitsun!

*English "Tommies"

Aschersleben, 26.5.48

My dear Hans,

I have received your lovely letter of 24.4.48 with many thanks. I am one year older again and that is all. In the evening the Höhls and Ziemanns came to us for a cup of coffee. From Mum I got a nice wooden suitcase and a few little things. The Ziemanns gave me a bunch of flowers, a bow-tie and from the Höhls, three hundred grams of cotton wool. All in all I had ten bunches of flowers. How did Jean celebrate her birthday? I congratulate her belatedly and wish her all the best. Her birthday was certainly better, because things are altogether different abroad. Your parcel hasn't arrived yet, or haven't you sent it off yet. Why should I send a photo, the love has died, firstly she is four years older than me and secondly I am still young and have the choice. When your photos are ready please send us two, so that I have one of both of you too. I am going dancing this afternoon. Otherwise, there is nothing else to do. Last night Mum and I went to the cinema. "Es lebe die Liebe" was on. The Referendum starts today. They should at least give us back our homeland, that would go some way to satisfy us. I worked until around twelve o'clock again. I look after my clients every Sunday morning. Dear Hans, just be careful with your leg and don't always play football. And how are you, apart from that? It's super that you got a shirt - my shirts aren't shirts any more, they are rags. I can't take off my jacket. We certainly had a lot of work at Whitsun. Yesterday I didn't get home till 7 o'clock. Sometimes it gets a bit much. But you know those who are good-natured are exploited to the limit. You wouldn't believe how much they are earning. These people drink ground coffee and cocoa. We can't afford that. Although often one has a huge desire for it. Now I must finish. Many greetings, Hans and Jean, from your brother Horst, and mum. Looking forward to an early and healthy reunion. I would be enormously pleased if you could get some shoes for mum. Goodbye for now. Write soon again.

Aschersleben 30.5.48

My dear Hans

We thank you very much for your letters dated May 14th and 16th. Unfortunately Horst's parcel has not yet arrived, it seems to take longer than you expected. I was a little surprised not to have had any greetings from you either for Mother's Day or Whitsun. Although it is not absolutely necessary, it would have made me happy. Did you actually ever send a parcel, having written on 13/4/48 that you were going to send it in the next few days, but this one has not arrived either, meaning it will have been en route for over six weeks. I could well use the sweetener, as we now have lettuce and there is never enough sugar.* We've not had any fat since Whitsun, food isn't really food without any fat. Let us hope the weather tomorrow will be nice, as we are planning to collect wood again. That will then be all for the time being. Yesterday I've had our wood sawn, and in the afternoon and this morning I split it all into logs and sweated so much that I had to change my clothes. Another few hours, and then all will be done, and we will have enough for the whole winter. I am really pleased to have done it all – it is of course essential. I have slept for an hour and my muscles are aching like mad. Have you still not got your pictures? It seems to take a very long time. If you have sweetener you can just enclose it in a letter. Mrs Brandt's husband sent her some in a letter and it arrived without a problem. The grain is doing well, hopefully it will be a good harvest. That means the difficult times for me will start all over again, and I am dreading it already. Horst has gone out for a little while. Now my dear boy, stay well, give our regards to Jean, lots of love and kisses from your mum and your brother Horst

* It was common to put quite a bit of sugar in salad dressings

LAEC Hostel.
Stathern.
June, 4th 1948.

My dearest, darling Jean,
Thank you very much for your postcard and letter I got this morning. That makes four days without a word. Anyway I was glad to get a few lines after all. I really don't feel like writing this afternoon, because I am waiting to see Mr Shilton this afternoon. The warden received a letter from Leicester today saying that Mr Barker-Swaine was surprised

to hear about trouble at Stathern Hostel AJV. The last sentence was, 'Mr Shilton is coming to Stathern on Friday to arrange reallocation with regard to hostel staff.' So I told her straight away what that means to me – leaving here – she was sent as cook-warden and as soon as she does the cooking, I'll have to be transferred. So I have to wait now for Shilton to know where they are going to send me to. I hope somewhere near you if it must be. I am sure the men will cause her lots of trouble because of her cooking. I shan't worry about it thou. Everybody was quite satisfied up till now. You can't run a place cheaper as we ran it. I'll post this letter tonight after Mr Shilton has been and let you know about everything. If he doesn't come till 4 o'clock I'll post it and you ring here on Sunday morning. I shall leave word about my new place if I happen to leave today or tomorrow. I may ring you (only if they move me) at about 9.00 Saturday night. Well, darling that's the newest so far. I posted my last letter to Eastbourne on Thursday afternoon and hope you got it alright. This one will be waiting for you when you get home. I am really sorry the weather wasn't too good. I didn't uncross my fingers. Don't think the warden may read postcards because I am looking out for the postman every morning and get the mail off him.

You don't think I am so old that the wind may blow cobwebs off me. That takes a lot more years. I hope you found your mothers scarf again. Well, darling don't tell me you want me to settle down at the other place when I leave here. Please come Sunday wherever I might be. I am longing to see you again.

I'll say cheerio now. Just be good and think of me.

All my love and kisses

Forever yours

Hans.

Hans Klawitter.

L.A.E.C. Hostel, Saltby,
nr Melton M.

My darling Jean,   Sunday 6.6.48.

I am very sorry about tonight darling. I know I wasn't in a good mood and please forgive me. I was upset about something but don't even know what it was. When your bus left I went into town and met Horst. We went to the picture and just arrived here. It is 10.45. I just feel I must write to you. I was surprised when you said. 'Wouldn't we be happy' Well, sweetheart, you know yourself quite well we would be. You only said it in such a sarcastic tone. Did you forget me telling you I could do everything for you? Remember it always darling, I only want to live for you. Please make sure and come next Sunday. You know I am longing to see you. Do you know what I meant with translating that letter to you? I wanted to show you I really finished and don't even care a tiny bit. Always remember it is only you that matters to me. Nobody else. Well, I'll say goodnight and God bless. A goodnight kiss only yours, darling, Hans.

Tuesday 8.00am

I am awfully sorry, darling you didn't get this letter today. After all I landed at my new place and had to take over straight away. Are you surprised to hear I am in Saltby again? There were lots of work to do when I came yesterday. I went to bed at 11.30 last night and got up at 4.30 this morning. There are 6 men (Poles, Ukrainian, Hungarian a.s.v) with me. I have nothing else to do than watch the cooking as chief cook. But the only trouble is the cooks don't know much. I hope it won't be so late again tonight.

Didn't you say once you like the lovely spots around Croxton? There we are again. Please come down on Sunday and let me know.

Mr Coy will take the letter and post it in Waltham, I'll ring you during the day.

Well, sweetheart, I'll say cheerio. Just be my best girl.

All my love and kisses
Forever yours
Hans.

Hans Klawitter,
LAEC Hostel, Saltby,
Melton Mowbray.
June, 8th 1948.

My dearest darling Jean

Wasn't it a nice surprise to call you from Buckminster 2772. And how glad the operator in Grantham will be to hear well known voices again? I was a bit surprised myself as Mr Sanders told me, but I really don't mind because it is better for you. You needn't change the bus in Melton and wait in the queue.

I shan't take tomorrow afternoon off because I like to see everything through at first. People sometimes say 'new brooms sweep good' but I am trying to get this place as far as I got Stathern Hostel. Everybody always satisfied. It really is nice when you can see smiling faces at dinner times. I've started today with steam pudding and the men ask me to do it again tomorrow. They've never seen any before. You know I don't mind work and the 6 men I've as help in the kitchen is very good to work with. Unfortunately nobody can bake so I think you can imagine what it means to bake for 80 men. That means one night without sleep during the week. The warden is good to work with, so everything is going alright.

Please, darling, come on Sunday. Don't tell me you're going to cancel it. You know the nice spots around Croxton don't you?

I took my little pup along. At first I was going to leave it in Stathern. When Mr Sanders came and saw it laying on my kitbag he told me to take it along. I am glad now I did, because he's going on nice. Everybody wants to play with him. Cheerio my sweetheart and God bless. Just be good.

All my love and a goodnight kiss

Only yours, my love

Hans.

Kitchen staff at Saltby
Hans centre back

92 Wharf St.

June 9th.

My dearest Hans

Thank you very much for your letter, what does it feel like to be back at Saltby. I was very surprised when you said you were there. Do you feel like a prisoner again of the United Nations? For heaven's sake darling, never join in any discussion about the war or politics and when they do start, go and find a safe place and wait until they have finished. You did not say whether you had taken the puppy (Bonzo) with you. It is NOT you that's to blame for Sunday it is me, I know I am so bossy. I don't mean to be. I wish you would stop me, and I am very sorry I was sarcastic, but I was mad on Sunday too and I don't know why. But darling I wish you would try to understand. You are always saying that I must be ashamed or something of you. I wish you wouldn't, I know it must seem funny to you, when I don't want people to know about us. It isn't that I mind people knowing. It is that I should get an awful lot of criticism. I think sometimes I don't care what they think. Anyway, darling I will try and explain what I mean sometime.

About Sunday what should we do if it's raining, go to Grantham or you meet me in Melton? You had better let me now.

I will say cheeri'O. I will take this letter to the General then you may get it tomorrow.

All my love
Jean

L.A.E.C. Hostel, Saltby.
June, 10th 1948.

My dearest, darling Jean,

Thank you so very much for your letter I received this morning. You can imagine how I was longing for. It's a good thing everything is going nicely so we could finish at 7.30 tonight. I hope shortly they'll call Saltby the best fed hostel on the job. Anyway I am going to try it. It was a bit chinese to me when I first saw how the hostel has been run, but we changed already. Also the warden agreed. He's rather new on the job and likes to take on advice. There's quite a good understanding with him. In any case better than with the new warden at Stathern. I wonder how she's getting on. I wouldn't mind staying here if it only were nearer to you darling.

Don't be afraid about me getting into trouble with them folks here. You know I won't start anything and if someone else wants something, he most certainly can have it. You needn't worry at all. They warm up now and get rather friendly. I am awfully sorry I didn't write to you last night, but I was really busy. I was just starting a letter for you when one of the men came and asked me a favour. So after all I wrote a letter- and even a love letter- but in German. When I read it through I found it rather dry. I felt sorry for that fellow but couldn't help it.

Didn't I tell you in my last letter that I took Bonzo along. I am used to the name now. He is laying across my shoes now. My other shoes and slippers have to be in a safe place now. Look, darling, don't say you're to blame for last Sunday. I don't call you bossy. Didn't I tell you often that I like you as you are? And that includes everything.

Alright, sweetheart, I won't talk again about being ashamed of me. I didn't mean to hurt you. So, please, forgive me. But, darling, you should never pay attention to what other people say. I told you I did so at home and found out it worked alright.

Now about Sunday. I am working up to something, but I am not quite sure of it. If it should be raining there'll be a place to go to. Anyway I am coming down to Melton to meet you there. I shall let you know on Saturday during the morning. Just make sure what bus you're coming on. I went to Melton today with Mr Coy, doing some shopping. After all I bought an electric iron for there is none here. You know I like to keep my suits in a good condition. So that makes another thing fo "us"

Well, darling, time is getting on and I'll say cheerio. I still have to write to my mother. Just be good and think of me.
All my love and kisses
Forever yours, my love
Hans

Bonzo

L.A.E.C. Hostel, Saltby.
June, 12th. 1948.

My dearest, darling, Jean,
Only a night and half a day to go till I see you tomorrow. So my first week is over without difficulties. I was so glad last night when the dinner was over because it was a hard job to cook with the rest the other fellow left for me. Bonzo is chewing my slippers and trousers and I already had to take

my shoes away. He is sitting on my bed trying to make two blankets out of one. That means I always have to get up and stop him. How's your pup? Did Susan say anything about seeing the little dog?

I have to try to keep my eyes open. I went to bed at 00.15 am and got up again at 4.00. No wonder I was so tired this afternoon. I had to lay down for an hour. I would like to get the kitchen in a state I like. Afterwards it is much easier to work for me. It is just 10 o'clock, but I still have to wait for the men to leave the sitting room (second half of the dining hall) to switch the light off.

Do you think we'll have nice weather tomorrow? If it is too wet we better go to Grantham. I always felt very sorry for you walking about in the rain last year, but you know I am always happy being with you. I went down to the pub tonight because Mr Selby told me this morning Mr Edwards would probably be there tonight. He wasn't so I went straight back without having a drink. Mr Selby offered me one and was surprised to hear me refuse the beer.

Well, my love I'll say goodnight and God bless. Just be a good girl.

All my love and a goodnight kiss
    Forever yours
        Hans.

            L.A.E.C. Hostel, Saltby.
            June 14th 1948.

My darling Jean,
I can spare a few minutes now, so I'll start to write a letter. I arrived back at 10.15 last night, had some supper and went to bed at 11.00. It must have been the time you arrived home. Thanks very much, darling for a wonderful afternoon. I like to see you always so happy. Life is worth it then. It is always the same after your leaving. I feel rotten and ask myself why we have to part. Anyway I am so sure our time will

come soon. Make sure, my love, as soon as possible. After a Sunday like yesterday I know what I've to miss. Nobody else could make me happier than you would. I arranged about next Sunday. The warden told me his bungalow is mine for the day. So we'll enjoy ourself. The birthday is only once a year, that means we'll make the best of it. The warden said if he'd known I had somebody coming yesterday he certainly would have told me to come to his place. I felt so sorry for you being without any food or drink for 11 hours. It was my fault and it shan't happen again. I don't mind about myself, but I don't like to see you as you were yesterday.

I had a word from Mr Pickering this morning. He's in plaster now for about five weeks and therefore of course very uncomfortable. He asked me if I want to come along if he should happen to take another hostel. That just depends on where and what hostel it is. If it is somewhere near you, darling, at once. He asked me to remember him to you. He hasn't heard from the office yet where he's to go and hasn't had any money yet. I think they don't care much if anybody is on the sick.

My room looked nice when I came back last night. One of my slippers was all over the place. He's done that job well. Anyway he kept quiet during the night so I was able to get some sleep at last.

I think I better take your advice about my money and leave the matter for the time being. Anyway I'll wait till Mr Sanders comes again next Friday. There's an old saying in Germany "wait but hang on to it" I hope that'll be the best.

Well, my love I'll say cheerio now. I've to find out what time the last mail is to be put in the letter box so you may get it in the morning.

Be good and think of me and better times.

All my love and kisses

Only yours, darling

Hans.

L.A.E.C. Hostel, Saltby.
June 14th 1948.

My dearest, darling, Jean,

Well, here I am again. I hope you don't mind me writing every day. Tell me when you get tired of it. I would like to get one every day.

Was it raining in Leicester today? We had a thunder storm coming this way, but without rain. The air is still close and I am sweating whilst I write this. It is 7.30, rather an unusual time for me to finish. I won't say I am fed up, but I feel rotten. Mr Sanders was here again tonight and told me there's a letter on the way from Mr Barker-Swaine about my money. I wonder what he's to say. Did you see or read it. Perhaps you know about it earlier than I do.

I am off tonight so I'll wash my shirt and then there's some time left to read your letters. I like to do that. If you only would be here everything would be alright. I am so lonely. But don't you worry, sweetheart, I know I have to wait. It only is a shame that the best time (when we are together) flies. I wish it could be endless. I am quite sure the next Sunday will make up for years and every one in future will be better- in your company.

Well, my love, I'll say goodnight and God bless always and write a few more lines tomorrow morning. A goodnight kiss and sweet dreams. Your Hans

June 15th 7.45 am

Well, my love another day's started. Unfortunately there was no letter for me this morning. You've had it, chum and better wait until tomorrow. There is still a lot of work to do today. Come and give me a hand. Just some tarts to be made and only for 90 men. I went to bed at 11.30 last night. The reason is I found something to do, mending socks and shirts. When I woke up it was 6.00.

Well, my sweetheart, I'll say cheerio now for Mr Coy is leaving and I asked him to post the letter for me. Just be good and think of me.

All my love and kisses

  Forever yours

Hans.

    92 Wharf St.

    June 15th 1948.

My dearest Hans.

Thank you very much for your letter. I am sorry you did not get one from me, but you know how busy I am (rushed to death). I wasn't really in the mood yesterday to write. I am not today but I had better make the effort otherwise you will be wondering what is the matter with me. I arrived home safe at about 11.10. I had an Irishman talking to me from Melton to Rotherby telling me how beautiful Ireland was when he got off the bus he said maybe we could meet in Melton for a pint. I had to laugh.

Last night I went to see the auntie I went away with. They did not come back until Saturday and the weather last week was lovely. My cousin was weeding the garden so I spent most of the time watching her. I took my dog with me and he loved it in the garden walking where he shouldn't. I didn't make up my mind whether or not to go to the pictures tonight. I'll have to see after I have my tea. Anyway darling I will write a long letter tomorrow so till then

    All my love

    Jean

                L.A.E.C. Hostel, Saltby.

                June, **16**th 1948.

My darling Jean,

Well, what do you think of my new messenger? I bet you're a bit surprised. Don't you think it is nice to start the day with a nice letter? Mr Coy just told me you helped him to escape the police. Remember when I parked my lorry there for an hour? A few times I've seen bobbies walking about, but didn't pay any attention. I always walked by, jumped in and drove straight off. They always had patience with us.

I wonder if I shall get your long letter tomorrow morning as you said. And now about Sunday. Please come for the day. That means before midday. I arranged everything for our dinner here without taking a thing off the men's rations. It'll be a nice one anyway. I really miss my trip to Leicester on Wednesday afternoon. The warden told me to take more time off working 16 hours day after day. You know I am not very particular about it except Sunday afternoons when you come, but it even might be possible to come over one afternoon next week. That is if you don't mind and are able to spare me the evening.

Well, my love, I'll say cheerio for now and have a look around how the supper is going on. All my love and sweet dreams. Do you think of me. A goodnight kiss. Your Hans.

Thursday 17th. 1948.

Don't be surprised, darling, but I slept til 11.30 today. Of course I got up at 5.00, gave the men the rations for breakfast and went straight to bed again. I didn't sleep at all last night so I had to make up for it in the morning. My cold is getting better. That's why I couldn't sleep. I received the letter about my money today, but I am not satisfied. I'll show you on Sunday.

Unfortunately there was no private letter from Leicester, but 2 from my mother instead. She and Horst are alright and send their greetings to you.

Well, my sweetheart, I shall have to wait for your letter until tomorrow. So cheerio and just be my best girl. Think of me. All my love and kisses

Forever yours

Hans.

L.A.E.C. Hostel, Saltby.
June, 16th 1948.

My dearest, darling Jean

Thank you very much for your letter. At first I was rather disappointed as the warden told me there's nothing for me and when I turned around he put it in my pocket. Otherwise I would have rung you up this morning to find out if you're at work. You might have catched a cold I thought and stayed at home.

Why didn't you tell him there's already an Irish girl at your office you're arguing with. That would have given him the rest, I think. Anyway you weren't too lonely then on the bus. Was he a nice fellow? I bet you've had a laugh. Isn't it nice taking the dog along and it goes where it shouldn't go. Bonzo has that habit too. But he gets better in time.

I shan't see many pictures here. It is too difficult and fussy to get to Grantham or Melton. Really I don't mind because I don't enjoy a picture very much being on my own.

I didn't get the letter from the office yet. Doesn't it take a long time for them people to make up their mind? Anyway I wonder what the big white chief has to say. I think I better get that particular order of the ministry meanwhile if they don't want to pay my full wage. Be sure I'll get it.

Well, my sweetheart, I'll say cheerio for the present. Mr Coy is the postman and just called for it. Aren't you a lucky girl, getting a letter every day?

Just be good and think of me.

All my love and kisses
Forever yours, my love
Hans

Aschersleben , 4.6.1948

17/6.48

My dear Hans,

451

As I still have not received any news from you, I'd like to send a few lines to you. Firstly I'd like to send a big toast to you on your birthday and would like to wish you many happy returns and hope we will be able to celebrate a reunion this year. It would be even better if we could celebrate your birthday together. The parcel still has not arrived, I hope it will arrive before my holiday. This Thursday I am invited to the Höhl's wedding and on Wednesday we are going to Western Pomerania. Here we have our Spring Festival until Sunday, carousels, Ferris wheel, and a huge number of stalls; it's all a big nonsense. It would be much better if they would sell delicious sweets, but I doubt that will come back again. It looks like they are going to do the currency reform; there is much talk about it. But we have nothing to lose anyway. We are just about making ends meet on a day to day basis. Prices are incredibly high. Dear Hans, I'd like to ask you again, did you actually already post the parcel you promised? Disappointments are rather frequent and therefore it is better avoided. You sent the last parcel in November and that's so long ago. It is only because you then wrote that you wanted to support us, but not that you think you have to send us a lot! It is only that we see how many parcels and food others are getting, and we have to stand by and watch. I don't know how you are standing financially, but our situation is really bad. We can't pay 15 Reichsmark for one herring. And if we get a different currency, we are lost anyway. Dear Hans, are your pictures done yet? How is your leg, take care of it and don't play too much football. How is Jean, has she done her journey yet? Still no news from our Pappa, we are hoping every day, lots of people are arriving from Russia every day. I want to finish now. All our love to you and Jean from your brother Horst. Write again soon. Once again I wish you a very happy birthday, hope you have a good one. Hoping for a healthy and happy reunion soon. Bye for now!

R 17/6.48   Aschersleben, 4.6.1948

17/6.48

My dear Hans,
Many thanks for your lovely letter from 26.5.48 , which we

received yesterday, it actually arrived within 7 days, that's not happening very often. Above all, I would like to send you all my best wishes for your 23rd birthday, I would like to wish you for this new year all the very best and good luck and health and may all your wishes come true and may we be able to experience a healthy reunion. I am sure Jean will come and see you, as this year your birthday is on a Sunday. You will bake a nice cake and a mokka coffee to go with it. I did tell you before that I wanted to go to Berlin!! I don't have Bahr's address, but perhaps I will bump into him again at some point. Yes, it is Gerhard Franz who had sent you his regards. Your parcel for Horst is still not here, I am really sad for him that he hasn't got the new shirt for his travels; his own ones are in really very bad shape. Did you actually send off the parcel for us in April? Because you wrote on the 13th of April that you would send it in the next few days. We have been waiting for it every day, in vain, and we were so much looking forward to it, to a nice cup of coffee or hot chocolate, but I think we will have to give up that hope. Horst is going to Höhl's wedding on Tuesday; at least he will be able to fill his stomach for once. We have not had any fat for the last 3 weeks. No meat for the whole month, all in all already 6 weeks, because we had no meat since Pentecost. It's really hard to survive like this over a long period. How shall we be strong enough to go foraging for potatoes!!! Every week I have been 3 times to the office of trade in order to get a dress, just for wearing during the week. It is too much; one is queuing for hours and again nothing. We are hoping that all goes well with our trip, and we will stay until the 22.6.48. We are dreading the long journey, but we are so much looking forward to seeing all the relatives again. It would be wonderful if only we didn't have to go to so many different places, because we are wasting such a lot of time on the train. Now, my boy, I'm sending all my love and kisses to you, stay well, from your Mum who is always thinking of you and your brother Horst. Give all our love to Jean too.

92 Wharf St.
June 18th 1948.

Only two more days and you will be a year older. 23. My, aren't you getting old you will soon be drawing the old age pension. I will be coming on the 2.30 bus from Leicester and we can walk down to Saltby if it is a nice day (that is if we are going to Saltby) and ride back at night. Lucy has gone home for a fortnight. I think I miss her more than I miss Iris when she is away and Iris is with me all day.   I took the dog to the vet again last night. The vet told me it would be a lot of trouble to get rid of his mange, but I don't mind that as long as I can get him well again. He gave me a bottle of white lotion and I have to rub it well into the places he has lost his hair. I did it last night and it took me over an hour. It is a good job he isn't very big else it might have taken all night. Alice came to see me last night. I haven't seen her for ages. I am seeing her next week. I don't know what we shall do, probably go to the pictures as usual.

Well, darling I had better say cheerio be good. I'll see you on sunday.

All my love

Jean

L.A.E.C. Hostel, Saltby.
June, 18th 1948.

My darling Jean,

Good morning and thank you very much for the long but invisible letter. It looks as if I shall get only one letter this week too. Anyway it is alright as long as you get one almost every day. I really would like you to let me know about Sunday, but I think there's plenty of time left to talk it over on the phone tomorrow morning.

Of course I had something at least this morning. A letter from my aunt and cousin but you know what I am waiting for. It wouldn't matter if we could talk on the phone every other day. I made steam puddings last night and the warden told me they were the best one he's ever had. It is easy doing here putting 25 puddings in a steam oven at one time. And almost everything steam heating. Anyway I'll show you around on Sunday.

It looks like rain today and if it should be raining on Sunday, we'll stay in.

Well, my sweetheart I'll get cracking again. My pudding is still to be done.

So long, darling and just be good.

> All my love and kisses
> > Eternally yours
> > > Hans.

> L.A.E.C. Hostel, Saltby.
> June, 18th 1948.

My darling Jean,

I am in a good mood tonight and I think I've never been upset as I am now. Mr Whiteman has just been and asked me rather a nice question. I was asked it the first time in my life. The warden from Stathern has made a report of some food being missing. So Mr W naturally asked me if I'd taken something away or given away. I was the last one to be asked and everybody's answer was "no". I couldn't find out when she made the report and if she mentioned me. But I'll know that in time. You know how I hate those two-faced persons. Didn't I tell you so from the very beginning? It is a good thing I gave her the key back on Friday afternoon when she told me I am to be moved. I just heard Mr Barker-Swaine was also here.

Well, my sweetheart, I better say goodnight now. I've got a nice headache and the best thing to do is to go to bed. I hope I will be fresh again in the morning and there might be a letter from you to cheer me up. Goodnight and God bless always. A goodnight kiss from Hans.

Saturday, 19th. 1948

Good morning, darling and how are you? I've had a nice rest, but woke up with a headache again. I did take no end of Aspro's lately without success. It really was a very nice surprise when I got 2 letters this morning. The one you wrote day before yesterday has been to Old Dalby by mistake and therefore arrived a day later. Mr Coy told me he asked you about taking something back and seemed to be sorry leaving without. I wonder how Mr Edwards knew about me being moved? Perhaps Horst told him for he went to Billesdon. He may come here one day, but that'll take him a long time.

Yes, only one more day to go and I'll be a year older. Today I really feel to retire and draw old age pension. I hope I can change your mind about coming on the 2.30. I've got meat and everything for our dinner and would be very sorry if I had to cancel all the arrangements I made. Well, I shall hear when I ring you during the morning.

Well, my love, I'll say cheerio and do the cakes straight the way. I'll write a few more lines tonight. All my love and kisses yours Hans.

It's a pity, really, you aren't able to come earlier, but it's alright, darling. It can't be helped. You know I don't want you to get into trouble at home.

I've fixed the men up with everything for tomorrow so there's nothing to worry about. The warden asked me to take the whole day and spend it at his place.

Well, my sweetheart, I'll go to bed now and have a nice, long rest. Good night to you and God bless. Just be good and think of me.

> All my love and kisses
> Forever yours
> Hans.

92 Wharf St.

June 1948.

My dearest Hans

Thank you very much for both the letters. I was very surprised when Mr Coy brought me a letter. I think he expected to take one back, he asked twice if I had anything for him. Even if I had a letter I would not have asked him to take it. Mr Edwards rang this afternoon. I told him you had moved back to Saltby, but he already knew. He thought you had only gone to Saltby temporarily then you were going to Market Harborough Hostel. I told him you went to see if you could see him on Saturday night. He said he was going but Clive was ill. He will be coming to see you one day, so he said. Mr Whitemans son John is in hospital, he had his appendix out last night, when I rang this morning his condition was satisfactory.

You wanted to know what the Irishman was like, well he was tight and when an Irishman is in that state it is best to be nice to them otherwise they get very nasty.

You nearly did not get a letter this morning. I wrote yesterday afternoon and I almost forgot to post it so I had to take it to the General. Then I went to the pictures, they were 2 old ones. I had seen both before but they were very funny. I rang Dora today and I am seeing her on Friday night. I suppose we shall go to the pictures. There isn't anything else to do.

I have been bathing the dog tonight. I know I shouldn't really bath him until he is older, but I have bought some kur-mange to put on him and it is on the directions that if you've put greasy things on before wash it off, so I did. I think he will be ok. I have dried him well and my mother lit a fire. I have also washed my hair so you see how busy I am. I have to try to set it somehow. I had started but then I remembered I had a letter to write and I know if I finished my hair the letter would never get written. I have two letters to write. I ought

to write both this week, one is to Bernhard and the other is to Muriel, my friend in London. She sent me a purse for my birthday a week last Saturday so I really ought to write and thank her. I think she has gone away this week to Weymouth. I will have to say goodnight and God bless otherwise I will be up half the night setting my hair.
All my love
Jean.

Many Happy Returns

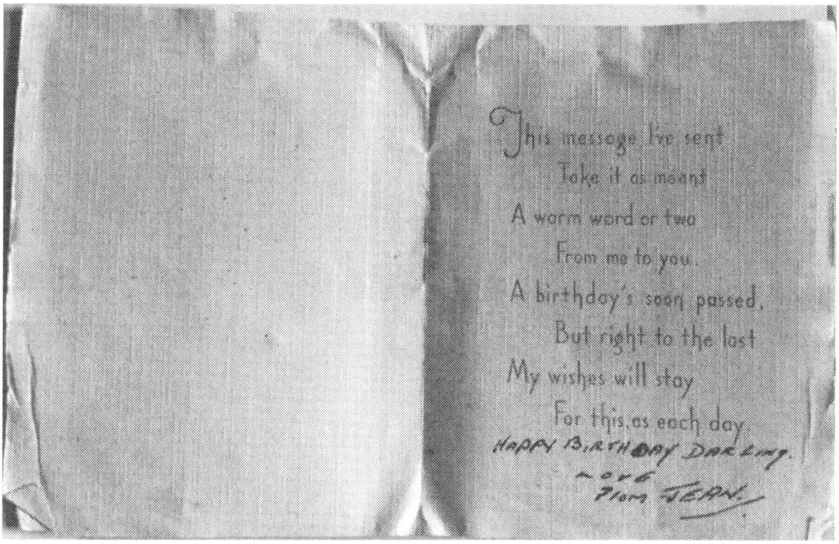

92 Wharf St.
June 21st.

My dearest Hans

Letter for the week beginning June 21st ending June 26th No 1. I am sorry you did not get one on Tuesday. <u>BUT</u> I was going to write this afternoon. I really intended to, but one of the fellows in Water Supplies Dept is leaving at the end of the month and he wanted to take some photographs and I was one of the honoured ones. So I went up to have a cup of tea and then on the roof to have the snaps taken. So you see I have a good excuse for not writing at least I think it is.

Well, I arrived home safe and sound at 11.5. I put the meat on a plate. I couldn't remember if you said put the meat in water or put it in a basin then in water so I asked my mother and she said put it on a plate it will be alright until in the morning. And it was. We had some for breakfast. I had a nasty shock when I arrived home, my mother had gone to bed so I put the meat on a plate, took the eggs out of the box and was going to take the dog a little run when I heard something move in the fireplace. My heart turned over and upstairs I went. The poor dog had to be disappointed. I took the dog to the vet again tonight, he was a lot worse and he seemed as if he couldn't rest. The vet has given me some tablets to give him and some ointment to put on him every day for the next few days, so it looks as though I will have to stay in every night to rub the dog. I don't mind that as long as I can get him well again, he is in a poor way really. I ought to have the V.C. for rubbing him. I can hardly stand the sight of it.

Well, darling I hope you really had a very happy birthday and that you will have still happier ones.

Mr Coy asked me today if I had a good time yesterday, he said he was coming but could not get there because he wasn't too well. I think Mr C the warden knows where I work because he was in the office when Mr Coy spoke to me.

Well I will have to say goodnight and God bless. Give my love to Bonzo.

Love and kisses

Jean

P.S.
What a long letter

On the roof at L.A.E.C.

L.A.E.C. Hostel, Saltby.

June 21st 1948.

My dearest, darling, Jean,

I am so sorry that wonderful day went so quick. You made it my best birthday for years. And I want to thank you very much for the lovely present. You probably don't know what it means to me that there's someone who cares for me after all those terrible years. It makes me <u>so</u> happy. I shall always be thankful to you and I'll never forget that you made life worth again for me. I really was surprised when I asked you about next Sunday and you said yes straight away. You know it only makes a nice weekend when you're with me. Please yourself where you like to go Melton or Grantham. I don't mind for myself as long as I see you pleased.

Did you get home well? I arrived here at 10.20 and picked one of the men up on the way so he took the second cycle. After bringing the bikes back to the bungalow I went and saw the cooks in their quarters. They had a german station on the wireless and there was such a nice music that I sat listening until 11.15. Bonzo was still asleep when I came over and he still is now. He's had some exercise yesterday. Did you remember what I told you about the meat? Anyway it'll make a nice meal for you and your mother. Everything was so homely yesterday and I only wish that our time won't be too far away.

Well, my sweetheart, I'll say cheerio. Mr Coy is just leaving and I like to have the letters posted in Melton. I am sure you'll get it tomorrow morning. Thanks again, darling, for everything.

Just be my best girl and think of me.

> All my love and kisses
>> Eternally yours
>>> Hans.

> 92 Wharf St,
> June.

My dearest Hans.

Letter No 2. That is so you don't tell me at the end of the

week you have had only one letter when it is 3. I haven't very much to say. I went to the pictures last night with Dora. We went to the Odeon to see "Miranda", it was very funny, it was about a mermaid that comes on land for three weeks. I will have to give Alice a ring sometime this week. I said I would see her one night but I have not had time this week, what with having to look after the dog and one thing and another. I had a letter this morning from Germany, someone by the name of Harry Gohns. I looked at the name and I couldn't remember any Germans by that name. I know I have a bad memory but I didn't think it was that bad. Anyway when I opened it and read it I got an awful shock and I'm not kidding this time, it was from a friend of Willi Shafers to say that he died last Tuesday, from something the matter with his throat. It is thought he may have had something wrong with him whilst he was a P.O.W. because they say he seemed to know he was going to die. This fellow asked me if I knew anything or anyone that might know, and that would I write to let them know. I rang up Stoughton to see if anyone could tell me anything but no good, but I will write tomorrow.

Well darling I will say cheeri'O. I have to catch up with my sleep so goodnight and God bless.

All my love

Jean.

Jean with Bonzo

L.A.E.C. Hostel Saltby.
June 22nd 1948.

My dearest, darling Jean,

Another day is gone and that makes me nearer to Sunday. I hope you don't mind not getting a letter tomorrow morning, for I was really busy last night and early this morning. I was going to bed at 9.30 last night when one of the fellows came and asked to read a letter to him. So I did, and after finishing that he of course wanted the reply written. I didn't say anything and after all the writing was done, it was 11.15. She wanted a long letter just as you do. It looks as I get used to writing other people's letters. I don't mind as long as they don't come too often and disturb me writing to you. That's far more important for me.

Very well, darling, how are you today. We had a few heavy showers and thunderstorms in the early afternoon, but it is so nice outside now. I would love to go for a walk with you, but unfortunately I would have to walk 29 miles at first to get to your place. And then it would be a bit too late for a walk. What would you do in that case? Just move nearer or tell me to walk alone? Anyway, I'll take Bonzo a short walk now and, "try" to go to bed. I'll write a few more lines when I get your letter in the morning. Good night, my love and God bless. Just be good.

     All my love and kisses

       Yours Hans

Wednesday 23rd 1948 8.15. A.m. sunshine.

Good morning darling, I hope you've had a good rest. It seems as if everybody wants photographs of you. I myself for instance. By now I can always tell when you're really busy. That means no letter for me in the morning. Anyway I hope you enjoyed the cup of tea and the wonderful view of Leicester or the back of the house. By the way, could you see Saltby? Maybe we can see each other when I stand on top of my house.

I would have loved to see you rushing upstairs when you heard something moving in the fireplace. Remember what I told you so often!! Don't be afraid, they won't do you any harm. So you'd better stay in every night and nurse your pup. I hope he'll be better shortly. I most certainly will give you the V.C. if you're successful. The warden bought himself a dog yesterday. I'll have a look today.

It might be possible that Mr Coy told Mr Chandler where you're working. Anyway I didn't, otherwise he would have mentioned it last Sunday. I gave your love to Bonzo, but he doesn't seem to be satisfied. He told me he would like to see you again soon. I agree with him.

So that was the letter for the whole week!! You better make an effort and tell me in the next one where you want me to come next Sunday for you didn't mention it yet.

Well, my sweetheart, I'll say cheerio. My messenger just called. Be good, darling and think of me.

> All my love and kisses
>> Forever yours
> Hans.

Mr Chandler at Saltby

Mr Chandler at Saltby

Schmiedenfelde, 10.6.1948

22/6.48

My dear Hans,

Today you shall receive a few words from Schmiedenfelde. Tuesday evening we left home traveling all the way through the night with the D-train to Berlin, there we had a good connection at 7 AM and then arrived at Schmiedenfelde at 1.30PM. But we were very tired as we didn't have seats and you can imagine how incredibly exhausting such a long journey is. Today we wanted to visit Uncle Erich, but we missed the train and had to walk back again the 6km to Uncle Gustav. We will be going tomorrow at 5 AM, leaving the house at 3 AM to catch the train. Tuesday we will go to Aunt Lina and then come back here on Friday. Sunday the 20th of June we will have to head back home again at 9.30PM and will hopefully be back home in the evening of the 21.6. We are really having a good time here, everybody sends their love to you, they are very happy that we came here. At least we for once can fill our tummies. They all send their love for your birthday and wish you lots of good luck. Have a nice celebration and think of us. The weather is changing all the time, one day it's very hot, the other cold and I still have not got rid of my cold. Horst has already got a proper tan. Now, my dear Hans, stay healthy, give my regards to Jean, and I'm sending you all my love and kisses- from your Mum and brother Horst. Hope to see you soon healthy.

> LAEC Hostel Saltby.
> Wyville Road.
> June 24$\underline{th}$ 1948.

My dearest darling Jean

How are you today, sweetheart? It was such a nice day and really a shame to stay inside, but the year has more workdays than holidays I found out. Otherwise we'd have to pay for getting a job. Well, Thursday is gone so far and only another two and a half days to go. I just took Bonzo a walk, but there's no park about to go to. Maybe I could meet you and your pup there, but I've said once before it would be too far to walk. Bonzo wouldn't do it. By the way can you get a collar for him and bring it along on Sunday. I think you know the size (not mine of course, I don't want to be put in a chain). You can do that later on if you're not satisfied.

There are lots of work to do tonight. Socks want mending, I like to have a bath and so on. What about coming to help me with the socks. It's awkward for me.

What did you think about Sunday? It was homely I think and would have been still better just the two of us. The warden is going away this weekend so Mr Bentley ask me what I am going to do. I told him we're not coming here. He seemed disappointed, but we'll see a nice picture together. I myself like it very much to be at a nice place but with you being here only Sundays, I enjoy it much more being on our own. Do you agree? I think that's what was the matter with me when you brought Susan along. Maybe you felt the same about it because you wanted to take the blame. Anyway that day is gone and another nice Sunday ahead. We'll certainly make the best of it.

I think I'll better start with my work now. A few more lines tomorrow morning.

Goodnight my love and God bless. A goodnight kiss, your Hans.

June 25th 1948

Good morning darling. How are you? It is 8.00 now and you might believe it or not, I just got up. It's a bad habit to stay in bed until your letter comes, but I like it very much. I think you're doing the same. Thank you very much for letter no. 2. Talking about no. 3 that means it'll follow tomorrow morning.

I did all the odd jobs last night, had my bath and then read a few of your letters. At 10.45 I went to bed and had a very good sleep.

So Willi passed away. Poor chap. I knew a fellow I was with in America. He knew there was something wrong with him, but didn't want to see a doctor. He also died on the ship when we came back. It is only funny how they know your address and why they write to you instead to Stoughton Camp. Maybe he's had one of your letters with him. You better find out and let them know.

Well, my love I'll say cheerio. I'll ring you tomorrow morning. So just be good and think of me.

All my love and kisses always

Your Hans

92 Wharf St.

June 25th.

My dearest Hans

I thank you so much for your letter. I really expected one today. But when I looked there was no letter. If I am lucky there may be one at lunch time. It is now 11.30 (morning) am. I thought I had better post it early to make sure you receive it tomorrow. I think it takes longer to get to Saltby than it did to Starthern. Have you noticed that whenever I start to write to you whilst I am at work I always run out of ink, and I don't like to fill my pen with the ink the ministry supplies. So I have had to get another pen.

I took Freddie to the vet last night. He is much better than he was last Monday. I asked the vet what was the possibility of curing him. He said he had seen dogs much worse than him get over it. I'm hoping he will get over it in any case. I wrote to that friend of Willi's to say how sorry I was. I also wrote to Bernhard. Then I got my bike out and took them up to Campbell Street post office. I couldn't find out if anyone knew if Willi had any seriously wrong with him while he was in England, the fellow at Stoughton camp gave me an address in London to write to. I will be doing that when I know his P.O.W number.

I will come to Melton on Sunday on the 3.15. We can see what we will do when we meet in Melton.

I will have to say cheeri'O. I'll be seeing you on Sunday.

All my love
Jean

___.

L.A.E.C. Hostel Slatby.
June 27th 48.

My dearest, darling Jean,
Good morning- or I'd better say good afternoon it's 1.45. I am
leaving here on the 2.50 that makes me in Melton at 3.15.
Well, knowing that you like to get a letter today I think I
better write a few lines. Thank you very much for the letter
I received yesterday. I'm awfully sorry our conversation on
the phone was so short, but I was very much in a hurry. My
bus or better Mr Coy left at 2.00 and I had to get everything
ready before. There was a good picture on "Snowbound" it
was called. The supporting one was "Beauty for the asking".
Anyway it was the last time I went round the shops with a
few of these fellows. I was almost ashamed of myself. They
are just like little children having some money to spend.
After all it was 6 o'clock when everybody was satisfied and
I able to see the picture. I went back on the 8.30 and had a
nice walk from Croxton to the camp. It really did me good.
Mr Bentley has his fiancee and his brother coming this afternoon. I felt sorry for him yesterday dinner time when 2 Poles
from here brought their wives along, being here on 7 days
leave and he didn't know what to do. I was sitting in the van
already when he told me " you're going away and leave me on
my own to face this ~~awquard~~ awkward ~~sirtuaition~~ situation"
and that because the women went right up to their husbands
sleeping quarters.
Well, my love, I'll have to say cheerio. It's 2.00 and I've to get
ready till 2.30. Just be good till I see you.
All my love and kisses
　　　Forever yours, darling
　　　　　　　Hans

L.A.E.C. Hostel Saltby.
June 27th 1948.

My dearest, darling Jean
I just arrived back at the hostel. When I left the bus I saw a shower coming up and it really was a good thing there were no policeman behind me for I was speeding. It only took me 7 minutes from Croxton to Saltby. A good exercise before going to bed, isn't it? Don't you think I should join a race club. You know I already liked speeding when I drove a lorry. So I just made it. I brought the bike back to the bungalow and it started to rain when I left.

Well, darling I thank you very much for the enjoyable afternoon. I told you already you make me very happy telling me straight away you're coming the next Sunday. When I arrived here I had a look at the cooks quarters and stopped there for quarter of an hour. They had a sandwich and a cup of coffee waiting for me. Very nice isn't it? There is such a wonderful music at a German station and I would like it so much to be with you now, just the two of us, listening to the wireless. You know how I am longing for a particular day- for a few words- when everything comes true. Well, my love I think I better go to bed now and have a good rest. Six more days to go till next Sunday. So sleep well and pleasant dreams.

All my love and kisses
Forever yours
Hans.

Hans and Mr Chandler at Saltby Hostel

L.A.E.C. Hostel Saltby.

June 28th 1948.

My darling Jean

It's 10.50 now and I've finished. Mr Sanders and Mr Shilton have been here and left at 10.00. There was something like a conference and everybody asked about complaints. After talking for a couple of hours I found out there were no complaints about the food so I am quite satisfied. Mr Shilton and the warden also are. So there's nothing to worry about. Anyway it proves best that I am getting it right. You know I am not afraid of a failure. Mr Sanders came to the steam-table and asked me. "Am I right here for a cup of tea and a packet of cigarettes?" I told him he may get a cup of tea without paying for but I just sold out of cigarettes. So everybody was laughing.

Well, sweetheart I think I better say good night. I can hardly keep my eyes open. Just be good and think of me. A good night kiss as every night.

Friday, 29th 48

Good morning, my darling. How are you? I hope you feel better than what the weather is like this morning. It looks as if the summertime is over already. I got up at the usual time and found out that Mr Coy had left already for Waltham, and I hope now he's going to Melton later on to take my letter along.

One of my cooks is leaving on Friday and so I hope to get somebody else for the kitchen. What about you? Don't you want to make an assistant cook? Come and have a go. Mr Chandler gave me the photos this morning. I'll show you when you come on Sunday.

So long then, darling and just be my best girl. Do you think of me?

All my love and kisses
Always yours
Hans.

NO 1   92 Wharf St.
      June 29th.
My dearest Hans
What has happened. Have you cut your hand or have you been too busy? I was surprised when there was not a letter for me this morning. I thought there would be a letter at lunchtime. But no there wasn't. I am sorry you did not have a letter from me today. I believe I said I would write so you would get it on Tuesday. Yesterday afternoon I went to the tea party in Water Supplies. I believe I told you Mr Worsley is going to the West Sussex A.E.C. and he gave a little party. We had quite a good feed. I could not make up my mind whether or not to go to the pictures last night. Some of the films that have been on lately have been terrible. It should stop me going to the pictures so much. I went to see my aunty at Birstall in the end. I didn't go until 9.45. I came home on the 10.30 bus. I was speaking to Mr Chandler this morning he has been telling me that he had been home for his relatives wedding and what a marvellous time he had had. I have just remembered. When I arrived home on Sunday I couldn't find my key. I had left it in my coat pocket. I thought I would have to stay in the yard until my mother came, that meant I would have to wait half an hour. So I got a ladder out and I went through the bedroom window. I am now thinking of taking up burglary as a profession.
I will say cheerio
      til next time
      All my love
      Jean

¨   NO 3
                              L.A.E.C. Hostel Saltby.
                              June 30th 1948.
My dearest, darling Jean,

475

Good morning, sweetheart. How are you? Thank you so much for your letter I received 5 minutes ago. Of course I haven't cut my hand and I also wasn't too busy. I kept my promise. I wrote to you on Monday and it was posted on Monday afternoon so I am very sorry, darling, you didn't get it yesterday morning. You also should have got one today. Sometimes it seems as if it takes longer than a day. Anyway I hope you've got two letters this morning.

I've had a nice surprise today. The first letter from Alfred's arrived. He apologised about not writing earlier. I am not sure if you had one from him lately. Alfred told me that he hasn't got his job back yet and is still working on his brothers farm. So he at least gets his full meals. He said something about his rations and the black market. I haven't had any mail from my mother for about a fortnight.

Well, darling I hope you enjoyed yourself at the tea party (water supplies). You know I used to go to the pictures two or three times the week. But I've stopped it now. It's awkward to go to Melton or Grantham from here. I played table tennis yesterday and walk like a little baby today. I've got to get used to it again.

I asked Mr Chandler yesterday if he's spoken to you already. He said he doesn't know where you're working. Funny, isn't it? Talking to you and doesn't know who he's talking to.

You poor little girl forgot your keys? Don't take a ladder again. You might fall down. I just wonder how you managed to get the ladder up to the window and all that on your own. Is the bedroom upstairs?

I think that new job you want to take up isn't bad at all. Sometimes you may get something worth it, even a couple of years free work and- as the War Ag always says- plus board and lodging. Anyway it is nothing for me. I better like the straight way of earning my living.

I might go along to Melton with Mr Coy this morning. I'll certainly ring you from there that is if the call box is in order. Last time I went down it wasn't.

Well, my love I'll get ready and say cheerio hoping that you've got two letters today. Just be good and think of me. All my love and kisses

Forever yours, darling

Hans.

L.A.E.C. Hostel Saltby.
June 30$^{\underline{th}}$ 1948.

My dearest, darling Jean,

I am back at the hostel. We came back later than expected. Mr Coy told me to be at his office here at 10 o'clock and we at last left at 11.00. We left Melton at 1.30 and went around a few villages before we arrived here.

So you received both my letters today. Have a look at what time it was posted. Listen darling when I say I'll write on Monday I do it. There must be something very important to stop me from doing so. And that doesn't happen very often. I wrote a letter to Alfred this afternoon. He told me to remember him to you and I hope you don't mind me sending your greetings too. Alfred wrote he didn't smoke since he arrived because the German cigarettes are horrible. So I've put 2 fags into the envelope and told him to have a decent smoke the Sunday after he gets my letter. I was waiting for about ten minutes till I got your number. Always engaged. Who was that you're talking to just before we finished our conversation? One of the fellows from the office? I am very sorry about your pup. But don't you think yourself it is the best for him? Bonzo gets big now. He got onto my raincoat yesterday and I had to mend it afterwards. I can't leave anything in the room now. At first he took everything he could get hold of outside, then brought things in here and now takes them out again. I only hope he'll get over it soon.

I got a good book from one of the fellows here so it'll make a change to read a few pages tonight, because I decided to go to bed as early as possible. Good night, darling and pleasant

dreams. Xxx
Thursday July 1st 1948
Good morning, my love. How are you today? Isn't it cold for this time of year! I had it nice warm last night and think I start a fire again straight the way. You were pretty definite yesterday when you said there shan't be a letter for me in the morning. Anyway I hope to get one tomorrow and on Saturday. And not to forget, see you on Sunday. Did you notice that the first half of my year is gone? Isn't it surprising how time flies and to think how many wonderful days we'll be able to spend together. You know what I am longing to hear. Well, my sweetheart, I"ll say cheerio. I hope Mr Coy hasn't left yet. So just be good and think of me.

All my love and kisses
    Eternally yours
            Hans

    92 Wharf Street.
    July 1st.

My dearest Hans

I suppose I had better start by thanking you for your letters 1, 2 and 3. Haven't I been lucky this week!!! Eh but I am not complaining. If I had only one letter from you a week I couldn't say anything, because I don't write much more than that myself. Anyway darling thank you very much for writing and telephoning. You don't have the opportunity to talk from Melton very often. If you are wondering why I prefer you ring me from Melton, it is because then it isn't a time call. It was Tom Burton that came in to see me whilst I was talking to you. He had been to the County Court about the burglary at the Braunstone Depot. They had not taken very much but got sent away. They were only young boys. I still don't know what to do about my dog. I hate having to part with him. He seemed a little better today but he is still very quiet. I suppose the wisest and safest thing would be to have him put to sleep. If we keep him I don't think he would be a very healthy dog. Did I tell you Alice was coming last night? Well, she came, we didn't stay in, we went to visit a cousin of Alice's. I have to ring her, she was going at lunchtime to see if there were any seats at the Palace Theatre. There is supposed to be a very good show on. I will ring her if you wait a moment. So, she couldn't get any seats, they were all booked up, but we have arranged to go to the pictures. I spoke to Mr Edwards this afternoon. I gave him your message, he said he would be coming over to Saltby one day and he will call at the hostel to see you.

I will say cheerio be good if you can.

Love

Jean

PS I almost forgot about Sunday I will be on the 2.30 from Leicester.

Jean

LAEC Hostel Saltby.

July 2nd 1948.

My dearest darling Jean

I just finished the work I like so much. I washed three shirts and some other little things. It didn't take me long, but I think I've got them rather clean this time. It is getting late so I'll go to bed. Goodnight, darling and God bless.

Saturday 3rd July 1948

After all I decided to go to Grantham in the afternoon and before then I want to iron my shirts and prepare things for tea and supper.

I am sorry, sweetheart, but I was unable to ring you. I tried a few times but always engaged. So I didn't bother any more for you'd told me in the last letter what bus you're coming on. I saw 'The two Mr Carolls' at Grantham but unfortunately that sort of film I don't like very much. The warden asked me to come to his place for supper. He's on his own. Mr

Bentley went home for the day. I just came back and think it the best to go to bed straight the way (after taking a couple of asprins). Only 16 hours left till I'll see you tomorrow. I found a nice mess when I came back. The grocer had been this afternoon whilst I was away so the boys put the eggs in here on the floor not thinking of Bonzo. He was very pleased and just took his weekly ration: 2 eggs. I only found the shells.

Well, my love, good night. I'll be dreaming of you. Just be good.

All my love and kisses
Forever yours
Hans

LAEC Hostel Saltby.
July 2nd 1948.

My dearest Jean

Thank you very much for your letter. I was still in bed when Mr Chandler brought it. You got a letter almost every day this week. It has nothing to do with being lucky. You know how I love writing to you. It'll always be more than one, anyway. You didn't expect me at the office yesterday morning did you? Mr Chandler said he was talking to you for about half an hour. It's a good thing to ring from Melton. We can talk longer but you're right I haven't got the opportunity to go to Melton very often. Mr Coy is going down every day but it takes such an awful long time to get because he's to see farmers on his way and that would make it late for me.

Look, darling as I told you I think if the best thing for you and for the dog to have him destroyed. You're right he wouldn't make a very healthy dog. Do you want Bonzo instead? He grows rapidly and you'll be surprised when you see him on Sunday. By the way, only 2 more days to go. I am longing so much for that day.

Thank you for giving the message to Mr Edwards I just wonder when it'll be. Till xmas is still a long time. Them two women I told you about left this morning. Mr Barker-Swaine gave permission for them to stay and have their meals here. I don't know where they slept. Probably in one of the empty huts around here and I think it was pretty cold lately. Don't you want to come for a week to the 'Saltby Seaside' but I would furnish a hut for you.

Well, my sweetheart, I'll say cheerio. I'll be at the bus stop in time for your bus with a bike and both tyres flat.

> Just be good, my best girl and think of me,
>> All my love and kisses
>>> Only yours, darling
>>>> Hans.

> 92 Wharf Street.
> July 4th 1948.

My dearest Hans

I hope you are not too annoyed with me for not turning up this afternoon, it is really too wet to come. If I thought it would turn fine I would have risked coming, but I am afraid it is going to rain all day. I hope you will understand. I tried to ring you but I got no reply. I thought I had better try to tell you I wouldn't be coming. I hope you did not go down to meet the bus, but knowing you I know you would. I have just lit the fire and I am going to do some of the table cloth I brought whilst I was at Eastbourne. I haven't done any of it since I came home. I haven't got rid of the dog yet and I don't think I will because he seems a lot better today. I have been giving him some M&B tablets. My mother came home last Thursday and someone had told her that they give greyhounds them. I remembered I had some left from when I had tonsillitis so I have been giving him them on Friday and Saturday. I give him half every 6 hours I gave him one this morning. I will give him one tonight before I go to bed. The lump under his chin has gone down and his mange isn't any worse. This morning I was rubbing him with castor oil for 2 hours. Darling I have just looked outside and it has stopped raining. It is now 3.15 and you will be on your way to meet me. I wish there was some way to let you know that I won't be on the bus. I hope you won't be too mad at me. I am really very sorry I did not come. I went to the Palace on Thursday after all. I met Alice out of work and we were going to the pictures. We were going by the Palace when we decided to ask if they had any cancellations, they had 2 single seats so we had them. The show was not bad but it wasn't good. Alice is going to Jersey for a fortnight holiday, she goes a week on Monday. I haven't spent any of my sweet ration for this month yet. I will have to get all of them next week now. I believe we have 1lbs or so next week. I will have some sweets when I come to Saltby (that is if I am forgiven and I can come next week).

My cousin's girl friend has just been in. She wanted to dry her stockings by the fire. They were hoping that my aunt and uncle were going out this afternoon. I believe I have told you they do not get on too well together. My auntie is always treating him as if he is still a child and every now and again the sparks fly. So they are going out even though it is raining, by the way it has started again.

Susan has got the chicken pox, it isn't anything serious but it is catching. She slept with me on Friday night so I hope I don't get it.

Well darling I will have to say cheeri'O and I hope I'm forgiven, but it was really too wet to come. So till next time I see you.

All my love and kisses
Jean

LAEC Hostel Saltby.
6pm July 4th 1948.

My dearest Jean

The Sunday afternoon is over and a new week ahead. You didn't come so it wasn't a decent weekend for me. It was raining here at 2.30, but not too bad. I remembered you saying you don't mind being in the rain whilst we're together so I didn't even think you wouldn't come. I went to Croxton to the 3.40 and met Olive on the way for the bus was a bit earlier. She told me she hadn't seen you. My suggestion was you might be on the second bus, but both buses were through when I arrived. You'll remember me talking about going to Grantham if the weather would be too bad to go on the cycle. What else was to do for me than race back to Saltby and expect a call at 4.00 , the time the bus gets into G. I gave you time until 4.25 for the possibility to come up in a taxi, raced back to Croxton for the 4.40, got there in time, ring Saltby and asked if you'd arrived meanwhile. The answer was, no, so I waited a few minutes till the Leicester bus came, didn't see you there and went back to Saltby. After trying to get on the phone (the first time at 4.00 was successless) I knew at least you're at home safe and sound. I really got wet through. Don't worry I've had my Sunday exercises at least. 10 miles wouldn't be so bad, I found out.

There really was nothing better to do than going to Saltby even if it was raining. We couldn't have stayed in the cinema till the bus left. Otherwise it would have meant walking about in the rain. So after all darling I think it was the best for you not to come.

You might have catched a cold and you know I don't want that. I hope I wasn't too rude on the phone for it wasn't your fault that it was raining. If I was, please forgive me.

Well, sweetheart, I'll have a look if Olive is still there. Maybe she could post the letter in Leicester and you'll have it in the morning. So just be good till I see you next Sunday (for sure).

All my love and kisses

Eternally yours my darling

Hans

My dearest darling Jean,
Didn't you say yesterday there should be a letter for me this morning. I was waiting, but rather successless. Anyway, darling there's only a night between today and tomorrow morning. It's 8.30 now and I just finished work. I've done all the cooking myself today and that means a bit more than it was at Stathern Hostel. We make a competition who's cooking the best meal. I cooked twice as much as usually tonight, nothing came back, in fact, there was nothing left for myself and poor little Bonzo. He always wants to help me writing the letter, but he's too big now to be taken on the knee. We need two chairs then. I wrote one of the love letters to Germany. One gets used to, anyway.
Well, darling I'll go to bed now. It was a hard day. Hoping to hear from you in the morning. I kiss you good night. God Bless.
Tuesday 6th July 1948
Good morning my sweetheart. How are you? The first thing this morning was your letter. And now I am able to tell you why it didn't arrive yesterday. You better complain to the postmaster for the letter went to London at first and afterwards found its way to Saltby. I think Saltby was more popular when our fellows were here. Now nobody knows it.
Isn't it funny, it was nice yesterday and it reminds me of the picture. It always rains on Sundays! I've told you I am not annoyed with you, in fact I think it was better you didn't come. You might have got wet and catched a cold. I hope the best for your pup. It would be very nice if you could get him cured. I haven't seen him yet so you'd better bring him along one day when he's alright again.
So after all you went to see the show at the palace. I would like to go with you and see something nice, but you hardly

give me a chance. Anyway, we'll talk it over sometime. Here is the possibility to stay away for a whole day, but where should I go to in Leicester? Look, darling, don't bother about bringing the sweets along. They should be for you, that's why I gave the points to you.

You said you would come next Sunday if you're forgiven and can come again. You like a good joke, don't you? You know quite well how I am longing to see you.

Bonzo woke me up dead 5 o'clock this morning and continued pulling the blankets and sheets away till 7.00. The next thing I knew than was Mr Chandler bringing my letter. I still was half asleep when I read it.

Well, my love I'll say cheerio and bring the letter to the Labour Office to be taken to Melton. I hope I'll get one tomorrow morning.

So just be my best girl and don't worry your head too much about being forgiven. I am longing for you to come next Sunday.

All my love and kisses

Forever yours, darling

Hans.

92 Wharf St.

    July 6th 1948.

My dearest Hans

I thank you very much for the very nice letter you wrote on Sunday afternoon. I quite expected to get a nasty letter after the telephone call on Sunday. I am very sorry I couldn't say very much, but my aunt, uncle, cousin and his girl friend were there, and they were all listening to what I had to say. Even though I wanted to speak to you, I just couldn't say what I wanted to say. Now I am very sorry about all the trouble I caused you. By the way, how was it Olive was able to get through to Saltby! Mr Coy came in this afternoon he said Mr Chandler was with him, but I did not see him. I have been to the pictures tonight, to the Odeon, there were 2 good films on. I quite enjoyed them.

Well darling it is getting late, but I thought I had better write now, I may not get a chance at work so good night, God Bless.

All my love

Jean

PS It is my mother's pen

J

LAEC Hostel Saltby.
July 7$\underline{th}$ 1948.

My dearest, darling Jean

Unfortunately no letter this morning, but I had one from my mother. The first one here at Saltby. My parcel arrived on the 14.6.48, almost a month later than it should have been. It was in perfect order and still contained everything. Horst is going to thank for it himself. As my mother told me, he was very pleased with the shirt and the sweets for they didn't have any for years. In the very next future I'll get the shoes for my mother and send another parcel. You'll be surprised to hear I've got plenty of coupons, or at least enough to last me some time. I shall also get 12 more on the 21st July. I'll look through my mothers mail again and make sure, what size she wants. Would you do me the favour of buying them for me. You know it's awkward for me at present to come to Leicester myself and I miss going to the pictures with you so much. I hope I can arrange it sometimes or don't you want to see me during the week?

Bonzo is annoyed with me. I bought a nice collar for him yesterday and also a lead. Putting his collar on he was just like a wild horse. I only put the lead on for a couple of minutes last night. He doesn't even look up when I called him, but seems to be a bit more pleased with me this morning.

Well, my sweetheart I hope there's everything alright for Sunday. Please, don't let me down again.

I shall have to say cheerio. Just be good till I see you again.

All my love and kisses

Forever yours darling

Hans

R 7/7.48   Aschersleben, 22.6.1948

7/7.48

My dear Hans,

When we got back from our trip last night, we found the 3 lovely letters from you, from 1.6, 8.6 and 5.6 and today we got the letter from the 14.6 and the parcel for Horst. It made us very happy and we thank you so much .The parcel had already been at the post office for 8 days, it was damaged, the side was open, and it weighed 3 pounds. It contained one shirt, chocolates, 3 bobbins of black yarn, 2 bobbins of white yarn, and another 2 bobbins of fine white yarn, sewing needles, safety pins, 1 soap, 1 jar of black pepper, 1 nutmeg, 1 ball of black wool and rubber band and 4 sweeteners. You cannot imagine how much pleasure you gave us, so many many thanks again, the shirt is also wonderful, Horstel is very happy with it and then the fantastic chocolates! We can hardly remember when we had something like that last. It's such a shame that the photos were messed up; we have been looking forward to them for such a long time. We were really surprised that you have changed jobs, as long as it's better for you and you feel good there. I'm glad you got such a good reference from your boss. You have a great weekly salary and can afford things which we unfortunately can't. The currency reform is coming soon and it looks like our hard earned money will be gone and we are starting again from zero. The trip also cost us 250 Mark, but it doesn't matter, at least we had a nice holiday and we could eat a lot, the delicious milk and the bread with butter which we have missed out on for so long. We had the best time at Uncle Gustav's; we were there for 7 days and everybody was keen on making our holiday as nice as possible. We were with Uncle Erich from Sunday until Tuesday, then 2 days with Aunt Lina, and it hurts that she is even worse off than we are; she works all day for a farmer on the field, only for food for lunch and dinner, without a salary. She doesn't have bedsheets or a pillowcase. We have at least one sheet each. Christel works in the nursery with plants. Aunt Lina hasn't heard anything from Bruno either. Everybody sends their love to you. We have also visited Grandma. I am very pleased that you bought yourself a suit and shoes. We can't buy anything like that at the moment and I think that won't change in the near future. Your offer to buy shoes for me makes me very happy, do you really think it's possible; it's a big worry when you have nothing to put on your feet. You would do me an enormous favour with this, but can Jean really sacrifice her points for me? Life is not fun when you cannot afford anything. One thing after the other goes to pieces and you can't get anything new. Soon the tough season of picking potatoes will begin, I'm really dreading it, but it has to be, if only it goes well and we stay healthy, I'm still fighting with my cold. We have such changing weather, one day very hot, and a few hours later cold again. Finally the rain, it was long overdue. The grain has grown well this year and we hope that the weather during harvest will be good. Aunt Else has also received a parcel from Heinz with coffee and beautiful Palmolive soap and other things. He is only allowed to send a 2 pound parcel each time. But it's a big joy every time. We have just finished our soap. The soap we can buy here, is made out of clay, you cannot wash yourself even if you try very hard. Therefore I am incredibly grateful when you send something; everything is so valuable to us and so helpful. I can imagine that it is hard to bake for a hundred men. It is almost 8PM and Horst is still not back from the shop, I'm sure they are very busy there; everyone wants to have a perm before the currency reform will kick in. Now, my dear Hans, please stay healthy. Sending all my love and kisses from your Mum and your brother Horst, he will say thank you in his own letter. Please send my regards to Jean. Hope to see you soon in good health.

92 Wharf Street.
July 8th 1948.
My dearest Hans
I had a letter yesterday from that friend of Willi Schafer, he asked if I would mind writing to him as he likes to write in English. I had to smile when he said he had told Willi's mother that he had asked me to write to him. I think they must think I was very friendly with Willi. Last night I went to see Alice. I told you she goes to Jersey on Monday. We had a gossip. Alice washed her hair and I tried to set it for her but it wasn't very successful. Iris is very excited, she goes to Paris for a fortnight, she is making me very envious, I wish I was going with her. She is going to take a letter for a fellow at the Loughboro' Hostel. He was stationed in Paris for 2 years.
I am staying in tonight, Dora is coming round. I have not seen her for about 3 weeks. So I suppose I will be busy talking this evening too.
I will write tonight all being well.
All my love
Jean

92 Wharf Street.
July 8th 1948.
My dearest Hans
I don't think you will be able to recover from getting 2 letters written in one day and I don't think I will either. Heaven only knows what I can write about because I don't. Your not ringing me last Saturday had nothing to do with my not coming on Sunday. I was coming up until 12.15. I had even put the buttons on my mac. I looked at the weather and I couldn't face having to bike 2 miles in that. Mr Chandler

spoke to me yesterday, he said you could have dried me out at Saltby. You had plenty of fires. Anyway I will be there on Sunday 2.30 bus and bring a bicycle with a chain on it. You need not bother to ring me on Saturday. As I told you in my earlier letter, I did not go out tonight. Dora came and told me all about her boyfriend and so on. I was going to wash my air but didn't have time. By the time I had finished rubbing the dog it was 8.0. I like to start to wash it at 6.30, then it gives me plenty of time to dry it. Freddy is getting on alright (that is my dog's name in case you have forgotten), He seems very lively today.

I will say goodnight, God Bless see you on Sunday.

All my love and kisses

Jean

LAEC Hostel Saltby.

July 8th 1948.

My dearest darling Jean,

I thank you so very much for the letter I received this morning. Look, darling, why did you expect a nasty letter after the phone call? I think that's one point for you, because you made me look at things from both sides, not only taking myself as example. You know I had nothing else to do as just waiting for you. That's the reason I went to the bus the second time. I thought it might have been raining too hard at 2.30 so you took the next bus. How Olive got through to Saltby? Mr Bentley rung here just before 1 o'clock when the bus arrived he took a second bike over to fetch her.

I just took Bonzo a walk on the lead. He's quite good and gets used to it. I am very sorry you didn't get a letter today but I burnt my left hand badly yesterday and didn't feel like writing at all. It's the worst burning yourself with steam. Anyway it's a lot better tonight. Today I had to make jam cakes for all the men so I've been pretty busy.

I'll ring you on Saturday morning.

Well, my love I'll say good night and God Bless. Just be good.

All my love and kisses

Eternally yours

Hans

LAEC Hostel Saltby.

July 9th 1948.

My dearest darling Jean

Good morning, sweetheart and how do you feel today? Fine, I hope. It's 9.00am and the sun shining already. I'll cross my fingers for Sunday. Thanks very much for your letter. I was most surprised to hear you didn't get a letter on Thursday. I wrote of course and gave it to the interpreter to have it posted in Leicester on Wednesday afternoon. Now you told me you didn't get it, I got him to explain. He went to L alright but forgot to post them, giving the letters to Mr Coy when he came back and he also forgot, left them on the table. He was going to post the letters last night and after all I hope he did. That means you should have got it this morning. I think I better go down to Melton everyday and post the mail myself.

You'll have a big correspondence shortly, writing to Germany. They surely think you're very friendly with Willi. Listen, darling don't let other people make you envious. I always say that 'who laughs last has the best laugh.' Iris might be very excited because she's going to see her boyfriend, but let me tell you Paris is too hot for a girl to go on her own. As you know I've been there and should know what it looks like. I would be worrying about you every minute. Be sure we will go there once, both of us. We'll enjoy ourselves as much as possible and then let other people be curious. I'll try and show you round all them places I've been to, but it's up to you if that time ever comes. You know my answer!

Well, darling, I'll go and do my work now. I've to fry fish today and that takes some doing. Anyway, this letter will be a long one writing more tonight, tomorrow and Sunday. Only two and a half more days to go. The warden said yesterday he's going to send his assistant home for the weekend so we can have the Sunday afternoon on our own. I got something nice for tea, so come and get it. I expect you in any case even if it is raining dogs.

Well, my love so long and just be my best girl. All my love and kisses to you.

Here I am again. I hope you don't mind me writing so much. Mr Edwards has been this afternoon with the money. He'd two visitors with him a man and a woman, staying at his place. They wanted to have a look around the kitchen. He said he was very surprised to hear I am here amongst this lot of strange people. We just talked for half an hour and he left after having a cup of tea. Some of my weekend work is done, so I hope it'll be a bit easier tomorrow. I'll have a bath tonight and go straight to bed afterwards. Isn't it cold today? I expected such a nice summer but there's still some time to go. I certainly keep my fingers crossed for Sunday.

Sunday

Good morning, sweetheart. I got up early this morning and the first thing I noticed was the rain. I hope you're coming for I told you I am expecting you in any case.

Thanks very much for your letter. I am glad to know you got both my letters on Saturday. After all I went to Grantham yesterday afternoon. I really wasn't in the mood to go but I'd promised one of the cooks to go to the pictures with him. We left on the 2.30 went to the pictures twice and I took the next bus at 9.00 back to Saltby. He, of course, went dancing with one of the other fellows. I spoke to Mrs Betts yesterday. She sent a message up with one of the drivers asking me to come for tea. Unfortunately I'd made other arrangements already. I'll go down one evening next week. She was on her own, Mrs Baxter being in Leicester. She also told me Mrs B doesn't want to stay longer.

Well, darling I'll see you 3.40 waiting with two bikes (both with a chain on).

So long darling and just be good.

All my love and kisses

Eternally yours

Hans

92 Wharf Street.

July 12th 1948.

My dearest Hans

I arrived home quite safe at 11.0. The bus stopped for 5 minutes at Waltham, then again for 7 mins at Melton, that happened before, I should think they have changed their system whilst you were at Stathern. When I get near Leicester I always get my key out ready but last night I couldn't find it. I remember that I had left it in my coat pocket on Saturday night so I had to wake my mother up. I have just been speaking to Kath at Melton. It is her first day back. I told you her mother had been ill. She wanted to know if I had a boyfriend, but you know I don't like telling anyone my business. Don't you think you could find her a boyfriend at Saltby, she seems to be giving up hope. Well, darling I'm not going out tonight there isn't anywhere to go, nothing on the pictures. I'll see what I can do for the dog. He does not seem too well.

I will write again tomorrow, all being well, so till then be good.

All my love and kisses

Jean

LAEC Hostel Saltby.

July 12th 1948.

My dearest darling Jean

I hope you can read my handwriting today for I am doing just the same you did some time ago. I am writing this in bed. As I told you in my last letter I didn't have a good rest last night. I got up at 8.00 this morning, but could hardly stand on my feet. So to bed again I went till 10.00. Then I got up and it got worse and worse. I am that far now not being able to stand up, sit or lay down. And my leg looks just nice. Anyway I've seen it worse in the hospital. It's nothing serious so don't worry your little head about it. It'll be over in a couple of days. Till Sunday anyway. Won't you come over and look after me? There is nobody here to do it.

I've got myself some books for the night in case I can't get asleep. It's 7.30 now and I think I'll be able to write a bit more later on.

It's 2.30am now and I just finished my first book. I am thinking of you all the time darling and hope you've a good rest. Well I'll switch the light off and try it that way. Good night and God bless. All my love and kisses to you.

Tuesday 8.55am

It's just time for you to go to the office. Good morning sweetheart and thanks very much for your letter. I am still in bed. I don't know if my leg is better today but I shall know when I get up in a few minutes.

I am sorry to hear you'd to wake your mother. It seems there was no ladder about this time. I'll put a notice up here asking if there's one who would like to become acquainted with a ginger headed girl. Maybe invitation for tea but cigarettes are to be paid for before leaving the house.

Well my love I'll say cheerio for the present. I hope Mr Coy hasn't left yet. So just be good and think of the 23 year old cripple at Saltby.

All my love and kisses
Eternally yours
Hans.

LAEC Hostel Saltby.
July 12th 1948.

My darling Jean

Good morning sweetheart. How are you? I hope you feel lots better than I do, I couldn't sleep till 4.30 this morning. It is worse than yesterday, but the best sign I am getting better. It only last a few days. Did you come home well last night? I arrived here at 10.25 rather late because I had a little accident going along the wood so that I had to walk the last half a mile. I should have gone round the main road but thought it's nearer that way. It was my own fault.

You looked so tired when you got on to the bus. I think sitting inside all afternoon and evening didn't do you much good. It was rather warm in front of that stove.

I thank you so much for the very nice afternoon. I felt like being at home. As I told you it's awkward to part after such a nice time. You don't know how much I am longing to be with you forever. My only wish is that it'll be soon. May it become true before long.

Well, my love, this is only a very short letter but I hope you don't mind. I can't sit any longer and better lay down for half an hour.

Cheerio darling and remember always what I told you yesterday. Just be a good girl.

All my love and kisses
Eternally yours darling
Hans.

92 Wharf St.
July 13th 1948.

My dearest Hans

Well I didn't have a letter today. I know there will be 2 tomorrow, that is if Mr C remembered to post the other one.

I told you this morning I was going to write that letter to the War Office first, well I have not started it yet, but I know what I am going to put. Though to me it seems a waste of time writing because if he had had a serious illness whilst he was here there isn't anything they can do about it now.

We have another mouse running around again. I have just heard it. I have been outside to see if I could see the cat but I don't know where he can be, but I have let Bill come in. I don't think he will be any good but he may frighten it and Freddy, in his state of health could not do anything. Dora rang me this afternoon to see if I would go round for tea, but I had already told my mother I would be home so I went round about 6.15. About 7.30 my mother rang up to say my aunty had got her some black currants and would I fetch them. I was annoyed, but in the finish I went. That is the aunty whose daughter is in Hamburg, I believe I told you her sister and husband were going to see her this August but only her sister can go, it has to be a blood relation to be able to go. I have found the cat now so I feel safer. He just sits there watching and waits. I don't know what will happen if he catches it. I will most likely have a fit. How is your leg today, much better I hope. If I marry you I had better get myself some eye shields and ear plugs if you have to read until 4.30 in the morning.

I will have to say goodnight now. The dog is waiting for a drink. The cat has not caught the mouse yet and before I go to bed I will have to put her outside, I dare not leave her in all night so she will have to come again in the morning. So once again goodnight and God Bless. All my love and kisses for tonight.

Good morning. Thank you very much for your letters. I received them both this morning. The first one was posted in Grantham at 9.45am the other Melton 12.15pm but what does it matter as long as I get them.

You ought to have seen me this morning. I did have a rush. I thought it was about 8.45 instead the man on the radio said it was 9.1. I hadn't got my dress or shoes on or even my hair combed. I arrived at the office at 9.10 so I didn't do so badly did I? I have just bought a camera off Mr Smith, he is going on holiday today and he hadn't got much money. He was saying he would sell it for £3. Mr Brown (he works in the Labour Dept, and at one time he had a photography business) said it was worth 90/- and not to ask less than £4. I told him I would give him £3 for it. I had asked Mr Brown if he could get me one about a week ago. Mr Smith said he may bring it in this afternoon otherwise I will have to wait until he comes back, that is in a fortnight's time. Are you wondering what has happened getting 5 pages, if you are lucky I will try and make it 6 pages then I am at the end of this pad.

I can't make up my mind whether or not to stay in tonight, and go to the pictures Thursday, or the other way round, I could find plenty to do at home. I have just been speaking to the fellow at Low Hostel. He said I would have made a very good spy as I have such a nice way of finding things out.

Well darling I will say Cheeri'O and I hope your leg is much better next week. I should go to see a doctor if I were you. Do we go to Grantham or what do we do next Sunday?

All my love and kisses

Jean

.

Jean with Bill at 92 Wharf St

LAEC Hostel Saltby.
July 13th 1948   8pm.

My dearest, darling Jean,

So you're very much surprised when I called you this morning? It only took me 15 minutes to go from the kitchen to the office, but it's worth it, having a little chat with you from time to time. I would love to do it every day, but I think the LAEC can't afford to pay for those calls (I hope those is right this time). Can you tell I am writing this in bed again? I could hardly stand it any longer tonight so I got strict orders to go to bed and stay in bed tomorrow all day long. Otherwise there'll be somebody to knock my head off. Isn't that terrible? I don't know what to do in bed all day. Anyway I've put some books on the table in case of tonight. Take a day off tomorrow and come over. I guarantee for good meals and nothing else to do as sitting beside the bed telling me fairy tales. I don't ask for much do I? I thought about that fellow from the 'Good Listening Co' but he hasn't been yet with the wireless. So I just have to be patient and wait.

I've got a nice book now. Mr Sherlock Holmes. After the first 10 pages I'd solved the problem, made sure on the last page and there you are. That makes one less for tonight. Can you recommend any good books out of your library? The only stuff I get here are murder stories and cowboy books for children between 14 and 16 and I've passed that age.

Well, sweetheart, enough of that nonsense for now. About Sunday I think it the best to go to Grantham or if you don't mind me coming to Leicester I would be delighted to oblige you that way. Just please yourself. Let me know about it you can count on me in any case. By the way I just thought of it. Tomorrow's breakfast will be the first one to have in bed (except hospital) I shall see then what I'll have to do every morning!!!

Well, darling that's all for now. I hope my supper is coming soon for I've ordered it for 9.30. (There's no hurry to catch a bus tonight).

So just be good, my love, and think of me.

Goodnight and God bless always.

All my love and kisses

Eternally yours

Hans.

PS I'll see what I can do for Kath. You can tell her to send me a few snaps to be shown around. H

LAEC Hostel Saltby.

July 14th 1948.

My dearest darling Jean

What, no letter today? That means two tomorrow morning doesn't it? I am in the right mood for joking and can only say I never felt better than I feel today. It's 4 o'clock now and I am ashamed to say that I slept 3 parts of the day. No wonder I feel better. I thought it terrible to stay in bed but after all two days rest isn't bad at all. Sleeping 20 hours out of 24 and the rest of the time I gave personal interviews to the cooks and answered questions how to cook the meals.

Mr Whiteman has been here 10 minutes ago and delivered a letter from Ellen addressed to Stathern. I thought at first it was from you. I'll show Ellen's letter to you on Sunday. She's got some good information but unfortunately I don't know where from, I couldn't help laughing when I read it the first time.

How are you today darling? Did you have time to write today?

I still wonder what Whiteman was doing here. The only thing I don't like is that he found me in bed. As long as I was up nobody came but stay in bed one day and there you are. I only heard Mr Chandler say I think he's asleep when they came in. Mr W gave me the letter and told me to sleep again. I obeyed, turned round and closed my eyes again. I'll ask the warden tonight what he wanted.

Haven't you got something nice for me for tea? I've a good appetite today but must be something special. A kiss would satisfy me darling.

I just bought a working shirt. 2 guys have been with a van and lots of stuff. Even shoes and suits. You see, there's no need for us to go to town. Everything is brought right to the door.

I've got two letters from my mother this morning, one of them written after the change of the currency. Everybody lost 90% that means they lost almost the lot for the second time. The trouble is the prices and wages are just the same as before. I always admire her courage. She said in the letter 'They can't get us down in that way. We'll start again' And I know she means it. She said she's so glad I stayed here. I hope there's somebody else who was glad, even if it only was a tiny bit!!! I hope there'll be a possibility to get the two out of the Russian zone sometime. Both send all the best to you. When I send the next parcel I'll put some more chocolate in. They must have enjoyed it according to the letter.

Well, my sweetheart, I'll say cheerio for now. Just be my best girl and think of me.

All my love and kisses

Eternally yours, my love,

Hans

PS Come and join me with my dinner, it'll be here in ten minutes. H

R 14/7.48   Aschersleben, 23.6.1948

14/7.48

My dear Hans,

I want to grab the chance and send you a few lines again today. From tomorrow we will have the new currency and then postage for a letter will be 10 times more than before. Our hard earned money will be once again worth nothing. It had been said that the refugees would get more value for their money but when it came to it, it was empty words again. And we won't be ever get to the point where we are able to afford anything; we will be beggars all our life. It is such a sad world. All we have left, all we own is 500 Reichsmark. When I have changed them tomorrow, we will have 176 Marks, 23 are to be paid for rent on July 1st, 6 Marks for the radio and so on. What will be left? Life is an eternal fight for survival. If we hadn't done our trip yet, we certainly couldn't do it now. It's good that they have not paid out your money yet, it would have also gone. So we won't be able to take the train when we are going to collect potatoes this year, it will all have to be by foot. I am so glad that at least you can buy yourself things, for us it will be sheer impossible. We are happy that at least you are better off. People have bought everything they could get in order to get rid of their money, even if it was for rubbish things. What sense does it make to throw out all the money for such rubbish? One has to wait to see how things are developing now. Horst will also write to you today. Now my dear Hans, keep well and let us hear from you as soon as possible. I'm sending all my love, from Mum and your brother Horst. Lots of love to Jean. Hope to see you soon in good health.

Aschersleben , 23.6.1948

Dear Hans,

Many many thanks for the beautiful shirt, the chocolates, and all the other great things. You can imagine how excited we were about it. First of all I want to take back what I wrote in my last letter, I was very nervous and I had troubles and I didn't know what I was doing. Please forgive me. What do you think about our situation, isn't it terrible? The little money we earnt and saved is all gone now. We are in a really bad state of affairs. You did really well to stay where you are, otherwise your money would have gone too. We were lucky that we could go on our trip, because now we could not afford it now. Wages are staying the same and prices too, so it's the same as before, only we have been fleeced for a good part of our money. Now Germany has been torn up. The Streeses wanted to come and visit us next month, but that won't happen now. One disappointment after the other. Your parcel has arrived just in time, because from now on only letters are allowed, the rest is forbidden. We have now got over our journey, but it's hard to travel for over 26 hours. But it was really nice and I got a really nice tan, we had enough to eat and drink, which is the most important thing. Herta is due on June 29; she is such a decent and pretty girl and has had to suffer so much. We were amazed how much everyone had grown up. We are forwarding all the many regards from all our relatives. Dear Hans, how is Miss Jean, did she have a good holiday and please send my regards to her and please thank her for her efforts in getting the shirt for me. I would also like to thank you again for it. Do you still have the radio? How are you feeling , being the head chef now? I will finish now. I am sending heartfelt greetings to you my dear Hans and to Jean from your brother Horst and Mum. Hope to see you soon. Listen to our radio channels, then you know how bad it is here. Write to us soon.

14/7.48   Aschersleben, 27.6.1948

14/7.48

     My dear Hans,

Today is Sunday and I would like to send you many greetings. Yesterday I went to pick blueberries with Mrs Lehmann and it was so very cold that our fingers got frozen; one doesn't know what to say to this. We have survived the currency reform; we have been fleeced of our last few quid but it's not worth shedding any tears over it. We already had to leave everything behind we ever owned, had to move on and make a living. So now we have to start from fresh again, it seems to be our destiny. Yesterday we walked to the Harz mountains to pick berries and tomorrow we want to go again, but then I will take the train. It is so exhausting to walk such a long distance and then be bent over all day, it is a very painstaking business this year, the berries are very small, but one needs to have some fruits too. Horst has worn his new shirt for the first time, it suits him very well and he is so happy. Here you can't get your hands on anything, it's such a beautiful fabric and very different in the way it is tailored, buttoned all the way. It is raining now. In fact, it had better not rain today, as it is "dormouse day ", meaning if it rains today, it will rain for 7 weeks. I wonder what will happen in Berlin, I am sure you have heard it on the radio. One is longing to know what's going to happen. One would hope that all is well in the end. Dear Hans, I would really appreciate it if you could get hold of some brown and white darning yarn, there is always so much darning to do for me. Hope you are fit and well. I am sure Jean will have visited you today , please give her my best regards. Write again soon. I am sending you all my love and kisses from your Mum and brother Horst. We have thoroughly enjoyed your chocolates, they were truly delicious.

LAEC Hostel Saltby.
July, 15th 1948 10.00am.

My dearest darling Jean

I thank you so very much for your nice long letter I received this morning. Mr Chandler brought it and told me it's a fat one, but when he looked through the mail he couldn't find it. Afterwards he remembered putting it separate in his pocket. It was very kind of him bringing his wireless over last night. He said why didn't I ask him earlier, I told him I couldn't have asked knowing that he likes to listen to the programmes. He went to Leicester today and left the set here. So I have to stay in bed for another day and make sure to be fit for Sunday.
Don't get too much excited over your little mouse. It isn't fair to chase that poor little thing with a big cat and it won't do you any harm. So just leave it alone. Maybe you get it tame in time. So you feel safer with the cat about. But be

careful and don't jump on the table yourself.

My leg is much better today, almost alright again. There's no need for you buying eye shields and ear plugs. By the way what are the earplugs for? Do you think I cry? Don't make me laugh. After all you told me how you're nursing your dog I think a dog's life isn't bad at all.

I really would have liked to see you the other morning. What time do you get up? I thought you said something about 8.00. I am surprised to hear you dressed and run all the way in 9 minutes. Poor girl and what about the breakfast? No wonder you're hungry by 11.00

So you bought a camera. That's very nice. I hope you've got it already. £3 isn't dear.

I didn't wonder what happened to get 6 pages. I think I know. Are you in love darling? I long to see your shiny eyes on Sunday.

It's 11.00. Felix Mendelsohn and his Hawaiian Serenaders just started playing 'My sweetheart' I love to hear guitars playing. Believe, I am quite comfortable today. Only one thing missing can you guess?

Don't worry about me, sweetheart I am alright. Nothing doing about spying, it's too dangerous. I don't like that business. So 90% you loose the neck. How many letters did you get this week? Tell me on Sunday. I hope you're satisfied with me. I did my best.

Don't be surprised darling. I am out of bed. Half an hour after I got up my wireless came. It's a nice one. I am satisfied after the first few hours. It makes the room a bit more alive. Playing all day long, you be sure. One of our station is just talking about POW. Bit too late for me. I even found a new station. Guess which one! Leicester Wharf St, so be careful!!!

I've got our snaps today and had one postcard made of us. It's not too bad, but I have seen better ones. There's one each for you if you want them. I'll show you on Sunday.

About Sunday. Tell me what bus you're coming on and I'll wait for the bus at Croxton. If possible sit on the left side so

I can see what bus you're on. Then off to Grantham. Remember! Even if it rains dogs as big as Bonzo. Well, my love, be good now and think of me.

All my love and a kiss

Forever yours

Hans.

92 Wharf Street.
July 16th 1948.

My dearest Hans

Thank you so much for your letter. I am very annoyed with the Post Office, all the trouble I went to on Wednesday so you would get a letter yesterday then you didn't get it. Well you should have had it by now. Were you surprised to get such a long letter? Did you find out what Mr Whiteman wanted? He has just been in the showroom, he said he was in a play next week at the Little Theatre called 'The Middle Watch'. I think he tells just about everyone to go so it is packed with his friends, I don't think I will go. I can't stand amateur plays. I went to the pictures last night to see 'Good time girl'. It was a very good programme, it started at 6.40 and I didn't come out until 10.15, the other picture was a cowboy. I think you would like that. Then I got to take the dog a walk. He loves me to take him out everytime I put on my coat on he gets out of his basket, and that is about the only time he bothers to move, but he seems to be getting better, anyway he isn't any worse.

About Sunday I will be on the 2.30 to Grantham. If you don't get on the bus that I am on I will meet you under the clock. I think you know where that is.

I hope you are quite better now after having a day in bed: So cherri'O.

All my love

Jean

LAEC Hostel Saltby.
July 16th1948 (payday).

My dearest, darling Jean,

How are you today? I hope well. It's 7.45 and I just finished work. I really was surprised when I saw Mr B-Swaine coming with the money today. The big white chief himself. I've had a busy day after staying in bed for almost 2 days. Mr Chandler is going home tomorrow so Mr Bentley takes over. I shall be glad when the next week is gone by without difficulties. He's just the contrary to Mr Chandler. I haven't made up my mind yet whether to go to Grantham tomorrow or not. We are going on Sunday to see a picture so there's no use to go Saturday.

There's such a nice music on the wireless, maybe you're also listening. I've had a letter from my mother this morning. She sends her greetings to you. Well, my sweetheart I'll say cheerio or better good night. I'll write tomorrow and Sunday. A kiss from Hans.

Saturday July 17th 1948

After all I did not go to Grantham. My leg was worse that ever so I lay down this afternoon to be fit for tomorrow.

Who was on the phone this morning? She asked me what number I was speaking from. She said you're gone upstairs and would ring me back. However I told her I've plenty of time to wait for you. I think she just wanted to know where the call came from.

507

Thanks very much for your letter. Mr Whiteman just had a look around all the hostels when he came the other day. Mr Chandler has told him he's had to force me on pistol point because I didn't want to lay down.

I've decided to see the doctor on Monday morning. It's better that way. It might be something serious inside and I am not going to take a risk. Maybe an operation to get rid of once and for all. I only hope I'll get to Croxton alright tomorrow. Don't worry I'll be there even if I've to take two sticks.

Well, my love I'll say goodnight now. Only 20 more hours to wait. Just be good now and think of me.

All my love and kisses
Eternally yours
Hans.

17/7.48   Aschersleben, 4.7.48

16/7.48

My dear Hans,

I would like to write a few lines to you today. It's been 19 days now that we have not heard anything from you. With all this currency turmoil, it seems that the postal system is also troubled now. Over the border it seems that one can get one's hands on everything. Here nothing has changed. I wanted to have a new foot put on my stockings, but she needed good material for it, but where can it get it from? Nothing will change for us. How often did I go to the trade office to ask for a raincoat or a cape, but always in vain, but the shop windows are packed with it. The prices are the same, but who will be able to pay for it. For the last few weeks we had really changeable weather, a lot of rain and rather cool. The grains and the vegetables are growing well in the fields, which leaves us the hope that we will get more to eat this year. Not long, and the arduous task of collecting potatoes will start again, I hope I'll be able to stick it out, my heart is troubling me a lot again. But nothing can happen to us unless it is not meant to be. On Thursday there is the funeral of Mrs Klingebeil's father, he is also from Stettin, he was not even bedridden but died from heart failure. It is very difficult for the old people to give away their last saved penny.

I am continuing my letter now, we went for a walk in the afternoon and in the evening we are going to the cinema. Today is Papa's birthday, how will he be doing? We still have not had any news from him. I wonder when the day will come. Next month you will get your holiday, have you already made your travel plans. I hope you have a really good time. I hope it will work out ok with my shoes, because I got a pair from Miss Ellen, but the soles come off all the time. They are the last ones I own and there is nothing to buy. My dear Hans, if it was at all possible, could you please look for black and brown shoelaces and shoe polish. Please send our regards to Jean. Stay healthy, I am sending you greetings and kisses from your Mum and Horst. Hope to see you healthy again soon.

Aschersleben, 4.7. 1948

My dear Hans,

Today is Sunday and I would like to send you a few lines. It's been a long time since I received any mail from you. How are you? I really hope that you are healthy and cheerful, which I can report from us too. Today we actually had really beautiful weather and so Mum, Mrs Liemann and I went for a walk, we went to Stephan's Park and to the Fort. Last night I went to a dance, it's always the same. We have survived the currency reform; we really didn't have much more to lose. In the West the situation is much much better, there is everything available, everything you want to buy as if it was real peacetime. But here it is the same as before, everything is so expensive, so nothing has changed but all our money is gone. Tonight Mum and I want to go to the cinema, they are showing "Journey into the adventure". We have now been back from holiday for 2 weeks, how the time flies! How do you like your new job? How do you feel being the head chef? I'm sure you now don't have as much work, do you? Oh, how much I love cooking! Is this flat as nice as the other one? The shirt you sent me is impeccable and I have already worn it twice, it fits like it's been measured for me and I love the colour. Many thanks again. The situation in Berlin looks rather depressing .Are you listening to the radio? Then you will know what's going on. Dear Hans, would you be able to get hair nets for Mum, you could send them in a letter. But only if it's not too difficult for you. Mum doesn't like to ask all the time. She says, she is bothering you all the time. How is Miss Jean, please send our regards to her. What's going on with the pictures? We would love to see them. Today some farmers have already harvested the summer barley. Mum is already dreading the picking of the leftover potatoes; it is such a massive agony to preserve our life. Now I want to end my letter, sending our love to you, dear Hans and to Jean from Horst and Mum. Write to us soon , hoping to see you soon in good health.

LAEC Hostel Saltby.
July 19th 1948.

My dearest darling Jean.

Thank you very much for a lovely afternoon darling. I felt so lonely after you left. It was so strange for me seeing you leave here without me. It won't happen again. I was so happy, happy as I was never before in my life. Everything looking so bright. Well, darling don't worry we'll find a way and master the situation. I am not afraid of anything. It'll be a lovely time I'm sure.

Well, darling I've seen the doctor this morning, he just said he can't help me and is going to transfer the case to the Royal Infirmary Leicester. After I'd left Waltham the doctor rung Mr Bentley but he won't tell me. He just said I needn't worry about it, it isn't serious. But just now I found out that the doctor wants me to go this afternoon or tomorrow morning. That means it is time to have something done about it. So Mr Bentley rung Mr Shilton and ask him for transport. He was told either bus or ambulance but I would have to pay for the ambulance myself. I didn't know that was the new health scheme. The doctor told me not to go on a bus. So I'll have to wait now. Mr Bentley was going to ring Barker-Swaine about transport. Anyway I'll see.

I've told you now what's going to happen. Maybe I am coming tomorrow, who knows. Well, darling don't you worry if they keep me there. I am not afraid because I know what an operation is. Just kids play. It was terrible again last night but this'll be the last night I hope.

Well, my love, I'll say cheerio for now. If I am coming I'll ring you again from here, otherwise I'll write at once. Just be my best little girl and keep smiling, My thought will be with you always.

All my love and kisses

Eternally yours

Hans.

92 Wharf Street.

July 19th 1948.

My dearest Hans

It is now 4.30 and I don't suppose you will be going to the Infirmary this afternoon. Every call I have taken my heart turns over in case it may be you. I hope everything will be alright. Please darling let me know what they going to do to you, but don't worry they say everything happens for the best.

I arrived home safe but that fellow who went to the back of the bus was a dead loss, he didn't try to understand. I was hungry until I got in. I remembered my supper but it was quite alright I was not a bit hungry. I took Freddy a walk and

I wasn't long before I was in bed.

What is there left for me to say now that I have just been speaking to you to say you were on your way. I was hoping you would be, the worst part is waiting. I think it would be best if they keep you at the Infirmary until Mr Chandler is back. Mr B would be able to upset the camp and you wouldn't be there to get mixed up in it.

Well darling I will so cheeri'O and God Bless you.

    All my love
    Jean
PS Get someone reliable to look after Bonzo.

    92 Wharf Street.
    July 20th.
My dearest Hans

I was so very glad you rang me. I was wondering what they had told you. I have been terribly worried all day, but I don't know what there is to worry about, the time to start to worry will be when you have the operation. I waited until 5.15 for you to ring me but no, so I thought maybe they had kept you in. I rang you from a call box on the way home. I went through to about 2 departments before I got anywhere. The person I spoke to was very nice, she told me you had had to wait for the ambulance to come from Melton and that you were going back on Thursday. I asked if you would be staying in the infirmary on Thursday, she said she did not think so. If you had to have an operation it wouldn't be just yet. I was hoping you would stay in today and get it over with but I was very relieved when she said you had gone back. I met Dora last night. We went to get our railway tickets for Llandudno. They only issue so many tickets to a train and there were only 2 trains which we could go on that left on July 31st. .There was a 5.20 and 3.30. We thought we may as well take the 3.30 in the morning, by the way I think that will just about finish me off for the week. I have been scrubbing my raincoat tonight, it looks a bit better but not much. I am going to put it in the case just in case it is wet when I am away. The railway is fetching my case next Monday and I have an awful lot to do, but you know me very inefficient, I leave everything until the last minute. Dora is as different again to me, she has almost everything ready. She wants me to stay at their house Friday night to make sure we get there in time for the train. You know what happened when I went to Eastbourne, but I have never missed a train yet. Touch wood.

Susan is staying the night, Betty and Cyril have gone out with some friends in a car. It isn't very often they go out to-gether because Betty doesn't like to leave Susan much and I don't think she likes to ask Cyril's mother. I told you her and Betty were not on very good terms at the moment. Betty has no any idea why she does not speak, and she doesn't bother to ask. She couldn't care less. They are hoping to get a house soon.

Well darling I will say cheeri'O. I hope everything will be alright on Thursday, don't worry about anything. I am sure everything will turn out OK for you, and I. Be good. Good-night and God Bless you.

All my love
Jean.

LAEC Hostel Saltby.
July 20th · 1948.

My dearest darling Jean

At Saltby again, darling. As I told you only for 48 hours. I don't know what'll happen then. It made me so happy when you told me you'd rung the infirmary asking for me. So, you thought of me did you? It's very nice of you, but don't worry so much darling. I'll be alright and not in the least afraid.

They can do with me whatever they want as long as I get rid of it once and for all. I couldn't help laughing when I went to have the x-ray taken. I undressed, had one taken, told to dress again and wait outside for it. After five minutes waiting I had to undergo the same again because the first one wasn't quite perfect. My bones are too thick I was told. After a quick glance on the paper I found out what it was: bony infection.

Well, sweetheart, cross your fingers that I'll be fit again for going to Grantham on our first anniversary next month. I hope it won't take long for I don't like to stay in bed for weeks. If I have to stay I only have one wish. Please come and see me as often as possible. I felt pretty bad when I came back tonight. Nothing to eat and not even a 'lousy' cup of tea during the day. Therefore I had about half a gallon tonight. The fellows in the kitchen were cheering when I came back and disappointed when I told them about Thursday. Mr Bentley almost got a shock when I told him I'll take charge again till I leave. That gives him only 3 days for his own ideas. Last night he held a meeting with the cooks. When they came at 10.00pm they all came to see me and we had a good laugh whilst he was next door to us. I've been together with hundreds of strange people so it's only amusing for me because I've met that kind of people before. He's still going round telling everybody he's the hostel chief now.

There's such a nice music on tonight. Come and enjoy it. I won't forget the last Sunday. Never in my life.

Well, my love it's 10.30 now and I am tired out today. My leg doesn't hurt very much (touch wood) so I'll try to get some sleep. Goodnight and God bless. Just be good.

All my love and kisses to you darling,
eternally yours.
Hans.

92 Wharf Street.
July 21st 1948.

My dearest Hans

Thank you so very much for your letter. I didn't get it until dinner time. I hope you got the photographs alright, the one that is just head and shoulders of me belonged to my mother. She doesn't know I have taken it, but she had 2 and she never looked at it so I don't think it will be missed.

Well darling you should know by now what is going to happen to you. I won't post this letter until I know where you are, and it isn't any good making any arrangements about Saturday until we know.

I have not been out at all this week. I have been washing Freddy tonight with some kur-mange and it is working wonders. His hair is beginning to grow in parts so it looks as though we are going to have 2 dogs instead for one. I was going to wash my hair tonight but I have a bit of a cold (I don't know how I got it). It's nothing much, only I feel a bit dozy and I thought it may turn into a bad one if I washed it, so I will do it one night next week.

I will write a few lines to this tomorrow after I know where you are. I will be thinking of you all day wondering what is happening to you.

LAEC Hostel Saltby.
July, 21st 1948.

My dearest, darling Jean,

Another day is gone. I feel fairly well today but that doesn't stop me from going tomorrow. I've started it and shall see it through to the end for my own – and your sake. You may understand I don't want you to have trouble with me later on. That's one of the main reasons why I like to have it done now.

How are you today darling? I hope fine. It's such a lovely day again except for the wind. It almost blows us away up here at

Saltby. Never mind, better days are ahead. I wrote a letter to my mother today, but didn't say anything about going to the hospital. It's better to tell her afterwards for I don't want her to worry about it.

Didn't you go to the pictures last night. I really was surprised when I rung you and found you at home. Mr Bentley was rather polite and friendly today. He went to Melton this morning and I asked him to buy a few things for me. He did and also brought new illustrated papers without taking any money for them.

On my way to Leicester I'll go to the Food Office in Melton and get my 12 clothing coupons due on the 21st July. I also asked Bentley for my ration book in case I've to stay. And be sure I'll take a sandwich along this time. It's a pity I can't take a cup of tea!! I'll come to you for it at 10.30.

You should have seen the mess here last night. One of the cooks brought about 2lbs of bones for Bonzo and put it down on the stove. This morning I found them all over the room and had to take a broom before I could get to the door. Well, sweetheart I'll say cheerio now and God bless. Keep smiling and be good.

All my love and kisses
Eternally yours

Hans.

LAEC Hostel Saltby.
July 22nd 1948.

My darling Jean

Thanks very much for arranging everything for me, darling. When the bus got into Croxton Fred drove up and I changed. So off we went without a minute's delay. He asked me who was speaking on the phone. I said it was the War Ag because

I went there. Well, sweetheart in one way I am glad I didn't have to stay. I just thought of it if they'd kept me there on Tuesday and operated on me according to the first diagnosis, they wouldn't have found anything wrong. It was better this way I don't like the cutting business if there's a way to avoid it.

I've two letters to answer tonight. The one I got this morning and the one you gave me. So you've been worried all day on Tuesday. That's so much to me for it shows me how much you really care. Don't worry about me whatever may happen to me, I've had enough happening to me so I think I can handle situations and take a lot whatever it might be, except one thing, and that is if you would leave me or tell me off. But I am almost sure that won't happen. Don't you tell me you're 'going on the 3.30am train' on the 31st July. That's far too early for you, even when going on a holiday. Don't take the proverb: "the early bird catches the bone" too serious. Anyway better stay at Dora's for the last night or you'll miss the train for the first time in your life. Thanks so much again for the nice photos. As soon as I came home tonight I took the others out of the frame and put this one in. It looks beautiful but the person it was taken of looks much more beautiful. I hope your mother doesn't miss it. If she does tell her whom you gave it to. Are you packing all next week? It should only take you a few minutes I think. Well, I don't mind having two dogs instead of one as long as they keep quiet. Not like Lester and Bonzo here.

And now about Saturday. I was very glad to hear you're coming on the 1.30 from Leicester. That gives us another hour. Don't you think we'd better come here instead of going to Grantham? Remember how crowded Grantham is on Saturdays. We can stay in here if it rains. If the sun shines I'll get some sandwiches and a' bottle of black coffee 'ready to take along and we can stay outside all afternoon. Don't you think it'll be more enjoyable being on our own without anybody else around?

517

Tomorrow morning I'll have to see the local doctor again about fit or unfit for work. It's getting a bit worse now. I hope it'll be quite alright shortly. Well, my love I'll say good night and God bless you. Mr Bentley wants me to come over to his house to make the menu out and discuss a few things.
Just be good and keep smiling.

All my love and kisses yours
Hans.

LAEC Hostel Saltby.
July, 23ʳᵈ 1948.

My dearest darling Jean

As usually your weekend letter. How are you today darling? I am really sorry I'll have to wait until Monday to get the next letter. Anyway there's a nice Saturday afternoon between. As I told you in my last letter Mr Bentley asked me yesterday to see the local doctor today for a certificate 'fit for work.' So I went down to Waltham and the doctor told me to give the leg an entire rest. I gave Mr Bentley the certificate and he almost got a shock when he looked at it. Do you suggest what the doctor put down? 'Incapable for work for some weeks.' I shan't take it that serious. It just depends whether I've got pains or not. After I came back last night and went over to his house he said: 'Honestly I am glad you're back.' He is on his own and I away for a couple of weeks would have brought him into a nice mess. He got stuck with the menu last night already.
You would've had a good laugh last night. Mr Bentley asked me where you're working. I said "Didn't you notice what she said last Sunday about Mr Barker-Swaine?" You should have seen his face when I said, Oh, she's working for the War Ag for years and that's why she knows B-Swaine so well. He didn't know what to say for a minute. The shock was a complete one. I started the conversation again and asked him if he's

said anything wrong last Sunday. He only said "one has to be very careful."

My leg is still the same as it was yesterday. I think I shall be able to come to Croxton myself. Anyway we'll have a nice afternoon for the weather forecast said bright periods for tomorrow.

Well, sweetheart, I'll ring you tomorrow morning to make sure. Goodnight for now and God bless you. Just be good. A goodnight kiss to you.

Saturday, July 24th 1948

I am so awfully sorry darling I can't come to Croxton. I hope you don't mind. Mr Bentley went to see the doctor this morning and he asked how I was. B told him I am resting most of the time, but do a few odd jobs during the day, looking around the kitchen and so on. The doctor got quite annoyed about that for he ordered complete rest and told Mr Bentley I am not at all allowed to walk around. I have to stay in bed and for a week at least. Alright but I shall be glad when the week is over. You know how much I like staying in bed. After all I think the doctor is right, but if they would only tell me what it is. There must be something one can do about it not just resting it.

Well, my sweetheart I hope you'll get here alright. Only four more hours to wait.

So long, darling and be a nice girl.

All my love and kisses
Eternally yours
Hans.

       92 Wharf Street.
       July 25th.

My dearest Hans

Well darling how is being in bed going down today? Isn't it a lovely afternoon, I wish I was with you at Saltby. I shall have to wait now for another 2 weeks. I only just got the bus last night, it came down early 8.47 I was still on the bike when I heard the bus coming. I put the bike in and ran to the top of the lane, it stopped a few yards down the road. If I had missed that one I could have got one 20 minutes after. I think that 2 buses go to Grantham together, but one goes back at 9.40 and the other one at 10.0. I arrived home at 10.55 and I had not even cracked the eggs or squashed the tomatoes. I did not feel hungry so I left them and had the eggs for breakfast this morning. I will eat the pie tonight for my tea come supper. My mother has gone to Rothley, I am on my own except for the 2 dogs and cat, so I am not going to bother to mash a cup of tea. I will wait until 7.0 then I am going to make a pig of myself.

I have not started to do what I stayed at home to do. I took Freddy to the park this morning and after I had had my lunch, I felt so tired that I went to sleep in the chair till 3.30, then I thought I had better start to write to you. I have answered the invitation I have had to go to a wedding on August 28th from one of the girls that I worked with at Corah's. Alice is being bridesmaid. I think that is why I have had an invitation, because I have never had much to do with her.

Well darling if you want to get this in the morning, I will have to say cheeri'O. The post goes at 4.15 Sundays and if I miss that I will have to go to the GPO in Campbell Street.

All my love and kisses
Jeanny.

Jean with Freddie

LAEC Hostel Saltby.
July, 24th 1948.

My darling Jean

I cleared things away and went straight to bed. Well my love to be honest I feel rotten as I always do after you've left. Why can't we stay together!! I don't want to be impatient. You gave me so much this afternoon and told me what I was longing for. One day I'll thank you for everything and that shall be the greatest day in our lifes.

I hope you've got the bus alright. It's 10.25 and you probably just left Melton. I am so very sorry you've to go back all that way. You looked so tired tonight. I can hardly keep my eyes open, but I won't sleep before I think you're at home. It's 10.50 now and you'll be near Leicester. I've got the Yank Station on now. There is some lovely music on. I am thinking of you all the time. You are on your way home now. I hope you'll make it alright.

Well, sweetheart I'll say goodnight and God bless you always. All my love forever and lots of kisses to you.

Sunday 25/7/48 12.30

Hello darling how are you? Busy today? Don't pack too much and remember you're only going for a week. Then I shall have you back again.

I've just finished my last work before I start my weeks rest. The supper for the big white chief is ready. Everybody is licking his fingers after having a look at the rabbit.

I only hope the weather will keep nice for your holidays. Enjoy it darling. I am only sorry I can't join you, but we'll wait till I get my holidays and then spend a few days together. I am longing for it.

Well, my love, please don't mind this short letter. I've to give it along to Grantham and I want you to get it in the morning. You'll get another one on Tuesday.

So just be good and think of me.
All my love and lots of kisses
Eternally yours
Hans.

My darling Jean

Hello, ma'am! Have you finished your packing? I hope you didn't stay in all day. It really would be a shame. Can you imagine how I look laying in bed and the sun shining? I told Bentley to buy a pair of shorts tomorrow and then I shall have my headquarter outside. Don't come home after your holidays and look still white. Remember, dark brown is the colour darling during the summer month. I shall try it next week.

I am quite comfortable and almost without pains when I rest the leg. Mr Bentley asked me to come over the bungalow for a while because I was on my own all afternoon and therefore rather lonely. I of course got up and walked over there, sat down for a few minutes. Mr Chandler came in the meantime so it was a good excuse for me to leave. I just made it the way back. After all I found out better to stick to the doctors orders. I want to be fit when you come back in a fortnight. Don't you like to come here for a week to nurse me? I think I would be cured within a week. Consider that and direct your suitcases to Saltby station. I'll fetch them.

Wasn't it warm today? It's 10.20 now and I've still door and windows open to get a bit of cool air. It's lovely outside and just right to take you a walk. Unfortunately --! You probably know the rest already.

Well, my sweetheart, I'll get some sleep now. Just be good and think of me. I'll be dreaming of you. God bless you.

All my love and kisses
Eternally yours
Hans.

My dearest, darling Jean

I really missed your letter this morning, but after all I had one from Ellen. I wrote to her last week in reply to the letter and told her that I was going to the infirmary. So she wrote just a few lines asking if there's anything she could do for me or send me whilst I am sick. It's really nice of her but I wrote today and told her not to trouble herself.

I did not get up since last night, but it's getting worse again. Don't you think I am a bit too impatient? I notice it now myself. It looks as if it can't be cured in a day or two. Anyway I've got a fortnights time till you come back and be sure I'll do my best.

Oh! By the way, you didn't tell me the new address for the time you're away. Please, let me know darling.

Are you going to see a picture tonight?

Mr and Mrs Chandler came in at lunchtime for a couple of minutes. She's rather tall beside him. About 6f I think. Looking down at her husband. He told me to come over and lay down outside his bungalow, but I prefer to stay here. I don't like answering questions all afternoon. Mr Chandler told me this morning how nice and tasty the rabbit was and how much they enjoyed the supper. He said his wife wrote home straight away and told her daughters about that nice supper. Bonzo seems to be rather uncomfortable today. He can't find a cool place. I think I better join him underneath the bed. One of the cooks went to Grantham today so I told him to buy a pair of shorts for me to start my sunbathing.

Are you listening, darling? Of course I mean to the same programme. It's 'Bandparade.' All the latest songs. 'Heartbreaker' is just on. One should always remember that one. It's very true. I know already every inch around my four walls. I'll get Fred to bring me some thrilling cowboy books tomorrow. That'll help me I hope.

If there would only be a bit of a brise tonight to cool the air off.

Anything you want me to say, sweetheart? Alright! I love you very very much and always will do. More than ever.

Well, my love, I'll say goodnight and God bless. Be a good girl and keep smiling.

All my love and kisses
Eternally yours
Hans.

92 Wharf St.
July 27th.

My darling Hans

Thank you very much for your letters. I got them both this morning. The weather is just about killing me off. I think if it lasts much longer it will do. I am so tired sitting here. I would just love to be you in bed, I think we had better go and live at the North Pole.

No, darling I have not read that novel you can tell me all about the story when I come next. Another thing, I still would not eat any rabbit even if it is cold, hot and not so hot. I still don't like rabbit. I didn't go anywhere last night. I did take the dog to the park for about an hour. I will be busy tonight, my mother has a crate to unpack. Betty was coming to do it this afternoon but she phoned to say she had a sore throat and would not be coming down, so my mother and I are going to unpack it tonight but not until it is cooler. Iris came back today, she will be getting married in a few weeks' time. Her boyfriend is coming here with his Mother in three weeks then in another 3 weeks they are going to be married, but Iris is not going back to Paris with him. She is going to wait until he can find a place to live. I should get the camera tomorrow, Mr Smith is back off his holiday. I still have one or two things to get before this week is out. I lent my sunglasses to my cousin about a month ago and I have to fetch them but when I do not know.

Well darling I hope your leg is better today. Please do what the doctor tells you and rest it. By the way the address I am staying at in Wales is on the back of this paper.

Be good

All my love xxx

Jean

Miss J Phillips
c/o Mrs M. H. Jones
'Rowena'
34 Madoc Street
Llandudno

LAEC Hostel Saltby.

July, 27th. 1948.

My darling Jeanny,

Thanks very much for your letter. Isn't the weather marvellous? And you dare asking me how it is to stay in bed? Don't be surprised what I'll look like in 2 weeks. I've started my sunbathing this afternoon, twice for half an hour. I hope you'll look the same after your weeks holidays. 2 weeks waiting makes a lot darling but then we'll have a nice day again.

Are you going to the wedding then? Maybe I am taking my holidays at that time, but don't let me spoil your plans.

Lofty came this afternoon and asked me how I am. He wants to arrange for two buses to go to Skegness. They want me to go along, but I probably can't in this state of health. So let's hope for the best for Monday. Anyway I shan't get up before it's perfectly alright again. The Sunday afterwards its far more important for me.

The warden has just been and ask me if I've been outside today? I look like a real life Indian. And that's only from the first half an hour. Mr Chandler took his wife around Redmile, Bottesford Kimpton today, but they didn't walk. Only on the bus. He said it was too warm to walk to the castle. They're coming to Leicester tomorrow and he'll post this letter there for me. I am sure then you'll get it Thursday morning.

Well, my little sweetheart I'll say goodnight now and God bless. Be a good girl and keep smiling.

All my love and kisses

Eternally yours

Hans.

LAEC Hostel Saltby.

July 27th 1948.

My dearest, darling Jean,

It's 9.00pm and I just heard a very nice programme from the Russ. zone. If I could only get hold of that skunk I would wring his neck. Such nonsense makes me upset.

Isn't the weather just wonderful? I got used to it after all. Don't you think staying in bed is the best thing. Be sure it's pretty hot inside these huts. Our margarine is running away. I've been outside for 2 hours this afternoon and look just nice. Perhaps the sun is good for my leg. He just said on the wireless the highest temperature today was 94. Still another 26 to go to get to the temperature in our dear old Louisiana. Wouldn't that be nice? I bet you get tired sitting at your switchboard all day. The only thing to do is going on holiday. Only 2 more days darling. It'll be nice for you all the week and enjoy yourself. You've only got 5 more days after this week and we'll make the best of those.

I just had a good laugh. After the news he said that the Olympic flame has arrived, but went out when it was handed over to the English runner. Dover must be a windy place.

There's no need to go and live at the North pole just move a bit to Northern Scotland. I think that would do. I'll tell you about that particular novel sometime.

Alright! Alright! Don't get excited about the cold, hot, not so hot rabbit. I've crossed it off already. Nothing to worry about at all. There's another invitation for a wedding for you, I guess. Iris is getting on alright then.

I hope you've got the camera alright. Bring a few nice photos home for me, will you darling?

My leg is alright as long as I rest it. I'll have to see the doctor again on Friday and probably get another week in bed.

Well my sweetheart, I'll say goodnight and God bless you. I'll post the next letter on Friday to the new address. So just be good and think of me.

All my love and kisses
Eternally yours
Hans.

R 30/7.48   **Aschersleben , 11.7.1948**

27/7.48

My dear Hans,

Thank God we have finally received mail from you again, the letters are dated 17.6 and 22.6.1948. I am so sorry that you have interpreted Horst's letter that way, and you know very well that my only aim has always been to raise you both as honourable people and it is my biggest pleasure that you both are such decent men. How could you think that you should send more than you can manage? Don't you ever do anything wrong and Horst also knows that honesty is the best policy. I am sure he is really sorry about the nonsense he has written and I also have told him off. He is often very nervous and overworked and you will understand if he tries to organise things for us as we have lost all our hard earned money. How shall we ever be able to afford things, one doesn't want to live with things that are borrowed for ever. If only Papa was with us again, so that we could manage things together. It is not easy for us. Prices stayed the same, but our saved money is all gone. You see, Horst rarely has a day off, he is working bank holidays and Sundays until after lunchtime, therefore I'm begging you, please don't be upset with him. One shouldn't always weigh one's words, who would want to call you a liar; there is no reason for that. Your parcel from the 16th of April has still not arrived. I hope your cold is better already. On Thursday we went to pick raspberries, on Friday we collected wood, and tomorrow we go again to pick raspberries, we have to have some fruit occasionally, if only the journey there wouldn't be so awfully long, that's the hardest bit. On Tuesday we have to go back to the fields to look for and pick the potato beetles, otherwise we won't get our coupons to be able to pick grains and I cannot do without that, because hunger is very painful. Then we have to collect winter barley, it's all without any break, it's on and on and on… I am sure you must have been so delighted about Jean's birthday present, we would have loved to make you happy too, but we cannot get anything decent here and there is no money to buy anything of value. Before the currency change I wanted to buy a purse for myself, but 22.50 Mark I thought was far too expensive, even if it had been a proper one, but to spend money for such poor quality? You wanted to know about the currency exchange. Ok, everybody could exchange 70 Reich Mark, for the rest you got 10 for every 100 Marks, we wouldn't have complained if the prices hadn't stayed as high. This week I will post a few newspapers for you but I need to get a big envelope first. We are still in mail contact with the Eichhorn family; I will send them your regards. Mr Eichhorn had plans to come to our area in order to organise some food but with this poor harvest he won't have much success. Regilde married a railway employee in Lauscha a few years ago; her first engagement didn't last long. I received a letter from Herta a few days ago, she got divorced on the 9th of June 1948, and she is relieved that that part of her life is over. She was supposed to be divorced on the grounds that both parties are guilty, as is the custom nowadays, but she said to the judge that she won't t take any blame. Heinz Ludwig is the bad guy, treating Herta and his child the way he did. She even has to claim support for Inge through the courts now. It was assumed that the reason for the divorce was that they had drifted apart. That morning there were 38 divorces, can you imagine? There are so many unhappy marriages nowadays as a result of the war. This week I went with Mrs Lehmann to the countryside to pick carrots, one has to be constantly on the go in order to have something to cook. I hope that this is going to change at some point. During June we still had no fat, as a meat substitute we get salt fish, and we have not had meat since the middle of May, and there is no prospect of getting any soon. At least we still have potatoes; lots of people have run out months ago. I did write to you that the Höhls had organised fabric for a coat for me- I can pick up the coat on Friday from the tailor's now, he is charging 70 Mark , for a tailor's wage that's incredible, isn't it? He was going to charge 100 Mark, but as I could provide the thread myself, it was reduced by 30Mark. Now my boy, I am wishing you well as usual. I am sending you all my love and kisses from you Mum and Horst. Please give my regards to Jean. Hoping to see you again soon in good health.

92 Wharf St.
July 28th.

My darling Hans
Have you melted yet? I hope not but oh, hasn't it been hot? I

hope it is like this next week, but I hope it is a bit cooler on Aug 8th. I hope your leg is better, if it isn't we can go some other time.

Thank you for your very nice long letter. It was very nice of Ellen. She must be a very nice person. Did she say anything about Alfred? I spoke to Mr Chandler this morning. Did he tell you? I asked him how Mrs C likes Saltby, he said his daughter was coming down in September for a week. I think you had better have your holiday that week. You know how jealous I am. I have the camera, Mr Smith brought it today. It looks alright but I will have to wait and see if it is.

I was looking in the shops the other night at the radios and saw that you only need pay 4/- per week if you buy one on the high purchase. You always pay more for a thing that way but at least you would have it today and not like you are doing now. It seems such a waste paying 4/- for the hire of a radio.

Dora came round this evening to make arrangements for Friday. I am going to stay at Dora's Friday night. I would have preferred to stay at home and meet her later but I did not like to say so, I think it will be best. My mother will have a good night's sleep. I still don't know if she is going away next week or not. If she goes I had better bring Freddy to you, only he isn't very keen on men he prefers the lady's (like most Germans!!!). Alice came tonight too. I told you she had been to Jersey for a holiday. We had a good chat. There always seems so much more to talk to Alice about than Dora. In between talking I have washed my hair you can see how busy I was tonight. I went to the pictures last night to see a very good picture, it was an old one 'Dark Journey', about two spies, one French and the other German in the first war. Someone told me how good it was. I told you I was going to help my mother unpack a crate but when I got home she and my cousin had already done it. So I was able to go to the pictures.

I have the 'Yanky' station on now, time 10.30. They are

playing your old German song 'You can't be true dear.' I was listening to the play tonight 8.0 to 9.15 (they are playing the German version of the song, I believe you now?) anyway, the play was good, it was called 'The First Mrs Fraser.' Did you listen to it?

Well darling I will have to say goodnight and God Bless. I have to take Fred his nightly walk.

All my love and kisses

Jean

LAEC Hostel Saltby.
July, 28th. 1948.

My dearest, darling Jeanny,

This letter will see you at Llandudno. Your holidays have started and please, sweetheart, enjoy yourself as much as possible. I hope you'll have the same weather all week. Are you comfortable there? Don't get lost and come back healthier than you went. I'll be thinking of you all the time. How nice it would be to spend a week together. I'll wait darling. Once our time will come.

Well, I was going to take my hour outside again when the opening of the Olympic Games came on the air. I was listening till it finished. Just the same as in 1936. The only thing I can say, marvellous. It's only a shame that our team isn't amongst them. Well, I hope for the next time.

It's 9.30 now. Where's the ink? I'll have another go but better take the other pen. Well, I've had my hour outside, dinner, a conversation with Mr Whiteman and a bath. Quite a lot within 4 hours isn't it? Mr Whiteman just asked how I was and went again. Do you remember when they stopped me bringing the meals to Redmile Hostel? Now the men get the food from here 3 times a week. And it is only to be taken in a van. 12 miles! Isn't it funny people always have to do what they forbid some time ago. It's ok with me. I am on the sick. Oh! There's such a funny programme on the wireless now. I think it's 'Blackpool night' That comedian brings some very nice things. Maybe you are also listening.

Mr Chandler came the other day and asked me how everything was during the previous week. I didn't say anything. If he wants to find out he better asks somebody else. I don't like to do anybody a bad turn, not even Mr Bentley. He's getting married the day after tomorrow. Olive will look after him alright. I bet she'll make a man out of him.

Tomorrow morning I shall have to see the doctor again and that means another week in bed. The knee is alright now, but it moved just up to the hip. I'll ask him about some ointment if there's anything for it.

Well, my love I'll say goodnight and God bless. Think of me and remember how much I love you. Let me know about you soon. Sleep well and pleasant dreams.

All my love and kisses
Eternally yours, darling
Hans.

92 Wharf St.

July 29th.

My darling Hans

Thank you very much for your letter. This one will be the last one I write from Leicester until after my holiday. I will write as often as I can next week, but you know what it is like when on holiday, you know what it's like when I'm not. I still have a lot to do, I bet I go without half the things I intend to take but I could not care less.

Mr Bodymore rang this afternoon. I asked if he had heard anything of Mr Pickering, imagine my surprise when he said that he was married last Saturday and was on his honeymoon at Torquay. Had he arranged to get married when he was at Stathern? He probably thought it would be cheaper to have a double room instead of 2 singles.

When did you decide to have your holiday in August? I wish you could go away somewhere for a week. I know it's useless to say that. If you did have a week on your own I could still have my 5 days with you. Because you can have your day off every week when you like and I could have a day off then we could go somewhere like Skegness. Are you going on Sunday, it would be nice if you did only I think Skegness will be very crowded this holiday.

Well darling I will send you a postcard as soon as I arrive. Think of me getting up at 2.0 Saturday morning. I will be thinking of you all week (except when I am with someone else) no darling I mean what I said.

Love all of it, Jeanny

LAEC Hostel Saltby.
July 29<u>th</u> 1948.

My dearest darling Jean

Thanks very much for the nice long letter I received this morning. Did you think I could let you go without ringing you before? Fortunately I was told by the doctor to try walking around. He can't do anything else and said it's just a matter of waiting. Well then, I'll walk and wait. So everything will be alright on August 8th. I might even go along to Skegness on Monday. Just depends on how I feel. Mr Saunders asked how I got so brown. I told him it's warm, very warm indeed, in this room. He laughed. My special friend Bentley has left tonight to get ready for tomorrow. I bet he'll be surprised.

It's quite nice to listen to the Olympic Games now. He talked about the swimming pool this afternoon and said everybody was nervous. So, I remembered 1942, the first year in the Labour Service, when I swum for the district championship at Stettin. The first start was a false one because I couldn't wait to get to the other end, but made it alright. Are you listening to 'adventure unlimited?' It's just started. Poor Mr Jackson!!

Ellen didn't say anything about Alfred. As I told you she just sent a few lines.

Well, ma'am your wish will be an order for me. My holidays

will be taken the week the 2 daughters come. You needn't be afraid.

Look, darling I am glad you looked at the radios in the shops. If there's anything cheaper than this I am going to think it over. If you didn't really like to stay at Dora's for the night why didn't you come here and take a train from Grantham at about 2 o'clock? 2 hours earlier doesn't make any difference, does it? Do you think the Germans always like lady's? Sweethearts or darlings, yes I am sure of that.

I got my pay tonight and they stopped me 13/- but I haven't had any sick pay from the National Health yet. 'Wait' is my motto.

Well, my love, I'll say cheerio now. Be careful and look after yourself well.

All my love and kisses
Eternally yours darling,
Hans.

R 30/7.48   ## Aschersleben, 18.7.1948
29/7.48

My dear Hans,

Today, Sunday, I would like to send you many greetings again. We have not had any mail from you for the last 12 days; the last one was from June 22. The postal service is very bad again at the moment, we've had no mail from anyone. I have been in the forest for 2 days picking raspberries and 2 days cleaning stones from 5.45AM to 3PM, without any payment, only for getting permission to collect left over grains on the fields, and I have still 2 more days to go. The weather is getting better and better and life harder and harder. Tomorrow we want to go and check how much winter barley we will have this year. The harvest is delayed as it rained so much, let's hope the weather is stable during harvest. I just had a little sleep, because we want to go and see a film tonight, but if I am so tired, I won't see much of the film. I hope you are better again, which is the case here too. On

Friday I picked up my new coat, it is really nice, but 70 Marks for tailoring is too mean, it's all my saved money. Now they are intending to pay wages proportionate to performance, then Horst will earn more. 27 Marks per week is really not much salary and tips are not big nowadays, money is tight because of the currency reform. Dear Hans, I so wish I could have sent you the newspapers you asked for but I am not allowed to send them, it is forbidden, I was so disappointed. We won't have many Sundays at home in the next few weeks when we start picking potatoes and grains, every day has to be used. If the weather doesn't change, it won't be good for us, as the ears of the grains won't break off and we won't be able to find any.Then we have nothing that we can exchange for food. Well, we won't worry now about what might happen, what will be will be. Stay well and send my love to Jean. I am sending all my deep love and kisses to you, your Mum and brother Horst. Hope to see you in good health soon.

LAEC Hostel Saltby.
July 31$\underline{st}$ ·1948.

My darling Jean,
Thanks very much for the last letter from Leicester. You'll be at your place already for a few hours and I hope you've had a seat all the way. What's the weather like at your place. I hope it's better than here otherwise it would've made a bad start for you. It was foggy all morning and didn't clear up yet. It's 7 o'clock now.
I hope I shall get a bit more than just a postcard darling the next week. How many items did you forget? I hope you don't mind me asking I am just curious that's all.
I really was surprised to hear that Mr Pickering got married. It must have been an effort after 14 years. Please, sweetheart, don't let's wait that long. One could never get Mr P talking about it. He was funny about it when we started jok-

ing.

Did I say anything definite about having my holidays in August? I can't remember. As I told you I decided for September, one particular week. We'll talk about it when you are back. After all there's no bus going to Skegness on Monday. No organisation at all and the main trouble, the men can't make up their mind. One day they want to go the next day they don't.

So, you'll be thinking of me all the time, except when you're with someone else. I'll remember that on August 8th. You know how much I trust and how much I love you, darling. Always think of it and nothing will ever go wrong..

Well, darling, I am so lonely today. Won't you come back and spend the rest of the week here? It would be much nicer.

I just had my supper with Mr Chandler and I think I'd better go to bed now. I don't feel too good. So, I'll say goodnight and God bless. Take care of yourself, darling and just be my best little girl.

> All my love and kisses
>> Eternally yours sweetheart
>>> Hans.

> Sunday, August 1st 1948.

'My darling'

I am awfully sorry, but there was no possibility to get the other letter posted today. I got it ready last night but none of the cooks went away to post it and I am afraid it's too late now. Time 7.30pm. I'll put both letters in one envelope and try to get them posted tomorrow. I think the mail van will be coming in the morning.

How are you, darling? I feel lots better these days. (Touch wood). What time will you be coming back on Saturday? Shall I ring you Sunday morning to make sure about the afternoon? I would like to hear your voice and know you're back home safely.

The weather here has changed completely. The sun is gone,

it's cloudy and rather cool. And the worst thing I haven't finished my sunbathing yet. What a shame!! I've just come back from the warden's place. Mr and Mrs Coy were there so the warden asked me to come over and have tea with them. Mr Coy has got the keys and is probably moving into his new house next week. She said she was sorry when I had to leave Stathern. But I am quite alright here. I don't like to get to familiar with them. She asked me to come down to Stathern when they have got settled. I said 'maybe.' I'll have to go and see Mrs Betts as well and have a look around his place then.

I decided to take over again on Tuesday morning. Not working, but just having a look around some funny things going on. 2 of the fellows started moaning yesterday when I told him to do something. Mr Bentley has spoilt the lot, but I'll get them straightened out again.

Mr Chandler gave me a tip last night. Mr Hilton asked him the other day if he could spare me for 5 weeks for a holiday camp. Probably Redmile. Why the hell is it always me? They've lots of cooks, maybe professional ones, in the other hostels, why don't they send one of them? I want to stay where I am and not move around hostels. It is almost the same as it was in prisoner times. Well, I shall see about that.

Well, my love I'll say goodnight and God bless always. Be careful and just be good. Think of me.

> All my love and kisses
> Eternally yours, darling
> > Hans.

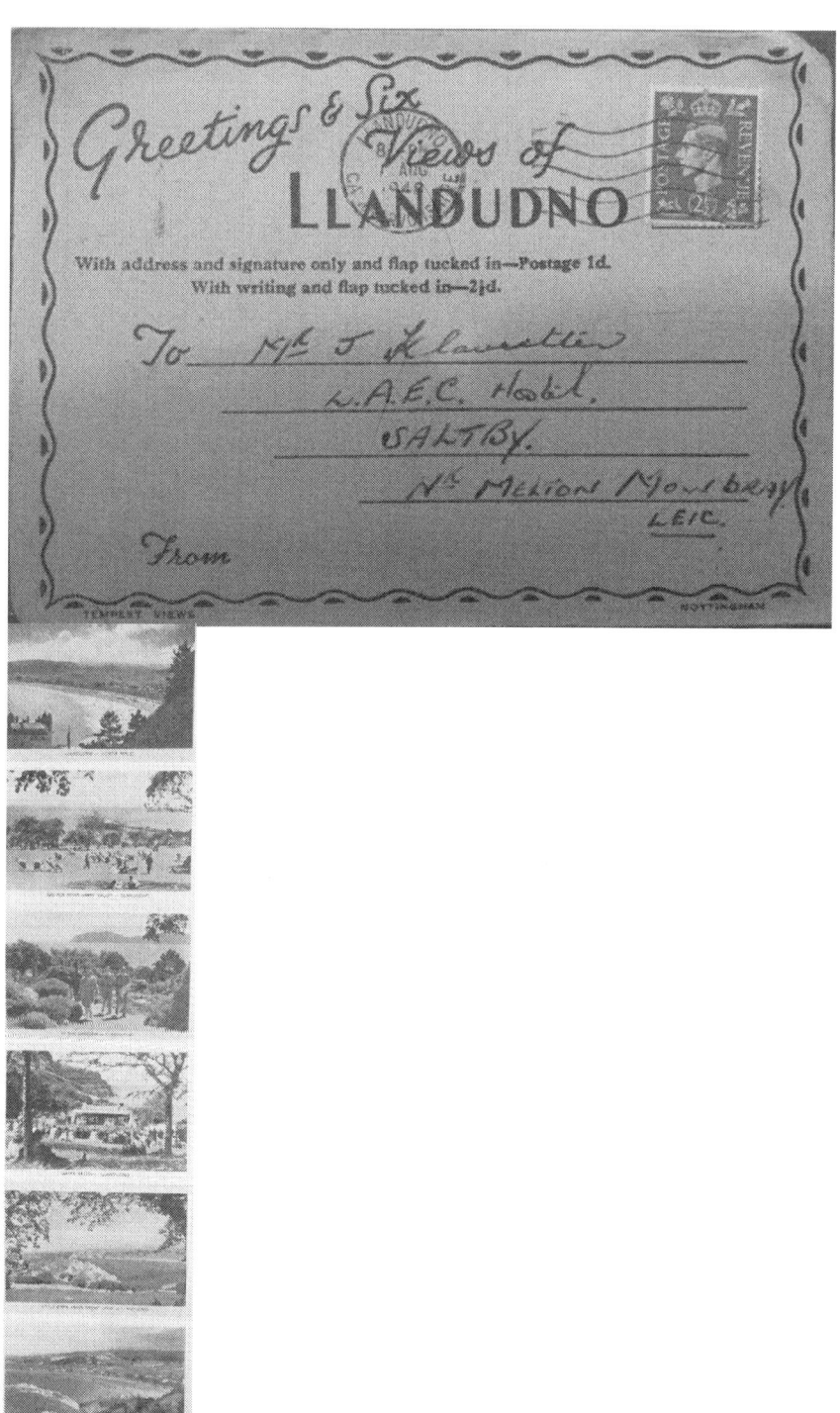

Greetings & Six Views of LLANDUDNO

With address and signature only and flap tucked in—Postage 1d.
With writing and flap tucked in—2½d.

To ___ _Mr J R lawretter_

L.A.E.C. Hotel.

SALTBY.

Nr MELTON MOWBRAY

LEIC.

From

TEMPEST VIEWS   NOTTINGHAM

"Rowena",
34 Madoc St,
Llandudno.
Aug 1st 1948.

My dearest Hans
I never expected to get a letter so soon when they said there was a letter for me. Dora said "good heavens he must be missing you" are you? Thank you very much for it. I managed to get the train in good time. The train wasn't a bit packed in fact we had a compartment to ourselves all the way and were to lay full out on the seats and try to sleep. We arrived in Llandudno about 8.30. In the morning we looked Llandudno over (I will let you know what I think at the end of the week). It started to rain and thunder after lunch so we went to the pictures to see " Gentleman's agreement" . It was very good. We went to a dance last night, got back to the place about 11.00 so you see I wasn't late. I slept like a top, I was so very tired. I'm sitting on the beach writing this. The weather seems to have changed, it isn't cold but the sun is not out. By the look of the sky it won't be coming out today. I know it should be out tomorrow because you ordered it. We are going for a paddle when I have finished this. Dora is writing to her boy. I should know him as well as Dora does by the end of the week. She talks of him all the time. I guess that it must be love. I can't find out if there is anything serious between them. I don't think there is yet.
Well darling how is your leg? I'm hoping it is alright. I wish you were here, but as you have said that time will come. We have the rest of our lives and that I hope will be one long holiday for the both of us. Well darling cheerio. Bye for now I will write sometime again. Just be good
All my love and kisses   Jean

LAEC Hostel Saltby.
August 2nd.1948.

540

My darling Jeanny,

How are you today, darling? I hope fine. I am all on my own. Mr Chandler went for a walk in the afternoon, so I laid down at 2 o'clock to have an hour's rest, but when I woke up and looked at my watch I found it was 5.30. That means the day is almost over and I am rather glad. It was so lonely for me and I am longing for the next Sunday. One of the cooks asked me yesterday to come along to Grantham to see a picture. I told him I can't go on a bike so he wanted to take me on tow. We had a good laugh.

I have to confess I get rather used to have breakfast in bed. After a rest yesterday afternoon I woke up at 6.00 this morning, watched the boys doing the breakfast and went to bed again at 7.15. My breakfast came half an hour later and then slept until 10.30. That's what I call a bank holiday. I'll have to see the doctor again on Friday and shall start working on Saturday. I feel quite well. Just came back. I took Bonzo for a walk down to the other camps and back. He's getting on nicely. Have you had a nice day?

Well, my sweetheart. I'll say cheerio and look after yourself well just be my best little girl.

Think of me and remember how much I am loving you.

> All my love and kisses
> Eternally yours, my sweet
> Hans.

L.A.E.C. Hostel Saltby.
August 3rd.1948.

My dearest, darling Jean

I thank you so very very much for your letter. You know how much I miss you, especially the last weekend. It must have been nice a compartment for yourself. Did you sleep a few hours? I still wonder how you managed to get up so early. You must have had a good connection in London. Only 5 hours to Wales. Have you had nice weather yesterday. Here it started to rain in the late afternoon and it was awful during the night. I had to get up and shut the windows. I heard about "Gentlemen's Agreement" on the wireless last week. Wasn't it something about a man in America who said he was jewish just to see how they're treated? I didn't hear it all. Did you enjoy the dance on Saturday? I hope it was a change for you. Who is talking most of her boyfriend? You or Dora. As far as I know you it'll be Dora. The men were surprised to see me in the kitchen early this morning. I was there before they came at 5.00. As I told you I've had a few hours yesterday afternoon, so I woke up at 4.30 this morning and as I didn't feel tired, I got up.

It has stopped raining now but by the look of the sky not for long. The weather is not the best for my leg, but in fact it is getting better day after day. Everything will be alright for Sunday. What bus are you coming on? Make it the 1.30 from Leicester if possible. I'll bring a few sandwiches along hoping it'll be fine.

I've just had my lunch and I think the best thing to do is to have a rest in the afternoon. Don't you agree? So long, my sweet I'll write a few more lines tonight. Xxx

Well, sweetheart, here I am again. It's 7.00 pm and I am going to bed straight the way. It looks as if it was a bit too much today. I ran about all day long because I had 10 extra men to work in the kitchen. Cleaning the stores and so on. After all I daren't leave them alone in the stores so I had to stay and watch them. Anyway I am very glad I am able to go to bed now. I better not say anything about not being 65 yet! Your answer will be the same so I know it well.

I'll say cheerio for now. When I get your next letter I shall see how long the mail goes and when to write the last one. When are you leaving there? Saturday morning?

Well, so long my love and just be good. Look after yourself and think of me
All my love and kisses
    Eternally yours, darling
                    Hans.

    "Rowena",
    34 Madoc St,
    Llandudno.
    Aug 3rd 1948.
My dearest Hans

I wrote a letter to you last night, and I hadn't had a letter from you yesterday but received 2 this morning. You ought to have heard Dora, I think she is envious because she has had only one letter so far. I am sorry you were not able to go to Skegness, but I don't think you would have liked it on a bank holiday, it would have been far too crowded. I have given up hope of seeing the sun, but it isn't cold. We put our beach dresses on hoping the sun would come out, but so far I have been sitting with my coat and cardigan. Dora has taken her dress off but is sitting in her cardigan.

You want to know what kind of a room we have, you would laugh if you could see it. It is only a small house where we are staying. There are 6 other people besides Dora and I. It's an old fashioned place but is very clean and the food is good. Our bedroom isn't very big but just enough room, there isn't any hot water and we have a jug and basin and an iron bed stead. And a feather mattress which is very comfortable.

We went on a sea trip to the Isle of Man yesterday, the journey is about 53 miles and it took 3 ½ hours to get there, and was I thankful to get there, you should have seen me hang over the side of the boat. I was quite alright ¾ hour before we reached Douglas. Dora went first, I thought I was going to make it ok but a little while after I had to go to the side and believe me I wish I could have got off that boat. Anyway it was very nice to get there. What we saw of Douglas was very nice. I can't make up my mind whether or not it would be worth going again for a holiday. Coming back we didn't feel anything, though Dora doesn't feel too good today. I was going to send a postcard from Douglas so you would have one today but I felt too ill to bother. Sunday morning we lay on the beach. We were going to do the same in the afternoon but it was a bit drizzly so we just messed around, went into an amusement place which had a machine that played any record you wished to hear for 2d. I found one of my favourites called "So Tired", I don't hear very often. It is sometimes played on the A.T.N after 10.00. I have been in twice since.

Monday we had a very lazy day, lay on the beach all day (I'm as red as an Indian it is going a bit now)

Sunday evening we went a walk round the Orme. I think it might be a mountain but I think you would call it a hill at the side of the Alps. We didn't go up just round it into the west shore of Llandudno. It is very nice there just at the mouth of the river Conway. I saw one or two houses that would just suit us. I think you and I had better open our own hotel don't you think? Why should Mr Bentley be surprised? You never said where you came from when you were at home. I have gone and bought a bicycle basket. I have been looking in Leicester for a big one but couldn't see one. Now I will not have to bother.

I know it isn't any good asking if you are missing me because it is only like an ordinary week. It doesn't make any difference whether I am 30 or 130 miles away, we are still apart. But one day we won't be will we? Or have you changed your mind. I don't think you need to ring me unless your leg isn't any better. If it is ok let us go to Gratham to the place you first took me. Do you remember those children asking if you were going to marry me. I felt so embarrassed.

Well darling be good till Sunday

All my love

Jeanny

THE MODEL YACHTING POOL, WEST SHORE, LLANDUDNO

Mr J Klawitter,
L.A.E.C Hostel, Saltby.
Nr Melton Mowbray.
 LEICS.

Dear Hans

Received the letter you wrote
On the 3rd arrived here on the 5th

But was posted in Melton on the 4th
I will be coming on the 2.30 bus there
isn't a 1.30 on Sunday to Grantham
The weather here hasn't been too bad
What rain there has been was at night. Will
Be seeing you in Grantham under the clock.
Jean

R 6/8.48   Aschersleben, 20.7.1948
4/8.48

     My dear Hans,
At long last we have received mail from you again, the letters

545

from July 6 and 7 have arrived, thank you so much. And tonight I want to answer straight away. Actually I am more than ready for bed, but then you'll have to wait much longer. We went to pick raspberries today, with great success, and for that I have to get up just after 3 AM to be at the train station at 4 and when I get back home again I am really very tired, because the march from the train station to the forest is very tough. Today we had the first really hot day for a long time. And now the harvest can begin. The day after tomorrow we want to look for wild mushrooms, and that will be a good substitute for meat, we have not had any for 9 weeks. Health wise we are more or less ok. Gertrud's visit was cancelled, the currency reform has cost them all their money and they have nothing left and Trude lost her job on top of it. So they are not doing well at all. You are quite spoilt to be able to sleep until 8 AM. I unfortunately can't sleep in, not even on Sundays as Horst has to leave at 7.30AM. I don't begrudge you at all, I'm glad that you can get some rest, 48 hours work is too much in the long run. And it's great when you can earn more money, especially as you can buy something with it. I am really very happy that you are trying to get some shoes for me, if you saw how bad my shoe situation is, I am constantly losing the soles of the shoes that Miss Ellen gave to me. If Jean is getting them ,please tell her to try and get some with a bit of heel, I am not very good at walking with very flat shoes, perhaps she could get some pumps, that's the ones I really liked to wear , but I don't know what you can get there. Are you using the points to buy them? I am sure they are going to be very expensive. Where are we supposed to get the money from if we need to buy something? One piece of clothing after the other, from the few pieces that we have left, is falling apart and we can't replace any of it. If I only think how hard Horst has worked for this, and now it is all gone. We are so lucky that at least Horst has the decent shirt from you and he really loves it. How many times did I go to the trade office, every time without success.

If it gets warmer now I will be sweating properly in my thick skirt and sweater, I still have an outfit for Sundays, but nothing for every day. We are supposed to get new money again, and who knows what worse is in store for us then. Sometimes we are close to desperation. Yesterday I was so upset that I could not answer your letters, it is better not to think about it all. Life is sometimes so totally pointless, an eternal fight for survival. Yesterday we got a letter from Eisleben, Uncle Hermann Gogolin passed away on July 1st, he had a corn cut from his toe, he got an infection from it, he went to hospital, where they discovered that he was diabetic. They then had to amputate his leg but he passed away soon after. He was 74 years old and otherwise pretty fit. Our nutrition certainly doesn't help things; one doesn't have any resistance any more. Blessed is the one who is at his eternal resting place, for he is relieved from heartache and pain. If we were not so longingly waiting for Papa and you it would all be pointless! Now, my dear Hans I want to come to an end, stay healthy. Sending lots of love and kisses from your Mum and your brother Horst, he is still with his clients. Please give our love to Jean.

Prenzlau 1.7.48

5/8.48
Dear Hans!

Many thanks for your lovely letter dated 1.6. It reached me a few days ago and made me very happy. It also made me think a lot. Today I am having a chance to write back to you. I am on my own in the house so at least it is quiet. Yes Hans, I have allowed myself to be persuaded and have returned here again. I already regretted my decision on the same day, but you will understand, some things are easier said than done. What I think about Otto, how he treats me etc. I told him not so long ago and in no uncertain terms. The result was that he has now got the hump. We only talk about the most necessary matters. It is an intolerable situation. But Hans, I don't want to bother you with my problems. I suppose a good portion of our troubles is my fault. Unfortunately, I am not able to change and adjust altogether. That's how one goes through this miserable life without any happiness. Years ago my motto was "If you want to get anywhere in life, you have to be happy". It now hangs above my bed. I slept and dreamt that life was happiness. I woke up and there was "obligation". I did not know how difficult an obligation could be. I only discovered it in the last weeks. If I did not have you, whom else could I turn to? I shall try to give my letters a different content in future. No Hans, you must not be angry about my last letter. Perhaps you misunderstood me. It is, as ever, my wish to see you once again, yes, I must see you, even if I have to wait a while. I am so busy every day that one does not realize how time flies. Working here, one has no time to think of oneself. Harvest is before us, so soon after the sugar beet work.

My health is not very good. I am still waiting for the operation. Hans, I am sure you are not serious when you say that I am thinking badly of you. I would ask you one thing please: when you write to me, would you mind leaving your surname out?*. It would look less official. But please, do as you wish. I must not forget to wish you all the best for your birthday. I am sure you will be spending it with Jean. Give her my regards, if you so wish. Now, Hänschen, I have used my last sheet of writing paper and will endeavour to get some more, so that I can answer your next letter.

I am sending you my very best wishes and greetings. Vera.

Mum and Manfred are also sending you their best wishes. Manfred is getting married on 31.7.

* every German person puts their name and address on the back of the envelope

R 6/8.48 Aschersleben , 22.7.1948

5 /8.48

My dear Hans,

548

When I got back home today at lunchtime I found your lovely letter with the pictures in it. The pictures have turned out really well. I got a right shock, because you look exactly like Uncle Erich when he was young, one could really think it was him in the pictures. Jean also looks really good, at least we now know her from the pictures.

* You my dear Hans also look very well. We don't see many here looking so well. Herr Schulz has been here now for five weeks and has lost a lot of weight, in spite of having eaten quite well. He brought back lots of things and they have been able to swap some of them, one pound of coffee, 60 pounds of rye, it helps a lot. If you have foodstuffs to swap it opens up further opportunities. This morning Mrs Lehmann, Mrs Schulz and I went out into the country to try and get a document which will allow us to glean the corn ears. It was pointless, because apparently this year, nobody from Aschersleben is allowed to go on the corn fields in the villages to pick the ears of the corn, except the villagers themselves. Well, our dream has come to an end. Here in our area there is nothing to be had. There are thousands of people anxiously waiting for an acre of land to become available. Up until now I have always diligently tried to make a living for ourselves as far as I possibly could, even though it was very hard for me at times. If they are now taking this away from us as well, and despite all our great efforts, we are still starving, this on top of all our worries and the sheer torment, then it's all done for me.

This year shall be the year of homecoming, believe me, dear Hans, if our Papa isn't to come home and we can't afford anything anymore, then it is finished for both of us, we can do nothing any more, there is nothing in this world that we have any more, nothing but worry, distress and effort. Look, you have Jean for support, and you are not alone, but we are not getting any further with our situation here, and for what reason are we enduring this ordeal any longer. Instead of getting better it gets even worse. Horst can work as much as he wants but it's leading to nothing. Sometimes we are so incredibly desperate. Sometimes I could just sit down and cry. This morning I went to the trade office, but again, always the same, there is absolutely nothing for the refugees. Not even a cape for the rain, but there are still people who can pay 200 Mark for ¾ ltr of oil and 4 Mark for an egg. The one who doesn't have the money goes home empty handed. For a while the farmers could freely sell off their surplus vegetables as long as they fulfilled their output target, but that is also forbidden now. The food for 10 days is enough for 2 meals and the other days we have to live on thin air. Dear boy, all the best for you, sending all my love and kisses from your Mum and brother Horst, please send our love to Jean.

In the following paragraph Mutti changed to writting in the Sutterlin script which was taught in German schools up until 1941

L.A.E.C. Hostel Saltby.
August 4$\underline{th}$·1948.

My dearest, darling Jean

I don't think it wise to post a letter tomorrow for I don't know what time you're leaving there on Saturday. As far as I can see now letters take 2 days that would make it Saturday. So I better keep writing and give it to you on Sunday.

Well, darling there's a lot of news. I am going to tell you. It was a shock to me, anyway. Mr Sanders has been this afternoon and as he saw me, just started smiling. I think I looked a bit bewildered when he asked if I was ready to go. Mr Chandler has told me before, but I didn't let Mr Sanders know. I just said " do I have to change again. It's almost like a prisoner changing the camps every few months." He said it wasn't that bad because it's only for 5 weeks and I'll go back here afterwards. After we had a few good jokes I asked him when I had to go and what kind of people are there. It's Redmile holiday camp and the people there are 25 girls and 25 men, Mr Goodman being the warden. He also told me that after a few girls from the office have already applied, "except Jean" and he smiled again. He was going to ask you for your application next week. Mr Sanders said you're surely going down to Redmile. We'll have a word about that on Sunday.

This morning Mr Chandler brought me my mail. A letter

from my mother and parcel. Still half sleeping I asked him where the parcel comes from. He said probably Jean because there's no senders name on. After rubbing my eyes, I found out it was from Ellen, containing two books to read for the time I was confined to bed. The titles are "Rebecca" by Daphne du Maurier and " The English Teacher" by R.K. Narayan. They're both very good books. I'll send them back as soon as I've finished with them. Anyway it's very nice of her sending the books.

Well, my darling, I'll say goodnight and God bless. I'll keep writing til Sunday so you shall have a long letter when you come. Just be careful and be my best girl. All my love and kisses- and thoughts-

Eternally yours, my love

Hans

Thursday August 5th 1948

Well, darling here I am again. Thank you ever so much for your nice long letter I got this morning. I only had 3 letters today. One from you, one from my mother and one from one of my cousins.

So you know how it is other people being envious. Tell Dora to train her boyfriend a bit better. I really didn't mind not going to Skegness, for I like to go along with you. I shall enjoy it much more.

So you found feather mattresses very comfortable. We at home always had those, but I think it's an old fashioned way. I would've loved to see you on your sea trip to the Isle of Man. Don't worry, I've seen sailors on our trip to the States hanging over board and feeding the fishes. Everybody can't stand it. It didn't affect me. Anyway you held out longer than Dora did.

Not a bad idea at all opening a hotel on our own. So it's just like an ordinary week for me and doesn't make any difference being 30 or 130 miles away. Let me tell you something. First it isn't like an ordinary week for I've to wait a fortnight and then it does make a difference you being away 130 instead of 30 miles.

You asked if I've changed my mind? You know I never will. I remember the children very well when we first went to Grantham. Oh! And you felt so embarrassed and today?!!? Time may change as you know, but as the song says " time won't change my love for you"

I have had a nice trip around today with Mr Coy and Mr Chandler. We went Melton, Waltham, Stathern, Redmile, Saltby. Mrs Betts told me she's leaving tomorrow, finishing with the War Ag. We had a look at Mr Coy's house and I must say I like it very much. 4 rooms kitchen, hot water and so on and, of course, stairs.

Well, my love I'll have to say cheerio. Day after tomorrow you'll be at home again. Be careful and look after yourself well. Be good til I see you Sunday.

All my love and kisses

Eternally yours, darling

Hans.

Friday August 6<u>th</u> 1948

I am very sorry to say it''s your last day at Llandudno. Isn't it a shame to wake me up before 8.00 in the morning and then find there's no transport to go to the doctor. Mr Coy came at lunchtime. Nothing else to do than get up early again tomorrow.

Well, darling tomorrow at this time you'll be at home again. Are you sorry to come back. The weather was awful today. Raining all day long.

I was surprised when I got my money today. Last week they deducted 13s, this week £1-6-0. And I haven't got anything from the N.H. When Mr Whiteman was here yesterday I asked him about it. He said as much as he found out about the new scheme, the War Ag deducts a certain amount and if you stay sick longer than 4 weeks you get the benefit from the National Health in the other case, however one gets the money paid back from the A.E.C. I only have to watch the certificates to be sent to the N.H. Tomorrow I shall see the doctor and ask him for the final certificate. I am really tired of messing about. One day the leg is quite alright, the other day it's not so good. He can't do anything else for me, in fact he said walking might do it good. So I'll walk.

Mr Sanders brought his wife along today. I think I've seen her before in Melton. She looks nice. The weather forecast said something about rain on Sunday. Don't you think it'll be better to come over here, because we can hardly go places when it rains. I was thinking of you all day. I thought you might be glad to come home again, are you? Anyway, I am longing for you. This last day and a half will be the worst. And then it's Sunday again.

Well, my love I'll say goodnight and God bless always. I still have to answer my mothers letter. Just be good and be careful on your way home tomorrow.

> All my love and kisses
> Eternally yours
> Hans

Saturday 7t$\underline{^h}$ Aug. 1948

I thank you very much for the postcard I received this morning. I expected a long letter but I am glad I got a postcard. It's 11.30 am now and you might be on your way home now 100 miles nearer. That'll make a lot of difference for me.

Well, darling I've been to see the doctor this morning. Cheeky fellow wouldn't give me the final certificate. He said I should rest another week. I insisted and told him I feel quite well and everything will be alright. So after all I got it.

Fancy there isn't a 1.30 bus to Grantham on Sunday. So that bus only goes to Melton? Well, it can't be helped.

I feel alright today, am able to ride a bike, so nothing to fear for tomorrow. The only thing I am thinking of is that it might be raining. The weather forecast said so. There still is a way out. I'll ring you tomorrow during the morning and if it is raining I'll get a car to pick us up at Croxton and bring us here to Saltby. We'll go to Grantham then another day when it is better.

This afternoon I shall be going to Grantham. I haven't been to the pictures for 3 weeks. Isn't that terrible? Anyway I hope there is a decent one on today. 3 of the fellows just asked me if they could go along to buy some things. I told them I am only going to the pictures and straight back.

Well, my darling I'll say cheerio for now. Be seeing you tomorrow. I would like to go to bed now and wake up tomorrow at 2.00 pm. Time goes so much quicker when sleeping. Just be good and take care of yourself on the way back home.

All my love and kisses

Eternally yours

Hans.

Saturday night, 9.30

Hello, darling I've been to Grantham and saw a good picture. "Possessed" it was called, the supporting one something about a Minstrel Show. It was also nice. After I came back I had plenty to do. I washed several shirts, socks, underwear, pressed my suit and so on. By the way before I forget to tell you, I've got something nice for you. I just fancied you would like it. Please darling, don't be curious. Everything at it's time.

I hope you've had a good journey back and are at home by now. I think Bonzo also wants to write a few lines to welcome you home. He's sitting in front of me, his legs on my knees and looks at the letter. You'll be tired tonight and so am I.

I'll say goodnight and God bless. Dream of us and be a good girl. Many kisses to you.

Sunday 1.30 pm

Good afternoon, sweetheart. After I've spoken to you I feel better. Alright, let's go to Grantham. I only hope it'll keep as it is now. We don't want rain do we? I'll get ready now so til I see you, cheerio. All my love forever

Hans.

92 Wharf St.

Aug 9th 1948.

My dearest Hans

I am home safe and sound. I arrived in Leicester about 11.0. I went straight to bed with the intention of reading your letter but susan was in my bed so I had to put the light out and read it at work today. It took about all day to get through it, but I liked reading it. Mr Sanders asked me today if I had seen my German friend, I said "yes", then he asked if I was going to Redmile. Mr Barker-Swain asked this morning when the wedding was. He said he was very surprised when he heard. He said I'll tell you what I told my daughter when the Americans were here. "There are 50001 English men that are not married and that odd one would be better". His daughter married an Englishman. I asked Mr Sanders if he had told him and he said B.S had seen my photograph in your room. I didn't know he had been in. Kathleen rang from Melton today and she said that she had heard that I was courting but it was a shot in the dark trying to find out. She said she had an idea that I was. So I told her I had been seeing you for a year. I thought she knew but she said not.

It looks as though I am definitely being a bridesmaid to Iris. She has been speaking about it today. So I will have to be. It amuses me really, there are going to be 2 other girls and they are not great friends of hers either.

I meant to tell you yesterday that Betty has got a flat, she is busy cleaning it. It is only 5 minutes away from here, that is why Susan is staying. Alice came tonight, one of her brothers is a builder and he is going to do some odd jobs for Betty. The brother that is home from America came with her. I have just been thinking (don't say what with) I had not better send another letter to Saltby. I will wait until I hear from Redmile.

Well darling I will say cheeri'O. I will be thinking of you all night

All my love

And kisses

Jean

L.A.E.C. Hostel Saltby.
August 9th 1948.

My darling Jean,

I am very sorry you won't get a letter on Tuesday, the more because I said last night you would get one. Please forgive me, but I was really busy all day long. Soon after breakfast we talked about getting the second dining hall ready as a dancehall and decided to start at once. The stage looked a mess. No electricity, nothing, all wires cut two or three times. And the worst, about 200 wires hanging from the ceiling. So I made it my job to fix the lights. By lunchtime the lights in the dining hall were burning, leaving the stage for the afternoon. You know what bright lights we had on the stage, just about 75 bulbs. And then the wires cut all over the place. I almost went mad after one hour sorting out and marking the wires. At least I fixed that and the stage lights were alright when I noticed the fuses burning out. That means a wrong connection, so I finished for today. I have to have a good rest before I start that job again.

Thanks so much for a lovely afternoon and especially for the nice tie. It's lovely. Let's go the same place next year. Have you decided whether to go to Redmile for a week or not? It would be wonderful if you could make it possible. I told you I was going to cross my fingers for rain!!

I've had two letters and a registered parcel today. One letter from Barker-Swain saying he should be glad if I could take over duties at Redmile Hostel from August 12th till Sept 18th 1948 and I shall return to my position at Saltby Hostel after Redmile closes down on Sept 18th. The second letter was from the National Health and the parcel contained my watch. Well, it isn't the same watch I sent away, but it's the same type. Looks like a new one. I don't mind at all

My leg is just the same as it was Saturday morning. I am really glad after the walk yesterday, so I know I can stand a days hard work without staying in bed the next day. I don't like to spoil "our" week at the holiday camp.

Mr Chandler told me he was talking to you in the morning and you told him we've had a nice afternoon. It really was.

Are you listening to wireless? "Kentucky Minstrels" are on the air now. It's 7.20. I took Bonzo a good run this morning. The warden wanted me at his house so I went over on a bike twice and poor Bonzo ran all the way. I don't want him to get too fat and lazy. He's had his meal and is sleeping now.

Well, my sweetheart I'll say goodnight and God bless. Be good and think of me.

All my love and kisses

    Eternally yours, darling

                Hans.

Tuesday

I was speaking to Mr Chandler earlier on this afternoon, he said he had a letter in his pocket for me. Wanted to know if he should read it to me. I said if he did that there wouldn't be any need to send it. I asked how you were after all the walking you did on Sunday, he said he thought it had affected you. I hope it didn't or else if it had you would have to take a bath chair. So Mr Bentley leaves you at the end of the week, it is a shame really especially just after his wedding, he will be able to stay at home while Olive goes out to work. He would probably make a good house wife.

Well darling, I am staying in tonight and I am going to wash the dog then wash my own hair if all goes well.

You would have laughed this morning. We have to ask if the calls that are made outside Leicestershire are private or office. Mr Sanders made a call to London and when I asked he said he wasn't going to ask after anyones health, it was official. About one hour after someone in the Labour asked for Saltby. Mr S picked up the phone and said it is official, they were not asking how Hans Klawitter was.

It is now time for me to go home so I'll say cheerio bye once again

Love
   Jean

L.A.E.C. Hostel Saltby.
August 10$\underline{th}$ 1948.

My dearest, darling Jean,
Isn't it funny none of us got a letter today. Mr Chandler posted one for you this afternoon and I guess you know.
Well, darling it's 9.15 and I just finished my work. It was a long day from 8.00 am til now. I promised to get all the lights in the hall and on the stage ready till tonight and I kept it, in fact I also fixed new cables and plugs for the wireless. I am only here another day and like to do my share. There is only one job left for tomorrow, putting an aerial up for the wireless. Then tomorrow night I like to pack my things to be ready Thursday morning.
Mr Chandler got his motor-cycle today. He came tonight asking if I would like a ride. I had a good ride around, but couldn't get more than 20 miles out of it. You know that is not the speed I like. Perhaps he thought I couldn't ride it. Did you listen to " A matter of life and death". I was listening all the time. "Miss Dangerfield" is on now. Mr and Mrs Coy were here half an hour ago. She said she saw us on Sunday in High St, called me but I didn't hear. I told her I seldom hear anything on a Sunday afternoon.
By the way, the new address for Redmile is- Redmile Adult Harvest Camp, Redmile. You can write to that address starting from tomorrow.
What did Mr Chandler say about you coming to a dance here and have supper and breakfast for 2/6s. I had a good laugh when he told me. I hope there'll be a letter for me in the morning. You'll certainly have one.
I can hardly write for I can't keep my eyes open. I am so tired today so I'll say goodnight now and God bless always. Remember always how much I love you and think of our time ahead. Just be good and think of me.

All my love and kisses
    Eternally yours
            Hans.

My darling Jean,
Thanks very much for your nice letter I got an hour ago. I thought I better answer it at once before I cool off. I am up since 5.30, did a bit of washing before breakfast to get it dried and ironed today. I like to have everything clean when I go tomorrow.

Look, darling, you shouldn't joke about about locking you up to keep you safe. I don't really know how that idea got into my head, but I daren't think of anything happening to you. It may show you how much I love you and I am only thinking about your happiness. I've asked you to marry me and therefore I am going to do for you everything I can because it's something to look forward to- our lifetime.

Well, I told you Mr Sanders was going to ask you about Redmile and so he did. I understand you now and quite agree with you in keeping your private affairs away from the War Ag, meaning the episode with Mr Barker-Swain. He certainly can tell his daughter whatever he likes, but he should not be so much interested in other peoples private affairs. If he thinks that just the odd 50001st would be better than anyone of us I hope to show him one day that he was wrong. I was really crossed when I read it. I'll make him change his mind. Didn't I tell you what I would like to do with people who try to step between us? It's a good thing you're old enough to know yourself what to do and don't care about other peoples gossip. I wish he could say something to me.

He would certainly get his answer. By the way, somebody must have told B.S. because he's never been in the kitchen as long as I am here and he's never seen my room, although he was in Saltby a few times. I hope he's said something for the first and last time.

You wondered Kathleen didn't know? She's asked me a few times how you were. I always told her I didn't know because I haven't heard from you for ages. She didn't suspect anything. Well, I have to be careful now when I see her again.

Betty will be glad now she's got a flat. I only hope we could get a nice one somewhere far away from anybody.

Look, darling, please keep writing, I've given you the new address in my last letter.

If Mr Chandler said the walk on Sunday affected me then he's wrong. I couldn't feel better. I am not due for a bath chair yet. Let's wait another 60 years. Yes Mr Bentley is leaving this weekend. He's finished his 3 month probation and he told me this morning they won't keep him. His attitude towards the men is not what it should be, he was told. He'll certainly make a good house wife.

Well, sweetheart I'll finish now. It's almost lunchtime and I haven't any of my work at the hall yet. After doing the job this afternoon I'll be able to write a few more lines. So long, darling and a kiss. Well, it's 9.30 and I've just finished. 3 shirts pressed, everything packed except the wireless and your picture on it. I leave all the other things here and just lock the door. The 18th Sept will see me back here. Mr Whiteman came tonight and he couldn't tell me what time the van is coming for me tomorrow. Maybe in the afternoon. I've had my supper in the meantime and also had a chat with Major. Surprising how time flies. It's 10.45. You'll be going to bed now I think.

So I'll say goodnight and God bless you. Remember how much I love you and dream of us. Just be good

All my love and many kisses

      Eternally yours, my sweetheart

Hans

P.S.
They're just playing " You can't be true, dear" He's wrong

92 Wharf St.
Aug 12th.

My dearest Hans

By now, you know what Redmile is like and whether you are going to like or not. I spoke to Mr Chandler 2 or 3 times today and he said you were late going to Redmile, did he go in the finish. So I have to take second place to the lights in the dining hall now do I, and I don't know yet whether or not to forgive you. What an hour to start cleaning a suit 10.15 Sunday night. Couldn't it have waited until the next day. Oh! I forgot you were too busy Monday.

You don't want to let Bonzo run at the side of the bicycle, it won't be any good for him. I had a dog that used to do that and we had to have him destroyed when he was 4 years old with a tumour. I was surprised this afternoon, someone rang up for the Labour Dept, and said is that you Jean? And guess who it was. Mr Pickering, but you probably know, as he has gone to Enderby Hostel where Mr Goodman has come from. Mr Pickering knows you were at Redmile. That is Mr Goodman junior. I do not know that one. I have been thinking, won't Sunday be your busiest time and especially this Sunday being the first one. Do you think if you can get the time off we had better find somewhere else to go. I would rather if there are going to be a lot of people there such as Mr Sanders and Whiteman or anyone else. If I don't hear from you I will be on the 1.30 bus from Leicester and catch the 2.45 bus to Redmile. I get off the bus at the corner just before the bus turns towards the cross roads to Bottesford, or if you do make arrangements to meet me off the bus in Melton, we can stay there. You have not had to take second place. But I went to Alice's and got home rather late. Betty was staying the night and I had to go straight up to bed. I didn't listen to the play.

Lucy came home tonight with me for tea. Peter, her husband is away on a course for 8 weeks and I feel rather sorry for Lucy because she hasn't got any friends here, only her in laws and she doesn't like to go there too often. So I asked her to come and we went to the pictures, to the Odeon. It was a good picture, one of the best laughs I have had for a long time. You will have to try and see it if you can when it goes to Melton, it was called "Sitting Pretty" it was very funny.

Old faithful is on my knee (Freddy). I had not ought to have him on really he makes such a mess of them, but what can I do when he looks so pitifully at me. I will have to close now. I am just about starving for something to eat. I wish you were here. I know you would get me something (or would you).

Well darling, be good and enjoy yourself at Redmile. I know you will have to work hard but it will be a change for you and a change of faces which will do you good. Don't work too hard I will see you on Sunday

    All my love and Kisses
    Love
       Jean.

P.S
At least I have made up for the missing letter
J.P.

Redmile Hostel

Hans Klawitter.

My dearest, darling Jean,
This is Redmile Harvest Camp calling Leicester. Well sweetheart, here I am and I don't think it'll take me long to settle down. Anyway the place looks terrible. I wonder how they're going to get everything ready for Saturday. Today they started to put lino into the huts then tomorrow the huts have to be furnished. In fact, I don't think it'll look bad in the end. The quarters have been painted and look smart. You'll see my little hut on Sunday. I've been speaking to Mr Sanders this afternoon and he said I could take that place for myself if I like. It was the barbers shop when it was a POW hostel. Mr Goodman, his wife and son and another woman with her little daughter arrived here in the afternoon. It's the Mr Goodman I met before at Stathern. He knew me at once. There's a big job ahead tomorrow. I am going to clean

the kitchen and make the place look like a master kitchen.

Mr Chandler told me he has been speaking to you a few times this morning. Well, darling I hope you have been writing so I shall get a letter on Saturday.

Now about Sunday. I don't know if I shall be able to meet you at Melton. If I am not there, take the Bottesford bus and I'll be here on the road waiting for you.

Mr Whiteman is here and I hope you don't mind if I give this letter along with him. It's the only possibility to get this letter away. I don't know yet how long it takes to Leicester.

Well, my love I'll say goodnight and God bless. Just be good and think of me.

All my love and kisses

Eternally yours

Hans.

92 Wharf St.

August 16th.

My dearest Hans

O well, here I am and aren't you lucky having a letter Tuesday morning. I arrived home at 10.50 the bus was earlier than it usually is when it gets into Leicester so I would be in bed by the time you arrived at the hostel. By the way did you go to sleep on the bus?

When I arrived home my mother said Alice had been round about 8.00. Her brother (the one that is home from America) has some coloured snaps that have to be shown like a film and he was going to show them. I will have to ring Alice and maybe I will go one night in the week.

I know there was something I had to tell you. I saw Horst on Saturday afternoon, did I tell you that he had gone to Knightthorpe hostel Loughborough. He seemed surprised to know that I knew he had gone there.

Mr Sanders said today that there is a lorry that leaves Charles St every Saturday afternoon and stays about one hour then comes back, and if I would like to go and have my tea there

I could. It won't be this Saturday, because we are both going to Melton. Aren't we!!!
By the way, I stayed on the line after Mr Goodman had been through to the Labour Dept, but we had been cut off.
Well darling be good
　　All my love
　　And kisses
　　　Jean

Redmile warden and kitchen staff

Hans Klawitter,
L.A.E.C Hostel Redmile,
Notts.
August, 10<u>th</u> 1948.

My dearest, darling Jean,
Thanks ever so much for your lovely long letter I received this morning. It only was two days late, but in any case better than no letter. Time is 9.30 and that makes my 16 hours full. I don't feel too well tonight, but everything will be al-

right after a few hours sleep.

I was waiting for you to come back on the phone, but the operator said the line had been cleared.

Did you get home alright last night darling. I only hope you slept already by the time I got home. It wasn't later than 11.45. It only made 7 ½ hours sleep, in fact I felt fresh when I got up. Anyway it'll be a bit earlier tonight.

Unfortunately I don't know yet about Saturday, but I'll let you know in time. I think I could go off because Mr Goodman will be here. There's only the tea and supper to do for the new people coming in the afternoon.

I think I've seen parts of that picture "Sitting Pretty" at Grantham when I went from Saltby the last time.

When I go down to my hut now I'll almost walk on my knees.

Well, darling, don't you worry about me working too hard. I'll be alright. It is a change for me, even in getting up 3 hrs earlier.

I hope you don't mind this short letter in reply to your 6 pages, but believe me I am dead tired. Goodnight and God bless. Just be good and think of me.

All my love and kisses
  Eternally yours
          Hans

                    L.A.E.C Hostel Redmile.
                    August, 18th·1948.

My dearest, darling Jean

Thanks ever so much for your very nice letter I received today. I only hope you aren't mad with me for not writing yesterday. I was so tired and went to bed at 10.00 after finishing my work. But don't worry it won't get me down. That takes a lot. Do you know why your letters always take 2 days? They go to Melton Mowbray (according to the address) from there to Nott. because it's Notts. And from there I get them.

It is very nice of Mr Sanders to offer you a trip every week. I'm sorry I can't tell you anything yet about Saturday. You know the new people are coming in the afternoon.

Mr Goodman asked back to the exchange after the call, however, they told him the line was cleared.

It's 11.40pm now. You'll wonder why I'm still up so late. Mr G wanted to go to Saltby so he asked me to go along with him. Mr Chandler was very pleased to see us. We had a nice cup of tea and came back 20 minutes ago. At first I didn't want to go, because I wanted to write to you. The trouble was he didn't know his way so I had to go.

Albert (the new fellow helping me) is very good and we really get on nicely. It's a bit easier for me now, but I can't cut the 16 hours down. It takes a lot of doing.

Well, darling I'll have to write more tomorrow morning after 4 hours sleep. The warden just switched the light off. I wish you a good night and give you all my love and kisses. Yours Hans.

Redmile kitchen

92 Wharf St.

Aug 19th.

My dearest Hans

Thank you very much for your letter (dated 16th), the only one I have had this week. I hoped there would be one this morning, but no. So I guessed you must be very busy.

I hope you will be able to get the half day on Saturday and will meet me in Melton. There is a bus at 2.00 from Leicester arrives M.M at 2.45. Then if I come on Saturday I can get some of my odd jobs done on Sunday. I have just asked one of the girls at Melton what was on the pictures, but she could only tell me what was on at one of them, "Paula" and I have seen that. I will try and find out what is on the other one. We will have to go to Nottingham whilst you're at Redmile, that is if you have time. I went to the pictures Monday night to see "The unfinished dance", the story wasn't so hot but the dancing was very good. Tuesday night I went round to see Dora. Wednesday I took the dog to the vet again. I had to be there at 6.00. I had to go home get the dog and run all the way there to be in time. I have to go again Friday. From the vet we went to my auntie's at Birstall. Alice is coming round tonight. That is all I have been doing this week, not very exciting.

Mr Sanders has been in with the photographs of the Harvest Camp, they are very good. He showed them to Lucy and the others. I wondered what he would say when he got to the one with you, fortunately he never said a word. Or if he had my life would not have been worth living for the next few days. I have just been to see Connie. I've been there ½ hour talking. I would have been there still if it hadn't been for Iris. She isn't with me this week, that is why I am able to write to you at the office. Her boyfriend is in this country, he is in London at the moment, he is staying there for a few days. The wedding is on the 11th September. I don't know yet what time. I am hoping it will be in the afternoon. I don't want to have a day off. I am going to a wedding on Aug 28th, that's at 11.30 Sat. I am going to try to get the hour off otherwise I have to have the day off and I don't think it is worth it. I hope I get a letter in the morning. In fact I had better have a letter in the morning otherwise- you can guess what I will do!!!

Well darling I will say cheeri'O I want to post this at lunchtime to make sure you get it on Friday.

All my love

Jean

P.S.

Not one of the photographs I took whilst I was away came out so I don't know what the others will be like. Do you know anything about cameras?

L.A.E.C Hostel Redmile.

August, 20<u>th</u> 1948.

My dearest, darling Jean

Well I just finished work. There's a farewell party in the village pub tonight. I was asked lots of times to go, but I shan't go. I really couldn't care less. You know I don't drink anything.

As I told you I was going to ask Mr Sanders about the lorries. When Mr Goodman brought my money Sanders had left. Anyway the warden knew the time so I'll let you know first thing tomorrow.

We had fried fish and steamed pudding tonight. About 10 people came and told me it was the nicest dinner they'd had for a month. I have never seen a steamed pudding as it was yesterday. Even at Stathern I never got it done like yesterday.

Well sweetheart it's 6.30 a.m. now, another half an hour and the people will be here for breakfast. After all I went to the party last night. I've had a bath after 9 o'clock and at 9.30 Mr Goodman asked me to go with him in the car. So I changed and we left at 9.50. A good thing for the pub closed at 10.00.

We just had a look round, I drank a lemonade (everybody was laughing about it) and arrived back at 10.10. It was half past eleven when I went to bed. I can hardly keep my eyes open this morning

People at Redmile Holiday Camp

      92 Wharf St.
      Aug 22nd 1948.
My dearest Hans
I hope you arrived back at Redmile safe and sound. The bus got into Leicester 10.35 I was at home 10.45. I took the dog a walk, sat by the fire for a few minutes to warm my feet, and then I went to bed, got upstairs and discovered my mother wasn't in. I had to go and unlock the door. I saw she was in next door so I went back to bed. When she came in she didn't think I was home she was expecting me to ring through to say I had missed the bus. I took the dog to the vet this morning, he said the dog was getting on very well and

that I would not have to take him much more. I have to take him on Tuesday again. He thought that the mange was bred in him, that means it is likely to break out in the spring! He is more trouble than a baby. From the vets I walked over the fields (one field) to my Auntie's at Birstall. Well darling, how are things going at the hostel today? I hope they are going on as if there had not been anything put in the paper. I hope you don't mind me telling you what I think. I know it isn't anything to do with me, but don't you think it's really the best thing to do? You don't have to work 16 hours a day unless you get paid for them, then you can't grumble about it if they do pay you. Why don't you ask Connie if she is supposed to supervise the kitchen, if she is, make sure she does her share. If she won't you can complain. After all it's only for 4 weeks and that will soon go.

I am on my own this afternoon, my mother has gone to Rothley with my aunt and uncle from next door so as you see I have not any neighbours, but I have the cat and 2 dogs to keep me company, but they won't argue. Do you think you will be able to put up with me for a lifetime? That is if you can stand it that long. Now you will say I am talking nonsense, but don't say you were not warned, that I argue and nag. Well darling I will say cheeri'O, I wonder if I will get a long letter or just one sheet!!! I have got to take it to Campbell St Post Office. The box down the street will have been emptied by now.

Well darling be good. I will see you next Sunday.

All my love

And kisses

Jean

P.S. Have you a soap coupon you don't want

Hans and Jean at Redmile

Aschersleben 1.8.1948.
22/8.48

My dear Hans,
Many thanks for your letter from 25.7.48, it only took 6 days
to arrive here. We were not expecting you to be ill and we
wish you better soon. We still have not received the letter
in which you told us about being ill. We are very glad that
it all turned out well in the end and that you did not need
an operation. But please dear Hans, do not play football anymore, because with that you put too much pressure on your
leg. I am quite relieved that Jean can come and look after you
from time to time and I can imagine that she was also very
worried about you. And as you also now have a radio there,
at least you are entertained and time goes by quicker. We've
been to collect potatoes twice now, and the outcome was
only minimal, I just hope that it is better next week. These

incredibly long trips, are aleays a real killer in this awful heat. We went to the countryside twice and got green beans and 25kg potatoes, each time it was a 3 hour walk. I put the beans in brine so that we have some vegetables for the winter. This morning I queued from 5-8 AM for tinned meat but from 100 grams only 60 grams this time, it's not worth the long wait. Tomorrow we are off to the fields again. If only we were at least allowed to go to the villages. Here we cannot get anything. Horst went for a swim, he was working until 2PM today and next Sunday he has to come to the fields with us. He wonders why he doesn't receive any letters from you anymore. Are you still upset with him? Now, my dear Hans, please recover quickly, sending all my love and kisses from your Mum, who thinks of you all the time and your brother Horst. Hope to see you soon in good health. Please send our love to Jean.

L.A.E.C Hostel Redmile.
August, 23rd 1948.

My dearest, darling, Jean
Thanks very much for your letter. I hope you got mine this morning. I gave it along last night to be posted in Leicester. You at least got home a bit earlier.
So your mother thought you'd missed the bus. I bet she wouldn't mind if you stayed away for a night.
Everything is going alright here. Maybe you heard Barker-Swain talking to Mr Goodman this morning. B-S played hell because they didn't put the cutlery on the tables when the people arrived on Saturday afternoon, as I did last week. Mr Sanders must have seen me in Melton because he told Mr G I was away and things weren't done properly. You know I don't mind you telling me what you think and I always take an advice. Anyway I will wait until Friday and see what's going on about overtime. It's the first weeks pay from here. I know I can't grumble if they pay it and I never will. As I told

you the only thing I don't like is other people making themselves a nice day and I have to do the work for them. I don't want to complain and do anybody a bad turn, but iI'll tell them straight what I think when I find out I am in the right. I like it down here, but in fact take it easier after 4 weeks back in Saltby. If the weather keeps as it is now I am afraid they'll keep the hostel open a few more weeks. In my opinion the work can't be finished in just 5 weeks.

I am sure I'll be able to put up for a lifetime and I can stand it even longer than that. Love will be the bridge and you know I love you more than my own life. If only the time would come soon. I am so much longing for it. If only there would be a possibility to find a flat or anything that would suit us. I don't know why you don't like to stay near Leicester. Anyway that's up to you.

I'll put two soap coupons in for you. I really don't need them because I have 6 left.

Well sweetheart time is getting on and I am pretty tired. I think everything will be alright for Sunday.

Goodnight and God bless. Just be good and think of me.

All my love and a goodnight kiss

       Eternally yours

           Hans.

                L.A.E.C Hostel Redmile.

                August, 24$\underline{th}$ 1948.

My dearest, darling Jean,

Shall I get a letter tomorrow morning? That's the main question at present. I hope so and cross both my fingers. Well, darling, how are you today? I am fine except the cold I've coming. Does Asprin stop it? I just took 2 and go to bed straight the way.

Mr Goodman asked me today if I want some of the original photos taken for the paper. I ordered one of the kitchen group, without saying anything or rubbing it in. I really had to control myself a few times not to start again, but that's a promise.

Connie tried this afternoon to make me change my mind. She asked me to take one of the girls, the teacher from Leicester, out for a walk to show her what I could do. Both she and Mrs Bailey were rather disappointed when I said no and never. What do they know about me and you. Be sure darling, I never touch anybody else. I love you too much to disappoint you. Real love and faithfulness belong together. There's no girl in the world who is more attractive and lovelier than you. We'll be happy together all our lifetime and you know how much it means to me to make you happy. Well, my sweetheart, it's 9.45 and I'll go to bed to be fresh in the morning. I'll be thinking and dreaming of you all night. God bless and as many kisses as stars in the sky. Love
Hans

Wednesday 25th

Well, darling another day is over. Connie and her husband went to Leicester this afternoon and , of course Mr Sanders came out. I've had a talk with him and as I told you last Saturday, asked him who is in charge of the kitchen. He asked straight away if I've had any interference in the kitchen and I told him that I only wanted to be sure in case of trouble. Anyway he said he's got me down here as cook and that means I am in charge of the cooking. I shall keep my temper, but in spite hope she will not say anything. Well' darling I have one request. Could you possibly try and get some cigarettes for me for the weekend? I smoked the last one yesterday and can't get any around here. Not even in Melton. But please don't buy Turkish Cigarettes.

The warden is going to let me know about Sunday afternoon. In any case I'll ring you on Saturday morning.

There was a game of football tonight. One of the fellows saw me playing at Stathern Hostel so he came and asked. Of course I refused. I am glad to have a rest at night.

Before I forget. I asked Mr Sanders about overtime pay. He said yes as soon as the warden puts the overtime on the timesheet. I thought everything was alright, but asked the warden if he's put it on the timesheet. His answer was "no". He said he was waiting for official information. So I found nothing was done. I shall probably ring Mr S tomorrow and ask him to arrange with Finance Dept. Otherwise I shall loose about £3.

Well, my sweetheart I'll go to bed now. It's a bit earlier to-night.

Goodnight and God bless

All my love and kisses

Yours forever

Hans.

92 Wharf St.

Aug 26th.

My dearest Hans

I'm sorry you have only 2 letters (including this) this week, but I have only had 2 so far and I will get one Saturday. So you have not been any better off than me. I told you this morning I was writing to you at the office, but I didn't get around to it. Iris has come back. I can't write and talk to her at the same time. I am writing it now 10.30. I will post it in the morning. I hope you get it on Saturday. I was going to write last night but I arrived home too late. I went round to Dora for tea. Her mother and father have gone on holiday. One of her sisters is looking after them, she has a baby about 3 months old, Dora has been round here 2 or 3 times to show him to me and I have been out. So last night I went especially to see it. You want to know why I want to get away from Leicester and If possible England. It is hard to explain to anyone that isn't British, then if you were British I wouldn't have to explain. When anyone British marries a foreigner people always look on them as if they have done something wrong. It does not matter what nationality it is. With Iris marrying a French-man I have seen it. Only this afternoon someone came in and they were talking about Iris and said they hope I would not marry a foreigner. When they asked if I would, I said "yes, if I thought I would be happy". And then there are lots of other things people say. I know it sounds silly to take any notice of that, but I think in time it would get me down. There is another reason why I would not live at home. I would want to be independent of everybody. I wish we could find a way and I believe in time we will, but not until things are more settled and you know what you are going to do. I hope you can understand what I have tried to say. I love you very much and could put up with hardship, but not where everyone is ready to find fault, and say I told you so. And that is what it would be here. Anyway darling it need not worry us too much we'll find a way.

Well darling about Sunday. I will catch the 2.0 bus to Nottingham and meet you near that café at the bus station.

Bye for now. No English Irishman or Scotsman could be better than you.

All my love &

        Kisses

        Jean

Redmile Hostel

L.A.E.C Hostel Redmile.

Bottesford/Notts.

My dearest, darling Jean,
Thank you very very much for a lovely weekend. Shall I start moaning? The only thing I didn't like was that I had to cook all morning. Well, my darling when I get back to Saltby I'll take a weekend off and then lets go to Skegness and spend a nice day there. I've told you how much I like swimming.
You'll be at home by now. Time 9.30. It was the best for you, darling to go in the car. More comfortable and it made you earlier at home. Mr Barker-Swain left at 8.15. He asked me if I got home alright last night and if you arrived home safe. He thought you'd gone with Mr Whiteman last night, because he said he thinks Mr Whiteman got lost. He hasn't reported to him today.
About this afternoon, I told you I understand you very well and I know you're right. Look darling you better stop me. I don't want to hurt you. I also understand why you don't want to live anywhere around here. I think it would have been the same in Germany. Of course independence is the first thing one really wants. To manage everything ourselves without taking anybody's advice. You know how much I like gossip. Anyway darling don't lose hope, everything will be alright in time.
Well, my love, I want you to get this letter tomorrow (Tuesday) morning. Otherwise I could've written a few more lines in the morning. So that'll make another one to be posted Tuesday morning. I'll say goodnight and God bless always. I'll be dreaming of you
All my love and kisses
        Eternally yours
                Hans.

Jean at Skegness

My dearest, darling Jean,
Well sweetheart today I am able to finish a bit earlier. It's a matter of having a good start in the morning. I almost fell asleep on the bus and went to bed at 11.00. This morning Albert had to call me twice before I got up.

Thanks very much for the lovely afternoon. I really enjoyed everything. It only was a shame the weather was so bad. But it didn't matter did it. I am sorry I upset you yesterday, but we shouldn't quarrel about other people. I was far enough this morning to say something when I remembered the promise I made to you. So I kept quiet. You know I am not the one looking for trouble and you probably know that. Other people should do the same.

Albert has the afternoon off so we had the washing up and sandwiches to ourselves. Connie asked me the other day if I am a slave driver, because I always start a job early enough to get it done in time. I don't like to leave things to the last minute and then do it in a hurry. She, however, likes an hours rest after lunch and I start with the packed lunch straight away.

The new people didn't give me such a nice impression than the last lot. Anyway it's only for a week. When the other fellows left Leicester yesterday they were asked by Mr Sanders if there's any complaints. None at all, was the answer. That means the meals were alright.

I've told Mr Goodman about taking the next Sunday afternoon off. They're going away on Saturday so I'll be able to go to Nottingham. I only hope the weather will be a bit better than it was yesterday.

Most of the people went away for the afternoon so there's not much to do for tea. I'll lay down for a couple of hours after I've finished it. I feel very tired.

Did you get home well last night? As I told you, how nice would it be if we could say "let's go home now". But that time will come. Everything will be alright and we'll be very happy. I could always tell you, darling, how much I love you and I always like to hear you telling me. Well, sweetheart, it's 4.30 now. So be good and think of me. (Nothing about 16 hours a day). My thoughts will be with you all the time.

Do I get a letter in the morning?

All my love and kisses

     Eternally yours, my love,

               Hans.

R 8/9.48

Aschersleben, 8.8.1948
27.8

     My dear Hans,

Thank you very much for your lovely letter from July 30, 1948 and we are delighted that you are feeling better again. Please be careful with your leg, you ought to look after it. You should never overexert it. I hope the splinters are not going to move. I have been collecting potatoes since Monday; we had received a coupon for collecting grains at a village far off the train line. But it is such an ordeal to walk those long distances and the farmers don't leave much behind, despite the fact that they have such a plentiful harvest. Instead of 15 litres of wheat per Morgen* they are threshing 21-25 litres per Morgen. This morning Horst joined us too, but we had to turn around again as it was raining so heavily.I hope the weather will be better tomorrow and the day after tomorrow, Horst has taken 2 days unpaid holiday in order to help. You won't believe how many people are out there, everybody is afraid of starvation. We have already been drenched for 2 days because of the constant downpours, if only we would be rewarded with a yield. I only get about 3-4 hours sleep per night at the moment, as I still have to prepare the food for the next day when I get home. Mr Schulz joined our search for food yesterday and he said that he would have stayed in England if he hadn't had his family here, as the food was so much better there. Have you already been at the seaside? Dear Hans, I am not as worried about you as before, at the end of the day you are old enough to know what you want and can do. Lots of parcels are arriving from there at the moment, but who knows how long they have been on the way. There is a lot of wind now and so the ears of the grains will be dry tomorrow. Today the rainy day was a welcome day of rest, I am so incredibly tired, but I did some laundry. My feet are so sore from the long walks, and my shoes and stockings are ripped to pieces. Now my dear Hans, we wish you a very speedy recovery. I am sending you all my love and kisses from your Mum and your brother Horst. Please send our love to Jean. Do you think it is possible to put some sweetener into one of the letters?

*1/4 of a hectare or 2/3 of an acre
        92 Wharf St.
        Aug 30th.

My dearest Hans

Thank you very much for a lovely weekend. I arrived home about 9.0. After going nearly to Nottingham I think he took a wrong turn. Mr Goodman told him to go to Walton but we turned to go to Barlestone. It seemed a much farther way than it did when I came. I got home and I could not get in. My mother had taken the back door key with her and the bolt was on the front door. So I went round to see Betty had a drink then came back, my mother had just arrived. Did Barker-Swain say anything about the visitor, and do you know whether or not he saw me? I forgot to tell you, but you know the first Sunday I went to Redmile and Whiteman came. He said to me a few days later "you're proud when you're out". So thinking he'd not seen me at Redmile, I asked "why" then he told me he was at the camp and stayed till 9.0. I should think Mr Goodman must have said something to him.

Well darling, how is everything going down today. Any better in the kitchen than yesterday. I hope it is. I wish you did not have to work so hard in that kitchen it won't do you any good.

Tuesday Afternoon

About next weekend, what do you want to do, go to Nottingham or anything else.

Barker-Swain has been pulling my leg ,he said you were very upset because you had not heard from me today, and that you were dressed up because Mr Sanders had told you he was bringing me out to Redmile this morning.

Well darling I will say cheerio. It is time for me to go. I will write a long letter in the week.

All my love

Jean

.

Muriel, Jean and Mary at Bottesford Pub

L.A.E.C. Hostel Redmile.
August 30th 1948.

My dearest ,darling Jean,
I said in my last letter I was going to write a few lines today
so I better start before I fall asleep. It's 9.30 and I just left
the kitchen. Albert took the afternoon off so I had his cook
to do as well. I really feel rotten tonight. Well, I'll go to bed
early and everything will be alright in the morning. By the
way if you're able to get some cigarettes for me, please bring
them along next weekend. I just finished the last one and
Albert didn't get any in Nottingham. And if possible bring
the photo's along as well. I hope you'll get them back til Saturday. I am drinking again but only lemonade. One of the

men went and got a few bottles for me.

Well, sweetheart I better close now. I can't keep my eyes open any longer. I never before was as tired as I am now. So goodnight and God bless you. All my love and kisses to you.

Tuesday 31.8.48.

Hello darling, and how are you today? I've just finished (8.45) and think about going to bed straight away. The staff from Leicester office was here with somebody from the Ministry. Barker-Swain's first question was "How is Jean today". I said I can't afford a call every morning. He only smiled. I bet he still thinks I ring you every morning at 9 o'clock. Anyway it doesn't matter what he thinks. By the way, Mr and Mrs Goodman and also Mrs Bailey are leaving the hostel day after tomorrow, Thursday! Mr Sanders told them today. I'll be all on my own then except Mr Sanders looking after the hostel. I don't think he will be here very often. You know he used to be in charge of Saltby Labour Office when Mr Edwards was on holidays. I haven't seen him once within a fortnight. Connie wants to have a farewell party tomorrow night. She asked me if I was glad she was leaving. To a question there has to be an answer, so I said yes. As far as I know there'll be less people in next week. Just about 26. I think we'll manage alright. Her work wasn't much anyway.

Isn't the weather terrible tonight. It started to rain at 5.00 p.m. and hasn't stopped for a minute.

Do you have anything in mind about the next weekend? I'll let you know in time if anything unexpected turns up.

Some of the girls wanted me to go down to the village tonight, but not 10 horses would get me out of here. There is only one I am going out with- you. I wouldn't even go for 5 gin. I've told you lots of times how much I love you and that I would never leave you. Believe me I mean it. I am only thinking of you all the time.

Well, my sweetheart, I'll say goodnight and wish you pleasant dreams.

All my love and kisses

Eternally yours
             Hans.

   92 Wharf St.
   Sept 1st 1948.
My dearest Darling Hans
I am so very sorry you did not get a letter until Thursday.
Are you still annoyed? Mr Goodman said today you had not
heard from me and that you were mad with me. It was not
that I did not want to write, but I have not had time until the
evening then I have been too tired to bother and now that
Iris is back with me it is impossible to write to you. Anyway
am I forgiven!!!! I was going to do just a lot of writing tonight.
I started to write to Muriel (my friend in London) she used to
be very friendly with Connie, they went on holiday together
once. I have told her I have seen Connie. She will be surprised
to hear what she is doing. I had a letter from Bernhard today.
I had not heard from him for 2 months. I was beginning to
wonder what had happened to him. I have another letter to
answer. I have not written to that other fellow yet. I will
have to make a special effort to do that. I haven't written to
the War Office yet and I don't want to if I can help, they can't
help Willi now.
I went to the pictures on Monday, one was the "Bride goes
wild" and the other was a french film with English speaking. It was about the German occupation in France. Oh! You
should have seen it. I have not taken the films in yet. I have
been meaning to take them but you know me- I forgot. Anyway I will take them tomorrow, but I don't think I will have
them for Sunday. I have bathed the dog tonight, he looks
very nice now. I wish he could get a bit fatter and that his
hair would grow. What are we going to do Sunday?
Well darling I am tired again, so goodnight my love and God
bless you
      Love all of it
      Jean

Redmile Hostel

My dearest, darling Jean,
No letter this morning! It almost looks as if there'll be only one this week. What's the matter darling. Are you too busy or sick? I only hope it isn't the latter that keeps you in silence. Anyway it's only another night to wait til the mailman comes again.

Well only half a day till Connie leaves the place. She started being funny again this afternoon and nothing but the promise made me keep my temper. If only she would notice how ridiculous her talking is. I've told her off in a rather gentle tone. I'm sure now there's always trouble where she has anything to say. Anyway I'll pretend a headache tonight because of that farewell party. I don't want to see more of her than necessary.

I really can't help wondering what's the matter with you for not writing. I don't know you like this. I'll be glad if there is one for me.

Please, let me know about the weekend. I'll ring you up before that anyway.

Well, my sweetheart, I hope you don't mind this short letter. I'll go to bed straight away. Be thinking of you all the time. Just be good.

All my love and a goodnight kiss

    Eternally yours

        Hans.

                L.A.E.C. Hostel Redmile.

                Sept 2$\underline{^{nd}}$1948.

My dearest, darling Jean,

Well, Mr & Mrs Goodman have left this afternoon and it is quieter now. But not for long because Mrs Scott (her husband at Melton- Office) is taking over on Saturday night. She's bringing her 2 children along. Til then I have to manage myself. Mr Sanders is coming out every night. Do you know what Mrs Scott is like. Anyway, I've made a few things clear with Mr Sanders tonight. I've asked him if Connie had said anything and his answer was "quite a lot". I bet she tried to do us a bad turn, but S knows me long enough. She was furious yesterday because I refused to give any of those Swiss-rolls. I couldn't care less. She said one can notice if you have never before cooked for women and so don't know they like such things. The trouble is in the last hostel the cooks really waited on her. If she thought I would do the same, she found out in time that she was wrong. I did my duties as a cook but not as a waiter. Anyway she didn't get what she wanted. It must have looked strange to her that I let the people come first and then the staff.

I asked Mr Sanders to let me see this weeks time-sheet and wasn't much surprised to find time put down from 6.00 a.m. to 6.30pm. I was allowed to do all the work on my own without pay. Altogether I was 12 hrs. overtime short. S told me to make another timesheet out with the right times on it and he'll sign for it. It would've been the same on the first weeks sheets. Maybe he couldn't see me getting more money than he gets. Anyway I am more than glad they've left.

It was quite alright for you, darling to go home on that car. It made you earlier. It was a shame you couldn't get in at home. So your mother expected you later. I didn't hear Barker-Swaine saying anything about the visitors. Anyway he didn't see you and I don't think Mr Whiteman saw you the first Sunday.

I'll let you know on Saturday morning about Sunday. I am not quite sure about it yet.

B-Swaine is a ~~cheeky~~ devil to pull your leg. I never said anything to him. I wasn't dressed up, but working when he came.

Well, sweetheart, I'll say goodnight now. It's 11.00 o'clock and I've to go to bed early as you told me. Be good and think of me. God bless you.

> All my love and kisses
> > Eternally yours
> > > Hans.

L.A.E.C. Hostel Redmile.
Sept 5th1948.

My dearest, darling Jean,

It was a rather quick farewell, wasn't it? Did he go back Melton way? If he did he won't get a cup of tea when he comes again. I wonder what he told you this time.

I don't know what I shall do now. It upset all my plans. I think I better stop here. That poor fellow will be waiting for me in Melton. It doesn't matter. I'll have to find an excuse, that's all.

Do you think I'll get a few more letters next week? There'll be one to come tomorrow morning. That's something.

I thank you very much for the nice couple of hours we're able to spend together. If it only wouldn't be such a short time. I think we better go to Nottingham next where there's no B-S crossing our way, so we can be together a bit longer. I know how awful it is to come this way down here. It'll be lots better when I go back to Saltby in a fortnight. I shall have more time of my own.

Think of anything we can do together when I get my holidays. Isn't there a possibility to go somewhere, just the two of us. I am quite sure you would enjoy it as well as I would. Think it over, darling and tell me any advices.

Well, it's 8.20 now and you'll probably be half the way home. I feel pretty tired tonight so there's only one thing to do: to bed. I'll go down to the village now and post the letter for you to get on Tuesday. Just be good and don't take any notice when he talks nonsense.

Goodnight and God bless you

Love all of it

Eternally yours

   Hans.

  92 Wharf St.

  Sept 6th 1948.

My dearest Hans.

I arrived home safe after hearing B-S's life story, but I would rather have someone that will talk. He went Six Hills way, as you know, then through to the Loughboro Rd and dropped me at Frears Bakery (that is near the Abbey Park). I was home at 9.00. I took the dog a walk and called to see Betty. I stayed for supper though I was not very hungry. I asked B-Swain how he got to know I was there. He said he asked who was there, she said the cook with a blonde, then her daughter said it was a blonde. So B.S said he would have to go to see as he had an interest in this. He never even lectured me either, Mr Scott came in this afternoon and said "you never came to see me". So I said you knew where I was.

This is only going to be a short letter, it is so you will have at least 2 letters in the week.

Well darling I will say cheerio and write later on in the week

All my love

Jean

L.A.E.C. Hostel Redmile.

Sept 5th 1948.

My dearest, darling Jean,

Thanks very much for your letter I received today. I am glad to hear you arrived home alright and earlier than usually. B.-S. could've dropped you at Melton Rd at least. So you've had to walk rather a long way.

Isn't he cheeky, being interested in it. Perhaps he thought to find me there with someone else and tell you then how right he was. But in that case he certainly doesn't know me and he has had it.

Mr Scott just told me he's asked you about getting films for me. You can make sure how the snaps turned out before you get more of Mr Brown. I am quite sure they are alright.

Well, sweetheart, don't you think we'd better go to Nottinham next Sunday? I would like to see a picture for a change. Will it be possible for you to be there at 3.00pm? I would take the 2 o'clock from here.

It's 9.30 now and Mr Scott's just finished his dinner. That's all I was waiting for and now I'll go to bed.

Well, my love, I'll say goodnight now and God bless. Think of me and be a good girl.

All my love and kisses

Eternally yours

Hans.

L.A.E.C. Hostel Redmile.

Sept 6th 1948.

My dearest, darling Jean,

I was rather disappointed there was no letter for me this

morning. When did you post it? It must have been Friday, and it should've arrived here today at least.

How are you, today, darling. Mr Scott said this morning he's going to tell you off for being here and not even saying "hello" to him. I've told him we're in a terrible hurry for the 7.30 bus. He took that for an excuse anyway.

A van from the store came this afternoon and brought kitchen cloth (white) for Albert and I, but it really is ridiculous only one suit each. What are we going to do when this one is dirty? I am not going to wash it myself. The laundry can do that and the War Ag may pay for it. Anyway Michel took a snap of us tonight before the cloth gets dirty!!!

After all I was playing table tennis with the same fellows until 11.00 last night. Not tonight for I felt very tired when I got up this morning. It's only 9.10 now, but I'll be in bed in a few minutes.

Did you write today. I hope to hear from you tomorrow. By the way I've told Mr Scott to ask Mr Sanders to get a couple of films for me off Mr Brown and bring them along when he comes this weekend.

Well, my sweetheart I'll say goodnight and God bless. I'll be thinking of you all the time.

> Lots of love and kisses
> Eternally yours
> > Hans.

> 92 Wharf St.
> Sept 7th 1948.

My dearest Darling Hans

Thank you very much for your letter. You didn't sound very pleased that I came back by car. Would you rather I had gone back by bus (which would have meant me getting home at 11.00), and would you have liked me to have stood kissing you farewell for 5 minutes in front of Barker-Swain? Because if you would just let me know another time and I will see what I can do. You know how I like a crowd watching. One other thing, we spent 4 hours together (came 3.30 and left 7.30) not a couple. I fetched the photograph today, on the first film not one came out, the other one 4 turned out. The gentleman that took the film at Boots said he would have a look at the camera if I took it in. So when you have used this film let me have the camera to take in. Mr Scott said you want a film and asked me to let someone have it that was going either to Melton or Redmile. I won't bother now. Until after it has been fixed.

Now darling about your holiday. I really wish we could go away somewhere for a week together, but I have tried to explain many times that I don't think my mother would like it. Do you have to take it off all at once, or can you have it off in odd days. Then I could have a couple of days off this month then 3 days in December. Then maybe by that time I would have enough courage to say I was going away and would not have to ask, but at the moment I am a coward. I could neither ask or go, but it is your holiday you must please yourself. I wish you could go to the sea for a week, it would do you good. Well darling do you still understand me. It is a wonder you still say that you love me after the way I treat you. Do you still ! ! ! I Well my love I will have to say goodnight. I am writing this to you in bed. The dog has been crying to come upstairs. Sunday and Monday he came up and slept on the bed. I think he gets a bit lonely downstairs, but tonight he has to stay down and I am not going to let him come up. I am very hard, don't you think?

Well darling I may add a few lines tomorrow or I may not, but in any case I send all my love and kisses

Jean

____.

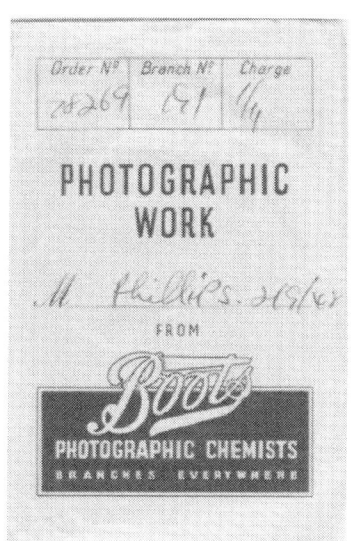

4.45 Wednesday afternoon

I was going to start this before but I have not had time you know how busy I am !!!

Well darling thank you very much for your letter. I was surprised to know that you have not had that letter yet I posted it Thursday lunch time so if you have not received it now you have had it.

It was Dora's birthday yesterday. I rung her to wish her many happy returns of the day. She is still going with her boyfriend, she asked if I was still friendly with you, funny asking a question like that. I did not ask her she told me I wasn't not being nosey either. It is time for me to powder my nose so cheerio

All my love

Jean

P.S.

I am staying in I'm going to wash my hair tonight

R 8/9.48   Aschersleben, 15.8.1948

7/9.48

My dear Hans,

Unfortunately we have not received a letter from you this week; I hope you are not ill. We now have had a few days of rain and so we could not go out and collect food and from today on it is forbidden, despite the fact that there is so much left over after the harvest. It is better that it is rotting instead of allowing the starving population to pick it up from the floor. In comparison to last year's yield, we only have a fraction this year; I don't know how we will be able to survive the winter. But I can't change it, I have done everything in my power, it was hard enough and in the meantime my energy is fading. I have lost a lot of weight again from the long walks, Horst could join for 2 days, but he couldn't get more time off. Last year I had been able to collect 8 pounds of poppy seed and so we had some additional fat, but that's not happening this year. We now have to do 2 days of reconstruction work in order to get coupons again to be allowed to pick potatoes and carrots, but that's not going to be a big success as there are so many people flooding the fields. Uncle Erich is sending his love. They are very busy with the harvest and they have to cut everything with the scythe as they don't have a reaper. Recently I found the packing paper, which you used to wrap Horst's Birthday shirt, and inside I found the letter you and Jean wrote to Horst for his birthday, we had not found it at the time! Horst was really delighted and will write himself. I am sure you were upset that he had not responded to your letter. If we hadn't found it through sheer coincidence, we would have never known. Dear Hans, could you please put some sweetener in the letter, because sugar is so very scarce, and occasionally Horst is able to get some fruit and then the tablets are so helpful. And now my dear boy I am sending you all my love and kisses, your Mutti and Horst. Lots of love to Jean

Translation *(by Hans)*   Aschersleben 15.8.48

594

Dear Jean

Today, after waiting for 3 month, I'll thank you very much for the lovely birthday letter. Please, don't be annoyed, but just now I found the letter amongst the paper in the parcel. I am very glad I got the shirt and it is nice and couldn't fit better. There is one thing I am able to dress properly now when I go out. My other shirts can't be called shirts anymore. It's a very difficult time for us and we're to bear it. The weather was very nice today, but it usually doesn't last long. It isn't too bad for me as I am working inside.

What do you think about a little journey to us and a nice fashioned hairdress? How is life going on over there? I am very glad Hans is well again. Don't let him play football! My mother and I went to the pictures yesterday and we always like to go when they show german ones. Most of them, however, are Russian pictures and we don't like those.

I'll finish now.

Please write again soon, we're always glad to hear from you.

Manny greetings to you, dear Jean and Hans from

Horst and Mum

R 8/9.48   **Aschersleben, 16.8.1948**

6/9.48

My dear Hans,

I would like to add a few lines to Horst's letter. Firstly I would like to thank you for your nice letter from August 8, 1948, which arrived today. I am so relieved that your leg is better again. So you want to cook for five weeks in the holiday camp? I wish you good luck with that. And who is then taking over your job? Is it far away from where you work at the moment. Then Jean won't be able to come and see you that often!! We are very sad that the Streeses won't be able to come for a visit. I am sure Gertrud has a stamp; It must have been a joke. But no one has anything in abundance, that's for sure. I soon won't dare to leave the house with my shoes any more, I still use the ones I got from Miss Ellen, but the soles are constantly coming off, and they can't be repaired any more. How destitute are we, that we won't even have a pair of shoes on our feet despite our hard work. But there is nothing we can do, it seems to be our fate and moaning won't improve our miserable situation. Now, my dear Hans, I am sending all my love and kisses, your Mum and brother Horst Lots of love to Jean, hope you enjoy your new job, looking forward to a healthy reunion soon.

Aschersleben 15.8.48

My dear Hans

Today I would like to send you a few lines again. Firstly, many thanks for your kind regards and Jean's letter, which I only found 3 months later. Can you imagine? Such a coincidence that we now found the letter. How are you doing? We are in the pink and hope you are the same. Take care of your leg and don't play football. Mum and I went to the cinema last night, they showed "Love, Passion and Sorrow", a really good film. Food picking is over now; it was over very quickly this year. But we only have a quarter of the yield of last year. I am sure it will be enough somehow. Mum is brooding; she is making herself very nervous. If only Papa would come home soon. Everything would be different then. Recently I had to go and see the doctor because of my nose, I still have a cold and now I have to put in drops all the time. Unfortunately your parcel has still not arrived here. Who knows if it will ever arrive? We would be really upset if we never got it. It has been on the way for a very long time. Dear Hans, do you think it is possible to send a few fine hair nets for Mum please? You could put it into a letter. Mum has a different haircut and therefore she needs a hairnet. The pictures you sent turned out really well. I absolutely love the picture with the two of you. Jean has a really good figure and I immediately went and got the magnifying glass and examined you both more closely. Do you think we will meet this year?

Sometimes it's getting all a bit much, and it is so very boring. It would be so much easier if we had enough and more decent food. At least you don't have the problem of not having enough food. All that worry about not having enough food makes Mum really sick. . I'd like to finish now. Sending my love to you and Jean, your Horst. Write soon again; hope to see you again soon in good health. Could you find tools for doing a manicure where you are?

L.A.E.C. Hostel Redmile.
Sept 8th 1 948.

My dearest, darling Jean,
How are you today, sweetheart? I feel alright if only the weather wouldn't be so awful. It started to rain at 4.00 and has not stopped yet for a minute.
The warden hasn't been in the kitchen since she came. She's asking for everything she wants, even a cup of water. Anyway it's very nice to work with her. She doesn't say a word although we talk sometimes. Mr Scott is also satisfied and really happy. So there's nothing to worry about for the last week. I don't know yet how many people there'll be, but hope only a few to make it a bit easier.
It's rather late tonight. I wrote a letter to my mother and at 10.00 one of the fellows came and asked me to play him a game of table tennis. I've just come back. Time 11.00. You'll be in bed by now. I wish you pleasant dreams and may all your wishes become true. There's no other girl in the world I could love as much as I love you. God bless you.
All my love and a goodnight kiss to you, my love
Thursday Sept 10th 1948
Well, darling, I thank you very much for your letter and the snaps enclosed. Listen, sweetheart, you know I don't like you to arrive home late if there's a possibility to make it earlier. And there was nothing said about my kissing my farewell in front of B.-S. I don't want that to be the reason for

gossip at the office. Knowing how interested people are. If he was waiting to see just that he's had it.

I am really surprised the other photos didn't turn out alright. The two of the camp are very nice. I wonder what's the matter with the camera. Anyway I'll bring it along to Nottingham on Sunday and you can let that gentleman a look at it. Alright, get a film when you get the camera back from Boots.

I'll have word with Mr Sanders tomorrow about taking my holidays in odd days. If that's the only possibility of being together I'll certainly try it. Do you think you'll have more courage in three month time? Well, I'll wait and I won't be impatient. Of course I understand your position. Look, darling, when I said I love you I meant it and I like to repeat it now that I always will do, no question how you treated me. I grew up amongst hardship and sometimes everything goes so easy, other times, however, I really don't know what I am doing. But one thing is very clear. "I love you more than my own life". I wouldn't give you up for anything in the world. It would just be the end for me. There's something I would like to talk to you about and that'll be on Sunday. I only hope there'll be a way to make my plans come true very soon. I'll do my best. It is something about both of us leaving the country to start our own life together. You can imagine, I think, how I am longing for it. And you? Well, I am sure it'll be grand. I really can't think of anything nicer.

Today I received the postal order from the N.H., but only for £2-16-4. My deductions were £3-5-0. I'll have to get the other 10s from the War Ag.

Well, my love, it's time for me to go to bed. 11.15. Only 5 ½ hrs sleep.

Just be good and think of me. Albert is taking the afternoon off tomorrow so that leaves everything to me.

Goodnight and God bless
All my love and thousand kisses

Eternally yours
Hans.

Aschersleben 22.8.48

My dear Hans

Today it is Sunday again. We have now finished gleaning and digging, if only the result had been remotely as good as the previous year, I have tried my best. If only later on it will work out better with the beet and the potatoes. Now it is forbidden to enter the fields, and there's nothing going with harvesting poppy seeds. Please do write to uncle Erich occasionally, he hasn't heard from you for so long. Dear Hans, are you already at your holiday camp? And will you go back to your old job? When will you have your holiday? I have already replied to your last letter which reached us last Monday. Tomorrow Mrs Lehmann and I are going into the woods to look for fungi and blackberries, it all helps a bit and a bit of variety on the daily menu is not a bad thing. Dear Hans, we would be really grateful if you could get us a few spices like pepper and cinnamon. On Friday I queued for three hours at the Wirtschaftsamt*, and after much kerfuffle I got an application for one shirt and one blouse, you never get as far as a dress or a slip and all my underwear is totally torn. We have been away from home for three and a half years now. Yesterday I asked at the post office about the whereabouts of the parcel sent on 16/4/48, but it seems to be a hopeless case. Many kind regards to Jean and let us hope that the new week will bring some mail from you. Stay well my dear Hans, love and kisses from your mum and your brother Horst. Here's to a speedy Wiedersehen

*(home economics service supplying people with basic provisions)

599

92 Wharf St.
Sept 9th.

Darling

This is going to be very short.

I will see you in Nottingham I'll be on the 2.0 bus from Leicester

I will to close now so you get it Saturday

So

   All my love

    Jean

    .

L.A.E.C. Hostel Redmile.
Sept 13th 1948.

My dearest, darling Jean,

Thank you very much for a lovely Sunday, even in spite of the rain. I didn't mind but you know there is something I would like better. Well, my sweetheart the time will come. Anyway we'll have a word about it when there's more time on Sunday. I got home alright last night, in fact I fell asleep soon after we'd left Nottingham and woke up in Plungar. I hope you arrived home safe and the door was open for you. Did you take Freddy his nightly walk again?

Please, darling don't forget the cigarettes next Sunday. I'll remind you again in the last letter. Fortunately the butcher brought me ten today.

Albert has had a row today with Willi again so I had to step between.

It didn't take them long to get upset. I don't want quarrel for the last few days.

I got my breakfast ready for tomorrow morning so it's rather late. Do you mind this short letter. I at least wanted you to get this on Wednesday morning.

Well, my love I'll say goodnight now and God Bless you.

> All my love and thousand kisses
>> Eternally yours
> Hans.

P.S.

I'll write a long letter tomorrow

Love

> Hans.

> 92 Wharf St.
> Sept 13th 1948.

Dearest darling Hans

I was glad to see that you had got on the bus alright. I was trying to see you in the queue, I noticed that one or two people were left behind. I wondered if you would be one, that is why I was glad to see you on the bus. I arrived in Leicester about 10.30 and it had stopped raining, It said in the paper tonight it had been the wettest day for 8 years. Mr Barker-Swain's in the office and asked if I went to Nottingham. Lucy was there and wanted to know how it was that B.S. knew I was going to Notts and she did not. She could not make it out, so I told her how he knew, after that she started firing questions at me, such as what does your mother say and your sister, how long had I known you, how did I know you and etc. I suppose she will have thought some more questions up for me in the morning. Mr Simpkin came in tonight he said he was going to Market Harborough to settle things up there and according to him they still won't have the keys to the stores, because no German is allowed to be responsible for food, because if a German got rid of the lot they can't do anything about it, but if the warden does they can take action against him. So by right you should not have the keys to the stores. They must trust you.

I will try to come next Sunday for the day, then we can have a talk about everything, but for now I will have to say good-night and God Bless you.

All my love and kisses

Jean.

92 Wharf St.

Sept 14th 1948.

My dearest darling Hans

I thank you very much for your letter. Even if it was only one page. Well darling I suppose by now you have heard or read in the papers that all German ex P.O.W's will be going home at the end of the year unless they were married before August 31st. Mr Simpkin came in this morning (I had not read anything about it) and asked me what I was going to do now. I thought he was pulling my leg until I got the "Daily Express" and saw for myself. Mr Simpkin said he had the leaflet about 8 weeks ago. Have you heard anything official yet? Barker-Swain asked me when I was going to be married this afternoon. He said " you've only got to the end of next month". I don't think anything will come of it, because there are a lot like Albert that have nothing to go home to. Was Albert going home at the end of the year? Anyway darling what about you and I. I would marry you tomorrow if I had not got anything to consider. When you get things settled about what you are going to do? I have not put that very well have I, but darling I don't mind where we go so long as we can have a place on our own where there isn't anyone to bother us, and there is another thing that worries me. It's my mother, I don't know what would happen. Anyway I think, in fact I know, everything will turn out alright. Have you written to Australia House yet? We will have a talk about it on Sunday. I have not been to the pictures this week. I was going tonight but my mother has gone out so I thought I would stay in and write some letters. At the moment I am trying to listen to a play and write this.

All my love and kisses

Jean.

My dearest, darling Jean,

I thank you very much for the letter I received today. There's not so much to do in the afternoon today, so I am able to start the long letter as I promised. Today I am rather ~~upse~~ fed up and it's a good thing there're only 3 more days to go. It is getting me down now after all. Well, I shall have an easy weekend and then take it easy at Saltby. I talked to Mr Chandler for about an hour last Saturday and he seems to be pleased to see me coming back.

Remember that Australian I told you about? He's gone back to London yesterday. He's sailing for Africa on Sunday. As he told me he's going to Australia House tomorrow and shall make enquiries in this case and also send me the necessary forms to fill in. He's a government official as I found out yesterday, I am going to wait now til Monday to get the forms from him and if I don't get them, write myself as we arranged.

If Lucy only wouldn't be so curious. I think I would've lost my temper already a long time ago.

Don't you worry I got on the bus alright. There was a long queue, but I stopped on the head of the queue, and kept talking to our fellows til the bus came in, but in fact I didn't see anyone that was left behind. I also arrived at 10.30 but it was still raining. It must have been worse here than in Nottingham. The land in front of the wardens office was flooded. A good thing my quarters are near the gate.

I got another letter today and was surprised to see the post stamp. Birmingham. It was from one of the girls who were here the first week. I told you about the one I used to play table tennis with. I'll show it to you on Sunday.

I know everything about not being allowed to have the keys

for the store. Well, they must trust me and, of course, it all depends on cooperation with the warden. However, I didn't know they can't do anything about it if the German gets rid of the lot. Anyway I am not going to sell anything. Everything is ready for supper and I am ready to go to bed. Last night it was 11.30 when I went. Michel asked me to go to the local with him and have a lemonade at least. It's his birthday today so he wanted to have a pint in advance. After we came back we sat down in the recreation room for half an hour.

Well, my sweetheart, how are you today? Fine, I hope. I'll write to my mother now and then go to bed. I am really dead tired tonight.

Shall I get a letter in the morning? I'll say goodnight and God bless you. Be a good girl and think of me.

All my love and thousand kisses

   Eternally yours

     Hans.

     L.A.E.C. Hostel Redmile.
      Sept 16th 1948.

My dearest, darling Jean,

Thank you very much for your letter and the call I've just had. Believe me it was a nice shock to me when I read your letter. I rushed round to the recreation room and looked for the paper. There it was , of course, as you said. Well, we'll see about it. When Mr Sanders comes on Saturday afternoon I shall have a word with him. Cross your fingers there may be a way. Nobody gets me back into the Russian Zone, because that would be a death sentence for me. They are just waiting for us to come home. As far as I know there are 10,000 here in England. I hope to be one of the remainers.

Well, sweetheart, don't lose hope. I know you would go where ever I go, and I thank you ever so much for saying so. Do you want to know my opinion now? Well, be brave and have the courage to tell your mother about everything. It must be one day and now the sooner the better. Please, darling, do it for me. Think of me and talk to her about it. She's your mother and will understand you. Anyway it won't stop me from writing to Australia House. I am not trying to write before Monday because the Australian is going there himself today and he promised to inquire and send necessary forms on to me at once.

I always thought of something like this happening before we got settled down properly. Now you may understand why I always kept talking about getting married. Well, we'll have a nice long chat on Sunday. Please, get up early and take the first bus at 8.30 that'll get you here about 10.45.

I couldn't help smiling when Mr Shilton tried to tell me about staying on for a few more days. As I told you Mr Sanders spoke about it already last Saturday. He was surprised I knew about it.

Well, darling, do what I asked you to do. I'll be thinking of you every minute. Believe me, you and also I will feel lots better after being through with it. May I remind you of bringing the cigarettes. Put them into your handbag on Saturday. I'll say cheerio for now. Be brave and think of me. Nobody will do you any harm and nobody can take you away from me. All my love and kisses

Eternally yours, my love Hans.

> 92 Wharf St.
> Sept 16th 1948.

My dearest darling Hans

Did you wonder why I did not say much the first time I rang. I did not know whether or not to say more to you or not as Mr B.S. was there, he had come to tell me the latest news. This is what he told me. All German friendly aliens who were not working for private farmers would have to go home. He was trying all day yesterday to keep the hostel staff, but has not had any success and I believe that those fellows that work in hostels have to get jobs on farms even if they are married to British girls. So darling if you wish to stay here you will have to get a job on a farm. They start sending you home in October, and that you all will be away by December. Time will tell what will happen.

With all this bother I had forgotten about the camera. I took it into Boots and they would have to send it away and that would take some time, so I thought I would see how the last film turns out before I let them have it. I will fetch the snaps tomorrow. I have not made up my mind ~~whether or not~~ what bus I will catch Sunday morning. The 8.30 is rather early. I might be able to make it. If I caught that one I would be in Melton 9.15, then catch the 9.45 to Redmile which would probably be in Redmile about 10.45. The next one would not get there until 12.45. So I think I had better try for the 8.30, but I won't promise.

Cheerio darling

All my love and kisses

Jean

——·

L.A.E.C. Hostel Redmile.
Sept 20th 1948.

My dearest, darling Jean,

Well, the new crowd is here and the first day is over. Mr Sanders told me I'll have to stay on for another four days, because there's only one ass. Cook amongst the lot and he was only cooking for 3 months about 2 years ago. Anyway I've asked him to let me go as soon as possible. It will be before the weekend, I hope. They've given me 3 more men for the kitchen. The new warden arrived in the afternoon.

Well, sweetheart, did you get home safe and sound? I was looking for you when our bus left, but couldn't see you. I stopped at Stathern on my way back and went round to see the Coy's. He asked me if you'd been to Redmile and was rather annoyed because he missed a chance as he said. Mrs Coy asked me again if you couldn't come down and stay with her for a weekend. You better like to come to Saltby, don't you? Remember, darling what I told you yesterday about telling your mother. Be brave and tell her. You'll see it doesn't take much courage after all.

I've had another word with Mr Sanders. He said I'd better make sure about a farmer. If something else turns up for me I can always take the better one then. Mr Scott came also this afternoon. He hasn't had a chance to get in touch with Mr Brown, but he'll see him at the market in Melton tomorrow and is going to ring me and tell me about it. I shall wait another two days for the forms that Australian was going to send me, if nothing arrives, I'll write myself. I am not going to lose hope, anyway I love you too much to leave you here and go away myself and you also told me yesterday that you want me to stay here. Alright, I'll do my best.

Thanks very much for a lovely Sunday. Well, my love, I only hope our time comes soon.

I'll say goodnight now and God bless. You're the best girl in the world. Just be good and think of me.

All my love and thousand kisses
Eternally yours, darling
Hans.

Replied 20/9.48

Prenzlau. 8.9.48

20/9.48

Dear Hans

Thank you very much for your lovely letter dated 5.8. It only reached me a few days ago.

Read and be astonished: I am also on leave. I spent a fortnight in Barta in Pommerania.

I think you have been there too. I was looking after a young boy, my brother-in-law's son. I took him back home and decided to stay there for a while. It was lovely. Unfortunately I was not able to settle properly. There were three children and they were all spoilt and badly brought up. They are very naughty prancing around all day, keeping you on your toes. Otto's brother has a gardening business on the Fliegerhorst in Barta where the sports ground used to be and he also owns the stretch of land next door. Perhaps you can remember where the Commander once lived. The brother leased his house and lives there now. The main thing was that I did not have to cook. Although we have the bare ingredients, it is nice to get a change in food. Otto makes his demands. They have nothing of nutritional value in their cupboards, mainly flour, peas and red berry compote and during harvest there were between 8 and 10 people at the table. I often had cold sweat attacks preparing their meals. First off I was terrified in case dinner was not ready in time, secondly that there might not be sufficient to go around. Sometimes, I felt really harassed but everything is behind me now and I can rest a little. The potatoes and turnips have to be harvested and that might be all for this year. I have not had even as much as an hour to read a book. There are loads of trousers and socks to be mended. You can see how efficient I am, but no, this is not the case, nobody is happy with me. How often I think of past memories, why my life had to turn out like this. What I would give if I could just relive one of those days.

Now, my dear Hans, Marga has also lost her husband. Ernst died three weeks ago and grief has returned to the family. The passing was a relief for Ernst because he had to suffer so much. His life was one enormous agony to him. But the children have lost their dad and Marga is feeling quite lost. She is very sad and homesick. However, she has no plans to travel and there is not much one can do from here. The whole situation is just very sad. If only the borders were taken down. It was quite easy last year for me but now I would not dare to cross the border. I would love to go and see her. If only I had stayed there last year. Why do I allow this constant humiliation. I don't know what I want. Then I ask myself again and again: Why did I get married in the first place? I am sure that you have never come across such a type of person. Enough of this.

The enclosed photo was taken at Fredi's wedding. I can introduce you to the whole family. Don't you think the little sister is lovely? When I go home it seems to me that every day is a Sunday. The house is filled with nothing but warmth and I am finding it very difficult to come back here again. Manfred lives upstairs in my flat. Otto does not like it when I visit them. I don't go there very often. The sister-in-law is a lovely person and I am getting on very well with father and son. I am very happy that everything has turned out so well. Only mum's health is not so good. At the moment I am quite well. Did you have a good time in your holiday camp? I must say that you have accepted a very difficult job as you have to be on your feet all day long. I hope you are getting some help. I am keeping my fingers crosses (on both hands) and wish you (from the bottom of my heart) a speedy recovery. You made a complete career change. I can imagine that you demonstrate a lot of skill and you are very successful. Unsurprising because I know how clever you are. You are not shy to take on new challenges and you master them brilliantly. You deserve every success and I congratulate you. Are you now going to change your plan? You wrote to me that you intend to come home at the beginning of next year. When you get married: it had to come, there was no other way, and I will getting used to this idea. Yes Hans, it does hurt me when you write it to me.

I managed to pour my heart out again today and it has done me good. I am looking forward to your next long letter.

Greetings from the heart and all the very best. Vera

If you don't want the photo, I will not feel offended if you send it back. Dear Hans, thank you for your photo. I do think that you look very slim for a Chef. I am looking forward to seeing you in the flesh. If only it did not take so long.

     92 Wharf St.

     Sept 21st 1948.

My dearest darling Hans.

I thank you for such a lovely day. I enjoyed it much more than the other Sunday I came. I think it was because we were alone. I was home by 9.45. I thought you should be back at Redmile by then. I took the dog a walk. I was hoping to be in bed early, to do this I had to be in bed before my mother got home. I was just pinning my hair up, when she came home, my auntie from next door came in with her. We were talking and I did not get into bed until gone 11.0. It isn't any good posting this letter until I know where you are. Mr Chandler rang this morning, he asked If I knew when you would be back at Saltby. I was talking to him for quite a while. I told him I would be seeing him on Sunday, all being well. He said he would be glad when you were back. We have a new relief telephonist. She started last week, but was at the Phoenix switchboard all last week. Her name is Mary. She has been on the board most of the afternoon so I have been able to get on with this without any interruption, but I am now back on the board. I have just had Mr Pickering on. He asked about you.

I had to stop writing whilst at work, I could not get on with it. It is now 8.45 and I am at home. I went to the pictures last night to see "I Remember Mama", it was fairly good. About a Norwegian (is that how you spell it) family that go to live in America, they had a nice family, 4 children (3 girls and 1 boy). I think you think I am joking when I say I would like 4 children, but I am not. I think a family like that is a much happier one than one where there is only one child. I know that our family will be a happy one, at least I hope it will, but one can never tell. I hope soon we will know what is going to happen. I feel sure that everything will turn out the way we want it to. I have not said anything to my mother yet. I will have to wait for my opportunity. It is hard for me, I have not got much courage when it comes to anything like that. I nearly always leave it and hope that everything will turn out for the best, but I know that sooner or later I will have to tell her. It would not be so bad if you had everything settled for the future. I don't think she would mind so much then, but I could not care less what my mother thinks or anyone else. I have to live with you and no one else (I hope).

I hope we are able to go to Australia where we can start a fresh life together where they will take us for what we are and not our nationality. If we are not able to go we will have to make the best of it. Do you remember me telling you about a girl Dora knew, married one of your fellows from Barkby Rd stores. He tried to get his release a few months ago. He tried a few times because he was not getting much money, and they would not give it to him. He rang me up this morning to say that he had got his release. He was trying to find a job, but had not been very successful. He wants to do clerical work, and if he has not found a job by Friday he has to report to the Ministry of Labour, they will send him into something, but I doubt if it will be into an office. He can not go into agriculture because of his health. Some of the girls at L.A.E.C went to take the civil service exam today to become permanent civil servants. We all had papers to fill in some months ago, but the 3 telephonists, Iris Clarice and I were informed that our wages would be reduced if we took it because when you pass tit you go on to a set wage, so we never bothered. I am glad I didn't. Lucy sent her papers in because she thought I would do so, now she is worried to death. She has about as many brains as me and that is not many (so if you want brainy children you had better not marry me). I took Fred to the vet again tonight. I don't think I told you my aunty (the one at Birstall) came in to see me at the office to say Mr Forman (the vet) would like to see Fred on Sunday morning. I had forgotten all about going to Redmile, so on Friday night I had to go on my bicycle to tell him I would not be able to go Sunday but would come on Tuesday. So I went this evening. He has put some ointment on him, I have to wash him on Saturday, then take him again Sunday morning at 10.0. I will have to be up early again to get there in time. Well darling I will say goodnight and God bless. Although I am not very good at saying this. I love you very much and will try to make you happy.

    All my love and kisses

                                        Jean

_____.

P.S.
I hope you can follow along the lines

L.A.E.C Hostel Redmile.
Sept 21st 1948.

My dearest, darling Jean,

How are you today, sweetheart? Fine, I hope. I've told the new cook this afternoon to cook the stew himself, but 5 minutes later he brought the interpreter to tell me he was only doing his cooking in 1942, and for a very short time. That meant to me, have another go yourself. The only thing I am waiting for is Mr Sanders to tell me "back to Saltby".I found out the A.E.C is very short of cooks. Why don't they try then to keep us as cooks?

Well, my love there was no letter this morning, but I hope for tomorrow. I've been to Nottingham today for a couple of hours and bought a very nice pair of shoes. Remember the ones I showed to you a fortnight ago? But please, don't ask for the price. I've also had a look around for sports suits, but couldn't find anything that satisfied me. When I come to Leicester again maybe there's something decent in the shops. Dinner is over. It doesn't take so long now as it did when the holiday makers were here. For 30 people it always took me 1 ½ hrs and now with 50 only 20 minutes. That makes it earlier for me. And besides that there're 3 more men in the kitchen.

Mr Coy came tonight and Mr Chandler has told him to ask when I am coming back. I am still waiting for Mr Sanders to tell me. Anyway I hope it'll be soon. I'll tell you in time about next Sunday. It'll be Saltby I think.

Well sweetheart, what do you think about courage? I think the best is to leave you to it. You'll tell your mother when you know it's time. I don't like to tell you what to do. You know yourself best. But always remember one thing. I love you more than anything else in the world and I hope nobody is making an attempt to part us, they would be unsuccessful.

Well, darling I'll say goodnight now and God bless you. Be thinking of you all the time. Just be good and pleasant dreams to you.

All my love and kisses
Eternally yours
Hans.

P.S.
Can you get any cartridges for these new "Rollerball Pens" please try to get a few when you've time.
Love
Hans.

Hans Klawitter,
LAEC Hostel Saltby,
Melton Mowbray/Leics.
Sept 23rd 1948.

My dearest, darling Jean,
I thank you ever so much for the lovely letter I received today. I thought you might not know whether I am still at Redmile or back here at Saltby. I didn't know anything definite when Mr Coy came at 4 o'clock and said he was going to take me back. Mr Wilkins rung Mr Hilton and he said yes, so I finished the dinner and got ready in ½ hour. Albert is left in charge as cook and when the warden asked him if he can do the cooking himself he said 'I don't know.' Anyway I hope they get on alright.

When we arrived here we went straight down to the bungalow where the promised cup of tea was waiting. And also a nice piece of cake.

Well, I dare say I've settled down again. You know it doesn't take me long. This morning I rung Mr Pickering and we've had a nice long chat. He seems to be alright there.

Mr Shilton came this morning. He smiled when he said 'you won't stay here long.' I asked him why and so he told me Mr Baker-Swaine had spoken with the Ministry this morning and they will definitely send all the domestic staff home.

They're to find 40 men British staff for the hostels and will be unsuccessful in that. Then I wonder why they don't want to keep our cooks. Everything seems to be in a mess. Shilton said it's the safest thing to find a farmer. As I haven't heard yet from Mr Scott I shall ring him in the afternoon. If he hasn't seen Mr Brown yet I am going to see him myself tomorrow morning. Then I'll know what I've to do.

Well, sweetheart, now to your letter. I really enjoyed the last Sunday much more than any other day before. I think it just was because we were all on our own. They've just played your favourite song 'Too tired' on the radio. Maybe you've heard it. It's 1.40

You'll have more time now to write at the office with your new relief being there. How do you get on with her?

You know, darling what I think about children. I know you aren't joking. I think just the same about it. Don't worry about anything, we'll be alright. The first thing is now to get everything straight. Haven't I told you times I know how difficult it is for you to tell your mother. As soon as I know where I stand we can talk about our future. I've posted my letter to Australia House yesterday and hope to get reply from there soon. We'll see about it then. I've told you I'll always try for the very best.

Mr Chandler told me this morning to ask you down for the day on Sunday. I've told him I'll try it anyway. What do you think about it? He was rather lonely the last weeks and said he likes to see us both around his place on Sunday. We're going to have lunch with him over at the bungalow. Can't you cancel your arrangements with the vet? And make it another day? Please, think it over and let me know in time.

Well, sweetheart, I'll have a look at Mr Chandler's car. That's to be fixed up again. She won't go.

Cheeri'o for now and God bless you. Remember I love you very, very much.

Love all of it and thousand kisses
             Eternally yours

Hans.

92 Wharf St.
Sept 24th.

Dearest darling Hans

I suppose Mr Chandler has told you that I am going to catch the 8.30 from Leicester. I remembered last night that I have to take Freddy to the vet on Sunday morning but I am going to take him tonight instead (Friday) and hope that the vet does not mind.

I was speaking to Heinz this morning. I got Billesdon hostel by mistake, I meant to ask for Mr Simkin number, then he began to tell me he had seen Mr Simkin and he had given him the Ministry of Agricultures leaflet about the conditions of those who have to go home and those that can stay. Mr Simkin came in this afternoon and I asked him about it and this is what he said. That if you could get a farmer to employ you before 30th Sept you have to have a form for the farmer to fill in. The farmer must not displace a British worker. So darling if it is possible to get on a farm before the 30th try and do so. That only gives you 4 days to try.

I spoke to Major this morning and I told him I would be going on Sunday. I longing to know what he wants to talk about. He asked me if I was happy I said 'yes are you' he said 'no' and he could not tell me why he was unhappy. I hope I am nothing to do with it anyway I shall find out on Sunday. The bus should arrive at Croxton 9.40.

All my love
Jean.

LAEC Hostel Saltby.
Sept 25th 1948.

My dearest, darling Jean,

Thank you very much for your letter I received this morning. Mr Chandler didn't say anything about you taking the 8.30. As far as I know Mr Scott has fixed Heinz up with a place. I rung Mr Brown this morning. He wasn't in so I've had a word with his wife. She remembered me well, but, in fact, they've got enough men working for them she said, they're going out over the weekend to see a few farmers and will ring me back Monday morning. Afterwards I went down to Melton and had a word with Mr Scott. He, however told me that a farmer at Pickwell wants 2 men, but Mr Barker-Swain has told him he's going to fix him up with two. He didn't mention any names. The best thing I can do is to ring the chief first thing Monday morning and ask him about this particular place. I'll see what he says.

You know, darling, I want to stay and I am trying hard to find a place. My love for you means more than getting home.

After I got your letter today I said to Major, "Jean is coming tomorrow so you can have a talk with her". His answer was, what should I talk about. He said on the phone, "I can't say it now, but that's because I always have to think 5 minutes what I want to say. And that's too long on the telephone". So I hope you aren't disappointed tomorrow. You're nothing to do with it. You'll see tomorrow.

Mr Chandler went out in his car tonight and when he came back and I took over I found the brakes blocked. So I had almost had it for fetching you in the morning. It only was another hours work to get it fixed again. Well, everything is ready so far.

I'll say goodnight now and God bless you. Just be good and think of me.

All my love and kisses

Eternally yours

Hans.

L.A.E.C. Hostel Saltby.

Sept 26th 1948.

"My darling"

It's 11.15 now and I hope you're at home by now. I arrived back at 10.20, coming down the back way. I still wonder how it happened I didn't take one of the trees. After I had put the bikes away I went to the warden, but only stopped for 5 minutes. I remembered just in time I still had to get tomorrows rations ready for the cooks, besides that my things for the laundry.

I noticed, darling, it gave you a bit of a shock when B-S started talking. Believe me, it was just the limit I could stand without getting rude. He changed a bit later on. I've told you not to give up hope. You know I always try to the very end, but never turn anything down because it looks hopeless. If I have to go after all, I'll have to the make best of it. Please, ask Mr Edwards for the reference and tell him not to forget to put on about driving vehicles. I was working with him from 12.12.46 till 31.12.47. After all it won't be too bad, knowing you're coming over as soon as I've fixed things up.

I felt so lonely when you got on to the bus and would have liked to go with you without bothering about anything. If we only could start our own life tomorrow. I love you so very much.

Well, my love, you'll be asleep by now. I wish you pleasant dreams. You forgot your letters so I'll put them in. Just be good and think of me.

Loads of love and thousand kisses,

      Eternally yours, darling

           Hans.

           LAEC Hostel Saltby.
           Sept 27th 1948.

My dearest, darling Jean,

Well, sweetheart it's 7.15 now and I am ready to go out for supper. Tomorrow morning I shall ring Mr Brown again. They didn't ring me today. Has Mr Barker-Swain mentioned anything today?

I am sorry, sweetheart, I've had to stop writing. Mr Chandler came over and asked if I was ready. We came home later as expected but, in fact, spent a very nice evening. I've eaten things I've never seen before. Egg and bacon pie, trifle made with wine etc Anyway I enjoyed it very much and they are a nice crowd.

How are things going on, darling? I haven't heard anything from Mr Barker-Swaine. Mr Sanders will be coming out today so I shall have a word with him. Only 2 more days to go, only one when you get this letter. Cross both your fingers my love. I'll ring Mr Brown again after I've had a word with Sanders. Please remind Mr Edwards of the reference. The best thing is if he gives it to you.

Well, I'll say cheerio. Mr Coy is leaving for Melton. Just be good and think of me.

All my love and kisses

Eternally yours

       Hans.

    92 Wharf St.

    Sept 28th 1948.

My dearest darling Hans

Thank you so very much for the letter. I am sorry I did not write yesterday, but as you know Iris came back and we were busy talking most of the day. I hope I am forgiven.

Well darling, Mr Chandler has been through and he told me you had to see a farmer this afternoon. I'm praying that you will get the job. At 4.15 Mr C said he had not been able to tell you as you had gone out, I was annoyed with you for not being there. You see Mr C said the first time he rang that you had to be there at 4.0, and when he rang at 4.15 he said you had not been back. I was so mad. B Swain asked me on Mon-

day morning if I could go up to his office. Up I went but I had better tell you about that some other time as it is now 5.15 and I have to take the dog to the vet and be there before 6.0.
So, all my love and kisses
Jean.

92 Wharf St.
Sept 28th.

My dearest darling Hans
This is the second letter I have written to you today, that is if you can call the one I did at the office a letter. I am very sorry but I could not get in the mood for writing.
I was so relieved when Mr Chandler said you had to go to see a farmer tonight. I am glad you rang to let me know how you got on, I have been thinking about you. I would not like you to go where you did not like the farmer, but as far as milking the cows, surely you could put up with that for a year. I thought you said you were not afraid of work!!! But it seems that you are afraid to milk a cow.
So I will try and tell you about B. Swain. He asked me to go up to his office. So up I went, I felt very embarrassed. He asked me how far things had gone between you and I. I felt very annoyed but I kept my temper and told him. Mr Sanders came in, he told Mr B.S. that you hadn't had any farming experience. Then Mr S. said that he could get you fixed up somewhere. Mr Shilton was in the office. When I came through on the phone he asked me if it did any good seeing B.S. I told him that I did not ask to see him. He sent for me, but according to him, B. S. said I had asked to see him.
Anyway darling, I hope you get somewhere you will be happy and I am sorry to say I hope you go where you have to

milk cows it will do you good eh!!!

I took the dog to the vet, he seems to have lost an awful lot of hair lately , the vet said he was bad again, but I will keep on taking him even if it is a rush for me to get him there for 6.0 in the hope that he will soon get better. I washed him last night and he really looked terrible afterwards. I hope you will be able to take Bonzo with you wherever you go.

I have not been able to think of anyone the Major could take out yet and I have no idea where I could find anyone for him, I will try and see what I can do. Even if I do think he is a traitor to his country.

I was talking to Kathleen this afternoon and she said she had seen you. She was saying that they had a German girl living with them (it is not any good going to see her, she is married).

Anyway darling, I will say goodnight and God Bless,

All my love and kisses
Jean

PS What about the weekend? I think we had better wait and see what is going to happen.
Jean xxxx

L.A.E.C. Hostel Saltby.
Sept 29th 1948.

My dearest, darling Jean,
Well, darling I've almost told you everything on the phone, but in spite I like to write a few lines. I am just listening to 'Take it from here' They talked about the new picture, 'I remember Mama' in a rather funny way. Did you listen to it? Did you hear her say 'Father hand me the hammer. There's a fly on the baby's forehead!!' I really couldn't help laughing. Well sweetheart, I thank you very much for your letter I re-

ceived this morning. I've got that farmers reply. He said he's sorry, but he wants a perfect milker. I wasn't really sorry he said so because Mr Coy said it isn't the place to stay at for 12 month. There was nothing else to do than taking matters in my own hands for nobody rung me from the office about the other place (Maclean, Pickwell). Mr Sanders has had another place for me in Willoughby, that's Nott's, so he had to ask permission from N.A.E.C. He'll ring me tomorrow morning as soon as he gets the call through from Nottingham. I myself rung Mr Maclean and unfortunately he wasn't in himself. I am trying again just after 8 o'clock.

I can imagine how mad you were yesterday when Mr Chandler told you he can't find me. Don't worry, sweetheart, you know I'll do my best to find anything. Tonight when the baker comes here I'll have a word with him for he mentioned something last Monday night when we talked about it. I am making other people feel sorry wherever I can.

Well, darling, I'll go over now to Mr Chandler and ring Mr Maclean again. I'll write a few more lines afterwards.

Here I am again. I've been on the phone for ½ hour and fixed things up. Mr Maclean is definitely going to take me if he gets the other two. He wants me to come over tomorrow and talk things over with him. I've got another 2 places in hand and we'll be successful after all.

Well, my love, I'll go to bed now and so say goodnight and God bless you. My dreams will be about you and remember how much I love you.

                    All my love and kisses
                    Eternally yours
                                Hans.

R 8/10.48   Aschersleben 5.9.48
                          29/9.48

My dear Hans

Finally after three weeks we have received your dear letter for which we thank you very much. I thought that you may have little time to write these days. We are happy to hear that you are fully recovered now, as nothing is more important than one's health. However please do not play football, as you know the consequences for your leg. We have wonderful late summer weather here, last week I went to collect fungi again. Found many, Horst so loves them. I guess you'll be glad to get back to your old job, where it is easier for you. But dear Hans, I have to say that I am very disappointed in you, as you have been promising to send me some shoes for the last four months, you have known about this for so long, but you do not quite understand the level of our needs here. I would so much like to be able to be properly dressed. If only it were possible for me to send you the money. Also, you were going to enclose some sweetener with your letters, but this has not happened either. These are not such big expenses and in fact we do not have any more soap, twisted thread or sewing yarn either. You know it's not like me to keep writing about these things, but the most basic items are not available and believe me I would not ask for them unless I thought you were able to help us out and I thought you would love doing it. You know dear Hans, I always have the feeling that Jean doesn't like it very much when you send us stuff, but I do not know if this is really so, but I cannot understand it otherwise. You are probably angry with me now, but you know that I never make promises I cannot keep!!! By the time you receive this letter you will have done your five weeks. It does not seem far from your other place, as the address is the same. Now I shall end this letter my dear Hans, please carry on being well and give regards to Jean. Lots of love and kisses from your mum and your brother Horst. Here's to a healthy Wiedersehen

r 8/10.48   Aschersleben 12.9.48
                                    29/9.48

    My dear Hans

Although we did not receive any mail from you this week I shall nevertheless send you our best Sunday greetings Llast week we had lovely summery weather, warm, up to 25 degrees. I hope it is nice where you are too. Is this the last week you will be cooking at the holiday camp? You'll have a bit more peace and quiet then! I have been depressed and in a bad mood for a while now, there's just too much going through my head. They say there will be more food, it certainly has been talked about enough, 50 grams of bread per day, and 125 grams of cereals and a few more potatoes, sugar does not even get mentioned. Yesterday a client of Horst's gave him 30lbs of plums, we were so happy, as we cannot but any – they are asking for 100 Mark per hundredweight. Soon it will be time to dig for potatoes, if only we will be more successful than with the grain. After that the beet, and a few trips into the woods to collect wood. It is such a pity that I was not able to collect any poppy seeds, at least we would have a bit more fat. Our landlady is buying herself a quarter of a pound of butter, something we cannot afford, so we have to go without and eat what we have. Who knows when the black market will finish? We had hoped to get some fat or meat, but unfortunately.... always the same. Will it ever change? On the whole we are reasonably healthy and hope the same for you. When will you get your break? And when will you come home to us? It is only another three months until Christmas, time just seems to fly, but we are hoping that our dear papa will be with us for Christmas. Now my dear Hans I will finish, please stay well, best regards to Jean and lots of love and kisses from your mum and your brother Horst. Here's to a healthy Wiedersehen

92 Wharf Street.
Sept 30th 1948.

My dearest darling Hans
I have been hoping that you would ring me to let me know how things are going. I suppose you would have let me know if you had found a farmer to take you. I shall be glad when this day is over, at least I will know whether or not you have to go home, I don't mind which way it is, the only thing that bothers me about going to Germany is the language. I am sure I could never speak it fluently but I am not very worried about that.

I rang Alice this morning to ask her to come for tea, she said she would not be able to come for tea but would come at 7.30, it is 8.15 and she has not arrived yet, but knowing Alice I would not be surprised if she does not come. When I rang Miss Batt was on the switchboard (she is at Corah's where I use to be relief telephonist) and she ask me to go to tea on Monday next, I have been a few times before, but this last year I have not rung her at all and when I ring Alice I usually try to ring when Miss Batt is not there. She is very nice, but it is so hard to try to hold a conversation with her. Anyway I have promised to go to tea Monday.

I have Family Favourites on, I thought just then he was going to play 'So tired' but instead he just mentioned that it had become a very popular record but he isn't going to play it tonight.

Alice has been and she has just gone (11.0) Berny an Irish girl came with her, I have just taken them a little way with Freddy I feel very sorry for Freddy tonight he has been trying to get on my knee all night but I won't have him, I took him to the vet and he has put some terrible stuff on him, it smells awful. I will be glad when he is better, it is getting me down

624

having to run home to get him then rush down to the vets. I only hope that it is worth it.

Well darling I will have to say goodnight and God Bless.

All my love and kisses

Jean

LAEC Hostel Saltby.
Sept 30th 1948.

My dearest darling Jean

Thanks so very much for your letter I received this morning. Well, sweetheart, you can be relieved now. Everything is settled with Mr Maclean, I've seen him this afternoon. Maybe you've heard him or Mr Coy calling Mr Wright and fixing things up.

The accommodations are not of the best, but I don't want to start grumbling. He promised to make the place as homely as he can. We don't pay any board, but have to pay for food and coal. One of the rooms is very small, but he's going to put a new grate in to do the cooking. I want the other room only as sleeping room, I am used to fix rooms up and make them look nice and homely. I'll do the cooking and work the other time on the farm, probably driving a tractor. Anyway the first impression of the farmer was good and that's what counts. You know I am not afraid of work and I think I've showed it. The only reason why I told the farmer I can't milk was because I didn't like him and that place. I know him when I drove a lorry and my squad was working for him. Miserable like anything. My Coy also wasn't keen on that place. I fancied Mr Maclean's and after all I managed alright. Remember, 'never give up hope' Even if it is the last day.

I also told the farmer I've worked on a farm before. I understood Sanders had told him I was only doing a job as a cook till now.

I just wonder why B-S is so interested in us. It isn't his concern at all and I wouldn't have been surprised if you'd lost your temper and told him off. In case he says anything again, tell him off. After all I arranged my job without him and so I needn't be thankful to him.

I forgot to ask the farmer about Bonzo, but I'll fix that up alright.

About the weekend! Would you like to come again for the day? Please!!! There's another Sunday left after this one to spend here together, but Mr Chandler would like to put a farewell party on for the last Sunday and wishes to see you here as well.

I'll say goodnight and God Bless you. I'll be dreaming of you so just be good.

    All my love and kisses,
     Eternally yours
       Hans.

R 8/10.48   **Aschersleben 19.9.48**

         2/10.48

  My dear Hans

Many thanks for your dear letter dated 8.9.48, which we received with thanks. We have had little mail from you, but hearing how much work you have, you clearly couldn't write that much. Well, you now have got over the 5 weeks and you can relax a little. Yesterday they started an eight-day folk festival, but I am not interested, I do not want to waste my hard-earned money on tatt, there is nothing decent to buy. Yes, Horst has very little free time, as he always strives to earn more money, so that we can move on. I often feel so sorry about the way he works himself to the bone. I would very much like to add to our income, but he won't allow it. And yet, in the end it will be too much for him, as we have to start to reorganise our home from scratch. Also, on Sundays he is never free before 15-15.30. In three weeks from now he is taking part in a hairdressing competition in Wernigerode in the Harz mountains, - it will cost a lot of money, but he needs to take part if he wants to move on in his profession. This afternoon Mrs Lessin from Guensten is visiting us again. In three months we will have got to Christmas again and you will have finished your time there!!! What are your thoughts about your future? You never write anything on that subject. Now my dear Hans, please stay well and lots of love and kisses from your mum and your brother Horst. Many kind regards to Jean. Here's to a healthy Wiedersehen

Addendum
Life for Hans and Jean has moved on to a new chapter. Can the romance survive in post-war England?
What path does life take for Mutti and Horst? Can they they break free from the endless suffering and rebuild their lives? Will Papa return home? What becomes of Vera? Their stories continue in "In search of home – love,life and longing on a journey in search of a better life"

Should you want to contact me please email

sendingsundaygreetings@gmail.com

Printed in Great Britain
by Amazon